CARL SCHMITT

D1522913

Twentieth-Century Political Thinkers
Series Editors: Kenneth L. Deutsch and Jean Bethke Elshtain

Raymond Aron: The Recovery of the Political
    by Brian C. Anderson, American Enterprise Institute
Jacques Maritain: The Philosopher in Society
    by James V. Schall, Georgetown University
Martin Buber: The Hidden Dialogue
    by Dan Avnon, Hebrew University of Jerusalem
John Dewey: America's Philosopher of Democracy
    by David Fott, University of Nevada
Simone Weil: The Way of Justice as Compassion
    by Richard H. Bell, The College of Wooster
Gandhi: Struggling for Autonomy
    by Ronald J. Terchek, University of Maryland at College Park
Paul Ricoeur: The Promise and Risk of Politics
    by Bernard P. Dauenhauer, University of Georgia
Carl Schmitt: The End of Law
    by William E. Scheuerman, University of Pittsburgh

FORDHAM
UNIVERSITY
LIBRARIES

WITHDRAWN
FROM
COLLECTION

CARL SCHMITT

The End of Law

WILLIAM E. SCHEUERMAN

ROWMAN & LITTLEFIELD PUBLISHERS, INC.
Lanham • Boulder • New York • Oxford

FORDHAM
UNIVERSITY
LIBRARY..
NEW YORK, NY
LINCOLN
CENTER

ROWMAN & LITTLEFIELD PUBLISHERS, INC.

Published in the United States of America
by Rowman & Littlefield Publishers, Inc.
4720 Boston Way, Lanham, Maryland 20706

12 Hid's Copse Road
Cumnor Hill, Oxford OX2 9JJ, England

Copyright © 1999 by Rowman & Littlefield Publishers, Inc.

All rights reserved. No part of this publication may be reproduced,
stored in a retrieval system, or transmitted in any form or by any
means, electronic, mechanical, photocopying, recording, or otherwise,
without the prior permission of the publisher.

British Library Cataloguing in Publication Information Available

Library of Congress Cataloging-in-Publication Data

Scheuerman, William E., 1965–
    Carl Schmitt : the end of law / William E. Scheuerman.
       p.   cm. — (Twentieth-century political thinkers)
    Includes bibliographical references and index.
    ISBN 0-8476-9417-8 (cloth : alk. paper). — ISBN 0-8476-9418-6
(pbk. : alk. paper)
      1. Schmitt, Carl, 1888– .   2. Laws—Philosophy. I. Title.
II. Series.
K230.S352S34   1999
340'.1—dc21   98-37287
                                  CIP

Printed in the United States of America

♾ ™ The paper used in this publication meets the minimum requirements of
American National Standard for Information Sciences—Permanence of Paper for
Printed Library Materials, ANSI Z39.48–1984.

*For Julia
and her dreams*

The doctrine has taken its place, if not as a received opinion, as one of the admitted sects or divisions of opinion: those who hold it have generally inherited, not adopted it; and conversion from one of these doctrines to another, being now an exceptional fact, occupies little place in the thoughts of their professors. Instead of being, as at first, constantly on the alert either to defend themselves against the world, or to bring the world over to them, they have subsided into acquiescence, and neither listen, when they can help it, to arguments against their creed, nor trouble dissentients (if there be such) with arguments in its favor. From this time may usually be dated the decline in the living power of the doctrine.

John Stuart Mill, *On Liberty*

CONTENTS

ACKNOWLEDGMENTS

I have incurred an enormous number of intellectual debts over the past five years in completing this study. My colleagues at the University of Pittsburgh have provided a lively intellectual environment from which I have benefited on more occasions than I can even begin to recount. In particular, Fred Whelan and Iris Young not only offered generous advice on the manuscript but also have made sure that I feel at home in Pittsburgh. Many others in Pittsburgh examined sections of the manuscript as well. Although I probably am forgetting some names, Vivian Curran, Albrecht Funk, and Guy Peters immediately come to mind.

Peter Caldwell and David Dyzenhaus also read more of the manuscript than they would probably care to recall. I have also gained from exchanges about Schmitt with Renato Cristi, John P. McCormick, and Stanley Paulson.

Belated thanks as well to Andy Markovits, who (for better or worse!) published my first essay on Carl Schmitt, as well as Richard Wolin, who has offered many words of encouragement.

Ingeborg Maus and Peter Niesen were gracious hosts while I completed this study in residence at the University of Frankfurt. I also would like to thank the Alexander von Humboldt Stiftung (Bonn) and the German Marshall Fund for making it possible for me to take time off from my teaching schedule to work on the manuscript.

Some earlier sections of the manuscript appeared in the *Cardozo Law Review*, *Constellations*, *History of Political Thought*, *Review of Politics*, and *Theory and Society*.

INTRODUCTION
WHY CARL SCHMITT?

Carl Schmitt belongs among the ranks of twentieth-century Europe's most influential political and legal theorists. Schmitt's ideas have long been familiar to intellectuals in many parts of Europe, and some of the indisputable theoretical giants of our century (including both Jürgen Habermas and Leo Strauss) have devoted significant energy to the task of critically responding to Schmitt. As I hope to show in this study, Schmitt exerted a subterranean influence on postwar American political thought as well. The ghost of Carl Schmitt haunts political and legal debates not only in Europe, but also in the contemporary United States.

Schmitt was also a reactionary critic of the Weimar Republic, Germany's first experiment in liberal democracy, who early on allied himself with Weimar's authoritarian opponents. In 1933, he joined the National Socialist Party and devoted his best years to the Nazi cause. As he aspired to formulate the outlines of an identifiably National Socialist system of law, Schmitt's Nazi period was his most prolific.

How are we to make sense of the nexus between Schmitt's theory and his political choices? For the most part, the reception of Schmitt in the English-speaking world thus far has taken two distinct but equally insufficient forms. Whereas some scholars have been satisfied with an apologetic discussion of Schmitt's ideas and their relationship to National Socialism, others criticize his views but succeed in doing so only by caricaturing them. The apologists downplay Schmitt's Nazi activities and the role he played in legitimizing a dictatorial alternative to the crisis-ridden Weimar Republic during the early 1930s, while the caricaturists obscure central elements of Schmitt's account and unwittingly provide intellectual fodder for Schmitt's defenders.[1]

This study sketches out an alternative course. Despite growing interest in Schmitt, too many scholars continue to miss the central place of Schmitt's ideas about law in his intellectual agenda. The fact that Schmitt's controversial reflections about sovereignty, dictatorship, parliamentary government, the welfare state, and international politics ultimately derive from a fundamental critique of liberal jurisprudence is often obscured. To provide a balanced picture of Schmitt's views, it is necessary to make an analysis of his ideas about law the focal point of that picture.[2] Furthermore, Schmitt's political and legal theory generates troublesome questions for those of us committed to defending liberalism's most basic protection against arbitrary power, the rule of law. If we are to preserve and strengthen the rule of law, we are intellectually and politically obliged to provide an answer to Schmitt's attack on it. We caricature or ignore Schmitt's ideas at our own risk.

I intend to demonstrate that Schmitt's political choices were intimately related to his critique of liberal jurisprudence. Schmitt embraced National Socialism because he (wrongly) believed that National Socialism could overcome the weaknesses of liberal legal theory and practice. For Schmitt, the bankruptcy of liberal law necessitated an authoritarian right-wing alternative to it. After 1933, Schmitt disastrously tried to solve what is now widely described within contemporary debates about the rule of law as the "crisis of legal indeterminacy"—by formulating a National Socialist alternative to liberal jurisprudence.

I

Who was Carl Schmitt? A fascination with Schmitt's eventful biography, together with a relative neglect of his complex political and legal theory, plagues much of the English-language literature on Schmitt.[3] In order to compensate for this tendency, the exegesis here tends to focus on Schmitt's published writings. Nonetheless, a preliminary biographical and historical backdrop for Schmitt's theory would be useful.[4]

Schmitt was born on July 11, 1888 to a Catholic family of modest means in the provincial town of Plettenberg in the western part of Germany, in what now is part of the state of North Rhine Westphalia. He died in the same town on the Monday following Easter Sunday in 1985 at the age of ninety-six. His life spanned the heyday of the *Kaiserreich* (German

Empire), the rise and fall of the Weimar Republic, Nazism, division of Germany by the Allies, the establishment and stabilization of the Federal Republic after 1945, as well as two world wars, the German Revolution (of 1918), the horrors of the Holocaust, the Cold War, and the construction of the Berlin Wall. Although he continued to write and correspond well into the final years of his life, Schmitt's most impressive intellectual achievements date roughly from World War I until the early 1950s.[5]

Schmitt studied law in Berlin, Munich, and Strasbourg, where he successfully earned his law degree in 1910, before completing his *Habilitationsschrift*, the traditional prerequisite for pursuing an academic career in Germany, in 1914.[6] Because of back injuries during basic training, he was exempted from service on the front during World War I. Instead Schmitt worked for the quasi-dictatorial military government in power in Germany at war's end, ultimately helping to oversee the activities of the peace movement and left-wing socialists (USPD) for the general staff. His first marriage in 1916 ended in embarrassment: Schmitt married a Serbian woman, Pawla Dorotic, who deceptively claimed an aristocratic background. Schmitt's attempt to divorce her brought him into conflict with the Catholic Church. When his plans to remarry in 1926 garnered a hostile response from the Church, he nonetheless went ahead and did so despite the fact that he seems to have been well aware that excommunication inevitably would follow.

In my view, Schmitt's subsequent estrangement from Catholicism was probably genuine. Religious themes play at most an insignificant role in his writings from the late 1920s, and during the Nazi period Schmitt clearly distanced himself from Catholicism. Although his Catholic background is self-evident in some of his works, one ought not to exaggerate the theological overtones of Schmitt's political and legal theory.[7] For most of his career, Schmitt was a relatively secular-minded jurist, not a "political theologian" concerned with waging an intellectual crusade against atheism. Even though the currently fashionable tendency in Germany to read Schmitt as a closet Catholic theologian has produced some illuminating results, it risks obfuscating the real significance of his ideas for contemporary political and legal theory.[8]

During the Weimar period, Schmitt taught at Munich, Bonn, and then Berlin. He served as a legal adviser to the executive-centered emergency regimes established in Germany in the wake of the economic depression in 1929, and helped coordinate the legal case of those who unconstitutionally dismantled the (Social Democrat–led) Prussian state government in the "coup against Prussia" (*Preussenschlag*) of 1932.[9] Although Schmitt before 1933 probably hoped for a right-wing authoritarian solution to Weimar's crisis along lines distinct from those of the Nazis, after the Nazi takeover he immediately linked hands with Germany's new rulers. On May 1, 1933, he joined the National Socialist Party and soon garnered a number of prominent posts within the Nazi hierarchy. Despite a feud with elements of the SS in 1936 that forced him to surrender some of his positions, Schmitt remained a vocal Nazi legal thinker who played a central role in heated debates within Germany about international law and politics. He continued on as an outspoken professor in Berlin until 1945. In my view, his writings from this period provide no support for his postwar self-exculpatory claim that after 1936 he opposed National Socialism.

After the war, Schmitt was banned from teaching in part because he refused to comply with the formalities of denazification. Nonetheless, his residence in Plettenberg served as an intellectual second home to both older and younger German conservatives hostile to democratic politics and the "Americanization" of West Germany that was such a striking facet of both popular and political culture there after World War II.[10]

Though Schmitt never publicly apologized for his complicity in the horrors of National Socialism, his influence within Europe at the time of his death in 1985 was clearly on the rise. Since then, a veritable "Schmitt renaissance" has taken place in some scholarly circles in North America as well.

II

No issue has excited the interest of jurists in our century more than the enigma of legal indeterminacy. No thinker has arguably had more to say about that enigma than Carl Schmitt.

According to the mainstream of modern liberal theory, the rule of law at a minimum requires that legal norms be (1) general in character, (2) relatively clear, (3) public, (4) prospective, and (5) stable. According to liberals, only laws of this type can help provide legal equality, assure fair notice, and preserve the accountability of government officials to citizens. The rule of law renders state action predictable and makes an indispensable contribution toward individual freedom. Generality protects against arbitrariness by helping to guarantee that *like cases be treated alike*. Clarity means that the activities of those applying or enforcing the law can be held to relatively coherent standards and thus effectively controlled. Publicity demands that citizens have fair notice of when and how the state will intervene. Similarly, laws must exist at the time an act is committed in order to furnish fair notice. Stability within law not only facilitates fair notice as well, but also helps bind officials to legal norms and minimizes potentially undesirable exercise of discretion.

Imagining how a legal system lacking the virtues of the rule of law would look provides a quick grasp of the strengths of the liberal argument. By permitting government to single out individuals in an unprincipled manner, norms treating like cases in an unlike way potentially represent an abrogation of minimal standards of fairness. Excessively vague laws risk giving judges and administrators unwarranted discretionary powers. Secret and retroactive laws make it impossible for citizens to know how government is permitted to act and, moreover, render the idea of the accountability of government to the governed anachronistic.[11] Confusing changes in the legal system exacerbate the problem of unaccountability, and potentially allow officials to usurp powers that may not properly belong to them. From the perspective of the ruled, such a political order means inconstancy and insecurity.[12]

Two trends in our century pose a considerable challenge to the liberal model of the rule of law. First, substantial evidence suggests that necessary forms of state intervention in the capitalist economy, as well as the concomitant expansion of the state's social welfare activities, result in placing significant discretionary power in the hands of judges and administrators. Faced with a series of arduous regulatory and social policy tasks, legislators have sometimes done little more than write blank checks to government officials, who then face the unenviable task of implementing laws that provide little meaningful guidance.[13] Second, the proliferation of powerful constitutional courts, endowed with generous powers of judicial review over legislation, has arguably accelerated trends toward discretionary government. Before 1945, judicial institutions along the lines of the mighty American Supreme Court were rare. Today they are relatively commonplace within liberal democracy. From a traditional perspective, this institutional development raises problems to the extent that constitutional norms are often by necessity relatively imprecise and vague (for example, "the due process of law"). In principle, the judicial review of legislation and the rule of law are consistent. But the rule of law probably requires that constitutional courts engage in relatively limited forms of judicial review.[14] For better or worse, constitutional judges have not always respected this maxim. In the name of constitutional clauses open to a multiplicity of competing interpretations, constitutional judges have often opted to exercise far-reaching power in opposition to relatively clear statutes promulgated by legislatures.

Contemporary legal theory has responded to these challenges in three ways.[15] One answer entails reformulating the rule of law in terms of what we might describe as the *limited indeterminacy thesis*. According to this view, it is advisable to accept the necessity of a relatively significant sphere of discretion. Even the most cogent rule can be interpreted in relatively distinct ways; a certain amount of open-endedness necessarily inheres even in clear linguistic utterances.[16] Moreover, administrative and judicial discretion can serve legitimate purposes, and it sometimes makes sense for a polity to delegate discretionary authority to courts or bureaucrats.[17] In short, the early liberal view, as suggested by Baron de Montesquieu and others deeply hostile to judicial discretion, that the rule of law implies that there is necessarily only *one determinate* answer to every legal question, is overstated. But even if the legal material fails to dictate a single correct answer, it still constitutes a framework in which only a relatively limited set of answers is acceptable.[18] A commitment to the rule of law requires that forms of "indeterminacy" within the law ultimately remain peripheral to the overall activities of the legal system. In this view, legal indeterminacy can be effectively contained: most cases are "easy," though the legal system inevitably contains some set of "hard" cases.

Most liberal legal thinkers described as "formalists" fall into this category.[19] Many contemporary legal positivists do as well, as do some nonpositivists who have tried to defend a relatively rigorous conception of the rule of law.[20]

Like the first view, the second answer grapples with present-day legal realities by acknowledging that the liberal state no longer operates, if it ever did, in accordance with ideal models of perfect legal determinacy. But according to those who endorse the *undeterminacy thesis*, the legal materials (rules, statutes, precedents), typically emphasized in traditional defenses of the rule of law, generally provide minimal guidance to those faced with the tasks of interpreting and enforcing the law. Rules allow decision makers to act in a surprising diversity of ways; vague standards are necessarily ubiquitous within the law; rules often collide. Inevitably, the application and enforcement of the law are vastly more open-ended, creative processes than those committed to the limited indeterminacy thesis acknowledge. Most cases are hard, and only a few are easy. For theorists in this second camp, conventional legal materials represent an indispensable component of legal interpretation. Yet they inevitably fail to take decision makers as far as formalists typically claim.

In their more cautious moments, the Legal Realists probably fall within this group.[21] The contemporary free-market jurist Richard Posner does as well. Hostile to legal formalism, Posner nonetheless claims allegiance to the traditional "desire for impersonality and objectivity, for government of laws and not of men."[22] Legal materials go some way toward guiding judges. But for Posner, legal regularity is guaranteed chiefly by free-market economics and its (alleged) capacity for generating predictable results. Economic thinking should guide judges faced with the task of interpreting the substantial array of legal materials characterized by ambiguity. Though in a different way, Ronald Dworkin falls under this rubric as well. Dworkin argues that a responsible legal decision maker is obliged to make sure that his interpretation of the law "fits" the legal materials at hand.[23] But Dworkin, like Posner, doubts that the traditional legal materials emphasized by formalist models of the rule of law are likely to render decision making sufficiently determinate. For Dworkin, legal interpretation, in accordance with what he describes as "integrity," means that judges necessarily must rely on the most coherent or "best possible" interpretation of the political morality of the community of which they are a part. Within the United States (and probably other liberal democracies as well), this means that the underlying coherence of law can be preserved only if judges grant a relatively significant place to controversial interpretations of liberal ideals of fairness and justice.[24]

A third group responds to the ubiquity of discretionary power within contemporary liberal democracy by embracing the *radical indeterminacy thesis*. Recent empirical challenges to the liberal state simply underline the bankruptcy of the liberal dream of regulating power by clear general norms. In this view, legal indeterminacy is both pervasive and irreparable. Every application and enforcement of the law is willful in the sense that legal materials allow for virtually any conceivable answer to the question at hand. All cases are hard. The rule of law is a myth insofar as it obscures the fact that legal materials are "empty vessels" into which judges and administra-

tors engage in freewheeling forms of political and social judgment uncon-
strained by the law. Posner and Dworkin simply do not go far enough. The
problem is not just that rules are notably incomplete and thus must be
supplemented by background methods or principles (in Posner's case, free-
market economics; in Dworkin's, liberal political morality). Legal interpretation entails creating meaning for rules where none existed beforehand.
Theorists within this camp are skeptical of attempts to reestablish the possibility of legal determinacy by appealing to ideals or principles allegedly
embedded within the liberal legal system since for them liberalism itself is
internally contradictory. Hence, principles implicit within every liberal
legal order are unavoidably inconsistent and contradictory as well. Determinacy in law thus cannot be established by appeal to liberal law's immanent principles since a deep indeterminacy exists also at that level.[25]

In the United States, this position has been embraced by radicals in the
legal academy hoping to discredit the claim that ours is a law-based state.
Certain variants of Legal Realism can be grouped under this category, as
well as some of the more drastic strands within Critical Legal Studies
(CLS).[26]

How does Carl Schmitt fit into these debates? Of course, Schmitt's
times and intellectual context were different from our own. It should come
as no surprise that Schmitt's theory resists neat codification into any of the
distinct categories of argumentation just descibed. Schmitt has no close
relations in legal theory in the United States today, and no influential
American legal theory even remotely resembles Schmitt's heinous Nazi-era
ideas. At most, there are potentially illuminating parallels between *some* of
his ideas and those of contemporary writers on the rule of law.[27]

As I show in chapter 1, Schmitt very early endorsed ideas about legal
indeterminacy that clearly took him well beyond traditional notions of the
limited determinacy of law. In some contrast to contemporary North
American defenders of both the underdeterminacy and radical indeterminacy theses, however, he believed that the critique of formalist jurisprudence necessarily pointed the way toward an assault on liberal models of
deliberative parliamentarism (chapter 2), constitutionalism (chapter 3), the
state/society divide (chapter 4), and international law (chapter 6). Schmitt
exploited what he took to be the Achilles' heel of liberalism—formalist
jurisprudence—in order to discredit liberalism altogether. Pace liberalism,
legal decision making inevitably rests on untrammeled discretion: the inevitability of a constitutive "pure decision" at the basis of every legal act

demonstrates the bankruptcy of "normativistic" liberalism as a whole. From Schmitt's perspective, the enigma of legal indeterminacy provided an effective intellectual weapon in the right-wing authoritarian assault on liberal democracy. Pervasive gaps within liberal law could be exploited for the sake of exploding the confines of liberalism.

Schmitt failed in his attack on liberalism. Too often, his theory depends on a problematic mix of intellectual caricature and historical myth. Even his critique of formalist liberal jurisprudence stumbles for this reason: like many more recent critics of formalism, Schmitt conveniently ignores its subtlety.

Yet his reflections on legal indeterminacy raise provocative questions for contemporary political and legal theory. Within North America, those who endorse radical conceptions of indeterminacy too often seem sure that the deconstruction of liberal jurisprudence constitutes a necessary first step toward establishing a progressive alternative to liberal democracy. Discrediting even modest versions of the idea of a determinate legal order is essential if we are to move beyond the sad status quo of contemporary liberal democracy. Allegedly, the attack on formalism prepares the way for a more just and equitable political and social order.[28]

The example of Carl Schmitt suggests otherwise. Schmitt's dramatic ideas about legal indeterminacy early on made him a defender of rightist dictatorship and then of National Socialism (chapter 5). For Schmitt, only authoritarian political systems can fully acknowledge the fundamentally bogus character of the liberal rule of law. In this theory, the systematic deconstruction of the rule of law clears the way not for left-wing utopia, but right-wing authoritarianism. Schmitt's writings remain a thorn in the side of all those jurists who have yet to explain adequately why the dismantling of the rule of law is likely to make more freedom and equality possible, rather than robbing us of the (insufficient) liberties and equality we presently possess. In my view, radical jurists express many legitimate anxieties about the profound dilemmas faced by capitalist liberal democracy today, whereas contemporary liberals too often close their eyes to the shocking ills of an increasingly bankrupt political system, growing economic inequality, and continuing racial injustice. But radical jurists are wrong to think that the best way to start dealing with such problems is by tossing the achievements of liberal jurisprudence out the window. No writer better illustrates the perils of a principled antiliberal jurisprudence than Carl Schmitt.

Schmitt also raises questions for liberal American jurists committed to the underdeterminacy thesis. It is true that Schmitt never directly grappled with liberal versions of the underdeterminacy thesis like those common in contemporary jurisprudence; Schmitt too readily assumes that liberalism necessarily entails a commitment to legal formalism. Yet it would be a mistake to dismiss the contemporary relevance of Schmitt's theory simply by noting that his views rest on a critique of traditional formalist jurisprudence at which prominent contemporary liberal jurists, such as Posner and Dworkin, look askance. Like many of his right-wing Weimar peers, Schmitt endorsed antiformalism within the law as a way of undermining Weimar's fledgling democratically elected parliament; in the German setting, antiformal jurisprudence served antidemocratic purposes.[29] Can contemporary critics of legal formalism avoid related dangers? Of course, Posner and Dworkin are committed to liberal democracy, and both would rightly express outrage at Schmitt's right-wing authoritarianism. Yet from the perspective of a traditional view of the legislature as the main site for lawmaking, both theorists provide some room for concern: according to one reading, Posner and Dworkin ultimately reduce the legislature to a junior partner in a decision-making structure dominated by judicial experts.[30] Within the context of a stable liberal polity, the attempt to compensate for the limits of traditional legal materials by heightened judicial reliance on free market economics (Posner) or interpretations of liberal political ideals (Dworkin) may seem relatively unproblematic; both Posner and Dworkin persuasively suggest that substantial elements of American legal practice correspond to their (respective economic and political) liberal agendas. But what if the legal and political system at hand lacks the deeply rooted liberalism of American legal culture?[31] What if its immanent political morality arguably rests, as in many parts of Europe between the two wars, on substantial doses of authoritarianism, illiberalism, or anti-Semitism?[32] In that setting, providing judges with substantial authority to interpret the law in terms of what Dworkin describes as the most coherent or "soundest" reading of the community's immanent political morality may help strengthen reactionary forces, especially if liberal and democratic values are relatively fragile and underdeveloped.

Schmitt similarly sought to reestablish legal determinacy by looking beyond traditional formalist legal sources and methods. But for him this required a frontal assault on modern pluralism: legal determinacy could be guaranteed only if legal decision makers were rendered fundamentally "homogeneous" in orientation. As early as 1912, Schmitt therefore suggested that only a homogeneous judiciary could resolve the crisis of legal indeterminacy. After 1933, Schmitt elaborated this idea into a full-fledged defense of National Socialist law. Interestingly, recent defenders of the underdeterminacy thesis have struggled to demonstrate that a far-reaching reliance on nontraditional legal materials and methods need not generate antipluralistic results. Posner, for example, argues—in my view unconvincingly—that his preference for a judiciary committed to free-market values is basically uncontroversial since the formal tenets of Law and Economics rest on a broad consensus within contemporary society.[33] Here as well, the example of Carl Schmitt highlights the seriousness of a dilemma that contemporary jurists often prefer to downplay. Within pluralistic societies, attempts to reestablish legal predictability and regularity by appeals to suprapositive methods are often more partisan than their defenders concede.

Schmitt's political and legal theory does *not* offer a reasonable alternative to any of the most influential currents in contemporary debates about the rule of law. Yet both proponents of the liberal rule of law and radical critics could do worse than by grappling seriously with Schmitt's terrible legacy.

III

The exegesis of Schmitt's political and legal theory in part 1 of this study is devoted to encouraging an exchange between contemporary political and legal theorists and Schmitt's legacy. Part 2 then examines a dialogue that has *already* taken place between Schmitt and American political thought.

Schmitt's influence on some of the most important voices within postwar American political and legal theory has been widely documented.[34] Yet the story of Schmitt's impact on postwar political thought in the United States remains incomplete. Take Joseph A. Schumpeter's enormously influential democratic theory (chapter 7), Friedrich A. Hayek's free-market critique of the welfare state (chapter 8), and Hans J. Morgenthau's "realist" theory of international relations (chapter 9): each was shaped profoundly by a more or less hidden debate with Carl Schmitt. This study concludes with a discussion of three authors who not only engaged in a relatively intense dialogue with Schmitt and his ideas, but also exerted a significant impact on postwar intellectual life in the United States. None of them was a principled "Schmittian" in any simple sense of the term, and each opposed Schmitt's own political preferences and significant parts of his theory. Nevertheless, each author was ultimately influenced substantially by Schmitt.

Until we tackle this revealing chapter in the history of contemporary American political thinking, our picture of it remains badly incomplete. Contrary to a widely shared intellectual bias, Schmitt, unfortunately, was more than a parochial "German thinker" lacking in significance for American political and legal thought. As a matter of fact, Schmitt helped determine the contours of political thinking in the United States—in the immediate aftermath of the Allied victory over National Socialism and fascism in 1945.

Part One

THE JURISPRUDENCE OF
LAWLESSNESS

1

THE CRISIS OF LEGAL INDETERMINACY

Carl Schmitt wasted no time before enthusiastically endorsing the National Socialist seizure of power in Germany. Immediately following passage of the fateful Enabling Act of March 23, 1933, Schmitt penned an array of apologetic essays in which he justified the Nazis' destruction of Weimar democracy as well as the persecution of Jews, Social Democrats, Communists and other so-called "national enemies."[1] Schmitt then helped draw up the *Reichstatthaltergesetz* of April 7, 1933, which effectively destroyed Germany's federal system and granted enormous legislative powers to Hitler and the Nazis.[2] Later that year, he put the finishing touches on *State, Movement, Folk*, which quickly became the object of a wide-ranging debate among German legal scholars anxious to influence the construction of a specifically Nazi legal alternative to the Weimar Republic's rendition of the liberal rule of law.[3] Although Schmitt probably preferred an alternative right-wing authoritarian solution to Weimar's crisis before 1933, he showed no reservations about embracing the Nazis in the immediate aftermath of their takeover. Both his academic and polemical writings from 1933 offer unambiguous evidence of Schmitt's fervent quest to ally himself with the National Socialist regime.

Central to understanding the relationship between Schmitt's horrible Nazi-era polemics and his often impressive pre-1933 writings, *State, Movement, Folk* both summarizes many of Schmitt's earlier criticisms of Weimar democracy and outlines the fundamental features of an alternative National Socialist legal order. Schmitt argues that the ongoing proliferation of vague, open-ended legal standards ("in good faith," "in the public interest," "public order"), already evident in the Weimar legal order and in every modern liberal democracy, suggests the anachronistic character of liberal

15

conceptions of the rule of law. Although classical defenders of the rule of law repeatedly emphasized the virtues of cogent, general legal norms, the liberal democratic legal order in fact decreasingly consists of such norms. According to Schmitt, vague legal standards potentially provide a starting point for transforming the remnants of liberal law in accordance with National Socialist ideals. Consequently, jurists sympathetic to the ongoing "national renewal" should exploit ambiguous legal clauses by interpreting them in a manner compatible with Nazi aspirations. In the process, the vessel of existing German law can be filled with National Socialist concepts of a homogeneous German "folk community," even before the Nazis succeed in generating statutes explicitly attuned to their political project.[4]

In response to those worried about the obvious dangers posed by this agenda to traditional legal protections, Schmitt's *State, Movement, Folk* offers a clever answer. Judicial actors cannot be meaningfully regulated or bound by open-ended legal clauses anyway. How can a vague standard such as "in good faith" possibly assure any determinacy within judicial decision making? Hence, the emergence of amorphous clauses within liberal democracy rendered traditional liberal conceptions of judicial decision making problematic well before the onset of the "national renewal" in Germany. Of course, one might respond to Schmitt's observation here by demanding a halt to the proliferation of amorphous law. But *State, Movement, Folk* identifies two reasons for questioning this possible course of action. First, the exigencies of the contemporary interventionist state render vague legal standards "unavoidable and indispensable."[5] Traditional concepts of the legal norm are made obsolete by the emergence of necessary but highly complex forms of state action. Second, the indeterminacy intrinsic to amorphous legal standards turns out to be nothing but the tip of the iceberg. In Schmitt's view, "[w]e have experienced that every [legal] word and every concept immediately becomes controversial, unsure, indeterminate and pliable in a fluctuating situation when different spirits and interests try to make use of them. . . . From this perspective, all existing legal concepts are 'indeterminate' legal concepts."[6] Classical liberal conceptions of a "mechanical and automatic binding" of the judge to the legal norm are clearly overstated. Pace liberal jurisprudence, *all* legal concepts are profoundly and unavoidably open-ended and indeterminate. Every legal decision is a *hard case*. Liberal demands to clarify and codify law are inherently flawed because no system of legal norms can hope to guarantee even a minimal degree of regularity and determinacy within legal decision making.

How then might the emerging Nazi political order guarantee some measure of control over the judiciary? Schmitt grasps that the expansion of possibilities for judicial discretion could work both *for* and *against* the Nazis; judges might exploit it in order to counter National Socialism. Just after endorsing the expulsion of Jews and purported political radicals from the civil service, Schmitt argues that only a "bindedness to the folk" [*Volksgebundenheit*] and "ethnic homogeneity" [*Artgleichheit*] within the ranks of German jurists could successfully assure a measure of coherence within judicial decision making. Judicial actors must partake of German ethnicity if they are to grasp in full the subtleties and particularities of German law; ethnic Germans alone are "capable of seeing the facts of the case correctly, listening to statements rightly, understanding words correctly and offering a correct evaluation of people and things" within the confines of an intrinsically German legal system.[7] Effective legal interpretation rests on implicit assumptions deriving from our participation in the racial and ethnic life of a particular *Volk*. No matter that "ethnic cleansing" necessitates terror: in Schmitt's view, the struggle to develop an intrinsically German form of postliberal legal determinacy demands nothing less. Legal reform requires a reform of legal *decision makers*. Legal determinacy can never be adequately achieved by means of a particular set of legal statutes or doctrines. Yet a deeper and more dependable degree of legal determinacy allegedly might be realized by establishing an ethnically homogeneous judiciary, free of alien [*artfremde*] ethnic and racial tendencies. Because legal decision making to a significant degree relies on "unconscious movements" of ethnic origin, only a judiciary possessing a homogeneous, ethnically predictable composition can guarantee legal predictability and determinacy.

Chapters 5 and 6 carefully scrutinize Schmitt's National Socialist legal and political theory. Here, I hope to trace its origins to Schmitt's pivotal early contributions to jurisprudence from the 1910s and early 1920s. First, I examine the roots of Schmitt's critique of liberal conceptions of judicial decision making, the crucial but oftentimes ignored *Law and Judgment* (1912) and *The Value of the State and Significance of the Individual* (1914) (I, II). Then I discuss the subsequent radicalization of Schmitt's hostility to liberal legal thinking that culminates in the militant antilegalism of *Political Theology* (1922) (III). I emphasize the role of Schmitt's reflections on the problem of the *indeterminacy* of law. Despite its central place within

Schmitt's thinking, his reflections on legal decision making have been repeatedly ignored by the ongoing "Schmitt renaissance" in English-speaking countries.[8] Yet Schmitt's analysis of the problem of legal indeterminacy, which he first formulates in some of his *earliest* writings, anticipates crucial elements of the ominous arguments found in *State, Movement, Folk*. Although it would be wrong to deny that Schmitt's ideas about liberal democratic political and legal ideas undergo an evolution, or that his theorizing after 1930 takes on increasingly radical hues, Schmitt's early analysis of the problem of legal indeterminacy shows that his Nazi-era legal theory represents less of a break within his thinking than many commentators have been willing to concede. Within the problematic contours of Schmitt's legal thinking, his option for National Socialism, unfortunately, rests on a terrible but consistent logic: Nazi law represented for Schmitt a logical answer to the most profound dilemmas of modern legal theory and practice.

I

In this study I hope to show that Carl Schmitt consistently relied on idealized and downright misleading interpretations of classical liberal political and legal ideals as instruments for mocking contemporary liberal democratic aspirations. In order to criticize the mundane realities of contemporary parliamentary government, Schmitt's *The Crisis of Parliamentary Democracy* (1923) hearkens back to a make-believe world of pristine nineteenth-century liberal parliamentarism. So as to debunk contemporary conceptions of liberal constitutionalism, Schmitt's *Constitutional Theory* (1928) offers a negative portrayal of twentieth-century *positivist* constitutionalist thinking and then contrasts it unfavorably to the ambitious constitutional ideals of early liberals like John Locke and Montesquieu. Schmitt's thinking on legal decision making similarly partakes of this rhetorically powerful, albeit intellectually suspect, ploy.

State, Movement, Folk asserts that liberal conceptions of legal decision making rest on a "normativistic faith" in a legal system free of loopholes and the corresponding view that all conceivable cases and situations can be unambiguously *subsumed* under a set of clear general norms. Liberals thus reduce the judge "to an automaton into which legal documents and fees are stuffed at the top in order that [they] may spill forth the verdict at the bottom along with the reasons, read mechanically from codified paragraphs."[9] In Schmitt's one-sided reading of liberal legal thought, Montesquieu's view of the judge as "*la bouche, qui prononce les paroles de la loi*" thus has exercised enormous influence.[10] Because of the impact of Montesquieu and those following in his footsteps, liberals allegedly believe that legal rules can guarantee a perfectly predictable and determinate decision in every conceivable case. Liberals believe that *all* legal decisions are "easy" cases, and *every* act of judicial subsumption can guarantee an unambiguously "right" answer.

Of course, one could argue against Schmitt here that the *underlying insight* of even relatively traditional liberal conceptions of judicial action takes a more modest—and defensible—form. Montesquieu is no more paradigmatic for liberal jurisprudence than Jean-Jacques Rousseau for democratic theory and practice; the resources of the liberal tradition are surely richer than Schmitt concedes. Even in the line of argumentation described above as the *limited indeterminacy thesis*, the idea of legal determinacy merely consists in claiming that a legal norm "cannot bind in every direction the act by which it is applied. There must always be more or less room for discretion, so that the . . . [legal norm] . . . can only have the character of a frame to be filled by this act."[11] In this more subtle reading of the idea of the binding character of law, the interpretation of the statute or norm surely can lead to several distinct decisions, though hardly to an infinite variety of decisions. This set of possible answers remains relatively limited and predictable, for legal determinacy is always necessarily imperfect. Montesquieu's Enlightenment conception of mechanical jurisprudence indeed is anachronistic. At the same time, we probably cannot assure a minimum of legal predictability and security without a commitment to some version, however modest, of the idea of the binding character of the semantic structure of legal norms. Unless legal materials can provide at least minimal guidance to judicial and administrative actors, the ideal of the rule of law loses any significance.

Yet it is precisely this highly misleading reading of liberal thinking about judicial action that constitutes the initial target of Schmitt's 1912 *Law and Judgment: An Examination of the Problem of Legal Practice*. Here as well, Schmitt associates the core of liberal jurisprudence with Montesquieu's view of judicial action in order to caricature traditional liberal legal ideals before, not surprisingly, dismissing them out of hand. *Law and Judgment* easily demonstrates the crudeness both of Montesquieu's views and modern legal movements influenced by him, such as the German Conceptual Jurists [*Begriffsjurisprudenz*].[12] If laws could be perfectly clear and transparent, Schmitt claims, then liberals' mechanical view of judicial decision making might possess some value. But in light of the fact that only a tiny number of cases involve both an adequately clear legal norm and an act obviously meant to be determined by it, the concept of a "smooth subsumption" applies only to exceptional cases. In the overwhelming majority of situations faced by a judge, the liberal view provides no real help. Thus, Schmitt believes that his own contribution to a theory of legal decision making can rightfully *commence* from the assumption that "the traditional hermeneutics of valid law" has already been effectively discredited.[13] Given the manifestly anachronistic character of liberal views of legal judgment, Schmitt seems to believe, *Law and Judgment* need not be concerned with reconstructing an identifiably liberal conception of judicial decision making. From this perspective, the path *beyond formalism* ultimately leads *beyond liberalism*.

Law and Judgment proceeds to offer a rigorous critique of influential attempts within modern jurisprudence to compensate for the inadequacies of formalistic jurisprudence. To those who admit that judges necessarily are forced to downplay the letter of the law and hence should instead focus on legislative intent, Schmitt responds that such views rest on a misleading conflation of state organs with concrete individual human beings. Recourse to concepts of "the will of the legislator" or "the will of the statute" simply obscures the nature of judicial action: the homogeneous, unified will implied by such terms is a fiction, a misleading personalization of state activity that made some sense in the context of Absolutism when lawmaking did rest on the will of a concrete individual.[14] But it makes no sense whatsoever as soon as numerous individual "wills" are implicated in the legislative process. And even if one disregards this initial problem, the fact remains that "it is factually impossible to ascertain the real, psychological content of the will of a definite human being . . . for a definite period of time."[15] An examination of legislative proceedings and historical documents related to the origins of a particular statute fails to resolve the dilemma at hand as well, for such materials should not be confused with the statute itself: "Only that published as a statute becomes a statute."[16] When relying on concepts of legislative intent, judges inevitably *construct* an ideal, rational legislator with little real relationship to the actual historical legislative process. "A 'will' suspended in the air above the judge is always first and foremost the result of an interpretation," and not, as defenders of this view posit, an objective

state of affairs that a judge merely concretizes when engaging in legal interpretation.[17] Legislative "will" or intent is the product of legal interpretation, not its starting point. A (discretionary) interpretive act first *makes
possible* those standards which judicial decision makers then, misleadingly,
claim compose the basis of their decisions.

What then of the prominent Free Law Movement, and its open acknowledgment of the discretionary character of all decision making? Anticipating many of the main arguments of American Legal Realism, the
politically heterogeneous German Free Law jurists similarly challenged formalistic conceptions of the law as a closed and unified set of norms. At first
glance, *Law and Judgment* seems to bring Schmitt into close proximity to
the Free Law Movement and its central claim that the unavoidability of
judicial discretion legitimizes the judge's reliance on open-ended, suprapositive legal standards (for example: "the needs of commerce").[18] But
Schmitt considers the Free Law School insufficiently rigorous. The Free
Law School extends the statutory basis of judicial action by introducing
new and more flexible standards into the legal system, thereby providing a
legal basis for judicial discretion. But according to Schmitt, its proponents
still implicitly assume that judges nonetheless "subsume" individual legal
acts under a set of legal rules, albeit a set of rules that has been substantially
broadened. For Schmitt, the formalistic spirit of Montesquieu haunts even
the most creative strands within modern legal thought, and a complete
break with Montesquieu's bankrupt intellectual legacy demands of us that
we undertake a frontal assault on the last vestiges of "normativistic" liberal
legalism. Schmitt insists that the addition of vague standards into the legal
system necessarily robs the concept of legal subsumption of any substance:
a vague standard such as "the needs of commerce" permits a panoply of
alternative—and potentially contradictory—answers to a particular legal
case.[19] The Free Law Movement thus points to the existence of a purely
discretionary moment inherent in judicial action. But its defenders ultimately prove unable to face the full implications of their discovery. Ultimately, they revert to the least defensible myth of traditional liberal legal
thinking, a moderate version of the idea of legal "subsumption," despite
the fact that their creative theoretical innovations rob the concept of subsumption of any real substance.

While openly building on the Free Law School's tension-ridden defense of judicial discretion, Schmitt's own model of judicial action strives to
explode its traditionalist confines. *Law and Judgment*'s answer to the central

problem of any theory of judicial decision making—"When is a judicial decision a correct decision?"—is already implied by Schmitt's critical comments about the Free Law Movement. According to Schmitt, the Free Law School correctly anticipated that legal decision making is always characterized by what Schmitt describes as a "moment" of "indifference in reference to the content" of law [*inhaltlicher Indifferenz*].[20] The relationship between the legal norm and the judicial actor inevitably involves an element of "indifference" or indeterminacy vis-à-vis the legal norm. In more familiar terms: an element of discretion characterizes judicial decision making.[21]

But how then is the political community to be spared the obvious ills of a discretionary judiciary unregulated by the letter of the law? The young Schmitt *is* worried about the specter of judicial arbitrariness and "subjectivism." Quite provocatively, *Law and Judgment* argues that indeterminacy at the level of the law's manifest structure need *not* generate judicial chaos. *Indeterminacy within the sphere of legal norms and standards still leaves open an alternative path to legal determinacy* [*Rechtsbestimmtheit*]. Anticipating a common argumentative move within recent American jurisprudential debates, Schmitt's initial answer to the purported ills of formalistic jurisprudence is an embrace of a (peculiar) version of the *underdeterminacy thesis*: although traditional legal materials emphasized by formalist jurists fail to assure legal determinacy, other sources available to the judicial actor can succeed in doing so. The task at hand involves reconceptualizing the problem of legal determinacy so as to break dramatically with formalistic liberal jurisprudence's traditional obsession with the relationship between the legal norm and the judicial actor; the task left unfinished by the Free Law School needs to be completed. Determinacy should no longer be conceptualized in terms of a "subsumption" of a particular act under a legal norm or standard. But if legal determinacy is no longer to be located in the nexus between the legal norm and the judge, where might we look to conceive of its possibility? Schmitt offers a novel answer to this question: legal determinacy still legitimately constitutes the guiding principle of the legal system. Yet the problem of legal determinacy must be conceptualized anew so as to focus on the *relationship between the individual judge and his peers*. In other words: the "normativistic" liberal focus on the relationship *between the norm and the judge* needs to be jettisoned for an emphasis on the relationship *between legal decision makers*. Legal determinacy indeed can be achieved by means of appeal to a shared legal/professional praxis.

In Schmitt's view, judges should acknowledge the obligatory status of a simple but absolutely pivotal principle: "a judicial decision is correct today when it can be assumed that another judge would have decided in the same way."[22] Judges can no longer seek recourse either to the letter of the law or to any of a series of compensatory mechanisms proposed by previous jurists in order to generate predictability and regularity. Instead, they need to engage in the thought experiment of asking themselves whether "another judge" would have acted in exactly the same manner. Existing legal practice already hints at the legitimacy of this principle: when judges write legal decisions, they appeal to their colleagues; when a particular case takes on special importance, it is common to insist that a number of judges cooperate in solving the case. But it now needs to gain open recognition as a superior source for an identifiably postliberal concept of legal determinacy. According to Schmitt, "[t]he 'other judge' here described is the empirical type of the modern expertly trained jurist."[23] The "normal" judicial professional of Schmitt's own day is the standard for his proposed test. In this model, judicial "practice justifies itself by means of its own practices."[24] Legal norms, standards, and concepts are no longer "containers into which the judge deposits a particular act." Instead, they represent mere "instruments for justifying an expectation," namely that other judges would have decided in the same way.[25] Traditional judicial strategies—a reference to the letter of the law, for example—can still legitimately be employed by the judge, but only if the judge in question understands the limits of such strategies by acknowledging that they are nothing but useful tools for ascertaining how the "other judge" would have acted.[26]

Schmitt's creative resolution of one of the perennial dilemmas of jurisprudence still leaves an obvious question unanswered: can it work? Might an appeal to the "empirical type of the modern expertly trained jurist" provide the judge with the meaningful guidance that liberals hope to provide by means of binding legal actors to the norm, and thereby guarantee a measure of determinacy within the law? Given the manifest diversity of types of "expertly trained jurists" in the modern world, there is certainly good reason to doubt Schmitt's assertion. Liberals and conservatives, socialists as well as defenders of economic laissez-faire, have composed the ranks of expertly trained modern jurists. Felix Frankfurter and Hans Kelsen, as well as the Nazi Roland Freisler, belong among them. A thought experiment in which the judge looks to the world of other "expertly trained jurists" is unlikely to provide unambiguous answers to difficult legal cases.

In my reading, Schmitt's argument probably only makes sense if the heterogeneity of modern jurisprudence is substantially downplayed. At least implicitly, Schmitt here probably presupposes a significant degree of political, social, and doctrinal homogeneity within the German judiciary; from Schmitt's perspective, the relative unanimity of socially conservative and deeply antidemocratic views among German jurists in 1912 certainly must have provided some empirical plausibility to this assumption.[27] Only in a relatively homogeneous judicial universe might the imperative to turn and consider the views of legal colleagues conceivably provide some minimal degree of determinacy within the legal system.

Law and Judgment leaves this crucial assumption unstated. But it is striking in light of Schmitt's subsequent claim in *State, Movement, Folk* that only homogeneity within the judiciary can guarantee some measure of legal determinacy. Clearly, there is no trace of the horrible racial and ethnic homogeneity later defended by Schmitt, and it would be indefensible to ignore the crucial differences between Schmitt's first contribution to legal theory and its Nazi period makeover. Nonetheless, well before the Nazi seizure of power, Schmitt offered a scathing critique of traditional liberal ideas of norm-based legal decision making that both emphasized the discretionary character of judicial action *and*, simultaneously, attempted to counteract the potent problems of discretion by pointing to the legal virtues of a "homogeneous" judiciary. Along with an emphasis on the inevitable indeterminacy of liberal jurisprudence, we find the anticipation of an alternative means for guaranteeing legal regularity: homogeneity.

II

The young Schmitt's second major contribution to political and legal thought, the 1914 *The Value of the State and the Significance of the Individual*, at first glance represents a polemic against precisely the cynical view of law that would later gain a wide following among Nazi jurists. Schmitt vehemently criticizes a diversity of "power-theories" of law that reduce the legal system to nothing but a "game" among competing power interests.[28] Such theories obscure law's essentially normative character. They provide no real place for the task of legal argumentation and justification. When pursued consistently, realist views of law deny the integrity of legal discourse by interpreting legal argumentation as a mere epiphenomenon of a more fundamental struggle among competing political and social constituencies. Thus, power realist views of law ultimately reduce law to nothing but *facticity*: they can only speak coherently about the social and political "facts" of empirical power, but hardly of "norms" and the problems of legal justification.

Schmitt then relies on this otherwise persuasive criticism of power realist conceptions of law in order to justify a conclusion that by no means automatically follows from it. He believes that an assault on a crude reductionist interpretation of law allows him to defend a thesis no less extreme than the view he challenges. Allegedly, law and power need to be seen as constituting two absolutely distinct spheres. Even those conceptions of law that permit power to be conceptualized as just one element of law, he now argues, inevitably "pollute" the normative core of law and thus distort its very essence. Law constitutes a "pure" set of norms, the realm of "ought" [*Sollen*], in stark contrast to the facticity [*Sein*] of empirical power struggles. Any attempt to mix the two spheres obscures law's essence: "pure law" is utterly distinct from "pure (that is, legally unregulated) power." "If law is to exist, it cannot be derived from power, for the gap between law and power simply cannot be bridged."[29] The realm of facticity, the sphere of concrete power, cannot ground normativity, the sphere of legal norms. Concrete power relations are essentially alien to law and its normative core. What lacks normative significance (power) cannot be transformed into something normative; an area of social existence "alien to values" [*Wertfremde*] cannot take the form of a set of values or norms. In a manner at times strikingly reminiscent of Hans Kelsen's neo-Kantian legal positivism and its insistence on a radical division between legal science and a sociology of empirical power relations, the young Schmitt similarly posits the existence of two altogether different "worlds."[30] Law consists of norms, but power is essentially a problem of the will, and even "a gradual transition [from the norm to the will] is unthinkable."[31]

The young Schmitt quickly parts company from Kelsen, however. Whereas Kelsen rests satisfied with positing an insurmountable divide between the spheres of pure law and concrete power, Schmitt struggles to overcome the antinomy between law and power.[32] Regrettably, his quest to do so suffers from the idiosyncrasies of his analytical starting point. Like water and oil, law and power cannot be properly fused or blended. Thus, when Schmitt tries to bring law and power into a more intimate relationship, he is forced to argue that the "purity of power" has to remain intact. Even though *The Value of the State and the Significance of the Individual* polemicizes against power-realist interpretations of law, Schmitt's own view ultimately proves closer to those of his opponents than he would prefer to have us acknowledge. Within Schmitt's vision of the legal system, expressions of unregulated "pure power" ultimately remain inescapable as well.

Although the spheres of power and law cannot be merged or fused, a means of linking the two spheres can be found. In Schmitt's account from World War I, this is precisely the function of the state. State organs undertake to translate the norms of the abstract legal universe into concrete reality. The state acts as a transmission belt between the legal sphere and the world of everyday power politics, between normativity and facticity. By undertaking to realize abstract legal norms, state institutions find themselves situated fruitfully between the realms of facticity and normativity, and thus capable of mediating between the two spheres. Yet this mediation comes at a price. To the extent that the state makes it possible to render the "heavenly" realm of legal normativity relevant for the mundane sphere of "earthly" reality, law is forced to surrender its heavenly character. More specifically: the realization of legal normativity in the world of everyday empirical facts makes it necessary to compromise its normative virginity. When law is *realized* and thus brought into the sphere of factual power relations, it is forced to make concessions to a universe alien to its own internal dynamics. What form must this compromise take? In light of Schmitt's formulation of the problem at hand, the answer is clear: law inevitably contains elements of that universe which it has been forced to enter into a compact with, namely the sphere of empirical power. When realized by governmental bodies, law includes a moment of normatively unregulated facticity, of *pure power* or *willfulness*.

The Value of the State and the Significance of the Individual thus represents a crucial evolutionary step within Schmitt's legal thinking. First, Schmitt now can offer a more detailed explanation of the underlying sources of indeterminacy in legal decision making. *Law and Judgment* generally focused on discarding relatively formalistic views of judicial action; *The Value of the State and the Significance of the Individual* now locates the fundamental source of the "indifference in reference to the content" of the law in the state's struggle to mediate between "pure power" and "pure law."[33] Owing to the unavoidable concessions that the sphere of normativity is forced to make to the realm of facticity, a "sovereign decision" is essential to legal experience. Law can never remain normatively pure if it is to become effective. From this perspective, legal indeterminacy is more than a narrow jurisprudential problem. Instead, it stems from the very heart of the political condition, conceived here as a tragic quest to link two profoundly distinct facets of human existence, normativity and facticity. Second, Schmitt now explicitly associates the "moment" of "indifference in reference to the content" of the law with an expression of "pure power"; this idea was probably suggested by *Law and Judgment*, but it was never formulated with sufficient clarity. Hence, Schmitt's claim is more ambitious than seemed evident in *Law and Judgment*. Not only is legal decision making inherently discretionary, but also discretion consists of perfect "willfulness," an expression of "pure power" unrestrained by the sphere of legal norms.

By suggesting that legal determinacy can be salvaged even if we acknowledge the inevitability of judicial discretion vis-à-vis the legal norm, *Law and Judgment* tended to downplay this more dramatic implication of Schmitt's critique of liberal jurisprudence. But *The Value of the State and the Significance of the Individual* points the way to an alternative—and more radical—course of argumentation.

III

In the shadow of World War I and then the German Revolution of 1918–1919, Schmitt's views on the indeterminacy of law undergo preciously the radicalization anticipated by *The Value of the State and the Significance of the Individual*. Schmitt formulates the outlines of an authoritarian legal theory that not only goes well beyond the critique of liberal jurisprudence outlined in *Law and Judgment*, but also already points in some ways toward the ominous *State, Movement, Folk*. As we have seen, Schmitt initially focused on debunking formalistic models of judicial action, before going on to trace their ills to the phenomenon of "pure power." His next move consists in underlining a conceptual link between dictatorship and the enigma of legal indeterminacy.

In a generally forgotten but crucial early essay, "Dictatorship and the State of Siege" (1917), Schmitt connects his abstract reflections on the problem of legal indeterminacy to one of the great political controversies of the war years. In subsequent years, Schmitt would exhibit enormous skill at making otherwise dry theoretical speculations in jurisprudence take on immediate political significance. "Dictatorship and the State of Siege" is an early example of this talent. By 1917, Germans were living under what amounted to a military dictatorship under Generals Paul von Hindenburg and Erich Ludendorff; vast arenas of political, social, and economic activity fell under the auspices of the emergency authorities. Not surprisingly, the generals and their political allies claimed that their dictatorial powers could not be legitimately controlled by traditional legal and political means. In their view, the world war required placing effectively unregulated political authority in their hands.[34] German scholars schooled in the tradition of the nineteenth-century German *Rechtsstaat* [law-based state] protested against the vast proliferation of dictatorial powers. Schmitt joined forces with those who sought to defend it.

Schmitt's essay begins by drawing a clear distinction between the institutions of a dictatorship and those of the state of siege. The former stems from French revolutionary *practice* and the experience of the war conditions of 1793, when revolutionary France was faced with universal hostility in Europe, and counterrevolutionary forces occupied parts of France itself. The Convention's dictatorship of 1793 was effectively "unlimited" [*schrankenlos*] in nature, and its success was predicated on the abandonment of an effective separation of executive and legislative powers.[35] In contrast, the institutions of the state of siege are indebted to French revolutionary *theory*; the Enlightenment rationalism of Locke, Montesquieu, and Rousseau plays a central role here. The crucial difference is that the state of siege continues, at least on the surface, to respect the principle of the separation of powers. No fusion of legislative and executive power occurs in the state of siege. By means of a legislative delegation, vast powers are centralized in the hands of military and executive authorities, in order to ward off a concrete threat to the well-being of the legal order as a whole. Nonetheless, these powers are to remain exclusively executive in nature. Those exercising the delegated authority are denied the right to issue orders having the status of legal statutes. In this spirit, Schmitt notes that in 1848 the French General Eugène Cavaignac gave back those powers delegated to him by the legislative authorities as soon as those tasks appointed him were completed.

What does this have to do with the German situation in World War I? At first glance, Schmitt appears to argue for limitations on the power of the military in Germany.[36] After all, Schmitt concedes that the Enlightenment-inspired French theory of the state of siege played a decisive role in shaping the German legal institutions of the emergency situation.[37] But what Schmitt gives with one hand he immediately takes away with the other. Developing his earlier ideas about legal indeterminacy, Schmitt systemati-

cally deconstructs the French conception of the state of siege. By the conclusion of the essay, Schmitt clearly suggests that its "rationalistic" attempt
to maintain the separation between legislative and executive powers is
doomed to fail. And at least by implication, Schmitt highlights the inevitability of a military dictatorship, in which legislative and executive powers
are fused, for the sake of defeating domestic and foreign foes during a dire
crisis.

Schmitt again mocks the Baron de Montesquieu's famous declaration
that the judge is nothing more than *la bouche qui prononce les paroles de la loi*,
suggesting that Jean-Jacques Rousseau's hostility to executive power needs
to be read as a radicalization of Montesquieu's exaggerated rationalistic hostility to judicial power. Montesquieu's mechanical conception of the judge
amounts to an attempt to reduce the judiciary to an accessory of the executive; for Montesquieu, the judge merely "pronounces" the law. Schmitt
then claims that Rousseau builds on this doomed quest by trying to eliminate executive power altogether. Rousseau replaces Montesquieu's tripartite separation of powers with the dualism of legislative and executive
powers, and the executive is described as engaging in a mechanical application of legislative norms. The legislator, undertaking action that is exclusively general in character, is the only real power in Rousseau's system.
Rousseau thereby exacerbates the fundamental weaknesses of Montesquieu's model.[38] Just as Montesquieu obscures the centrality of the discretionary decision constitutive of every judicial interpretation, so, too, does
Rousseau's model miss the creative character of every administrative decision. Schmitt goes so far as to suggest that it is absurd to believe that administrative decision making can be contained within a statute: "What is true
for the judicial decision . . . is even more true for the administration, for
which every aim to be achieved cannot be predetermined or formulated
by means of a statute."[39] In light of this problem, Schmitt argues that it
makes sense to see administrative discretion as a primordial or originary
form of political power [*Urzustand*]. Probably alluding to the origins of the
modern state in Absolutism, Schmitt asserts that "the starting point of all
state activity is administration."[40] Only later, as illustrated by the theories
of writers like Montesquieu and Rousseau, was the attempt undertaken to
subject situation-specific, administrative discretion to norm-based legislative and judicial devices. But Montesquieu and Rousseau fail to understand
that the originary discretionary power of the modern state can never be
extinguished. Unregulated discretion inevitably haunts the workings of

law-based government every time an administrator is asked to "apply" a statute, for no statute can succeed in fully capturing the creative [*schöpferisch*] activity of the administrator.[41]

Because of the congenital ills of the Enlightenment rationalism from which it derives, the institutions of the state of siege thus lack coherence. Representing nothing less than a return to the primordial origins of state power, the awesome discretionary power exhibited by the executive during the state of siege represents for Schmitt more than the mere "application" of a legislative statute. In reality, those holding this authority are ultimately unaffected by the legalistic dichotomy of legislative and executive power, and the separation of powers necessarily lacks the significance attributed to it by Enlightenment theory.[42] Although hesitant to state his dramatic conclusions openly, Schmitt thereby intimates that the institutions of the dictatorship and the state of siege share a crucial commonality: in the final analysis, both point to the necessity of overcoming the classical distinction between legislative and executive power in the face of a dire crisis.

The implications of this argument for Schmitt's account of legal indeterminacy are profound, even if Schmitt himself in 1917 failed to sketch them out immediately. Legally unregulated power is described as an outgrowth of an originary experience of discretionary power. Moreover, there is more than a faint suggestion in Schmitt's comments that this original *Urzustand* represents a more authentic or true form of politics than that acceptable to those who favor substantial legal limitations on the wartime exercises of emergency power; Schmitt seems delighted by the fact that the experience of World War I shatters the rationalistic illusions of naive Enlightenment political and legal thought. Wartime dictatorship and the exercise of discretion within the application and interpretation of legal norms both derive from the same source, the discretionary *Urzustand*. In short, legal indeterminacy and dictatorship are closely related. Wartime dictatorship is at best simply a more open expression of the unregulated discretion that plagues every act of legal interpretation and application.

On this reading, Schmitt's 1921 *Dictatorship* then simply makes the conceptual link between legal indeterminacy and dictatorial power explicit. Going well beyond the relatively simple theory of dictatorship offered in "Dictatorship and State of Siege," Schmitt in 1921 distinguishes between *commissarial* and *sovereign* dictatorship: the former is temporary and aims at the restoration of an existing legal order, whereas the latter brings about a revolutionary transformation of the status quo into a novel alternative political and legal order. In contrast to *Law and Judgment*, but in accordance with the 1917 "Dictatorship and State of Siege," the dilemma of legal indeterminacy is no longer conceived here chiefly as a problem of judicial discretion and thus of interest primarily as an element of judicial action. Rather, legal indeterminacy is seen as possessing profound relevance for understanding a variety of legal actors and institutions, the most revealing of which is dictatorship. For Schmitt, the concept of dictatorship constitutes the "missing link" of modern jurisprudence. Dictatorship represents a paradigmatic attempt to grapple seriously with the exigencies of legal indeterminacy.

The work's preface restates the now familiar idea that an "opposition" inevitably exists between a legal norm and the method of realizing it. In the language of Schmitt's prewar contributions to legal theory, a "moment of indifference in reference to the content" of the law results from the attempt to realize law in the sphere of concrete facticity. But here Schmitt argues that the omnipresent possibility of a gap between legal norms and the manner in which they gain realization in the concrete world is precisely "where the essence of dictatorship lies."[43] An analysis of the problem of dictatorship is crucial for acknowledging that the realization of a legal norm rests unavoidably on forms of (unregulated) discretionary action: "To speak in abstract terms, the problem of dictatorship, which far too rarely has been systematically analyzed, is the problem of the concrete exception within legal theory."[44] Schmitt's model of a commissarial dictatorship illustrates this point. In a commissarial dictatorship ordinary legal norms are abrogated for the sake of realizing a "concrete goal" essential to the preservation of the legal order. A commissarial dictator must restore the preexisting system of ordinary law; if he abandons this task, he becomes a mere despot.[45] Yet because the specific actions necessary for overcoming a dire political crisis cannot be predicted beforehand, even a limited form of commissarial dictatorship is rightfully free of normal legal restraints. A temporary emergency dictatorship of this type is forced to make use of individual and concrete measures in accord with the imperatives of the crisis at hand; ordinary general statutes are unlikely to suffice in the fulfillment of the task of overcoming the crisis. The general jurisprudential lesson here for Schmitt is that the survival of a functioning legal system presupposes highly discretionary forms of political power—in his earlier terminology, a moment of "indifference in reference to the content" of the law. The impressive discretionary authority of the emergency dictatorship is simply an unmediated expression of the irrepressible discretion that for Schmitt plagues even the "normal" process of judicial interpretation.

Dictatorship is a Janus-faced book. On the one hand, the "moment" of "indifference in reference to the content" of the law arguably remains just that in *Dictatorship*—a *moment* of legal existence. Schmitt's 1921 defense of a commissarial dictatorship might legitimately be read as nothing more than a defense of a temporary dictatorship, an instrument that even liberal democracy occasionally should employ amid a serious crisis in order to guarantee the very preconditions of legal and political order. But *Dictatorship* also lends itself to a more dramatic interpretation. For Schmitt, dictatorial power and legal indeterminacy exist in a relationship of "elective affinity" akin to the manner in which the faith in clear, determinate law is intimately related to parliamentary democracy.[46] Liberalism obscures the role of indeterminacy in the *legal* universe. In a parallel fashion, liberals naively believe that the specter of dictatorship can be driven from the *political* universe. As noted, for Schmitt dictatorship is simply an open expression of the discretionary power constitutive of every interpretation and application of the law. In this sense, dictatorship and legal indeterminacy go hand in hand. In light of this "elective affinity" between legal indeterminacy and dictatorship as well as the unavoidability of the former, why not then simply dump liberal democracy for a dictatorial alternative better attuned to the underlying structural logic of legal indeterminacy? If legal indeterminacy is as weighty a problem as Schmitt suggests, is not dictatorship preferable to liberal democracy and its "normativistic" failure to acknowledge the enigma of legal indeterminacy? To the extent that legally unregulated discretion represents the *Urzustand* of authentic politics, liberal democracy and the rule of law can probably at best represent a bad compromise with the structural imperatives of political and legal experience. Dictatorship (and a discretionary legal system) are more likely to accord with the imperatives of the discretionary *Urzustand*.

Schmitt ultimately embraces the latter, more radical position: as will be shown, he emphasizes the problem of legal indeterminacy in order to outline an authoritarian alternative to Weimar democracy during the late 1920s and early 1930s. But even in the early 1920s, this tendency in Schmitt's thinking is anticipated by core elements of his legal theory.

It is important to see why Schmitt's use of the expression "moment" in his account of the role of "indifference in reference to the content" of the law no longer is fully appropriate even by 1921. The term "moment" might suggest that indeterminacy is nothing but one among a number of distinct elements constitutive of legal experience, maybe even that law *for the most part* can be rendered determinate and predictable; that was one of the main aspirations of *Law and Judgment*. Yet if the "indifference in reference to the content of the law" consists, as Schmitt also claims, of pure power and perfect willfulness, it makes little sense to speak merely of a "moment" of arbitrariness within law. *If the element of arbitrary power within law is genuinely "pure," it would seem to follow that it is potentially unlimited: by definition, pure power or pure willfulness probably must remain an untamed and (normatively) unregulated form of power.* The "moment" of legal indeterminacy first conceptualized in *Law and Judgment* then very well probably has to be truly pervasive, law's dominant feature. Arbitrariness seems destined to make up a *ubiquitous* facet of all legal experience. Given the basic conceptual contours of his argument, Schmitt's idiosyncratic formulation of the *underdeterminacy thesis* prejudices him toward ultimately endorsing elements of the *radical indeterminacy thesis*. In turn, dictatorial power will have to take on a central role within Schmitt's theory as well.

This is precisely the thesis suggested by the *Political Theology* [1922]. Although Schmitt's terminology shifts slightly—he now speaks of the centrality of the "exception" for law[47]—he insists on the genuinely *universal* significance of the "indifference in reference to the content of law" first described in *Law and Judgment*: the exception refers to "a general concept in the theory of the state, and not merely to a construct applied to an emergency decree or state of siege."[48] It would be mistaken to associate the "moment of indifference" merely with a profound crisis or state of emergency, let alone a peripheral element of judicial decision making, for "[a]ll law is 'situational law.' "[49] *In its very essence, all legal experience is permeated by indeterminacy, by the ever-changing dictates of the "concrete exception."* Schmitt does admit that "the autonomous moment of the decision recedes to a minimum" during moments of relative political normalcy.[50] But even this "minimum" is probably destined to remain quite substantial given the undefinable and unlimited contours of a pure willfulness essential to legal experience. Law is to be conceived as based ultimately on a "pure decision not based on reason and discussion and not justifying itself . . . an absolute decision created out of nothingness."[51] Because the precise role of even the most unambiguous legal concepts depends on an act of "pure will" whose structure, by definition, remains open-ended, every abstract legal concept is "infinitely pliable."[52] Although the liberal rule of law may appear effective at a specific historical juncture, a closer look will reveal the utterly open-ended manner in which even general norms and concepts are manipulated by political and legal actors. Fundamentally, every judicial act is an intrinsically political act in which judges make "sovereign decisions" in favor of a particular set of political and aspirations: "in every [legal] transformation there is present an *auctoritatis interpositio*" in which the *auctoritatis interpositio* cannot be traced to the legal norm.[53] In this view, every judge or administrator who applies the law is simply a temporary "miniature" dictator, forced to resolve legal conflicts by an exercise of fundamentally discretionary power. As Schmitt comments later in *The Concept of the Political*, "the sovereignty of law means only the sovereignty of men who draw up and administer the law."[54] The general concepts and norms of the traditional liberal rule of law constitute at most a convenient mask for a "will to power," eagerly donned by legalistic bourgeois liberals who refuse to acknowledge the core imperatives of a violent and explosive political universe.

As John McCormick has observed, the idea of dictatorship similarly takes a more radical form in *Political Theology* than *Dictatorship*, published only a year earlier. Whereas *Dictatorship* can be read as a defense of a temporary commissarial dictatorship invested with exceptional powers in order to restore the state of legal normalcy, McCormick's assessment is that *Political Theology* allows "the ordinary rule of law [to be] dangerously encroached upon by exceptional absolutism."[55] In *Political Theology*, we can already detect the makings of Schmitt's vision of an authoritarian alternative to Weimar, a permanent dictatorship that rests on an appeal to the Weimar president, "as the personal embodiment of the popular will which cannot be procedurally ascertained in a time of crisis."[56] Although the sources of Schmitt's defense of a radical dictatorship are complex and multifaceted, my argument here should help explain one of them: to the extent that the logic of Schmitt's underlying argumentation leads him to make indeterminacy an all-important, omnipresent facet of law, the place of dictatorship similarly must gain in significance. If legal indeterminacy is a truly ubiquitous facet of legal experience, then dictatorship similarly must take on something close to an omnipresent, even permanent form. Not only do liberal democracy and the rule of law fail to deal adequately with the existence of irrepressible arbitrary power, but furthermore even a temporary, limited commissarial dictator is probably inadequate to the tasks at hand. For the enigma of legal indeterminacy necessitates a more radical form of dictatorship than that endorsed by Schmitt in 1921 in *Dictatorship*.

Interestingly, *Political Theology* says nothing about how legal indeterminacy might be combated. In contrast to *Law and Judgment*, Schmitt seems more concerned in *Political Theology* with discrediting *any* concept of legal determinacy than with formulating a postformalist version of it. In my reading, this shift in emphasis points to a crucial tension within Schmitt's legal thinking. To the extent that legal indeterminacy is identified with an act of unregulated, brute power, a "pure decision," is it possible for Schmitt to offer a coherent conception of legal determinacy? Does not the idea of a predictable, determinate legal system necessarily suggest the need for *some*, however minimal, *norm-based* restraints on the exercise of arbitrary power? Can Schmitt *both* conceive of the rule of law as nothing but "the sovereignty of men who draw up and administer the law" *and* posit, as he did in *Law and Judgment*, the possibility of a new form of legal determinacy?

State, Movement, Folk would again try to synthesize Schmitt's radical "decisionism" and its valorization of "a pure decision not based on reason and discussion and not justifying itself . . . an absolute decision created out of nothingness" with legal determinacy, albeit in an idiosyncratic postliberal form. Yet even at this juncture in our discussion we can begin to understand why that undertaking was destined to fail from the very outset. What type of grounding can Schmitt possibly provide for legal limits to the exercise of political power in light of his emphasis on the fundamentally openended character of all legal materials? A model of law that begins by associating legal experience with unregulated brute power—Schmitt himself seemed to grasp the limitations of this view in *The Value of the State and the Significance of the Individual*—is unlikely to allow for effective limits to the exercise of discretionary authority.

Not surprisingly, Schmitt's contributions to Nazi law helped bring about an assault on the foundations of the rule of law that was unprecedented in modern times. The "ethnic cleansing" of German jurists—enthusiastically endorsed by Schmitt in the 1930s—only exacerbated the Nazi regime's hostility to the modern legal tradition. Ethnic homogeneity within the judiciary hardly guaranteed legal determinacy, notwithstanding Schmitt's arguments to the contrary.

IV

In an October 1968 preface to the West German reissue of *Law and Judgment*, Schmitt commented that too many "heated polemics" had resulted in an unfair tendency to discredit his political and legal ideas. In his view, hostile critics had reduced "decisionism" to a "dangerous worldview," and the word "decision" was unfairly associated with a "fantastic act of willfulness." He adds that *Law and Judgment* points to "the simple origins of the starting point [of decisionism]. It makes the original meaning of judgment and decision making crystal clear." Thus, the eighty-year-old Schmitt hoped that a fair-minded reconsideration of the origins of decisionism in his early reflections on the problem of legal indeterminacy could help bring clarity to a "confused" and "polemical" debate.[57]

In this chapter, I have tried to show that a second look at the young Schmitt's legal thinking *does* bring clarity to the "confused" and "polemical" debate about his theoretical and political legacy. Pace Schmitt, it helps demonstrate that his embrace of German fascism was anticipated by key elements of his thinking about the dilemma of legal indeterminacy well before Hitler's rise to power.

Schmitt's reflections on legal indeterminacy potentially provide a valuable negative lesson for us today. As I noted in the introduction, those familiar with contemporary jurisprudential debates should be struck immediately by the often surprising commonalities between some strands of present-day jurisprudence and Schmitt's ideas about legal indeterminacy. Schmitt is hardly the only modern jurist to suggest that liberal legal interpretation rests on an expression of willful power. Although skeptical of extreme formulations of the radical indeterminacy thesis, Roberto Mangabeira Unger accuses traditional liberal legal practices of generating "forms of arbitrariness that are at least as troubling, intellectually and politically, as those of its familiar rivals."[58] The rule of law, as conceived by formalist-minded liberals and democrats, entails an "unacknowledged and unaccountable exercise of power."[59] Worst of all, legal traditionalists hypocritically deny the very existence of this constitutive moment of arbitrary power.

Whereas Unger at least still aspires to show that the purported ills of liberal democratic law could be overcome by a radical democratic alternative, Stanley Fish suggests that legal interpretation unavoidably rests on more or less arbitrary power. Fish argues that what passes for legal meaning is simply what those legal communities powerful enough to force their interpretations onto legal materials have determined.[60] Of course, Fish is hardly alone in endorsing nihilist views of this type. Others have tried to collapse the traditional distinction between law and politics in such a way as to conceive of legal decision making as necessarily expressing nothing more than a more or less arbitrary expression of power.[61]

To Schmitt's credit, he underlines the problematic implications of such extreme views. If, in fact, judicial (or, for that matter, administrative) action is overwhelmingly willful in character, then the foundations of traditional conceptions of the separation of power necessarily are shaken to the ground. The concept of an independent court, based traditionally on at least some, however minimal, distinction between judicial action and legislation, surely loses its traditional justification. Indeed, some form of dictatorship, in which the separation of powers has been abandoned altogether, may come to seem, as it did for Schmitt, a logical accompaniment to the inherent willfulness of all legal experience. If legal and administrative decision making inevitably is fundamentally arbitrary in character, then a political regime best attuned to the imperatives of radical legal indeterminacy might seem necessary. An authoritarian state, unregulated by legal and political restraints that hamper its reliance on ever-changing, discretionary law, would arguably provide the most logical institutional complement to the crisis of legal indeterminacy. Only an authoritarian state might "celebrate" the willfulness of legal experience, whereas a liberal democratic state committed to the rule of law hypocritically closes its eyes to the harsh realities of legal indeterminacy.

If I am not mistaken, those today who avidly endorse exaggerated ideas about the willfulness of liberal law have yet to face these implications. The example of Carl Schmitt suggests that it is incumbent on them to do so.

2

THE DECAY OF PARLIAMENTARISM

C arl Schmitt's idealized portrayal of nineteenth-century liberal parliamentarism and dramatic account of its alleged twentieth century decline have significantly shaped democratic theory in central Europe.[1] This influence is hardly surprising: Schmitt's arguments about modern representative democracy raise many difficult questions to which defenders of representative democracy need to respond. The recent North American revival of interest in Schmitt undoubtedly stems from this feature of his oeuvre as well. Too many contemporary liberal political theorists have been unwilling to acknowledge the depth of problems faced by liberal democracy today.[2] In this context, Schmitt's 1920s account of the "crisis of parliamentarism" may initially appear both original and timely.

Although understandable, this characteristic emphasis on Schmitt *the democratic theorist* obscures the eminent *jurisprudential* concerns of Schmitt's considerations on representative democracy. A central aim of Schmitt's analysis of the crisis tendencies of contemporary parliamentarism is to provide support for his radical views about the inevitability of a far-reaching indeterminacy within the law. The "crisis of parliamentarism" is part and parcel of a broader "crisis of legal indeterminacy." Chapter 1 tried to demonstrate that even before World War I Schmitt was critical of those who believed that legal predictability and regularity could be achieved by appeal to the "will of the statute" or the "will of the legislator." His attack on parliamentarism needs to be read in light of those earlier reflections. In order to underline his belief in the inherent indeterminacy of liberal law, Schmitt attempts to discredit the main source of law in contemporary liberal democracy, the *legislative* branch. Parliament produces the statutes interpreted by judges and applied by administrators; parliament is the prime maker of those legal materials which, according to modern liberal democratic doctrine, ultimately generate predictability and regularity within law and limitations on state action. If the bankruptcy of the liberal quest for determinate law is to be proven conclusively, the incoherence and the ineptness of the liberal lawmaker must be demonstrated as well.

Crude interpretations of Schmitt's ideas make deceptively easy the task of those of us concerned with defending and reconceiving representative government in a world unlike that of John Stuart Mill or Jeremy Bentham.[3] If we are to preserve representative government, we need to provide an answer to Schmitt's harsh "deconstruction" of it. After restating Schmitt's ideas about liberal parliamentarism (and their intimate relationship to the rule of law), I criticize important historical and sociological features of Schmitt's attack as well as his misleading description of the normative underpinnings of liberal parliamentarism (I, II). Contemporary representative institutions clearly suffer from many serious ills. But they are not, as Schmitt and a growing number of his defenders claim, anachronistic. Schmitt's critique of contemporary parliamentarism is badly overstated (III). In my view, a critique of Schmitt can rely to some extent on a number of inconsistencies and tensions within Schmitt's *own* account.

I

For Carl Schmitt, the ideal of free and unhindered discussion constitutes the essential principle of classical nineteenth-century parliamentarism. Formulated most clearly by liberal intellectuals like François Guizot and John Stuart Mill, the idea of a freewheeling, deliberative parliament, where rational public opinion would be able to crystallize and guide state action, had far-reaching implications and manifested itself in a rich variety of ways. In Schmitt's words, "[d]iscussion means an exchange of opinion that is governed by the purpose of persuading one's opponent through argument of the truth or justice of something, or allowing oneself to be persuaded of something as true and just."[4] The liberal model of free debate implied an elected representative's capacity to be guided by the "best" or most "truthful" argument rather than power- or interest-based demands. The underlying spirit of modern parliamentarism was fundamentally rationalistic. Yet this rationalism came in different shapes and sizes; the Marquis de Condorcet's "absolute rationalism," for example, competed with the "relative" rationalism of the American Federalists.[5] In important strands of modern political thought, representatives were not expected to be omniscient philosophers concerned with determining a set of "absolute" truths. In those cases, liberal parliamentarism's implicit brand of philosophical rationalism was of a "moderate" variety, concerned with the quest for situation-specific, "relative" truths about difficult practical questions. In this spirit, parliament was to secure a "balancing of outlooks and opinions," and a number of institutional devices, including bicameralism and federalism, were seen as making this balance of opinions among multiple parties possible.[6]

Parliamentary representatives were expected to engage in sophisticated forms of practical reflection and deliberation. If the most appropriate or the best argument guided representatives, parliamentary decision-making patterns would take a relatively flexible form; a good argument suddenly might conflict with a given set of preexisting political cleavages, and an elected representative might find himself allying with colleagues with whom he had just disagreed on a previous issue. Classical liberal parliamentarism hence presupposed an impressive degree of mutuality and reciprocity among elected representatives and the possession of a rich variety of argumentative and intellectual skills.

Of course, not all members of the political community were thought to possess such capabilities. Schmitt believes that it was more than coincidental that liberal defenses of parliament often presupposed the political hegemony of the propertied and well educated. On one level, he simply relies on a deeply antidemocratic assessment of the possibilities for broad, popular debate in developing this interpretation: since "the people itself cannot discuss . . . [and] it can only engage in acts of acclamation, voting, and saying yes or no to questions posed to it" from above, parliaments *necessarily* must be dominated by privileged, educated classes if they are to fulfill their deliberative functions.[7] Yet Schmitt simultaneously makes a crucial historical observation: he believes that the relative political and social homogeneity of many nineteenth-century liberal parliaments helped assure their discursive characteristics, in part because deeply divided parliaments occupied by profoundly antagonistic interests inevitably threaten the workings of "government by discussion." Separated by a deep social or political abyss, profoundly hostile political agents are likely to abandon the chivalrous mores of the "talking classes" and opt for more dramatic, potentially violent forms of political action. Schmitt hence is not claiming, as some of his formulations at first might seem to suggest, that nineteenth-century parliamentary institutions were pristine, deliberative institutions because representatives somehow were altogether free of down-to-earth interest-based claims like those common to contemporary mass democracies. Rather, Schmitt believes that a particular configuration of social interests, best captured by the idea of a parliament based on *Besitz und Bildung* (property and education), helped make the ideal of free discussion a reality within the halls of nineteenth-century parliaments.[8]

In Schmitt's account, a wide-ranging set of complementary institutions "receive[s] their meaning first through discussion and openness."[9] Discursive parliaments implied the necessity of genuinely independent representatives capable of looking beyond the narrow and parochial demands of party or region. Edmund Burke's famous theory of representation gave expression to this ideal. Elected representatives were expected to do more than mechanically register a set of political preferences that large bureaucratic institutions had already worked out beforehand. Political parties themselves were to rest on a free competition of ideas.

Deliberative parliamentarism also constituted the starting point for modern conceptions of the rule of law. For Schmitt, "the whole theory of the rule of law rests on the contrast between law which is general and already promulgated, universally binding without exception, and valid in principle for all times, and a personal order which varies case to case according to particular concrete circumstances."[10] But this distinction made sense only within the context of liberal rationalism, according to which universality is associated with rationality and particularity with "a concrete person 'moved by a variety of particular passions.' "[11] Closely related conceptions of the separation of powers were justified as ways of guaranteeing a competition of ideas, and an elected legislature was typically made the main site of political decision making chiefly because, in contrast to the executive, it was identified as that institution most thoroughly permeated with the ethos of rational debate and dialogue. The liberal ideal of the rule of law sought to assure the supremacy of discursive parliamentarians by privileging general parliamentary statutes in relation to executive decrees and measures, which were characteristically seen as stemming from a part of the governmental apparatus incapable of being guided by reasoned debate: "legislation is *deliberare*, executive *agere*."[12]

Here as well this rationalism took both extreme and moderate forms. Repeating arguments from the 1917 "Dictatorship and State of Siege," Schmitt notes that writers like Condorcet reduced administrative action altogether to "pronouncing a syllogism in which the law is the major premise."[13] In contrast, the moderate rationalism of the American Federalists supposedly maintained "a balance between the rational and irrational," presumably because the Federalists refused to dissolve executive power into legislation as Condorcet and others had sought.[14] Nonetheless, in Schmitt's exegesis, both forms of rationalism ultimately exhibit a vulnerability to the mechanical jurisprudence of Montesquieu; *The Federalist Papers* simply offers the least doctrinaire version of this model.[15] In Schmitt's gloss, a view of the judiciary and administration as nothing but different "mouth(s) that pronounce the words of the law" is a logical offshoot of the liberal rationalist quest to subject all facets of state activity to a system of rational, codified, legislative norms.

Finally, the "whole system of freedom of speech, assembly, and the press, of public meetings, parliamentary immunities and privileges" presupposes a deliberative vision of parliamentary practice.[16] According to Schmitt, many basic rights were justified on the basis of their contribution to parliamentary debate: a discursive civil society was to be protected by basic legal protections in order that parliamentarism could fulfill its promise of basing governmental action on an unhindered process of exchange and debate that would bring together "particles of reason that are strewn unequally among human beings."[17]

Schmitt's Weimar-era studies offer two main accounts of the demise of classical deliberative parliamentarism. In his early and highly influential *The Crisis of Parliamentary Democracy*, Schmitt relies upon nineteenth-century liberal arguments—Alexis de Tocqueville's is only the most well-known—to prove the irreversibility of egalitarian and democratic trends in the West. Schmitt similarly accepts the inevitability of democracy: today "the dominant concept of legitimacy is in fact democratic."[18] Yet while authors like Tocqueville develop this theme as a way of justifying an array of liberal restraints on popular decision making and ultimately endorsing a constitutional form of popular rule, Schmitt uses it to prove the basic *irrelevance* of liberalism and institutions such as parliament, which he interprets as embodying liberal ideals. At first glance Schmitt's argument may appear to rely on a theoretical sleight of hand. In *The Crisis of Parliamentary Democracy* he simply posits a basic incompatibility between democracy and liberalism. In Schmitt's problematic account of the history of democratic political thought, democracy is to be properly understood as an attempt to establish an "identity" between rulers and the ruled, the governed and the government, and the state and the people. For Schmitt, identity means establishing a set of "identifications" that, though unavoidably incomplete and thus never concrete "palpable realities," nonetheless involve the quest to establish a far-reaching, politically significant "sameness" or homogeneity in the community.[19] Allegedly, such an identity can be established by many means. Liberal parliamentarism need not play an essential role in establishing democratic identity. Because parliaments functioned as an important vehicle for broad-based democratic demands in much of the nineteenth century, traditional liberal thought misleadingly insisted on a relationship of mutual interdependence between liberal ideas (such as parliamentarism) and democratic ones. Schmitt, however, believes that twentieth-century mass movements should put such naive assumptions to rest. Because a genuine identity between rulers and the ruled can be established by many different means, dictatorial regimes very well might do a better job of accomplishing this task than liberal parliamentary ones. In Schmitt's view, fascism and Bolshevism could be eminently "democratic" political phenomena insofar as they successfully establish an identity between state and society, and between the governed and government.

This argument ominously depicts twentieth-century mass-based authoritarianism as a fulfillment of the democratic project. Schmitt thereby crudely reduces the democratic project to a quest for homogeneity and badly distorts the core of that project.[20] But for the moment, let us focus on the *immanent* tensions of Schmitt's presentation. They, too, are quite revealing.

Thus far, Schmitt's argument suggests only that democracy can rely on instruments *other* than traditional liberal parliamentarism. It nowhere proves an essential or necessary contradiction between democracy and liberal parliamentarism. To achieve that far more ambitious task, *The Crisis of Parliamentary Democracy* relies on a more fundamental argument about the essential core of political experience, or what Schmitt dubs the "concept of the political."[21] For Schmitt, politics is essentially conflictual, referring most basically to a potentially explosive struggle between political allies and opponents. The quintessence of political action is the ability to determine and act resolutely against a "foe," defined by Schmitt as "simply the Other, the Alien . . . [I]t is enough for his being that he is in a particularly intensive sense existentially something Other and Alien, so that in the case of conflict he means the negation of one's own form of existence and therefore must be guarded from and fought off, in order to preserve one's own appropriate form [*eigene seinsmässige Art*] of life."[22] The political foe is defined precisely by the fact that he may have to be killed at some juncture, and thus that he is an enemy or opponent in the most intense potential manner: "The concepts of friend, foe, and struggle only gain their real significance through the fact that they relate in particular to the real possibility of killing" an "alien" other.[23] Liberal parliamentarism's reliance on the principle of unhindered debate thus simply denies the core of authentic political experience. Parliamentarism presupposes that political conflicts and tensions can be resolved by recourse to debate and negotiation. But for Schmitt the essence of political experience is to be understood as "a pure decision not based on reason and discussion and not justifying itself . . . an absolute decision created out of nothingness," according to which political opponents are identified and preparations for the possibility of violent conflict commence.[24] Parliamentarism (along with the rule of law) is thus deeply "antipolitical." In contrast, the democratic tradition's attempt to establish identity supposedly has, in Schmitt's view, an authentically political character. As theorists such as Rousseau allegedly anticipated, the establishment of political identity may very well imply the necessity of "exterminating" [*vernichten*] heterogeneous minorities that fall outside the particular form of homogeneity upon which a given democracy rests.[25] In contrast to liberal parliamentarism, democracy thereby acknowledges the centrality of intense, potentially life-threatening crises.

This step in his argument is significant not only because it seems to allow Schmitt to demonstrate a fundamental tension between ("antipolitical") liberal parliamentarism and ("political") democracy, but additionally because it permits him to explain the decline of the former and the rise of the latter. Insofar as identity-based democratic politics corresponds more closely to the basic, existential core of all genuine political experience (the so-called concept of the political), Schmitt can suggest that it is not surprising that discursive liberal parliamentarism becomes historically anachronistic. Concrete social and historical trends can be interpreted as supporting Schmitt's abstract theoretical claims about the most basic features of political experience. History, it seems, follows political theory.

In the same vein, Schmitt intimates that liberal parliamentarism is incapable of fulfilling the minimal functions of authentic political representation. For Schmitt, representation means providing a visible presence to the otherwise unseen and absent. Representation is an eminently political phenomenon; it underlines the political virtues of those represented. A political community possessing "a higher and more intense type of existence," capable of distinguishing and defending itself from other political communities, can be successfully represented, whereas something "dead, inferior or worthless" necessarily lacks the prerequisites of true representation. When a political leader represents a unified political entity, for example, the person of the political leader can hope to provide a visible expression of the strength of the political community at hand. In that case, "[w]ords like greatness, nobility, majesty, glory, dignity and honor" become appropriate descriptions of both the representative and those represented by him.[26] In contrast, a divided, inept political entity, unable to assert its "own appropriate form of life" in relation to other communities, is unlikely to gain a representative possessing such attributes. More often than not, its leaders will seem weak and incompetent.

Schmitt tends to emphasize the personalistic character of authentic representation. Representation cannot be achieved by general norms, for "[t]he idea of representation is fully governed by the idea of personal authority. . . . Representation in an eminent sense, in contrast to mere 'standing in for' [*Stellvertretung*], can only be achieved by a person possessing authority or an idea which, as soon as it gains representation, is personified."[27] Unfortunately, liberal parliamentarism stands in an uneasy relation to the prerequisites of authentic representation. Parliamentarism tries to dissolve politics into (antipolitical) deliberation and debate. And parliamentarism obfuscates the personalistic character of representation, conceiving of liberal government as an impersonal rule of law when, in fact, representation always entails the concrete "rule of men." In this way as well, liberal parliamentarism contradicts the concept of the political.

But the problem with this strand of Schmitt's critique of parliamentarism is precisely that it relies so heavily on the "concept of the political." To put the problem most simply, if one refuses to accept his idiosyncratic claims about the concept of the political, we need not accept his view in *The Crisis of Parliamentary Democracy* that parliamentarism is somehow antipolitical in character and thus, unlike identity-based democratic politics, is probably doomed. Schmitt's conceptualization of politics, which places special emphasis on the crisis situation, distorts what much of everyday politics seems to be about, namely more or less peaceful forms of dispute and exchange.[28] Schmitt's emphasis on the criterion of intense hostility for political experience also risks romanticizing the use of political force or violence, which clearly is a highly intense form of political conflict. The essence of political experience need not be identified with a life-threatening, existential crisis, but rather with the quest to avoid or overcome such crises. When political action is based on an abstract "decision not based on reason and discussion and not justifying itself," the political sphere is likely to be overwhelmed by irresponsible and even irrational forms of behavior. Of course, Max Weber at some junctures similarly formulated a "decisionist" view of moral and political action, according to which our political and moral choices cannot be deduced from general ethical standards, given the "disenchanted" character of our universe. But in dramatic contrast to Weber, Schmitt seems unconcerned with the crucial task of minimizing the dangers of decisionism; Schmitt is unconvinced by Weber's argument in favor of an "ethic of responsibility." For Schmitt, this element of Weber's thinking is a remnant of liberal rationalism that is basically inconsistent with the core of political experience.[29]

Admittedly, Schmitt's *The Crisis of Parliamentary Democracy* provides a telling description of how contemporary parliamentarism no longer lives up to the standards of much of nineteenth-century liberal theory—most significantly, the idea of a deliberative legislature as the supreme lawmaker. Little genuinely freewheeling discussion goes on within the halls of elected legislatures today. Representatives seek to have a particular set of interests acknowledged or "registered" by governmental decision-makers, but hardly expect to sway their peers by means of rational argumentation. Similarly, political parties rarely rely on the free competition of ideas envisioned by nineteenth-century theorists, but instead depend on an impressive propaganda apparatus aimed at mobilizing—often, at least in some settings, by means of a manipulative use of emotions and symbols—a limited portion of the political community. Representatives are no longer independent in the fashion described by theorists like Edmund Burke. His ideas are taken seriously in university seminars, but not as a guide to real-life parliamentary practice. Few elected representatives are able to sacrifice the parochial interests of a specific constituency in favor of a quest for a (seemingly ephemeral) common good; few decisions are actually determined within the halls of the legislature. They now tend to be *pre*determined by the leadership of bureaucratized mass-based parties and a panoply of nonparliamentary actors, and the legislature may do little but ratify decisions made elsewhere. Whereas many classical liberals insisted on the nondelegation of legislative authority to administrative agencies, major political decisions now often are made by corporatist decision-making units dominated by powerful and well-organized interest groups. The state administration undertakes significant lawmaking functions, and bureaucratic decrees increasingly take on greater de facto significance than parliamentary general law. As Schmitt predicted, crisis tendencies within contemporary parliamentarism are intimately related to the proliferation of vague, open-ended laws, often incapable of providing adequate direction to judges and administrators. Inevitably, rule of law virtues are sacrificed: as statutes become increasingly amorphous, highly discretionary forms of judicial and administrative decision making flourish. Significant legal *in*determinacy indeed becomes a striking feature of many arenas of legal experience. In short, there are a number of disturbing signs not only that contemporary parliaments in the West are becoming an "empty formality," but that the traditional ideal of the rule of law is under attack as well.[30]

Schmitt's description of contemporary parliamentarism, repeated in a number of essays and larger studies during the Weimar period, surely amounts to more than the rantings of a fascist ideologue. Substantial scholarship confirms many of its features. Nearly seventy-five years ago, James Bryce articulated a number of analogous concerns.[31] More recently, Charles Maier has demonstrated that the proliferation of corporatist decision-making structures in 1920s Europe functioned to deny parliaments many of their traditional legislative prerogatives; perhaps Schmitt's account can be interpreted as an attempt to come to grips with this development.[32] Similarly, many jurists and legal scholars have scrambled to explain the sources of the vast discretionary powers today enjoyed by administrators and judges.[33] Still, Schmitt's observations hardly seem to justify the apocalyptic argumentative structure of *The Crisis of Parliamentary Democracy*: Schmitt really seems to think that his account can show us that "the age of discussion is coming to an end after all."[34] His dramatic contrast between the ambitious aspirations and alleged reality of nineteenth-century liberal parliamentarism and the disappointing contours of twentieth-century representative government hardly suffices as an adequate sociological and historical *explanation* for the purported decline of deliberative parliamentarism. For that matter, unless we accept Schmitt's broader claims about liberal parliamentarism's profoundly "antipolitical" character, *The Crisis of Parliamentary Democracy* ultimately presents us with no sufficient reason for accepting Schmitt's belief there that deliberative parliamentarism could not be reestablished in conditions very much unlike those that helped generate it. In short, what first appears to be an empirical study of the transformation of parliamentary government turns out to be an unambitious gloss on an abstract and highly problematic claim about the so-called "concept of the political."

Perhaps these inadequacies encouraged Schmitt to try to formulate a somewhat more nuanced sociological-historical explanation of parliamentarism's transformations. A set of subsequent texts—most importantly, the crucial but often ignored *Constitutional Theory* (1928)—does a superior job of tracing the history of parliamentarism in the nineteenth and twentieth centuries. In these texts, Schmitt relies on an impressive survey of nineteenth- and twentieth-century European parliaments to refurbish his basic argument. It now turns out that parliamentary bodies in some parts of Europe *were* able to acquire, in Schmitt's theoretical terms, some authentically "political" characteristics. Positioned between hostile monarchical forces based in the executive branch and militant, emerging workers' movements, parliaments dominated by educated, middle-class strata [*Bildung und Besitz*] played a pivotal role in the political community's chief friend/foe divisions. For a brief moment in the nineteenth century, parliament was able to function as an authentic representative body; *Bildung* was a "personal quality and therefore capable of being used in a system of representation."[35] Parliament constituted "a gathering of educated people, who represented education and reason, indeed the education and reason of the whole nation."[36] Liberal parliamentary representatives were a concrete personal embodiment of the political hegemony of the educated and economically privileged. Allegedly, they exhibited something of the "greatness, nobility, majesty, glory, dignity and honor" constitutive of effective representation. According to Schmitt, the nineteenth-century liberal bourgeoisie clearly grasped the authentic political character of its position. "Relativistic" and "formalistic" defenses of parliamentarism, like those endorsed by twentieth-century liberal theorists such as Weber and Kelsen, were alien to nineteenth-century liberals because they understood the political uses of a parliament dominated by those with education and property.[37]

But in Schmitt's account, bourgeois strata in much of Europe abandoned the more ambitious facets of the agenda of liberal parliamentarism as they discovered that alternative regime-types (French Bonapartism, Prussian constitutional monarchy, or a British-style quasi-plebiscitary democratic republic) would protect their basic interest in the preservation of private property. Challenged from below, the liberal bourgeoisie increasingly reduced parliament to an instrument for the protection of class privilege. Parliament soon lost its representative functions; Schmitt argues that a parliament primarily concerned with protecting economic interests can no longer perform authentic representative functions.[38] Particularly after the revolutions of 1848, the tendency to abandon parliament among the educated and propertied became commonplace, and Schmitt thinks that it explains why "since 1848 no systematic, ideal justification of the parliamentary system is brought forward" anymore.[39] Thereafter, liberal parliamentarism's intellectual roots in a set of "normativistic" illusions about the nature of politics increasingly manifested themselves in concrete terms. Propertied liberal strata made fateful, politically naive concessions to their opponents and obscured the existential threat posed by such foes. Most importantly, parliamentary representation—Schmitt mentions the growing electoral might of the British Labor Party as an example of what he has in mind[40]—was permitted to take on a heterogeneous and decreasingly bourgeois character. The emergence of electoral socialism means that many European parliaments no longer were unambiguously controlled by those strata that Schmitt considers alone capable of living up to the demands of unhindered discourse. Remember: for Schmitt, "the people cannot discuss—it can only engage in acts of acclamation, vote, or say yes or no to questions posed to it" from above. In Schmitt's theory, the people can do nothing but generate an "unorganized answer" given "to a question which may be posed by an authority whose existence is assumed."[41] Allegedly, to expect anything more of popular decision making would be utopian. The successful functioning of parliamentarism presupposes the political hegemony of educated, propertied classes. Without them, it is unlikely that parliament can perform its classical deliberative tasks.

According to Schmitt, the expansion of suffrage and the subsequent emergence of a parliamentary universe populated by deeply antagonistic class-based parties tend to mean (as Schmitt believes to be evident in Weimar Germany) that intense political cleavages now are located *within* parliament. Whereas the key friend/foe divisions in the nineteenth century to some extent corresponded to the separation between parliament and the executive, intense political cleavages in the twentieth century cripple parliament and make traditional forms of parliamentary politics impossible. Parliament becomes a mere forum for political majorities chiefly concerned with reorganizing the political community's underlying system of political legitimacy and institutions so as better to satisfy their particular power needs. Deeply hostile political blocs located within parliament are not simply increasingly uninterested in polite liberal debate or the traditional mores of the educated classes; now, appeals to traditional liberal parliamentary ideals and procedures, such as majority rule, are likely to serve as little but an ideological front for the power-interests and the particularistic agendas of hostile, distinct constituencies.[42] Inevitably, parliament in the twentieth century tends to become an instrument by means of which antagonistic power blocs hope to make sure that the state apparatus acknowledges the legitimacy of their private interests, but hardly a source of open-ended contemplation of the "common good." Legal trends mirror this development as well: the proliferation of nontraditional forms of law stems from the difficulties of achieving political compromises within the context of socially divided political communities.[43] Schmitt's *Guardian of the Constitution* (1931) asserts that early liberalism envisioned an autonomous society distinct from the state but able to maintain control over governmental action by means of its dominance of a deliberative parliament. But working-class-based political parties spawn new forms of state intervention in society and ultimately a fusion of state and society. In Schmitt's dramatic account, the legislature then becomes little more than a "showplace for pluralist interests" controlled by polarized interest blocs closely linked to particular facets of the interventionist state and representative of narrow elements of a political community often lacking, like the mass-based bureaucratic parties and increasingly plebiscitary elections that put legislators into power, any interest in engaging in quaint rationalistic discourse with political opponents.[44]

Parliament corresponded to the imperatives of a bourgeois-dominated political era. But in the age of mass democracy and organized working-class politics, it becomes transformed into a "technical transmission belt" for nonparliamentary decision-making complexes. "Parliament is no longer the site where political decisions are made. Key decisions are made outside of parliament."[45]

II

Schmitt's revised and far richer sociological-historical account of liberal parliamentarism undoubtedly is superior to the original provided in the 1923 *The Crisis of Parliamentary Democracy*. Nonetheless, it still contains a number of flaws. Let me begin by mentioning just a few of the more immediate ones.

First, it is empirically implausible that the limited quality of political deliberation in most contemporary parliamentary bodies, as Schmitt occasionally suggests, can be easily blamed on the emergence of popular and working-class political movements. Although the percentage of elected representatives with working-class and lower middle-class backgrounds increased significantly in many European legislatures at the beginning of the twentieth century, those percentages leveled out and even decreased after the 1930s and 1940s. Schmitt sees the deliberative functionings of parliament as inextricably tied to the middle-class social background of its members, but it is really only in the twentieth century—when parliaments, in Schmitt's account, *lose* their discursive capacities—that middle-class groups (and, in particular, lawyers) become truly well represented in most legislatures.[46] Of course, Schmitt also tries to present a more subtle version of this basic argument. But even the observation that labor and socialist political parties often contributed to political polarization and the paralysis of many legislative bodies at best applies, and even there only with a number of important qualifications, to a few central European countries (such as Weimar Germany), yet hardly can be taken as a universal explanation for parliamentary failure.[47] Arguably, some polities experienced important features of parliamentary decay *despite* the fact that mass-based workers' or social democratic parties never gained a foothold there.[48] The growing complexity of state activities in the twentieth century, which is surely the most immediate source of the growing autonomy of the state's administrative apparatus and many of the ills of representative government, cannot be explained chiefly, as Schmitt sometimes suggests, as a consequence of social democratic style interventions in the economy. Similarly, the relatively indeterminate character of much parliamentary legislation surely has many sources; the rise of labor and social democratic parties is at best one of them.[49]

A far more fundamental failing underlies Schmitt's sociological and historical argument, however. Much of the power of his analysis of liberal parliamentarism stems from the dramatic claim that liberal societies in fact *did* once have truly freewheeling, deliberative elected legislatures but, more or less abruptly, have *lost* them. Schmitt is not intent simply to contrast liberal democratic *ideals* with liberal democratic *reality*. He wants us to believe that at some point a "golden age" of parliamentary government existed, whose precious treasures are beyond the reach of everyone unlucky enough to be born in the twentieth century.

Yet *The Crisis of Parliamentary Democracy* never provides an *historical* account of classical liberal parliaments. Only in *Constitutional Theory*, in a crucial section entitled "An Historical Survey of the Development of the Parliamentary System," does Schmitt attempt to provide some concrete historical backing for his idealized portrayal of nineteenth-century liberal parliaments. And there its results are remarkably meager.

Where in the world of real parliaments did independent representatives square off intellectually so as to bring together "particles of reason that are strewn unequally among human beings"? Did liberal parliamentarism as Schmitt describes it ever gain a significant foothold in nineteenth-century Europe? Given the importance of Schmitt's implicit empirical claims about nineteenth-century liberal parliaments for his claims about parliamentary decay, the reader of *Constitutional Theory* will be surprised to find out that Schmitt himself apparently did not think his model of deliberative parliaments had very much to do with political reality, or at least *Constitutional Theory* seems to suggest as much. In this work, Schmitt argues that it was primarily German and French theorists (such as Lorenz von Stein, Rudolf Gneist, François Guizot, and Benjamin Constant) who, during the first half of the nineteenth century, developed the most mature theoretical conceptions of discursive parliamentarism;[50] in contrast, Britain provided a "practical" inspiration for European liberals. But Schmitt is forced to acknowledge that nineteenth-century German liberals never managed to establish anything close to the ideal of parliamentary government outlined in advanced century liberal theory. The German *Reichstag* became politically dominant only after the revolution of 1918, and according to Schmitt, by then "the political and social situation was so fully transformed" in Germany—most importantly, because of the ascent of the political left—that the fulfillment of the agenda of parliamentarism amounted to a "posthumous" victory for representative government.[51] By 1918, what Schmitt considers the necessary social presuppositions of liberal parliamentarism had dissipated to such an extent in Germany that it no longer could function in the manner sought by nineteenth-century liberals. Schmitt's presentation of the French case similarly gives the reader little to work with. He acknowledges that the post-Napoleonic "constitutional parliamentary" regime after 1815 and then Louis Phillip's "parliamentary monarchy" of 1830–48 guaranteed extensive discretionary authority to the crown and executive. It is difficult to imagine that Schmitt intends these regimes to be seen as the site of the powerful, deliberative legislatures described elsewhere in his writings. In fact, Schmitt never makes an argument for the virtues of parliamentarism under the auspices of Louis Phillip; perhaps he realizes that many contemporary observers of French parliamentarism during this period—most prominently, Tocqueville—chronicled extensive bribery, patronage, and corruption among parliamentarians.[52] Another candidate, for Schmitt, might be the French Third Republic. Despite the fact that Schmitt correctly notes that the 1875 constitution attributed unprecedented authority to the legislature, he again nowhere explicitly points to the Third Republic as an example of the broader model of liberal parliamentarism that he has in mind. Perhaps Schmitt simply knows too much about the sorry state of many features of French parliamentary politics during this period, or maybe he acknowledges that parliament by then already had begun to include working-class and lower middle-class representatives.[53]

Nineteenth-century Britain would be the obvious source for Schmitt's idealized account of liberal parliaments. Some recent commentators claim that he builds upon the British experience in order to formulate his critique of contemporary parliaments.[54] But Schmitt explicitly admits in *Constitutional Theory* that the House of Commons before the electoral reforms of 1832 relied upon an illiberal electoral system and was an "overwhelmingly aristocratic assembly of a medieval type."[55] He goes on to note that as early as the 1850s parliamentary elections began to take an increasingly plebiscitary character and that, by 1867, parliament no longer possessed a decisive or central position in the British system. In Schmitt's view, parliament had become little but a "connecting link" [*Bindeglied*] between the cabinet and the electorate, which increasingly had become an object of mass political mobilization.[56] Schmitt is forced to acknowledge that British politics by midcentury was increasingly dominated by charismatic party leaders, like William Gladstone, effective at building mass support by means of emotional appeals. This is already the beginning of the era of Weber's "caesaristic" party leader, but hardly that of the rationally discursive, independent liberal parliamentarian.[57]

Still, Schmitt's discussion of the British experience remains revealing for one important reason. In *Constitutional Theory* Schmitt is fascinated with how, since Montesquieu's deceptive portrayal of English political institutions in *The Spirit of the Laws*, various "constructions, schematizations, idealizations, and interpretations" of English parliamentarism served "the liberal bourgeoisie on the European continent in the struggle against Absolutism."[58] After Montesquieu's idealization of eighteenth-century England, further idealizations ensued: Schmitt claims that "the nineteenth-century English parliament became a *mythical picture* [emphasis added] for a significant portion of the liberal bourgeoisie, the historical correctness and accuracy of which does not matter."[59]

Schmitt's use of the term "myth" is significant for two reasons. Reminiscent of earlier comments about the methodological merits of relying on "juridical fictions,"[60] it lends credence to the suspicion that Schmitt himself does not really believe there ever was such a thing as a freewheeling, deliberative liberal parliament anywhere in the nineteenth century; his own historical account provides little, if any, basis for this thesis. His comments suggest strongly that the picture of a discursive English parliament was nothing but a politically efficacious "myth" employed by the liberal middle classes in their life-or-death struggle against the ancien régime and its aristocratic allies.

Even more significantly, the use of the term "myth" unveils a great deal about Schmitt's own project. In *The Crisis of Parliamentary Democracy* and other texts, Schmitt praises Georges Sorel's *Reflections on Violence* and its interpretation of the "myth" as an instrument by which a political constituency "pushes its energy forward and gives it the strength for martyrdom as well as the courage to use force."[61] In Schmitt's view, Sorel understands that politics ultimately involves potentially violent conflicts between "friends" and "foes," and that the irrational myth, in contrast to liberal ideals of peaceful deliberation and exchange, can play an effective role in mobilizing political agents so that they can "become the engine of world history."[62] Though hostile to Sorel's socialism, Schmitt delights in the French radical's thesis that, once a political and social order lacks an adequate basis in irrational myths, it "no longer can remain standing, and no mechanical apparatus can build a dam if a new storm of historical life has broken loose."[63] In short, Sorel implicitly understands the Schmittian concept of the political, and Sorel's theory of the political myth provides helpful advice to those ready to engage in conflict-ridden, life-threatening, authentically political forms of action.

Schmitt's emphasis on the "mythical" quality of discursive liberal parliamentarism here makes it difficult to avoid the following conclusions. For Carl Schmitt himself, an idealized and even unreal account of nineteenth-century liberal-parliamentarism is a convenient political myth that takes on new functions for friend/foe politics in the twentieth century. Whereas liberals in the nineteenth century looked to Britain and the "myth" of discursive parliamentarism in order to defeat a set of deeply hostile political opponents, Schmitt now unleashes the myth of a freewheeling, discursive parliament against an extremely threatening set of contemporary foes, namely, the working-class movement and the socialist political parties. In Schmitt's view, these constituencies now constitute the main threat to those, like Schmitt himself, who hope to preserve crucial components of the increasingly fragile project of premodern, elite-dominated politics. Left-wing political movements, he believes, lead the working classes astray by demanding political and social democratization and by falsely suggesting that they can do more than simply say yes or no to simple questions posed from above by an undemocratic elite. They thereby dislodge traditional patterns of deference long shown by the broad mass of the population to a narrow elite that, in Schmitt's account, alone possesses genuine political skills. Labor, social democratic, and communist parties, at least, become the main target of Schmitt's political fury in many of his Weimar-era writings[64] and certainly the object of his ire in his discussion of the development of parliamentary democracy in the nineteenth and twentieth centuries.

III

But perhaps Schmitt should be read more modestly. Maybe his basic argument can be salvaged if it is interpreted simply as an attempt to contrast the ambitious *ideals* of liberal parliamentarism, as they were formulated by liberalism's most impressive nineteenth-century theorists, with the unsatisfactory state of contemporary parliamentary *reality*. After all, does that not suffice? Should not liberals and democrats at least be somewhat worried if parliamentarism no longer lives up to the norms by means of which it was originally justified? Undoubtedly, parliaments today serve numerous functions unforeseen by nineteenth-century liberal theorists—at least in *The Crisis of Parliamentary Democracy,* Schmitt does not deny this[65]—but it probably still should be a matter of concern if their pivotal deliberative tasks are no longer being performed very effectively. Liberal democratic theorists defeated their political opponents in part by arguing for the superior *reasonableness* or *rationality* of parliamentary government. But contemporary liberal democracy cannot make the same claim if parliament does little but

ratify decisions really made behind closed doors by the administrative apparatus and powerful organized interests.

Even this more sympathetic interpretation of Schmitt's critique of parliamentarism cannot save the core of his argument. If Schmitt is to succeed
in contrasting liberal parliamentary ideals with liberal parliamentary reality,
he needs to provide an accurate portrait of those ideals. He fails in this task.

Recall Schmitt's assertion in *The Crisis of Parliamentary Democracy* that
many classical liberal rights, such as free speech or parliamentary immunities
and privileges, lose their "rationale" with the (alleged) demise of a deliberative parliament.[66] This is a revealing assertion. For Schmitt, many basic legal
protections make sense only because they guarantee parliamentary debate
and exchange. Insofar as parliament no longer performs deliberative functions, liberal protections, including free speech and freedom of assembly,
necessarily become anachronistic. In short, the fate of central liberal political institutions is determined by the destiny of deliberative parliamentarism.

This claim, as Jean Cohen and Andrew Arato have perceptively noted,
is a preposterous interpretation of basic liberal and democratic legal protections.[67] Such protections clearly perform many functions beyond the preservation of parliamentary debate. In some of his texts, Schmitt offers a
misleading, highly concretistic reading of the noble, old-fashioned ideal
of government by discussion.[68] This reading allows him to underplay the
importance and broader significance of a host of basic democratic institutions and rights. At some crucial junctures in his writings, Schmitt reduces
the liberal democratic ideal of government by discussion, which implied a
discursive and self-regulating *public sphere* in opposition to the state, to the
far more narrow ideal of a discursive, autonomous *parliament*. But many
classical liberal democratic conceptions of representative government envisioned *both* a deliberative parliament *and* a much broader, discursive public
that, by virtue of its own deliberative features, would choose representatives who would advance the most reasonable or rational governmental
policies and contribute in manifold ways to a relatively thoughtful expression of public opinion.[69]

Perhaps Schmitt would claim that this criticism is irrelevant to his basic
argument. As we will see in chapter 4, Schmitt suggests in the early 1930s
that the demise of the classical liberal state/society divide, and its replacement by an interventionist "total" state that permeates all aspects of social
and economic existence in the twentieth century, obliterate any vestiges of
the self-regulating, autonomous society depicted by early liberal theory.

Indeed, to the extent that deliberative processes within the political community at large are deeply threatened by state bureaucracies, problematic modes of surveillance, massive private corporations, and poorly regulated forms of corporatist-style public/private authority, this second facet of the ideal of government by discussion undoubtedly becomes fragile today; many facets of the contemporary political universe suggest that such threats are authentic. By the same token, if it turns out that some type of independent public sphere in contemporary liberal democracy—though, undoubtedly, one very distinct from the property-based, privatistic civil society pictured by classical liberal theory—still provides meaningful possibilities for at least some relatively meaningful deliberation and rational exchange, then one could respond to Schmitt by claiming that representative government has by no means exhausted all elements of its original normative agenda. Even if open discourse is hindered within some contemporary parliaments, the fact that liberal democracies may rest on a broader network of society-wide political debate and discourse would mean that the ideal of government by discussion has a future.

As part of his attack on liberal jurisprudence, Schmitt hopes to discredit the liberal legislature. Yet insofar as legislators are chosen at least to some extent on the basis of freewheeling argumentative debate and exchange, parliamentary lawmaking could still claim to rest on a minimal discursive basis. The liberal lawmaker is hardly as unambiguously incompetent, inept, or irrational as Schmitt wants to suggest. Parliamentary decision making's discursive origins, a broader societywide process of political debate, in which opposing arguments are exchanged and contested in a host of both traditional and new settings, certainly make *some* contribution to the reasonableness of liberal law.

Indeed, broad-based, popularly elected parliamentary bodies conceivably are more effective at representing a greater diversity and heterogeneity of argumentative viewpoints than other, competing state institutions and thus gain a renewed basis for insisting on their supremacy in the legislative process: parliament still may be the site where "particles of reason that are strewn together unequally among human beings" are able to manifest themselves, in a much richer, diverse, and multifaceted way than in alternative aspects of the political apparatus. A single, *univocal* elected executive cannot possibly stand for or represent all possible argumentative perspectives in civil society, whereas a broad-based, *multivocal* elected legislature with hundreds of members arguably may be quite effective at reflecting the heterogeneity of "particles of reason" found in contemporary society. While a large, popularly elected parliament may be fairly well suited to the task of reaching practical compromises among differing argumentative standpoints and thus in contributing to the reasonableness of governmental policy, a plebiscitary-style elected executive may find it hard to reflect the same diversity of argumentative perspectives. Insofar as parliaments can be shown to perform this somewhat more modest function as part of a broader set of complexes making up the project of government by discussion, they hardly deserve to be considered anachronistic or irrelevant. Contra Carl Schmitt, parliamentarism today is not an "empty formality."

Admittedly, these "particles of reason" effect governmental policy in a much more indirect manner than probably would have satisfied many nineteenth-century liberals. We also seriously need to examine a number of substantial reform proposals if the deliberative and legislative tasks of representative institutions are to be refurbished. Similarly, there are good reasons for worrying about the proliferation of open-ended law and corresponding modes of discretionary judicial and administrative decision making. But the need for reform still does not justify Schmitt's denial of the very existence of "particles of reason" in the interstices of contemporary representative democracy.

IV

I do not mean to conclude here on what may seem, in light of the evident ills of representative democracy today, an overly optimistic tone. Substantial threats obviously challenge the ideal of government by discussion even if one focuses on the merits of a deliberation outside of parliament proper.

Nonetheless, it is an empirical question whether contemporary liberal democracy has been robbed of *all* deliberative spaces; Schmitt's apocalyptic account tends to obscure the significance and complexity of this question. In the same vein, many challenges to the rule of law diagnosed by Schmitt are more ambivalent than he concedes. Vagueness in law sometimes facilitates arbitrariness and exacerbates political and social inequality; on occasion, it instead helps generate increased possibilities for political participation and greater social justice.[70] Schmitt seems uninterested in the complex texture of antiformal trends within the law. For him, trends toward the *deformalization* of law simply demonstrate the bankruptcy of the liberal rule of law and its longtime ally, deliberative parliamentarism.

Here as well, Schmitt offers an important negative lesson for us. His discussion of parliamentarism points directly to the potential dangers of one-sided, deconstructive interpretations of contemporary representative democracy, which too often have flourished on both the left and right. Obscuring the complexity of the traditional liberal ideal of government by deliberation, Schmitt rushes to conclude that contemporary parliaments (and the rule of law) are an "empty formality." In part because of this mistake, he ultimately embraces a dictatorial alternative to the Weimar Republic.

In light of this fateful choice, it is imperative to strive to avoid reproducing Schmitt's errors. We can begin to do so by honestly recognizing the real ills of contemporary representative democracy while simultaneously acknowledging liberal parliamentarism's immanent normative kernel as a starting point for reforms directed at overcoming those ills.

3

THE CRITIQUE OF LIBERAL
CONSTITUTIONALISM

C arl Schmitt's critique of liberal constitutionalism makes up the center-piece of his political and legal thinking during the mid- and late 1920s.[1] The 1928 *Constitutional Theory* not only is Schmitt's magnum opus from the Weimar period, but also represents one of the most ambitious attempts in this century to formulate a theoretical antipode to liberal consti-tutionalism. As a prominent German jurist has recently noted, "[n]o one has formulated the antiliberal alternative to the modern constitutional state as clearly, tersely, and pitilessly as" Carl Schmitt.[2] Because of the centrality of Schmitt's analysis of constitutionalism for our examination of Schmitt's hostility to liberal legalism, this chapter takes a careful look at it.

In chapter 1, we saw how Schmitt relied on a theory of the discretion-ary legal decision to deconstruct traditional models of judicial action. Schmitt's constitutional theory builds directly on this agenda by arguing that the *liberal constitutional order* as a whole rests on arbitrary, normatively unregulated power. Just as Schmitt's theory of judicial and administrative action ultimately privileges an irrational moment of decision in relation to the statute, so, too, does his constitutional theory grant a special place to arbitrary power. The moment of primordial arbitrariness thematized in Schmitt's World War I writings on military dictatorship is now located at the foundations of constitutional government. In Schmitt's constitutional theory, this originary arbitrariness not only haunts the everyday workings of liberal constitutionalism, but it also offers a starting point for developing an antiliberal alternative to it. Because liberal constitutionalism itself hints at the existence of profound problems unresolvable within its own intellectual parameters, Schmitt deems it deeply inadequate. Liberal constitutionalism is unable to grapple adequately with core features of political life (I).

I respond to Schmitt by suggesting that his argument reproduces certain errors of a mode of legal thought, Kelsen's legal positivism, that inspired Schmitt's assault in the first place. Consequently, Schmitt ultimately criticizes little more than an idiosyncratic version of liberal constitutionalism. Leo Strauss's famous observation that Schmitt's "critique of liberalism takes place within the horizon of liberalism" is accurate, but *only* if we acknowledge that Schmitt's interpretation of the "horizon of liberalism" is limited.[3] However provocative, Schmitt's critique is untenable (II). Finally, this chapter concludes with a series of tentative critical comments about the disturbingly contemporary quality of Schmitt's reflections on constitutional government. At a historical moment when liberal constitutionalism once again is subject to a series of one-sided criticisms, we would do well to recall the ideas of one of its most provocative—and troublesome— midcentury critics (III).

I

For Carl Schmitt, the essence of liberal constitutionalism is best captured by a term that he uses in an undeniably deprecatory fashion throughout his writings: *normativism*. Notwithstanding the immense diversity of liberal ideas about constitutional government, Schmitt claims that liberals have always sought to subject political power to a system of *norms*, to some type of rule-based legal regulation. Whether by means of a polemical contrast between "the rule of law" and the "rule of men," or an espousal of the now commonplace view that governmental power is legitimate only when derived from a fixed, written constitution, liberals repeatedly emphasize the political virtues of subordinating every conceivable expression of state authority to codified legal standards.

Early liberals were most rigorous in this quest; Schmitt's *Constitutional Theory* sees them as pursuing a "consistent normativity."[4] They not only aspired to regulate state power in accordance with a system of neatly codified legal and constitutional standards, but also sought a higher legitimacy for positive law within a system of natural right; in turn, natural right was typically conceived in a highly legalistic manner. In this early version, normativism still took an expressly *moral* form. Liberals believed unabashedly in the rightness and rationality of their legal and constitutional ideals. Early liberal conceptions of the legal statute best embodied this spirit. For John

Locke and other Enlightenment liberals, for example, state action was acceptable only when based on cogent, general laws, which Locke saw as constituting an attempt by mortals to reproduce the universalism of divine natural law. Individual legal measures were deemed potentially arbitrary and, moreover, utterly incompatible with early liberalism's ambitious moral universalistic worldview.[5]

Despite Schmitt's at times surprisingly flattering description of early liberal constitutionalism—his argumentative strategy in the 1928 *Constitutional Theory* represents another example of Schmitt's tendency to criticize contemporary liberal democracy by contrasting it unfavorably to an idealized, even romanticized interpretation of its classical predecessor—he still believes that the early liberal constitutionalist quest was ultimately doomed. Like its longtime institutional and intellectual ally, parliamentarism, liberal constitutionalism is destined to rot away. For Schmitt, normativism is always an eminently utopian worldview. Inevitably, liberals are forced to abandon consistent normativism in favor of more modest versions of normativistic thinking. Modern liberals hence ultimately surrender traditional liberalism's emphasis on the sanctity of the generality of the legal norm, and liberals increasingly tolerate legal forms incompatible with the ambitious legal ideals articulated in the theories of writers like Locke, Montesquieu, and Cesare Beccaria. In this vein, Schmitt is obsessed by the fact that his liberal peers in Weimar jurisprudence unabashedly endorse a concept of the statute, according to which *any* act of the legislature, even one taking an individual or open-ended form, deserves the status of law.[6] Schmitt argues that this trend contributes to an ominous legislative "absolutism" that, as we will see, allegedly threatens to undermine the very foundations of liberal constitutional government. Liberals thereby not only abandon their traditional emphasis on the importance of generality within law, but also simultaneously minimize the closely related requirements of the classical liberal ideal of *equality before the law*. Whereas early liberals like Locke interpreted this ideal as requiring the legislature to avoid actions directed at particular individuals or groups, for Weimar liberals it means nothing more than that administrators and judges should apply statutes equitably. For Schmitt the problem here is that those statutes themselves are permitted to take a discriminatory and inequitable form, which means that "equality before the law" is reduced to the absurd demand to apply unjust laws "justly": equality before the law is a farce if it merely requires a "blind" application by judges or administrators of laws fundamentally arbitrary in character. Occasionally reminiscent of some strands of recent liberal legal thought, Schmitt often points to the ways in the contemporary administrative state increasingly conflicts with traditional liberal general law. In stark contrast to liberals like Theodore Lowi or Friedrich A. Hayek, however, Schmitt's *Constitutional Theory* posits that illiberal legal trends are little more than a concrete manifestation of a fundamental failing inherent in normativistic liberal thinking. For Schmitt, liberal normativism lacks political efficacy. Thus, the ongoing decline of traditional liberal law is both predetermined *and* irreversible.[7]

For Schmitt, two recent manifestations of liberal constitutionalist "decay" [*Verfall*] possess special significance. First, Hans Kelsen's influential brand of legal positivism continues to envision the legal system as consisting of a set of norms, ultimately derivable in Kelsen's view from a "basic norm," defined in *The Pure Theory of Law* as "nothing more than the basic rule, according to which norms of the legal order are produced."[8] But Kelsen breaks with traditional liberalism by demanding a clear separation between legal and moral inquiry. In this system, Schmitt mockingly comments, a legal norm is "valid if it is valid and because it is valid," but not because it refers to a more fundamental moral ideal.[9] Consistent normativism thereby evolves into a mode of "bourgeois relativism."[10] All that remains of the utopian pathos of early liberal legalism is the meager belief that law consists of a coherently structured "hierarchy" of norms. Second, Kelsen's positivism exercises an unambiguously deleterious influence on contemporary constitutional jurisprudence. For Schmitt, relativism makes it impossible for jurists to conceive of a "basic norm" or even a "system" or "hierarchy" of constitutional norms in even the most minimally coherent fashion; Kelsen is internally inconsistent. In the aftermath of the demise of natural law, "the [liberal] constitution is transformed into a series of individual positive constitutional laws. Even if there is still talk of a 'basic norm' or 'basic law' . . . this happens only as a result of leftover formulas long emptied of their original meaning. It is thus just as imprecise and confusing to speak of 'the' constitution. In reality, what is meant by this is an unsystematic majority or plurality of constitutional regulations."[11] If values are relative, a constitution can embody no set of core moral values, and all constitutional standards have to be seen as possessing equal worth. None then deserves special protective status. A clause guaranteeing that "theological faculties should remain part of the universities," like that found in Article 149 of the Weimar Constitution, can be no less vital from a consis-

tent positivist standpoint than a basic guarantee of free speech, freedom
of assembly, or free elections. From the perspective of legal positivism,
constitutional amendment procedures need to treat such clauses with absolute neutrality. Hence, if nothing but a parliamentary supermajority is
needed to amend the constitution, then parliament necessarily deserves as
much of a right to alter (or even abrogate) the core procedures of liberal
democracy as to reform the theological faculties in the university. For
Schmitt, this suggests the self-evident incoherence of legal positivism: positivism offers no way to distinguish between essential and peripheral elements of the constitutional system. Kelsen's positivism culminates in a
brand of nihilism unable to provide a proper defense of its *own* purportedly
liberal aspirations. Because legal positivism can provide no moral justification for liberal democracy, it unwittingly equips illiberal political forces
with a real opportunity for destroying the final remnants of liberal normativism: as soon as illiberal political groupings garner, for example, two-thirds
of legislative votes, positivists are powerless in the face of a likely decision
to dissolve parliament itself. In its final, relativistic form, normativism arms
its own enemies.[12]

From this perspective, the contemporary liberal tendency to downplay
or even to abandon the classical conception of the generality of the statute
represents just another example of the liberal mistake of providing potential
political foes with awesome power. Although often unwittingly, legal positivists who endorse nonclassical modes of law prepare the (legal) way for
radical intrusions into liberal basic rights—including, of course, the right to
private property, which Schmitt considers constitutive of the liberal rule of
law.[13] Writing at a juncture in the history of Weimar when the specter of a
parliamentary road to democratic socialism still loomed large in the minds
of many, Schmitt is clearly worried that the left might rely on the positivist
critique of general law for the sake of attacking capitalist private property.[14]
In criticizing legal positivism, Schmitt thus appeals to classical ideals of
liberal law, *not* because he intends to defend classical liberal jurisprudence,
but solely because he wants to discredit contemporary versions of liberalism. Given his radical ideas about the indeterminacy of law, Schmitt is
incapable of consistently endorsing traditional conceptions of clear legal
norms capable of directing judges and administrators. But it is intellectually
opportune for him to refer to traditional liberal ideas in order to underline
the (purported) bankruptcy of contemporary liberalism.[15]

Why, however, did liberalism inevitably have to abandon "consistent normativity"? Why is self-destructive, nihilistic legal positivism the inexorable "final offshoot" [*letzten Ausläufer*] of classical liberalism, as Schmitt believes?[16]

Regrettably, Schmitt provides only scant historical details when sketching out his dramatic thesis about normativistic constitutionalism's inevitable decay. His argument is primarily legal-philosophical in nature. Even the most coherent brand of liberal normativism is intellectually flawed, and thus normativism must undergo a long process of historical deterioration. History, once again, follows political and legal theory: Schmitt assumes that the *immanent conceptual* limits of liberal constitutional theory can explain both its intellectual decline *and* its (alleged) real-life political ills.

Schmitt employs a variety of arguments in order to illustrate liberal constitutionalism's immanent flaws. Most importantly, he points out that liberals regularly presuppose the existence of a viable political apparatus; liberal constitutionalism's own stated aim is merely the *limitation* of a (preexisting) institutional complex. This assumption might seem trivial. But for Schmitt, it implies that liberals themselves concede, albeit in a backhanded manner, that the existence of a functioning political entity is necessarily *prior* to any normativistic restraints on it. Allegedly, liberals thereby begin to admit that normativism can never provide an adequate basis for a political community. Normativism fails when forced to grapple with the most basic, "existential" elements of political experience. A people is "constituted" first and foremost by means of possessing a capacity for undertaking violence against external threats, by the fact that it is "awakened" and "capable of action" against potential political enemies.[17] According to Schmitt's *Concept of the Political*, political experience inevitably is characterized by potentially life-threatening situations in which political entities face off against "the other, the stranger," a foe, who "in a specially intense way, [is] existentially something different and alien, so that in the extreme case conflicts . . . are possible."[18] Only if a political entity can successfully ward off the "stranger" and thus guarantee its survival do liberal legal normativities even have a chance to function successfully. Normativities are ineffective for resolving truly life-threatening political conflicts: "[t]hese can neither be decided by a previously determined general norm nor by the judgment of a disinterested and therefore neutral third party."[19] The very intensity of such "existential" conflicts excludes the possibility of regulating them by liberal legal devices. Schmitt is thus dismissive of theorists, like Kelsen, who believed that Weimar's deep tensions could in part be healed by means of judicial intervention. In a revealing 1931 feud with Kelsen, Schmitt argues that a constitutional court was unlikely to help guarantee political stability in Weimar. In crisis situations, judicial devices are necessarily so politicized—that is, they become nothing but an unmediated battleground for warring, "existentially" opposed political entities—that they no longer can meaningfully claim to embody liberal legalistic concepts of neutrality or equality before the law. They become nothing but the weapons of an explosive, potentially violent political struggle.[20] Liberal constitutionalism becomes worthless precisely when the political integrity of the community is at stake.

Liberals refuse to concede the unavoidable limits of normativism. Nonetheless, they still must grapple with the exigencies of a political universe inconsistent with their normativistic inclinations. Hence, when liberals do try to come to grips with the imperatives of friend/foe politics, they can do so only in bad faith. Although liberal jurisprudence is hostile to dictatorship, even liberals bestow far-reaching powers on state authorities during an emergency situation. Similarly, liberals shrink at any mention of the concept of sovereignty. Nonetheless, they often make effective use of state power in order to defeat life-threatening foes. Notwithstanding liberal aspirations, constitutional government has never taken an exclusively normativistic form; it necessarily is always mixed with supranormative, "existential" elements, functioning to guarantee political self-preservation in an unavoidably violent political universe. Liberals repeatedly transgress the narrow confines of their normativistic worldview. Yet to admit this flaw openly would demand of them that they acknowledge the political irrelevance of much of their worldview.

Normativistic assumptions similarly hinder liberals from adequately conceptualizing the problem of constitutional validity. Building on his previous analysis of judicial discretion, Schmitt argues that a constitutional system is valid only when it rests on an authoritative "decision" made by a concrete "will." Just as in judicial interpretation "the legal idea cannot realize itself," so too must every constitutional system rest on a concrete decision possessing a substantial amount of autonomy from the norm.[21] In the terminology of *Constitutional Theory*, a constitution is legitimate "when the power and authority of the constituent power . . . is recognized."[22] Early liberals may have been more intellectually consistent than their successors, but even they allegedly failed to see that legitimacy requires no "justification by means of an ethical or juridical norm."[23] Early liberal conceptions of natural law remained imprisoned in the (characteristic normativistic) failure to acknowledge the primacy of those aspects of political experience incapable of being deduced from a legal norm or standard. Although Schmitt's critique of legal positivism at first seems to share many of the concerns of contemporary natural law-based jurisprudence, his argument is thus ultimately quite distinct: because core elements of political experience are essentially supranormative, legitimacy ultimately can refer to nothing more than the efficacy of a particular set of political power holders or decision makers. Here, *legitimacy is essentially a question of power.*[24] Schmitt cannot deny the obvious point that liberals *aspire* to make sense of the problem of legal validity. But in his view, they inevitably provide a distorted view of the problem at hand. For Schmitt, Kelsen's insistence on the need to separate an empirical analysis of political power and one of legal science is the most blatant example of this danger. Insisting on a radical distinction between an empirical analysis of political power and legal science, Kelsen cannot even begin to make sense of the inherently coercive character of his "hierarchy" of legal norms, let alone provide a satisfying account of the political dynamics of constitution-making. Contra Kelsen, only if we acknowledge that a constitution gains validity on the basis of a coherent political decision by a particular "will" can we begin to conceive of it as a unified, hierarchically ordered whole, where some constitutional clauses are undoubtedly more vital than others. Those who acted to establish the Weimar Constitution, for example, surely would have seen its basic liberal-democratic principles as more significant than Article 149's special protections for divinity school professors. In Schmitt's view, they might rightfully have interpreted the positivist attempt to confuse this issue as constituting a starting point for undertaking potentially illegitimate forms of action against the German people's original basic "decision" in favor of a particular political form. Positivists who insist on treating every constitutional clause in a perfectly neutral manner obscure the absolutely pivotal significance of the "will" that decided in favor of a particular political system in the first place.[25]

Furthermore, normativism prevents liberals from properly understanding the origins and the underlying dynamics of their own constitutional system. Just as liberals are hesitant to admit the necessity of dictatorial emergency powers in order to guarantee the self-preservation of a liberal democracy, so, too, do liberals prefer to obfuscate the fact that liberal constitutional systems always *presuppose* and *perpetuate* a dictatorial act: normatively unregulated power is crucial to every political system. The primordial arbitrariness earlier attributed to the judicial decision also lies at the foundations of liberal constitutional government. Furthermore, this arbitrary *Urzustand* necessarily shapes every facet of constitutional government, akin to the manner in which Schmitt earlier considered it determinative of judicial and administrative decision making. In his previous writings on legal interpretation, Schmitt saw this originary arbitrariness as the main source of indeterminacy within the interpretation and application of statutes. In his constitutional theory, it analogously becomes the source of a profound indeterminacy that threatens to plague constitutional government as a whole.

Schmitt argues that the Weimar National Assembly of 1919 possessed dictatorial powers.[26] More ambitiously, he looks to the theory and practice of the French Revolution to unmask the purported hypocrisy of liberal jurisprudence. By means of a reinterpretation of Abbeé Sieyès's constitutional theory, Schmitt argues that liberal democratic jurisprudence implicitly recognizes the existence of an omnipotent, inalienable, and indivisible founding subject, the *pouvoir constituant*.[27] For Schmitt, Sieyès's theory gives expression to the fundamental truth that the modern sovereign, the "people" is capable only of giving itself a constitution once it has proven its ability to undertake resolute action against potential foes.[28] But the very act of demonstrating its political integrity may require that a "people" revert to utterly illiberal means. Why? A political entity must guarantee its self-preservation if it is even to begin to launch itself down the path towards liberal constitutionalism. But political self-preservation rests on the possibility of relying on instruments incompatible with liberal constitutionalism's obsession with restraining and hemming in political power. The very *differentiation* of a people from the "alien foe" is inevitably supranormative; Schmitt doubts that political identity can rest meaningfully on "normativistic" ideas, in part, as noted, because political conflict with "existential" enemies reaches such a pitch of intensity that "normativities" are likely to prove meaningless. Thus liberal democracy necessarily presupposes the existence of a normatively unrestrained, potentially all-powerful sovereign able to ward off the "foe." In contrast to so much contemporary liberal theory, Sieyès's concept of the unrestrained *pouvoir constituant* thus openly expresses the fact that every constitutional founding rests on "a pure decision" unlimited by liberal forms of normative justification.[29]

For Schmitt, it is thus hardly surprising that the French Revolution has always been something of an embarrassment to liberals. The French experience underlines the Achilles' heel of liberal constitutional theory, namely its failure to take the concept of the constituent power seriously enough. Revealingly, Schmitt admires the fact that the French attributed the exercise of arbitrary, supralegal constituent power to the "nation," conceived in an ethnically and nationally particularistic fashion. In this view, French theory and practice magnificently capture the political verity that constitution-making rests on the preexistence of an ethnically homogeneous nation, capable of effectively distinguishing itself from other peoples and, if necessary, waging war against them.[30] The indivisibility and omnipotence of the *pouvoir constituant* can be understood only in this context. The constituent power is no mere conceptual fiction. French theory correctly grasps that a concrete *Volk*, as noted, is always "constituted" by defining itself in opposition to "the stranger . . . existentially something different and alien."

Just as liberal jurisprudence falsely posits that the irrational decision can be subjected to the legal statute, so, too, does liberal constitutional theory wrongly assume that the unregulated will of the original *pouvoir constituant* can be absorbed or replaced by the procedures and institutions of the resultant constitutional system, the *pouvoir constitué*. Schmitt considers the attempt to subject the *pouvoir constituant* to the "normativities" of the *pouvoir constitué* incoherent. If both Sieyès's original theory and much of subsequent political practice are right to see the *pouvoir constituant* as omnipotent, inalienable, and indivisible, then the liberal attempt to absorb it into the path of "normal" liberal politics is incoherent. To make the *pouvoir constituant* subject to the legal rules and procedures of constitutional government would rob it of all those elements that made it the *pouvoir constituant* in the first place. If the foundation of government presupposes the existence of a popular subject possessing unlimited powers, and if the very nature of this founding authority prevents it from being absorbed into the (normativities) of functioning liberal democracy, *then we have to assume that the omnipotent founding subject of liberal democracy has never been disbanded.*

Schmitt believes that we need to take the idea of the inalienability, indivisibility, and absoluteness of the *pouvoir constituant* seriously. The *pouvoir constituant* remains a power to be reckoned with even after the act of founding is complete; the omnipotent subject of every liberal democracy, the people, necessarily continues to have a real existence above and beyond liberal constitutionalism's institutional complex. *The authoritarian founding act upon which liberal democracy rests is never complete. Its dictatorial spirit haunts the mundane world of everyday liberal politics.* The omnipotent founding popular sovereign "remains the real origin of all political events, the source of all power. It gives expression to this power by means of ever-new forms, and generates new forms and organizations out of itself, but it never conclusively subordinates its political existence to a particular form."[31] The *pouvoir constituant* makes use of normativistic liberal institutional devices, but it can also rightfully discard them at will. As Sieyès allegedly taught us, "it suffices if the nation wills it."[32] Because liberal procedures and institutions are mere instruments of the absolutely sovereign people, they inevitably lack the permanence that liberals attribute to them. The sovereign people is not to be found in the halls of parliament; it cannot be identified with constitutional or statutory rules that it may (temporarily) have decided to accept; even a legally ordained constitutional convention remains an inadequate expression of the sovereign's true nature unless the potentially unlimited exercise of its authority has been acknowledged. In addition, "[e]very genuine constitutional conflict concerning the political order's underlying decision can only be resolved by means of the will of the constitution-making authority itself."[33] Or, as one of Schmitt's Weimar contemporaries bluntly commented: meaningful constitutional reform can take place only by revolutionary means.[34]

For Schmitt, no "formalized" procedure or institution can capture the essence of the sovereign people, because formalization is incompatible with the willful, unrestrained nature of the *pouvoir constituant.* The *willfulness* of the constitutent power simply cannot be subjected to the mundane, everyday *lawfulness* of the *pouvoir constitué,* given the radically different principles at hand. The attempt to do so, for Schmitt, is akin to transforming fire into water—in short, a naive fantasy of liberal constitutional alchemists.

Where then is the *pouvoir constituant* located? Schmitt's answer to this question in the 1928 *Constitutional Theory* already anticipates his open espousal of a mass-based authoritarian regime during the Weimar Republic's final, tragic years. *Constitutional Theory* revealingly tells us where the *pouvoir constituant* is *not* found: in the universe of everyday liberal democratic politics, toward which Schmitt in the 1920s was openly hostile. Schmitt does his best to ward off possible radical-democratic interpretations of his constitutional theory. A superficial reader *might* conclude that Schmitt hopes to bring about some form of "permanent revolution" in which an original democratic *pouvoir constituant* continues to exercise political authority in as unlimited and unmediated a manner as possible; one even might see Schmitt as pursuing Rousseau's preference for periodic assemblies of the entire people as a way of counteracting political decay.[35] But this is not Schmitt's position. After attributing seemingly awesome powers to the democratic sovereign, Schmitt quickly adds that the people "can only engage in acts of acclamation, vote, say yes or no to questions" posed to it from above.[36] A few years later he comments that "it cannot counsel, deliberate, or discuss. It cannot govern or administer, nor can it posit norms; it can only sanction by its 'yes' the draft norms presented to it. Nor, above all, can it place a question, but only answer by 'yes' or 'no' a question put to it."[37] The sovereign people, it seems, can only *answer* simple questions, and the questions are best formulated and posed by a strong executive who stands unlimited by parliamentary procedures that potentially undermine his authority. As one of Schmitt's Weimar critics commented, popular political action here probably is reduced to "an unorganized answer . . . .given to a question which may be posed by an authority whose existence is assumed" and probably unquestioned as well.[38] Schmitt's "omnipotent" *Volk* turns out to possess a rather modest, even passive role.

In short, some form of executive-centered plebiscitarianism is likely to come closest to reliving the original founding dictatorship of the *pouvoir constituant*. "Normativistic" liberal legalism surely cannot. As will become clear shortly, Schmitt argues unambiguously during the early 1930s that only a mass-based dictatorship can hope to give adequate expression to the originary, arbitrary *Urzustand* of all political power. A "quantitative total state," wielding awesome discretionary state power to the imperatives of modern technological and economic developments, provides the best answer to the crisis of Weimar democracy.

II

This critical interpretation should place Schmitt's analysis of modern liberal jurisprudence in *Constitutional Theory* in a fresh light. Recall Schmitt's claims that contemporary liberals provide powerful weapons to their antiliberal opponents by permitting easy constitutional revision and tolerating nonclassical forms of law. In reality, Schmitt here develops a far more dangerous antiliberal weapon than anything defended by his Weimar

legal positivist foes. As I argued, even the 1928 *Constitutional Theory* probably already points to the outlines of a theoretical justification for an incipi-
ent dictator, unrestrained by the "normativities" of liberal democratic
politics, who lurks in the background of everyday politics, awaiting the
right moment for declaring that the "national will" has spoken in favor of
constitutional counterrevolution. Although there may be legitimate reasons
for worrying about the sovereign democratic legislature described by
Schmitt and endorsed by some of his positivist opponents, it surely is preferable to a dictator whose authority embodies the originary arbitrariness of
the Schmittian *pouvoir constituant.*[39] For the same reasons, Schmitt's occasional recourse to liberal conceptions of general, determinate law necessarily proves hollow. *Constitutional Theory* at first seems to describe a system of
general laws and rights as essential to constitutional government. Yet in
light of Schmitt's reflections on the constituent power, it is unclear what is
to keep an authoritarian stand-in for the *pouvoir constituant,* the willful originary source of every constitutional order, from altering or abrogating
these laws at will. An executive exercising power in the name of the *pouvoir
constituant* ultimately cannot, within the confines of Schmitt's theory, be
justifiably limited by any of the antipolitical "normativities" of liberal constitutionalism. Needless to say, this is potentially a recipe for legal indeterminacy with a vengeance: a legal system subordinate to the willfulness of a
mass-based dictator is unlikely to provide much legal regularity or security.
In comparison, recent liberal concessions to the need for *some* open-ended,
discretionary law, within a broader liberal legal system fundamentally committed to the principle of legality, look like child's play.

　　Nonetheless, it would be unfair to deny that Schmitt succeeds in identifying some vital questions for constitutional theory. We need not endorse
Schmitt's claim that liberal constitutionalism has undergone an inexorable
historical decay in order to respect his anxieties about its links to value-
relativism in the twentieth century. Schmitt raises tough questions about
the limits of positivist conceptions of constitutional interpretation and
amendment; we need only to recall that many contemporary liberal jurists
have expressed at times analogous worries about more recent positivist jurisprudence. Schmitt's preference for a decisionist over a normativist interpretation of constitutionalism is surely worrisome. Yet at least Schmitt's
formulation openly concedes that existing liberal democracies too often
rest on arbitrary forms of power and exclusion; the real question is whether
this development is as inevitable as Schmitt asserts. Schmitt's controversial

theory of the *pouvoir constituant* rests on a highly selective appropriation of French revolutionary political thought. By the same token, the relationship of democracy to constitutionally based limits on popular decision making remains a controversial issue within liberal theory.[40] Whatever the faults of Schmitt's argumentation, he at least helps remind us of one of the genuine paradoxes of modern constitutionalism: "the people" alone can found constitutional government, but constitutionalism then faces the difficult task of funneling and channeling popular politics by formal, legal means.

To leave the story there, however, might lead us to miss the depth of Schmitt's hostility to liberal constitutionalism. Schmitt *speaks to* important questions within liberal theory. But he lacks the conceptual instruments necessary for analyzing these questions adequately. As I hope to show, this failing ultimately derives from Schmitt's obsession with clearly distinguishing his intellectual perspective from that of liberalism's purported "final offshoot," Hans Kelsen's brand of legal positivism. Responding to Kelsen's peculiar variety of liberal political and legal theory, Schmitt exacerbates some of the methodological weaknesses of Kelsen's legal positivism. As a contemporary of both Schmitt and Kelsen recognized early on, Schmitt answers Kelsen's legal theory of the *will-less norm* with an alternative theory of the *norm-less will.*[41] In slightly different terms, Kelsen's pure theory of law becomes Schmitt's "pure theory of the will." Even more so than Kelsen's original, Schmitt's own radical juxtaposition of the *norm* to the *will* distorts the nature of legal and political experience. Thus, Schmitt never really succeeds in superseding Kelsen. He simply offers an authoritarian *complement* to Kelsen's legal positivism, while abandoning the numerous virtues of Kelsen's theory.

Of course, this is not the first time that Kelsen has figured in this study. Nor will it be the last. In my view, Kelsen was one of Schmitt's most impressive critics, and his reflections often provide a powerful starting point for examining the weaknesses of Schmitt's attack on the rule of law. Unlike Schmitt, Kelsen fought to the end to defend the Weimar Republic; postwar attempts to blame legal positivism for the readiness with which German jurists embraced the authoritarian state in 1933 are unconvincing.[42] At least within the sphere of constitutional theory, however, the results of Schmitt's engagement with Kelsen prove ambivalent. Notwithstanding the many virtues of Kelsen's theory, the methodology of his "pure theory" provides Schmitt with an opening for discrediting the project of liberal constitutionalism altogether.

As we saw above, Schmitt attributes the ills of liberal constitutionalism to its purported normativism. Recent commentators have interpreted Schmitt's use of this term (and many related ones, such as "normativity" and "normativization") as an instrument for criticizing *universalistic* elements of liberalism (liberal ideas about the basic equality of all persons, for example). But this reading probably attributes a degree of precision missing from Schmitt's own usage.[43] Normativism refers for Schmitt to a tremendous diversity of distinct ideas: it includes early liberal conceptions of natural law as well as modern legal positivism, robust and unabashedly (universalistic) *moral* ideals as well as value-relativistic theoretical positions, the rule of law (or rule of legal *norms*) and liberal aspirations to subject politics to *normative* (or moral) concerns, diverse liberal views on the origins of constitutional government alongside a panoply of liberal conceptions of judicial decision making. Although Schmitt offers countless *examples* of "normativism," "normativization," and "normativities," he never defines these terms with any real specificity. The reader will look at Schmitt's massive oeuvre in vain for an adequate definition of what precisely they entail.

However effective as a rhetorical instrument for discrediting liberalism, the concept of normativism simply does not provide as solid a basis for Schmitt's ambitious critique as he believes. Repeatedly, Schmitt crudely subsumes distinct liberal ideas under the (vague) category of normativism. This move precludes his formulating an adequately subtle interpretation of liberal ideals and their distinguishing characteristics; by grouping vastly different versions of liberal thinking (Montesquieu and Kelsen, for example) under the rubric of normativism, Schmitt has *already* taken substantial steps toward "demonstrating" the intellectual incoherence of liberalism even *before* he has even begun to articulate any real criticisms of liberal ideals. Furthermore, the straw man of normativism simply does not allow Schmitt to capture the essence of liberal constitutionalism in the first place. As any reader of Aristotle's *Politics* is well aware, modern liberals hardly stand alone in their praise of the rule of law; as Aquinas shows so well, the attempt to subject politics to "normativistic" (universalistic) moral ideals was essential to medieval Christian political thought. Yet Schmitt's use of the term normativism makes it difficult to determine what makes Locke or Kelsen more "normativistic" than Plato, Aristotle, Aquinas, or any of a host of competing classical authors.[44] Schmitt's attack on "normativism" may offer a starting point for criticizing the mainstream of Western political thought, but it is hardly the best way to identify and criticize the *specific* ills of liberal constitutionalism.

But perhaps this is a bit unfair to Schmitt. Surely, his Weimar-era writings devote substantial attention to the task of defining the liberal rule of law, which Schmitt considers the centerpiece of liberal constitutionalist thinking. Schmitt repeatedly argues that only *the generality of the legal norm* satisfies the conditions of the rule of law-ideal, for judicial independence "in the face of an individual measure is logically inconceivable."[45] Legislative action in the form of an individual act destroys any meaningful distinction between judicial and administrative decision making. When state action is directed at a particular object or individual, judicial activity no longer differs qualitatively from inherently discretionary, situation-specific modes of administrative action; a core element of the rule of law, the idea of determinate, norm-based judicial action, thus becomes obsolete. But even this seemingly sensible specification of the concept of normativism quickly turns out to be more slippery than is initially apparent. Like Schmitt's concept of normativism, his definition of general law is too open-ended. For the most part, the concept of general law in Schmitt's theory simply precludes the legal regulation of an individual object (a particular bank or newspaper, for example). But at other junctures, general law is seen as being incompatible with legal "dispensations and privileges, regardless of what form they take"—in short, with virtually *any* form of more or less specialized legislative activity.[46] The latter view is more far-reaching than the former: whereas the former provides a rather minimal restraint on governmental activity, the latter might imply that the rule of law is incompatible with much legislation essential to the modern welfare state. That most normativistic of liberal constitutional normativities, the idea of the general legal norm, is never consistently defined in Schmitt's writings. Of course, the reason for this ambiguity is clear enough in light of Schmitt's early reflections on the enigma of legal indeterminacy: Schmitt is chiefly interested in employing the traditional idea of general law as a weapon against contemporary liberal theories (like Kelsen's positivism) that seek to make some room for administrative and judicial discretion *without* abandoning the liberal dream of a norm-based rule of law. A principled defense of the traditional liberal ideal of general law simply cannot consistently make up a core element of Schmitt's own theory.

Let me try to suggest that Schmitt's failure to clarify the precise nature of his "normativistic" liberal foe derives from a more profound flaw in his theory. Schmitt never offers a coherent definition of normativism *because his dramatic juxtaposition of the norm to the decision itself is untenable.*

In Kelsen's pure theory of law, he resists a long tradition of methodological syncretism in legal scholarship, in which moral, sociological, and legal reflections are sloppily conflated. According to Kelsen, the failure to separate these different spheres has long proven disastrous to modern legal theory. Too often, what passes for legal science has been nothing but an ideological defense of the legal and political status quo, in which legal theory is reduced to apologetics for the existing political system and its dominant moral and political ideas. In this important sense, Kelsen's undertaking is eminently critical; he resists crude conflations of what "is" (for example, an existing legal system) with what "ought to be" (for example, the unfulfilled universalism of the liberal rule of law), and refuses to shroud the stark realities of political power in attractive moral and political ideas.

In Kelsen's view, the only way to overcome the ills of methodological syncretism is by insisting on a clear delineation of legal science from ethics, on the one side, and empirical sociology or political science, on the other. Legal inquiry needs to be given the status of an objective science, which means for Kelsen that it must undergo a rigorous separation from both moral and social scientific inquiries. In the simplest terms, Kelsen's methodological initiative takes the following form: the study of law is a *normative* science. But that is only to claim that a particular fact has a legal significance within a broader system of norms, according to which if a particular event takes place, then a certain consequence *ought* or *should* follow ("If A, then B *should be*."). Normativity here refers to the fact that a particular sanction is likely to follow when a particular norm is violated. Legal sociology obscures the normative quality of legal experience. It is concerned with factual relations between legal phenomena ("If A, then B *is*."). It comprehends law in the manner of a natural scientist concerned with shedding light on causal laws at work in the natural world. In Kelsen's view, empirical inquiry of this type is inherently limited, for an unavoidable gap exists between the realms of "is" and "ought." That is, an empirical analyst, in the fashion of a political scientist or legal sociologist, inevitably fails to provide insight into the normative or "*should be*" character of law. At the same time, the normative quality of legal experience hardly means that it is concerned with moral, ethical, or political questions. An objective, scientific study of law is normative to the extent that it is concerned with norms. Yet it cannot hope to answer the question of which norm is morally or ethically right. The *"should be"* of ethics is ultimately unrelated to the *"should be"* of law. For Kelsen, this view is tied to a broader belief that moral and political choices inevitably lack a universally binding character; in this respect, they are basically nonscientific. Because of the inherent relativism of moral and political experience, moral and political inquiries provide an inadequate basis for the scientific study of law.[47]

Schmitt's constitutional theory is clearly intended as a critical response to the methodological idiosyncrasies of Kelsen's pure theory of law. Although generally unconcerned with the complicated nuances of Kelsen's position, Schmitt is unsatisfied with Kelsen's attempt to differentiate legal science from an empirical analysis of concrete power relations. According to Schmitt, Kelsen thereby obscures the pivotal role of coercive state authority in legal relations: "Kelsen solved the problem of the concept of sovereignty by negating it."[48] Kelsen's "basic norm" is valid only because a particular set of empirical, real-life (political) institutions guarantees its validity. Yet his pure theory of law provides no role for an analysis of the concrete institutional sources of legal validity. Kelsen's legal theory thus not only reduces the state to a hierarchy of legal norms, but also ultimately has no way of making sense of law's dependence on state authority. The inherently political character of law, deriving from law's dependence on concrete political actors invested with the tasks of applying, interpreting, and enforcing it, is simply banned from legal inquiry by a methodological sleight of hand.

In his quest to criticize Kelsen's "normativistic" brand of legal positivism, Schmitt commits two fatal errors. First, he seems to read Kelsen's positivism *back into* earlier modes of liberal jurisprudence. Because Kelsen allegedly represents the *telos* of liberal legalism, his theory only manifests what was always *implicit* in previous brands of liberalism. Notwithstanding Schmitt's own statement that Kelsen embodies normativism's "final offshoot," he still seems to assume that many of his (legitimate) criticisms of Kelsen apply to each and every variant of liberal constitutionalism.[49] For example, Schmitt asserts that Kelsen's insistence on an absolute separation between legal science and an empirical analysis of state power expresses nothing but "the old liberal negation of the state vis-à-vis the law."[50]— surely an odd comment in light of the rich and detailed analyses of the concrete workings of state authority provided by liberal theorists like Montesquieu or Tocqueville, as well as the awareness by at least some liberal authors that "emergency powers" (Locke's prerogative, for example) make up an unavoidable element of modern political experience.[51] But Schmitt seems unimpressed by such obvious counterarguments, in part because he is more concerned with undermining the legitimacy of liberal constitutionalist ideals than providing a balanced assessment of their origins and evolution.

Second, Schmitt merely *reverses* Kelsen's juxtaposition of legal science (and its emphasis on the legal *norm*) to the problem of concrete political power (the *will*). But he fails to question the value of making this juxtaposition in the first place. Very much reminiscent of Kelsen's pure theory, Schmitt's constitutional theory repeatedly conceives of the "will" as something altogether distinct from the "norm." At the outset of *Constitutional Theory*, he emphatically observes that the will, "in contrast to mere norms," is something "existential" [*seinsmässige*] and thus qualitatively distinct from the "ought" [*Sollen*] character of norms. "The concept of the legal order contains *two totally different elements*: the normative element of the law and the existential [*seinsmässige*] element of a concrete order" [emphasis added].[52] Later, he adds that "the word 'will' describes—in contrast to every form of dependence on normative and abstract rightness—the essentially existential nature of the basis of [legal] validity."[53] Schmitt simply turns Kelsen's pure theory on its head. For Kelsen, the normative element of law (conceived of as distinct from state authority) is the centerpiece of legal experience, whereas Schmitt posits that the (decisionistically conceived) empirical will constitutes its core.

This shift fails to save Schmitt from the errors of his positivist opponent. Schmitt criticizes Kelsen's value relativism and worries about its alleged nihilistic overtones. But is Schmitt not far more vulnerable to nihilism in light of his uncritical endorsement of the "pure decision not based on reason or discussion and not justifying itself"? Schmitt believes that Kelsen's conception of the legal system in terms of "pure normativity" smacks of the realm of make-believe. But what about Schmitt's own "pure" decision, his "will" free of all conceivable normative restraints? Admittedly, Schmitt's extremely open-ended conception of the "normative" makes it difficult to imagine exactly *what* constitutes a "pure decision" or "norm-less will." A naive question may be in order here, however: is it not the case that the human will *always* and *inevitably* expresses itself in accordance with some type of norm or "normativistic" outlook? As Max Weber comments at the outset of *Economy and Society*, human action entails that the "acting individual attaches a subjective mean-

ing to his behavior—be it overt or covert, omission or acquiescence."[54]
This meaning may be simple or complicated, attractive or repellent, liberal
or illiberal: in any event, our common world is constituted by means of
purposeful human action, by modes of human activity having a practical or
normative significance for us. Meaning-constitutive human activity inevitably structures the social world, and facticity and normativity thus inevitably overlap in such a way as to render Schmitt's concept of the will-less
norm as one-sided and truncated as Kelsen's corresponding norm-less will.
Schmitt's idea of the norm-less will deceptively suggests the possibility of a
form of unbridled subjectivity probably incompatible with the basic principles of any identifiably *human* form of subjectivity. Animals and automatons
may act outside the parameters of "normative" concerns. But human beings cannot.

Schmitt believes that the primordial status of the norm-less will is demonstrated, as we saw above, by a host of practical examples. But is the
political and historical evidence quite as unambiguous as he suggests? We
surely might endorse some elements of Schmitt's critical account of crude,
mechanical theories of judicial action in which the decision vanishes as an
independent object of inquiry.[55] By the same token, we need to ask
whether judicial decision making could ever take a *fully* norm-less form; as
we will see, even the Nazi legal model envisioned by Schmitt during the
1930s entailed a "normative" agenda, albeit a rabidly nationalistic, deeply
illiberal, and profoundly anti-Semitic one. The idea of a legal system without a crucial "normativistic" component is even more problematic than
Kelsenian positivism's vision of a legal system without empirical, coercive,
political elements. In modern political history, constitution-making often
does presuppose explosive moments of political struggle in which a particular political entity "differentiates" itself from an alien "foe." Yet such struggles hardly occur in a normative vacuum: competing practical ideals and
"normativities" obviously play a crucial role even in the most violent, life-
threatening political moments—in revolutions, civil wars, and states of
emergency. For that matter, does constitutional history really present us
with even a single example of a normatively unregulated *pouvoir constituant*?
Even the Nazis and the Stalinists accepted the legitimacy of *some* procedural
rules and norms; even the most disturbing features of modern totalitarian
politics express some normative ideals and aspirations, however unattractive
they may be. Nazis and Stalinists may represent worrisome varieties of

"normativism," but their actions hardly embody "a pure decision not based on reason and discussion and not justifying itself."

A common criticism of Kelsen's legal positivism is that empirical concerns in fact inevitably enter his pure theory of law for the simple reason that a radical delineation of legal science as distinct from sociology is untenable. Kelsen allegedly "sneaks" empirical elements back into his "pure" legal categories because without them it would be impossible to offer a minimally coherent account of legal phenomena. Less appreciated is that Schmitt's corresponding pure theory of the will reproduces Kelsen's failing on this point as well. Despite its insistence on the purity of the will in relation to the norm, Schmitt's *Constitutional Theory* repeatedly concedes that the will (and volitional elements of political reality) and the norm (normative elements) are unavoidably fused in concrete political reality. Early on the reader is told that the "normatization" of the Weimar constitutional system is radically distinct from the German people's existential "decision" in favor of a particular regime-type. Yet Schmitt himself then openly declares that some constitutional clauses "are more than laws or normativizations" because they directly embody the original decision of the German people. In other words, although the "will" of the German people allegedly lacks all normative elements, it gains expression only by means of the (characteristically normativistic device) of the codified constitutional clause.[56] Schmitt then argues, as noted previously, that the liberal idea of general law is a quintessentially normativistic ideal. But he also suggests in *Constitutional Theory* that general law is "political" and thus, within the confines of his theoretical system, inherently antinormative.[57] After berating liberals for trying to subject the *pouvoir constituant* to an array of (allegedly normativistic) decision-making procedures, Schmitt offers his own model of mass-based plebiscitarianism. But the reader is left wondering why Schmitt's own proposals are necessarily more "norm-less": they certainly *seem* to constitute some type of "normativistic" regulation of popular decision making, albeit one with decidedly authoritarian credentials. In short: Schmitt himself suggests the mythical nature of his own "pure theory of the will."

Schmitt believes that he has succeeded in formulating a theoretical antipode to Kelsen's legal positivism. In reality, his alternative is little more than a distant cousin to Kelsen's positivism. Moreover, the cousin has abandoned the critical spirit of its positivist relative. Schmitt's theory simply exacerbates certain weaknesses of a highly idiosyncratic version of modern liberal jurisprudence. By no means can Schmitt legitimately claim to have superseded liberal constitutionalism. Schmitt has simply surrendered its most worthwhile achievements.

III

Let me conclude this discussion of Schmitt's Weimar-era constitutional theory with a brief comment on its contemporary relevance. Notwithstanding the manifest ills of Schmitt's constitutional theory, it haunts contemporary debates about the relationship between revolutionary politics and constitutional government.

One can easily imagine Schmitt applauding Jacques Derrida's recent statement that the American Declaration of Independence rests on a "fabulous retroactivity," according to which a "coup of force makes right, founds right or the law, gives right, *brings the law to the light of the day, gives both birth and day to the law.*"[58] In the words of one of Derrida's North American defenders, "every system is secured by placeholders that are irrevocably, structurally arbitrary and illegitimate. They enable the system but are illegitimate from its vantage point."[59] Of course, neither Schmitt nor Derrida is alone in arguing that constitutional government often rests on a vicious circle, in which violent willfulness alone generates a constitutional order inconsistent with the originary arbitrariness of foundational politics. For those familiar with the violent history of modern revolutionary politics, this claim is likely to appear trivial. But what Derrida and Schmitt also share is the far more controversial view that foundational politics *inevitably* rests on an arbitrary *coup de force*. The act of foundation is unavoidably arbitrary, notwithstanding liberal and democratic aspirations to conceive of the possibility of peaceful, norm-based political change (for example, by means of constitutional amendments). Moreover, the original sin of foundational violence means that the constitutionalist dream of "government of laws, not men" always suffers from a fundamental hypocrisy: it obscures the arbitrariness that haunts even "normal" legal experience.[60] The link between Derrida and Schmitt here is probably best captured by what Richard Wolin has described "as a shared fascination with 'limit situations' [*Grenzsituationen*] and extremes; an interest in transposing the fundamental experiences of aesthetic modernity—shock, disruption, experiential immediacy; an infatuation with the sinister and forbidden, with the 'flowers of evil'—to the plane of everyday life, thereby injecting an element of enthusiasm and vitality in what had otherwise become a rigid and lifeless mechanism."[61]

In a similar vein, the legal scholar Robert Cover has argued that "[r]evolutionary constitutional understandings are commonly staked in blood. In them, the violence of the law takes its most blatant form. But the relationship between legal interpretation and the infliction of pain remains operative even in the most routine of legal acts."[62] For Cover, as for Schmitt, legal experience unavoidably involves a moment of untamed violence. This violence manifests itself most clearly during a foundational act in which the framework of constitutional government is established. But it remains "operative" in the resultant legal order as well. In particular, the inherent violence of constitutionalism and the rule of law rears its ugly head in the criminal law (for example, in the act of sentencing).[63] Although occasionally ambiguous, Cover generally hopes to resist the traditional liberal attempt to distinguish clearly between legitimate (lawful) and illegitimate violence. When a criminal is punished, it is deceptive to believe that a "commonality of interpretation" or "common meaning" can be achieved according to which the judge is doing more than engaging in brute violence against the defendant. The divergent experiences of punishment—the criminal undergoes bodily harm, whereas the judge returns to his wife and kids in the suburbs—make a mockery of the "ideology" of legitimate punishment.[64] For Cover, the recent interpretativist turn in legal theory, exemplified most clearly by Ronald Dworkin, similarly obscures the fundamentally violent character of the law by emphasizing the moral character and coherence of judicial decision making.

Cover's argument can easily be translated into Schmittian language: the "normativities" of law are unavoidably abrogated by the unavoidable recurrence of "existential" politics within the everyday operations of liberal democracy.

Both Derrida and Cover see their reflections as part of a broader progressive political agenda: Derrida remains an important voice within France for the disenfranchised and powerless, and Cover argues for fundamental reforms of the sorry system of criminal punishment in the contemporary United States. But can these noble practical aspirations flow from a theoretical perspective that provides a privileged place to the experience of arbitrary power? Cover explicitly endorses the traditional ideal of an independent judiciary, and he continues to subscribe to the aspiration to "domesticate" violence.[65] Yet if the original sin of foundational arbitrariness is particularly evident in the exercise of judicial power, preserving the independence of the courts would seem a poor device for taming violence. For that matter, how is power to be domesticated in the first place, if not in part by the traditional instruments of the rule of law? Revealingly, some of Cover's enthusiasts have similarly pointed to the underlying tensions in Cover's writings on power and violence. But in trying to revise Cover, they simply accentuate those features most reminiscent of Schmitt. Austin Sarat and Thomas Kearns praise Cover for acknowledging that arbitrary violence plagues legal experience, while accusing him of naively succumbing to the humanistic "liberal apology for law" that keeps him from sketch-

√ ing out the most interesting implications of his vision of law as inherently willful and violent. In short: Cover's theory needs more Schmitt and less legal liberalism in order to take on a consistent texture. Unfortunately, Sarat and Kearns are unclear in reference to an obvious question posed by their antilegalism: what new institutional mechanisms could replace the rule of law and its (admittedly incomplete) quest to restrain arbitrary political power?[66]

A surprising number of theorists start, for the most part unwittingly, from Schmittian assumptions. Can they escape Schmitt's shocking conclusions?

4

THE TOTAL STATE

Left-wing legal theory is by no means the only place in contemporary
North American intellectual discourse haunted by the ghost of Carl
Schmitt. Among contemporary neoconservatives, it has long been a commonplace that the growth of the interventionist welfare state in the twentieth century has generated a potentially disastrous "crisis of governability,"
in which a rapid multiplication of demands for social and economic security
fragments state authority and delegitimizes liberal democracy. According to
this now familiar line of argumentation, growing state activity blurs the
traditional liberal distinction between state and society, "overloading" government and rendering effective state action unlikely: "the more decisions
the modern state has to handle, the more helpless it becomes."[1] Facing
unprecedented demands for democratic participation, traditional liberal institutions seem unsuited to the imperatives of a political universe in which
a highly mobilized citizenry exhibits a seemingly insatiable thirst for social
justice. In this view, virtually every polity now provides evidence of parliamentary decay, as legislatures prove unable to stand above the fray of spe-
cial-interest politics, the "generalized blackmailing game," and fulfill the
basic functions of governance.[2] Accordingly, there is now a "crisis of democracy," in which contemporary liberal democracy faces a dramatic
choice between continued decline—or a drastic curtailment of the alleged
excesses of democratic participation and its troublesome sidekick, the interventionist welfare state.[3] If liberal democracy is to survive, it needs to
counter the leveling winds of the "spirit of equality." Liberal democracy
can do so, but only if it strengthens popularly elected executives too long
subject to the whims of an excessively adversarial political culture.

Writing during the final crisis-ridden years of the Weimar Republic,
Carl Schmitt offered an eerily similar description of legal and political

trends in the twentieth century. For Schmitt, the outlines of the emerging interventionist welfare state in Weimar Germany and elsewhere in Europe suggested that we have entered the epoch of the "total state," in which traditional liberal conceptions of the state/society divide have been abandoned, and government intervenes in all spheres of human existence in order to grapple with a dramatic increase in political and social claims.[4] Traditional liberal democratic institutions increasingly are poorly attuned to the main political and social dictates of our era, and a dramatic strengthening of executive power is the only way by which the modern state now can hope to master those forces. Despite its far-reaching character, governmental action in the age of the total state generally proves ineffective. By taking the form of a democratic polity allied to the welfare state, political institutions exhibit evidence of disorganization and fragmentation.

In light of the surprisingly contemporaneous character of Schmitt's theory of the total state, it is pivotal that we tackle it head-on. Here, I begin with a discussion of Schmitt's central role in a wide-ranging debate among Weimar political and legal theorists about the status of the so-called *total state*. Most important for my purposes here, Schmitt ultimately reaches the conclusion that only an authoritarian alternative to contemporary liberal democracy is likely to prove capable of mastering the political and social tides of our era (I, II). I then argue that Schmitt's theory of the total state made him vulnerable to National Socialism (III), before criticizing the romanticized portrayal of nineteenth-century reality on which Schmitt's theory of the total state rests (IV).

I

In the final fateful years of the Weimar Republic, German jurists, political thinkers, and publicists focused an enormous amount of attention on the concept of the "total state." Once again, it was Carl Schmitt who played a pivotal role in this debate. Schmitt introduced the term total state into German political discourse in 1931, and it was Schmitt's initial conceptualization of it that spawned the controversial discussion that followed.[5]

In the exegesis offered here, Schmitt develops two distinct but nonetheless complementary lines of argumentation. First, Schmitt traces the transformation of the liberal state into the modern interventionist welfare state (A). Second, he supplements his political and economic account of the emergence of the so-called total state with a speculative philosophy of history, according to which our era is defined by "economic-technical" imperatives requiring that authentic political actors effectively manipulate modern economic and technological instruments if they are to engage successfully in friend/foe politics (B). Finally, Schmitt welds these two lines of argumentation to a defense of an authoritarian brand of executive-based plebiscitarianism.

Nonetheless, Schmitt's *initial* 1931 contribution to a theory of the total state remains tension-ridden: Schmitt builds his defense of an executive-centered political system on empirical foundations whose most problematic features are repeatedly emphasized in his own account. The first version of the theory of the total state seems to offer nothing less than a highly ambivalent right-wing defense of an intrusive, all-embracing popular despotism, at times reminiscent of the "democratic despotism" that worried writers like Alexis de Tocqueville and generations of conservatives who followed in his footsteps (C).

A

Schmitt's analysis of the economic and political origins of the total state represents an embellishment of his 1920s critique of liberal parliamentarism discussed in chapter 2. Relying on an idealized interpretation of modern political and social history, Schmitt's *The Guardian of the Constitution* (1931) suggests that European polities in the nineteenth century rested on a clear division between state and society.[6] Neutrality and nonintervention were the distinguishing principles of a generic liberal state, in which the autonomy of religion and of economic life was effectively guaranteed by a clear separation of state from society. Despite the purportedly limited character of the liberal state, it proved anything but weak in character. In accordance with his reflections on the short-lived political strengths of classical parliamentarism found in *Constitutional Theory* (1928), Schmitt now qualifies his earlier description of the classical liberal state as essentially "antipolitical."[7] For Schmitt, only because the liberal state was "strong enough to stand above and beyond all social forces" was it able to preserve its independence from society and to "relativize" potential conflicts—concerning religious, cultural, and economic differences—so as to prevent them from taking on explosive forms.[8] Though at first glance paradoxically, only a liberal state possessing elements of an "executive state" [*Regierungsstaat*] was able to maintain its political integrity and to gain the strength requisite for the protection of the liberal private sphere. Neutrality and nonintervention presuppose genuinely "political" capacities, and for Schmitt the nineteenth-century liberal state undoubtedly possessed such qualities. Whence the political attributes of the liberal state? *The Guardian of the Constitution* suggests that those elements of the liberal state generally considered *preliberal* by liberal theory in fact made classical liberalism possible. As an "executive state," resting on monarchical interests, it drew substantial prowess from the fact that it long faced off successfully against a genuine political foe, popular social and political forces unleashed by the modern liberal and democratic revolutions. The early liberal state still included vestiges of monarchical absolutism; this assured its autonomy vis-à-vis society. For Schmitt, the fact that the forces of the *ancien régime* long were able to fight off the life-or-death threat posed to its well-being suggests that the carriers of the "executive state" possessed impeccable political credentials.

In this interpretation, the early liberal state was always a tension-ridden and contradictory political creature. While deriving impressive political efficacy from its executive, a "monarchical state of civil servants" [*monarchischen Beamtenstaat*], hostile to democratization, it simultaneously included important elements of a parliamentary "legislative state" [*Gesetzgebungsstaat*], in which precisely those popular forces despised by the executive ultimately were able to gain a foothold. Of course, at first parliaments allowed only for the participation of the privileged and educated, those having *Besitz und Bildung*, the original carriers of liberal bourgeois civilization. But even at this early juncture, the liberal state manifested the dualistic character that would ultimately destroy it. In part, state intervention in society was limited precisely *because* parliaments increasingly sympathetic to liberal-bourgeois aspirations functioned as a counterweight to the executive *Regierungsstaat*. More fundamentally, parliament became the main institutional base for reform demands directed against traditional political and economic elites, meaning that the pivotal friend/foe divide between monarchical executive-based interests and comparatively broad-based political and social forces soon corresponded directly to the institutional separation of the executive from parliament. In Schmitt's interpretation, nineteenth-century liberal theory is simply incomprehensible without an appreciation of this dualistic core, which for Schmitt reveals itself in a host of related antitheses central to classical liberal thought. Most important, this underlying dualism is the source of the liberal delineation of the rule of law from arbitrary power, employed originally by defenders of the parliamentary "legislative state" who sought to contrast a vision of the parliament as resting on clear, prospective, general legal norms, to the purportedly willful actions of an "arbitrary" state executive.

For Schmitt, liberalism's dualistic structure inevitably leads to its self-destruction. As parliaments gain power over the executive (that is, as the "legislative state" supplants the "executive state"), and, as parliamentary suffrage is extended to include strata outside the ranks of the "propertied and educated," the traditional liberal division of state and society necessarily decays. The democratization of parliament, in conjunction with the simultaneous parliamentarization of the state, means that no element of the state now "stands above and beyond social forces." The dualism of executive and legislature, alongside a whole set of corresponding dualisms basic to nineteenth-century liberal theory and practice (including "state vs. society" and "executive vs. the people"), is destroyed, as "the people" (alternately, "society") occupies the state. State and society are fused, and the state becomes a mere expression of the "self-organization of society," as mass popular movements take over positions of political responsibility and exercise substantial political power for the first time.

In this way, liberalism loses its enigmatic dualistic structure. Yet for Schmitt it does so at the price of reducing the state to a mere instrument of mass democratic constituencies. In turn, these constituencies tend to see the state as little more than a means for satisfying a host of popular demands and needs—in particular, for increased economic and social security.

The conflation of state and society generates a total state that abandons liberal postulates of state neutrality and nonintervention: "If society organizes itself into the state, if state and society are to be basically identical, then all social and economic problems become immediate objects of the state."[9] The "societalization of the state" (and, simultaneously, the statization of society) means that the state becomes an interventionist state, a regulatory state, even a welfare state:

> the state as an outgrowth of society, and thus no longer objectively distinguishable from society, occupies everything societal, that is, anything that concerns the collective existence of human beings. There is no longer any sphere of society in relation to which the state must observe the principle of absolute neutrality in the sense of non-intervention.[10]

Writing amidst the darkest days of the economic depression, Schmitt tends to underline the *economic* facets of this development. Noting that state intervention in the economy in the twentieth century has grown in dramatic leaps and bounds, he repeatedly emphasizes that even defenders of capitalism are forced to acknowledge that state intervention in economic life is necessary if private ownership is to function effectively. In contemporary capitalism, nonintervention would simply permit the strongest and most privileged economic group to exploit unfair advantages in order to defeat its weaker economic competitors. For Schmitt, nonintervention in the economy therefore is no longer consistent with the concept of neutrality as conceived by classical liberal theorists. A dogmatic insistence on nonintervention amidst the crisis–ridden conditions of twentieth-century capitalism would merely exacerbate already explosive economic tensions. No state in the twentieth century can afford to abandon the instruments of economic interventionism.[11]

From this perspective, the total state not only is a product of the immanent contradictions of classical liberalism, but also represents a natural response to the social and economic conditions of an era in which few seriously doubt that the state can avoid playing a central role in social and economic affairs.

B

Along with his economic and political discussion of the origins of the total state, Schmitt develops a highly speculative account of the basic developmental tendencies of modern European civilization since the Renaissance. In this view, Western modernity is characterized first and foremost by a ceaseless quest for *neutrality*: the motor of cultural and spiritual development has been the struggle to locate "a neutral sphere in which there would be no conflict and they [the Europeans] could reach common agreement" by peaceful means.[12] This struggle has repeatedly determined what form the "central sphere" of human activity has taken at every juncture of modern Western development. Stated in the simplest terms, European culture fled the explosive controversies of theology in the seventeenth century in order to embrace a purportedly neutral sphere of metaphysics, before pursuing humanitarian ethics (in the eighteenth century) and finally economics (in the nineteenth century). Finally, our century is moving towards an "age of technicity," in which technological development is believed capable of overcoming political conflict. In this view, the course of European culture is predicated on a tragic quest to escape conflict and disagreement, an illusionary refusal to accept the inevitability of the "pure decision not based on reason and discussion and not justifying itself . . . an absolute decision created out of nothingness."[13] Each "central sphere" is initially seen as providing a basis for a relatively harmonious form of existence able to liberate humanity from conflicts that have long plagued it, only to be abandoned as disagreement and dissent inevitably surface precisely where they were deemed expendable. Nineteenth-century liberals, for example, imagined that they could produce a perfectly harmonious political and economic universe, only to face the fact that liberalism generates political and economic conflicts as explosive as any in history. Obsessed with the task of seeking escape from the decisionistic verities of moral and political action, European civilization marches relentlessly forward in its doomed quest for "neutralization and depoliticization."

For our purposes here, the "economic" nineteenth and the "technological" twentieth centuries are the most important elements of Schmitt's often apocalyptic account. In this view, the core categories of human existence in the nineteenth century became production and consumption, while the two dominant social philosophies of the nineteenth century, liberalism and Marxism, gave expression to this fundamentally economic orientation. Moral progress was conceived as a by-product of economic development; both liberals and Marxists aspired, though obviously by means of distinct paths, to achieve a harmonious economic order capable of reducing controversy and conflict to an absolute minimum. Yet the quest for neutralization via economics inevitably failed: "religious wars evolved into the still cultural yet already economically determined national wars of the nineteenth century and finally into economic wars."[14] Economic conflicts, in the form of explosive confrontations between competing autarchic economic and political blocs, ultimately took on unambiguously political characteristics as "the real possibility of physical killing" came to haunt the economic realm.

The twentieth century, the emerging "age of technicity," builds on the nineteenth century. Schmitt is somewhat obscure in his discussion of the relationship between the nineteenth and twentieth centuries, sometimes suggesting a radical break between the two eras, at other junctures pointing to an intimate link between them. On one level, the connection between the two eras is clear enough: faced with the failures of the eco-

nomically derived quest for neutrality, Europeans in the twentieth century
embrace a naive, apolitical interpretation of modern technology

> since apparently there is nothing more neutral. Technology serves every-
> one, just as radio is utilized for news of all kinds or as the postal service
> delivers packages regardless of their contents . . . With respect to theolog-
> ical, metaphysical, moral and even economic questions, which are debat-
> able, purely technical problems have something refreshingly factual about
> them. They are easy to solve, and it is easily understandable why there is
> a tendency to take refuge in technicity from the inextricable problems of
> all other spheres.[15]

The widespread faith in technology in our era derives in part from the
unfulfilled tasks of the nineteenth century, for technology is seen as capable
of overcoming economic scarcity and thus resolving economic conflict. At
some junctures, Schmitt suggests that his own era is best described as *economic-technical*, since the twentieth-century faith in technology stems from
its promise to resolve the unsolved dilemmas of the nineteenth century.[16]
At the very least, the *early* twentieth century is still a transitional era, positioned uneasily between the economic conflicts and ideologies of the nineteenth century and an emerging faith in the regenerative power of
advanced technology. Few in the twentieth century would deny the conflict-ridden and explosive character of economic life; we thereby seem to
have sacrificed that element of nineteenth-century ideology according to
which economics can succeed in depoliticizing Western culture. At the
same time, economic concerns remain predominant, and the new (allegedly) neutral sphere of technology has yet to supplant economics altogether. Both spheres continue to shape the contours of human existence in
the twentieth century, though neither is perfectly hegemonic.

How then do Schmitt's speculative concerns relate to his theory of the
total state? In a passage in what surely belongs among his most speculative
lectures, Schmitt declares that the modern state always "derives its actuality
and power from the given central sphere, because the decisive disputes of
friend-enemy groupings are also determined by it. As long as religious-
theological matters were the central focus, the maxim *cujus regio ejus religio*
had a political meaning."[17] When theology constituted the "central
sphere" of human culture, political leaders made sure that they alone decided on the religion of their subjects. By the same token, in our eco-

nomic-technical age, "a state which does not claim to understand and direct economic relations [and technology] must declare itself neutral with respect to political questions and decisions and thereby renounce its claim to rule."[18] In the economic-technical twentieth century, political leaders are forced to "master" economics and technology. If they fail to do so, they face political extinction, since the contours of friend/enemy politics are now permeated with economic and technological concerns.

This idea contains two parts. First, in an era in which economic differences take on a potentially violent and thus a directly political character, no effective political entity can afford to ignore economics. A state that refuses to address economic concerns in a universe defined by class conflict and antagonistic "autarchic world empires" is sure to prove a weak match for competing states actively involved with the task of channeling economic forces to suit their own political purposes. In Schmitt's view, Italy and the Soviet Union have already learned this lesson; Germany would do well to follow their example and acknowledge that extensive state intervention in the economy is imperative if Germany's political integrity is to be maintained.[19] Second, Schmitt anxiously comments that the twentieth century still awaits political forces "strong enough to master the new technology."[20] Pursuing an idea reminiscent of Machiavelli's *Prince*, Schmitt seems to believe that only authentic political actors are likely to prove capable of seeing through popular illusions—in our era, the naive belief in the potentialities of technology as a depoliticizing and neutralizing force. Efficacious political leaders understand that the age of technicity is destined to prove as controversial as any previous era, and they will make sure that technology works *for* them and not *against* them.

In a revealing but little known contribution to a discussion on "Freedom of the Press and Public Opinion" at the 1930 meeting of the German Sociological Association, Schmitt clarifies exactly *what* kind of technology he has in mind. Addressing some of Germany's most famous sociologists, Schmitt argues that the rapid development of the modern mass media contributes in an especially revealing manner to the demise of the traditional liberal state/society divide. Requiring unprecedented forms of *positive* state action, radio and film pose a real challenge to classical liberalism; even the most liberal polities have relied on extensive state action in order to cultivate and regulate the new media. Growing state involvement in the media—as demonstrated by the growth of state-run radio and the public financing of the film industry in many countries—raises troublesome questions about the possibility of state neutrality in the realm of communicative freedom. In this arena as well, the march of the total state seems inexorable: the public/private divide becomes most fuzzy precisely where the mass media are most highly developed. Most importantly for Schmitt, new media technology provides immense possibilities for mass persuasion and manipulation. Whoever proves most capable of employing the mass media effectively is likely to determine, to a great extent, the political course of the twentieth century.[21]

In accordance with the economic-technical imperatives of our times, the modern total state not only is an "economic state" [*Wirtschaftsstaat*], but also faces the difficult test of grappling successfully with the dictates of an "age of technicity" and its awesome arsenal of weapons of mass persuasion. At the very least, this development requires that government abandon any vestige of the liberal commitment to nonintervention in the realm of mass communication.

C

Contemporaries who confronted Schmitt's initial account of the total state in 1931 likely found themselves posing an obvious yet by no means trivial question: does Schmitt hope to place the development of the total state in a positive or negative light? And if we *are* to embrace the total state, what are its implications for liberal democratic politics? Schmitt's answer to this question—at least in 1931—was by no means crystal clear. No wonder his introduction of the concept of the total state into scholarly and political debate in Germany immediately generated an academic growth industry among right-wing political and legal thinkers.

Schmitt clearly hoped to gain political mileage from his empirical analysis of the origins of the total state. In the early 1930s, Schmitt was an outspoken defender of the Weimar executive and its constitutionally dubious use of emergency powers as a means of governing Germany during a period of profound political and economic crisis.[22] Given the fact that the executive was chosen by the German *Volk* as a whole, for Schmitt it provided a better expression of the homogeneous, unified people envisioned by Weimar's constitutional architects during the relatively hopeful days of 1918 and 1919, than Weimar's ineffective, divided parliament. In this view, only the Weimar Federal President was likely to fulfill authentic representative functions, and only he could provide a suitable embodiment of the awesome *pouvoir constituant* on which the Weimar polity necessarily rested.[23] Hindenburg's plebiscitary legitimacy was superior to the pathologies of Weimar's system of parliamentary legality. In 1931, Schmitt explicitly argued that the Weimar executive could legitimately "break through" [*durchbrechen*] constitutional norms of secondary importance to the constitutional order as whole.[24] Which norms did Schmitt have in mind? Schmitt was conveniently unclear in 1931 on this point. Yet he unambiguously stated that limits to the exercise of Weimar's emergency powers were primarily *institutional* in character: the Weimar Constitution provided the parliament with controls against the abuse of executive emergency authority.[25] As Schmitt was well aware, however, the deeply divided status of the legislature during this period meant that it was unlikely to take advantage of these controls. In (only somewhat) cruder terms: because parliament lacks the ability to ward off an authoritarian exceptional state, the Weimar executive can legitimately undertake to establish such a state.

Many who encountered Schmitt's analysis of the total state in 1931 legitimately interpreted it as a defense of Schmitt's own preference for an executive-based authoritarian regime possessing at best a dubious constitutional basis.[26] After all, on one point the theory of total state is unambiguous: for Schmitt, the rise of the total state demonstrates the anachronistic character of liberal parliamentarism and the rule of law, as well as the virtues of an executive-based authoritarian system allegedly better equipped to deal with the dictates of our economic-technical age. The total state requires jettisoning core liberal democratic institutions for an executive-centered regime equipped with impressive exceptional powers.

In *The Guardian of the Constitution* (1931), Schmitt describes contemporary parliaments as dominated by highly organized social and political blocs and parties, lacking even a minimal interest in rational debate. The "societalization of the state" manifests itself most clearly in a dysfunctional brand of parliamentarism having at best a faint resemblance to traditional liberal models of government by deliberation. The structure of the modern political party increasingly corresponds to the logic of the total state: in Schmitt's interpretation, parties fuse public and private by functioning as "total" institutions providing their members with tutelage from the crib to the grave. Social Democrats send their children to socialist youth camps, sign up for a socialist sports club, then spend their retirement years as members of the socialist stamp collectors' guild or bird-watchers' association; conservative parties offer a corresponding set of "total" institutions. The resulting "pluralist party-state," in which total parties ruthlessly carve up state authority for the benefit of profoundly antagonistic, all-encompassing political groupings, renders freewheeling parliamentary deliberation impossible. How could sensible debate and lawmaking ever take place between those who have undergone political socialization within the horizons of distinct, all-encompassing organizations pursuing altogether antagonistic aims?

The total state also rests on situation-specific forms of economic and social regulation incompatible with liberal models of the rule of law as resting on clear, general legal norms. State action now needs to adapt to the complex and ever-changing imperatives of a host of social and economic spheres, and for Schmitt it is unrealistic to expect traditional liberal legislative institutions or devices to succeed in tackling the immense tasks at hand. Only an executive-allocated far-reaching discretionary power is likely to do so. Schmitt goes so far as to suggest that in the twentieth century we find ourselves in an "economic state of emergency" [*Wirtschaftsnotstand*]. Economic crises are now widely seen as possessing the life-and-death quality once associated, for example, with the possibility of an armed attack or a violent uprising, and thus the management of the economy now concerns matters having a potential impact no less devastating than the "emergencies" described by classical liberal theorists in the eighteenth and nineteenth centuries. In line with this trend, emergency political and legal devices, long considered by liberal theorists appropriate solely to dire crises in which the polity faces an immediate existential threat, have now legitimately become a *pervasive* feature of economic and social regulation. For this reason, every modern executive inevitably relies on highly particularistic forms of administrative action, often lacking even a minimal basis in parliamentary general law.[27]

The theory of the total state thereby offers a crucial *sociological* complement to Schmitt's early jurisprudential reflections on the problem of legal indeterminacy. Given that the classical distinction between parliamentary law and administrative decree is *inevitably* blurred and that law today *unavoidably* becomes vague and open-ended, highly discretionary state action is simply unavoidable. Even if judges and administrators *could* be effectively bound by legal norms, contemporary legal systems nonetheless increasingly lack precisely those (clear, prospective) general norms alone capable of providing coherent guidance to those forced to interpret legal materials. For

Schmitt, liberal jurisprudence not only provides an anachronistic model of judicial and administrative action, but rests on bad legal sociology as well.

In the era of the total state, far-reaching *in*determinacy (in the form of irregular, highly discretionary state action) is necessarily a central feature of legal experience. In this respect as well, liberalism is simply outdated: its preference for the rule of law and relatively formalistic modes of decision making is inconsistent with the structural imperatives of our times.

As already discussed, Schmitt had previously hinted that the logical answer to the crisis of legal indeterminacy was a dictatorship, in which the unavoidability of arbitrary state action was taken as a given. In the early 1930s, this element of Schmitt's thinking becomes a pivotal feature of his theory of the total state. Schmitt's early jurisprudential writings suggest that the moment of arbitrary decision within state action might be contained— for example, by judges able to secure legal predictability and regularity despite the impossibility of binding state action to clear norms. By the early 1930s at the latest, the moment of arbitrary decision escapes even the modest limits outlined in Schmitt's jurisprudential writings. In the form of an awesome executive effectively unregulated by law, exercising power in the interests of the German *Volk* as a whole, the moment of willful decision liberates itself from any meaningful controls whatsoever.

Schmitt thereby relies on his empirical *diagnosis* of the total state in order to offer a normative *prognosis* possessing authoritarian credentials. Yet this strand within his argument clearly presents some problems for him; much of the subsequent debate about the total state debate focuses on these issues. In the simplest terms, the paradox at hand takes the following form: on the one hand, the concept of the total state is supposed to serve, at least implicitly, as a normative justification for Schmitt's own political agenda, namely an executive-based exceptional state. On the other hand, Schmitt often portrays the movement toward the total state as a *regression* having potentially disastrous implications: the inexorable transition from classical liberalism to the total state is hardly described as an altogether positive development. In effect, Schmitt undertakes to deduce his normative agenda from a series of historical transformations whose most unattractive features he repeatedly highlights.

Schmitt argues that the total state breeds clientelism and bureaucratic inefficacy. The state is "parceled out" [*parzelliert*] to competing political and social blocs struggling to gain their share of an apparatus that occupies an ever more paramount place in economic life. This "pluralistic splitting up of the state into a number of tightly organized social complexes" denies the state apparatus the minimum of integrity requisite for coherent state action.[28] The public economy (publicly operated services and firms, such as railroads or the post office) succumbs to disorganization and "planlessness" since antagonistic political and social interests exploit it for narrow purposes incompatible with the dictates of sound economics. In a 1931 essay, "Political Ideology and Political Reality in Germany and Western Europe," Schmitt's hostility to the total state's underlying "societalization of the state" becomes especially evident. Here, Schmitt describes the pluralist occupation of the state by popular political and social groupings as nothing less than the outgrowth of a foreign (American and Western European) political tradition inconsistent with Germany's indigenous authoritarian and statist traditions. In a passage foreshadowing Schmitt's worst xenophobic outbursts from the mid-1930s, he exhorts his countrymen to free themselves from such alien cultural influences and instead cultivate the "special type" [*Eigenart*] of political institutions appropriate to the special needs and conditions of Germany.[29] In this view, the total state is hardly an appropriate political and social form for contemporary Germany. On the contrary, Germany would do best to free herself from its "alien" tentacles.

In the final analysis, the movement toward an exceptional executive-based system of rule is depicted in 1931 as a more or less natural outgrowth of precisely the *same* forces that generate modern democracy's (allegedly) crippling clientelism, pluralism, and parceling out of state authority. Both the "positive" and the "negative" faces of the total state stem from a fusion of state and society engendered by the forces of political and social democratization. The inexorable trend toward an executive-dominated political system, *and* the worst ailments of the interventionist welfare state, constitute two sides of the same coin.

Schmitt thereby might be taken as suggesting that modern demands for political and social equality have culminated in a new form of political and social despotism, in which an all-embracing authoritarian state joins hands with the instruments of the welfare state. From this interpretative angle, Schmitt could be read as simply confirming Tocqueville's darkest anxieties about the democratic age: the total state is nothing more than a "democratic despotism" in which

> the will of man is not shattered, but softened, bent, and guided; men are seldom forced by it to act, but they are constantly restrained from acting.

Such a power does not destroy, but it prevents existence; it does not tyrannize, but it compresses, enervates, extinguishes, and stupefies a people, till each nation is reduced to nothing better than a flock of timid and industrious animals, of which government is the shepherd.[30]

Of course, Schmitt's assessment of this "democratic despotism" is obviously distinct from Tocqueville's. In light of Schmitt's outspoken defense of the total state's authoritarian political potentialities, he seems intent on *deepening* some of the trends that so alarmed Tocqueville and generations of political conservatives influenced by the French thinker.

Needless to say, this was an unusual agenda for a theorist of the authoritarian right, particularly given Schmitt's outspoken hostility to core components of the process of political democratization. Not surprisingly, his right-wing colleagues in German political and legal theory soon took him to task for it.

II

Between 1931 and 1933, Schmitt's theory of the total state generated a wide-ranging debate among many of the most important voices in German political and legal scholarship. Otto Hintze endorsed Schmitt's concept of the total state, suggesting that Schmitt had perceptively captured a series of novel political and social developments.[31] In a sympathetic review article, Ernst Rudolf Huber carefully summarized Schmitt's ideas, intimating that Schmitt simply had not gone far enough in underlining the challenges that the total state posed to traditional liberal civil liberties.[32] In a more critical tone, Gerhard Leibholz, who later became the most influential voice on the Federal Republic's constitutional court in the 1950s and 1960s, suggested that Schmitt had exaggerated the extent of political disarray and disintegration in Weimar Germany. Nonetheless, he endorsed the view that Weimar democracy seemed destined to evolve into some form of authoritarian state.[33] Meanwhile, the Nazi Party member Otto Koellreutter offered a rather confused discussion of Schmitt's theory in which he oddly characterized the total state as a "liberal power-state" [*liberaler Machtsstaat*].[34] Schmitt's own student, Ernst Forsthoff (later one of the most important voices in conservative jurisprudence in Germany after World War II), tried to defend his teacher against such criticisms in a book, appropriately entitled *Der totale Staat,* which seems to have gained some attention.[35] A slew of reactionary publicists and journalists embraced Schmitt's concept,[36] and even Social Democrats suggested that it contained some partial truths about the capitalist interventionist state.[37]

A critical response by a relatively unknown and now long-forgotten political sociologist, Heinz Ziegler, arguably played the main role in the ensuing debate. Ziegler's critique of Schmitt, sketched out in a pithy monograph entitled *Authoritarian or Total State,* not only defined the basic terms of much of the right-wing engagement with Schmitt during the final years of the Weimar Republic, but also led Schmitt to clarify and even to reformulate many of his initial claims about the total state.[38]

Ziegler's 1932 assault on Schmitt leaves few stones unturned. Like Schmitt, Ziegler argues that the days of liberal democracy are numbered. But Ziegler worries that Schmitt fails to go far enough in distancing himself from the legacy of modern democracy. Ziegler thematizes precisely that ambiguity in Schmitt's theory that we identified above: Schmitt's theory of the total state arguably offers a defense of a particularly modern form of popular despotism. For Ziegler, Schmitt's theory of the total state represents nothing less than the "end and perfection of democratization," a nightmarish "egalitarian collectivism" suitable to the needs of a "disordered mass society."[39] The total state is democratic majoritarianism run amok.[40] In *The Guardian of the Constitution,* Schmitt had sought to defend vast increases in executive power by reminding his readers that only the Weimar president is directly elected by the entire people; as noted above, only the executive provides a fair expression of the political unity of the German *Volk,* and for Schmitt, only he possesses an adequate form of plebiscitary legitimacy. In Ziegler's interpretation, this line of argumentation simply confirms his suspicion that Schmitt has abandoned the ranks of authentic conservatism in favor of the ominous egalitarianism of modern democracy; Schmitt seeks nothing less than a "democratic" dictator. Ziegler also criticizes Schmitt's interpretation of the fusion of state and society. Though acknowledging the basic accuracy of Schmitt's insistence on the unavoidability of state intervention in contemporary capitalism, Ziegler suggests that Schmitt's concept of the total state provides inadequate safeguards against those who might seek to interpret it in a statist manner. Schmitt's underdeveloped model of state/society relations in the total state *might* encourage the excessive bureaucratization and etatization of economic relations, and Schmitt's theory thus for Ziegler contains socialist implications.[41] Finally, Ziegler doubts that Schmitt's empirical diagnosis can succeed in sustaining Schmitt's authoritarian normative agenda. In Ziegler's view, a real solution to Germany's crisis necessitates a thoroughly "post-democratic" political and social system, in which leaders exercise truly autonomous and independent rule, unburdened by popular social and political demands. An authentic authoritarian state requires a radical break with the ineffective, parasitical total state described by Schmitt. Yet the plebiscitary origins of Schmitt's executive suggest that Schmitt ultimately fails to mark out a real alternative to the status quo. For Ziegler, no form of democratic mass-rule, including Schmitt's plebiscitary executive ruling by means of emergency decrees, can generate effective rulers. Plebiscitarianism suffers from the "anonymization of responsibility" and the "depersonalization" allegedly common to all forms of modern democracy. Instead of producing leaders possessing true "authority" and "personality," it is conducive to political incompetence and cheap demagoguery.[42]

Ziegler's critique clearly hit a raw nerve. Not surprisingly, Schmitt aggressively responded to it in 1932 and 1933. His response is especially revealing given the light it sheds on Schmitt's views about plebiscitarianism and modern democracy, and capitalism and state regulation. Here, political liberalism is systematically discarded, whereas some core features of economic liberalism are maintained. Capitalism and liberal democracy are separated: Schmitt's economic model *empowers* capital by freeing it from the regulatory burdens of the democratic welfare state, while his plebiscitarianism drastically *curtails* genuine popular participation. What Schmitt provides here is nothing less than a political theory of authoritarian capitalism, but one in which authoritarian political institutions are masked by an appearance of popular legitimacy.

In the 1932 *Legality and Legitimacy*, Schmitt offers a gracious acknowledgment of Ziegler's concerns, before declaring that popular *plebiscitarianism* is the *only* form of legitimacy available in the contemporary world. In the aftermath of the entrance of the masses onto the political scene, it is unrealistic to expect government to legitimize itself without *some* appeal to "the people."[43] *Traditional* forms of political authoritarianism, like those favored by Ziegler, are unlikely to prove effective in an era of mass politics. But Schmitt then goes to great pains to explain why his model of plebiscitary legitimacy both represents a genuinely postdemocratic form of legitimacy and provides room for authentic leadership along the lines desired by fellow reactionaries like Ziegler. Schmitt explains that the plebiscites that he has in mind have nothing to do with concepts of a *plebiscite de tous les jours* where popular participation and decision making constitute an active, ongoing process, and citizens exercise far-reaching political power. In Schmitt's plebiscites, the people "cannot counsel, deliberate, or discuss. It cannot govern or administer, nor can it posit norms; it can only sanction by its 'yes' the draft norms presented to it."[44] To be used effectively, plebiscites should take place only on a "momentary" [*augenblickweise*] and intermittent basis, and only an extremely limited choice should be presented to voters; voters only say "yes" or "no" to simple questions presented from above. The real driving force here is those who formulate and pose the questions at hand—in Schmitt's model, the executive. Schmitt adamantly comments that a plebiscite of this type is qualitatively distinct from traditional liberal democratic models of the popular election. In liberal democracy, an election provides an opportunity for freewheeling debate about candidates and political parties, and the election is seen as culminating in some "normativization" [*Normierung*], a piece of general law deriving its legitimacy from rational debate. In contrast, the Schmittian plebiscite is simply a "decision giving expression to an act of will" [*Entscheidung durch einen Willen*], a means by which the popular masses can hope to approximate "a pure decision not based on reason and discussion and not justifying itself."[45] It neither presupposes debate or contestation, nor does it generate a general legal norm intended to guide but also to bind and limit the executive. Pace Ziegler, plebiscitarianism hardly necessitates a principled commitment to either the normative or the institutional core of modern democracy.[46]

Schmitt simultaneously suggests that his model of plebiscitarianism provides an excellent test of aspirants for political leadership. The effective employment of the plebiscite is a risky affair. Those who succeed in posing "the right questions at the right time" can legitimately claim to have demonstrated impressive leadership skills; the successful use of the plebiscite presupposes "a very special and rare type of authority."[47] The demos is fickle and irrational, and only a select few will gain its support. In Schmitt's alternative to Ziegler's critical interpretation of plebiscitary decision making, the plebiscite hardly need subject political elites to the ills of incompetent, anonymous mass rule; instead, the true leader manipulates the plebiscite in order to mobilize the inarticulate masses in support of an agenda whose basic contours the leader has already set.[48]

Schmitt then introduces the crucial distinction between the "quantitative total state based on weakness" and the "qualitative total state based on strength" in order to underline his preference for private capitalism. In the simplest terms, the difference refers to two possible ways in which state and society can fuse. In the quantitative total state, the state ambitiously intervenes in *all* facets of social and economic existence, thus failing to acknowledge that *direct* state intervention in many areas of social life is likely to prove ineffective. Totality takes a "quantitative" form: the extent of governmental activity in the economy is what counts. In turn, the vast scope of state action in this pathological variant of the total state is driven by the fact that it remains a "pluralist party state" in which a panoply of competing political and social groupings extends the reach of government in order to increase the quantity of political and economic goods available for distribution to their members. Describing Weimar as an example of the quantitative total state, Schmitt highlights its political vulnerability: Weimar democracy is ineffective because it is forced to respond to conflicting demands from a vast array of conflicting social and political groups—in particular: labor unions, civil servants, and those claiming social welfare benefits. Schmitt even toys with the idea that the term total *state* may be misleading when applied to the "quantitative" fusion of state and society. In reality, the quantitative total state probably lacks even the minimal prerequisites of genuine statehood. In fact, its only "total" institutions are political parties, eagerly occupied with the task of occupying and extending governmental functions in order to extend their parasitical grip on political and economic life.[49]

Whereas Germany presently finds itself with a quantitative total state, according to Schmitt it desperately needs its distant qualitative cousin. In this alternative scenario, the state would still play a central role in social and economic affairs; the days of laissez-faire have come to an end. Yet the state would now simultaneously acknowledge the limits of direct interventionist devices.[50] More specifically, the state should provide the legal and institutional preconditions for a system in which capitalist proprietors engage in conscious forms of joint supervision of the economy. Schmitt is emphatically opposed to the collectivization of private property. But he does endorse "collective" decision making by capitalist proprietors. Where economic decisions are likely to have a "public" significance, state planners would not dominate the entrepreneur. Instead, entrepreneurs would engage in forms of planning. In Schmitt's own terms, the state planners should not dominate; rather, the (economically) dominant should plan. The final aim of this system would be an overall reduction of direct administrative regulation of the economy.[51] Here, totality is "qualitative" in the sense that the scope of state action is of secondary importance in relation to the effectiveness and coherence of state activity. In order for such coherence to be achieved, the state must do all it can to encourage private capitalists to engage in relatively far-sighted, sensible forms of economic coordination. But it needs to relinquish immediately many of the interventionist devices employed, in Schmitt's view unsuccessfully, by Weimar and other "quantitative" welfare total states.

How then is the qualitative total state to be established? Schmitt's analysis here of its deformed quantitative cousin already hints at his answer to this question. For Schmitt, the main source of the ills of the quantitative total state is that it is a polycratic "pluralist party state" in which political and social blocs prevent cogent state action while simultaneously overextending state authority. Given this diagnosis, there can be only one possible answer to Germany's ills: Germany must be liberated from the pluralism that, in Schmitt's view, is ferociously devouring her once impressive state apparatus.

As we have seen, as early as 1931 Schmitt had called on the Weimar president to "break through" constitutional norms inconsistent with the core of the Weimar Constitution. Which sections of the Constitution make up the core of the Constitution and thus earn the Federal President's tutelage? Whereas Schmitt's 1931 answer to this question remained somewhat unclear, the 1932 *Legality and Legitimacy* bluntly declares that the first part of the Weimar Constitution, in which liberal parliamentarism is made a central component of the German Republic, codifies nothing but a "relativistic" system of "formalistic value-neutrality" undeserving of Hindenburg's protection. Because "normativistic" parliamentarism and the rule of law are outdated in an era in which discretionary power is pervasive, the main institutional base for the pluralist party state, the democratic legislature, can legitimately be abrogated by the Weimar executive. An (undisclosed) set of "basic rights and duties," outlined in the Weimar Constitution's amorphous second part, should instead provide a constitutional basis for an authoritarian alternative better attuned to the imperatives of a legal universe in which highly discretionary state action is pervasive. According to *Legality and Legitimacy*, the second part of the Weimar Constitution should be "cleansed" and then used as a constitutional foundation for a dictatorship that breaks radically with the liberal democratic components of its first section.[52] In short, by relying on selected features of the Weimar Constitution, the executive should undertake a constitutional counterrevolution culminating in an authoritarian alternative to the weak "quantitative total state."

III

An examination of Schmitt's writings from the period immediately following the Nazi takeover suggests that he embraced National Socialism in part precisely because it promised to liberate Germany from the quantitative total state. In a front-page editorial penned shortly after Hitler's take-over for the *Westdeutscher Beobachter*, a Cologne-based National Socialist daily, Schmitt praises the Nazis for freeing Germany from the clientelistic and parasitic "heterogeneous power clumps" basic to the pluralist party state.[53] Schmitt's main work from the same year, *State, Movement, Folk*, bluntly asserts that the experience of the "weak" Weimar total state demonstrates the utter bankruptcy of liberal democracy in the contemporary world.[54] Only revolutionary change—and for Schmitt in 1933, the Nazis offered a genuine "national revolution"—can provide the political and legal devices essential to a truly contemporary polity, a "state for the twentieth century," capable of grappling effectively with the tasks of modern economic intervention. Having watched with frustration as Weimar's semi-authoritarian presidential regimes between 1930 and 1933 fumbled the task of cleansing the total state of its least attractive features, Schmitt turned to the Nazis with the hope that they might bring about reforms necessary for achieving the qualitative total state. For Schmitt in 1933, the Nazis alone seemed up to the demanding tasks of modernizing the German polity so as to accord with the dictates of our "economic-technical" era.

Leading National Socialists quickly reciprocated; particularly in the early years of the new regime, Nazi leaders were eager to develop ties to highly regarded intellectuals, particularly those possessing impressive political and legal know-how. Hitler himself employed the expression "total state" during public appearances in 1933, and the term soon became part of official National Socialist parlance. Not surprisingly, Schmitt seems to have gained credit for the concept. Its immediate popularity contributed to Schmitt's status as a "rising star" within the National Socialist ideological machinery.[55]

Of course, that the Nazis used the concept of the total state hardly proves that its basic contours were essentially National Socialist in character.[56] Some commentators have observed that Schmitt's idea of the qualitative total state might have proven compatible with support for competing forms of right-wing authoritarianism.[57] In fact, Schmitt's political favorite during Weimar's final days was clearly the reactionary General Kurt von Schleicher, who sought an authoritarian solution to Weimar somewhat distinct from National Socialism. By the same token, it is easy to see why the theory of the total state undoubtedly *predisposed* Schmitt to join forces with the Nazis, particularly after von Schleicher's maneuverings to establish an authoritarian state had failed so miserably.[58] The National Socialists not only promised an end to the crippling "pluralist party state," but also succeeded in doing so—*if* the pluralist party state is defined, as in Schmitt's theory, in reference to a plurality of independent political parties, and autonomous interest groups advancing the cause, first and foremost, of the socially and economically underprivileged.[59] Nazi economic ideas, though frequently contradictory, clearly meshed with Schmitt's own: like Schmitt, the National Socialists pushed for a private capitalist economy, but one in which quasi-public forms of "economic self-administration" by privileged economic groups played a decisive role.[60] Finally, the National Socialists' perverse manipulation of the instruments of mass popular mobilization arguably approximated Schmitt's own ideas about the plebiscite. Neither the Nazis nor Schmitt considered plebiscites incompatible with mass propaganda, censorship, or the elimination of political opposition. Both saw the plebiscite, first and foremost, as a means of *manufacturing consent from above*, not a gauge of an independent public opinion based on an autonomous, grassroots process of argumentative debate and contestation. From Schmitt's perspective during the early period of the National Socialist regime, the Nazi success in whipping up mass support surely suggested that they had passed precisely that test of authentic leadership outlined in the 1932 *Legality and Legitimacy*: Hitler and his advisors must have seemed to possess an uncanny ability to pose the right questions to the *Volk* at the right time. No wonder that Schmitt offered generous praise for Germany's new dictator after Hitler had demonstrated that "very special and rare type of authority" described by Schmitt in 1932.

Schmitt's 1933 comments on the modern mass media are particularly revealing for deciphering his political intentions during the fateful year in which Nazism overwhelmed Weimar democracy. Recall again that for

Schmitt our era is an *economic-technical* one, in which political actors face the task of mastering new instruments of mass persuasion, such as radio and film. What is striking about Schmitt's reflections on the mass media during this crucial year is that they *accord* with National Socialism while potentially *conflicting* with some elements of Schmitt's political theory: when Schmitt sketches out the concrete details of the qualitative total state, he strives to avoid any possible conflict with Nazi practice. Schmitt's present-day aficionados are likely to see this discrepancy as evidence for the fundamentally anti-Nazi orientation of Schmitt's theory. But it just as easily supports the interpretation that Schmitt ultimately formulated his ideas, at least in 1933, so as to suit Nazi needs.

In light of Schmitt's emphasis in the theory of the qualitative state on the relative autonomy of capitalist private property vis-à-vis the state, one might expect Schmitt to pursue a similar line of argumentation in his discussion of the development of mass communications and its implications for freedom of the press. Just as the qualitative total state is incompatible with a regimented state economy, so, too, in the sphere of mass communications—or so the theory of the qualitative state surely implies—new forms of "self-administration" and autonomy need to be established. Essential to the qualitative total state is that it acknowledges the anachronistic character of the traditional liberal state/society divide while still preserving meaningful freedom for capitalist proprietors; in a similar vein, the qualitative state should logically entail some form of press and communicative freedom, albeit of a type unfamiliar to classical liberalism. Neither in the economy, nor in the realm of mass communications, should a *qualitative* total state run roughshod over realms of independent activity free of *direct* state control.

Unfortunately, Schmitt's reader will search in vain for an argument along these lines. On the contrary, Schmitt now announces that any state that fails to subject the instruments of modern mass communication directly to its aims is destined to "denounce its own political existence."[61] In light of the mass-psychological impact of modern media technology, any state that hopes to maintain its political integrity inevitably is forced to engage in censorship and exercise monopolistic control over the new technologies at hand. Anticipating one of the most striking facets of modern totalitarianism, Schmitt suggests that successful regimes now are driven to employ the new technological devices of mass psychological manipulation in order to build popular support for their policies. From this perspective, traditional liberal conceptions of government as based on free consent are anachronistic. In the current technological age, "consent" must be manufactured by power holders who know best how to wield its awesome propaganda devices.[62]

IV

At the outset of this chapter, I pointed to a number of surprising commonalities between contemporary neoconservative accounts of the interventionist welfare state and Schmitt's theory of the total state. Of course, the decisive difference between Schmitt and more recent authors is that Schmitt ultimately concludes that a fundamental reform of the (allegedly) overloaded, fragmented, and increasingly powerless regulatory-welfare state requires an unabashedly authoritarian alternative to liberal democracy; as we have seen, this is surely one reason why Schmitt embraced National Socialism. Contemporary neoconservatives obviously shy away from similarly shocking conclusions. Although some of them occasionally do echo Schmitt's advice when advocating a dramatic expansion of executive power, their proposals surely remain within the parameters of the liberal democratic tradition; they remain committed to defensible conceptions of human equality and thus universal suffrage, parliamentarism, and the rule of law.[63] They often seek significant institutional changes, but hardly anything approximating Schmitt's mass-based dictatorship, in which the popular election is reduced to what Stephen Holmes has appropriately described as "soccer stadium democracy."[64]

Still, it is hard to ignore the possibility that Schmitt's disturbing prognosis, in some respects, offers a more consistent complement to the diagnosis of the welfare state found in both Schmitt and some contemporary neoconservatives. The paradox at hand takes the following form: if we believe that governmental decision making is crippled by powerful organized interests that, moreover, possess a popular basis in much of the citizenry, might it not then make sense for a would-be "reformer" to seek a curtailment of traditional democratic mechanisms and rights? How else might it be possible to "purge" government of the vast array of competing interests that allegedly overload it?

As we have seen, both Schmitt and some contemporary neoconservatives offer a dire picture of recent developments in state/society relations. If contemporary liberal democracy indeed has been undermined by an apocalyptic "generalized blackmailing game," maybe only the instruments of the authoritarian state can undertake the surgery required by both diagnoses? To the extent that both accounts tend to describe our era as one in which liberal democracy faces an emergency situation, authoritarianism may seem to provide a logical path beyond the state of emergency supposedly at hand.

In light of this disturbing consideration, it seems incumbent on us that we take a closer look at the diagnosis of the modern welfare state provided by Schmitt. After all, Schmitt's diagnosis and his (authoritarian) prognosis are inextricably linked. For now, I bracket the possibility that the contemporary neoconservative diagnosis of the welfare state suffers from the same ills evident in Schmitt's theory of the total state, in part because I hope to confront this possibility directly in chapter 8. Still, the striking similarities between these two accounts of the interventionist welfare state lend some plausibility to the possibility that the critical comments on Schmitt that follow can also be applied to recent neoconservative discourse about government "overload."

Schmitt's account suffers from a number of immediate flaws. On numerous occasions in this study, I have suggested that Schmitt's critique of contemporary democracy relies on a mythical portrayal of the liberal past, particularly when it suits his attempt to discredit contemporary democracy and the welfare state. Here again, this argumentative ploy figures prominently in Schmitt's thinking. The starting point of his theory of the total state is the deceptively simple idea that state and society have undergone a potentially disastrous *fusion* in the early twentieth century, whereby a traditional liberal state/society scenario is replaced by a total state resting on the "societalization of the state." In Schmitt's account, this fusion is the most fundamental source of the ills of the contemporary (quantitative version of the) total state. The starting point for a negative comparison of contemporary democracy is provided by Schmitt's (idiosyncratic) theory of the nineteenth-century liberal state, which for Schmitt allegedly lacked any of the ills of the modern interventionist welfare state.

But where in fact did state actors in the nineteenth century consistently respect the principle of absolute neutrality in the economy? Certainly not in Central Europe, where the state often functioned as a driving force in economic development. Even in England and the United States, the historical record meshes poorly with Schmitt's reflections, chiefly because the interventionist state is hardly a mere product of twentieth-century de-

mands.[65] Of course, decisive shifts did take place in the relationship be-
√ tween state and society between the nineteenth and the twentieth
centuries. In the United States, for example, at least three differences can
be immediately identified: economic intervention was undertaken primarily by state and municipal units, before being supplanted by far-reaching
federal activity in the twentieth century; the orientation of government
intervention was oriented primarily toward economic development and
basically pro-business in character, while after the New Deal at least *some*
forms of state action are supposed to empower the socially and economically vulnerable; in the nineteenth century, the idea of a "general expectation of justice, and a general expectation of recompense for injuries and
loss," so central to the modern welfare state, was relatively underdeveloped.[66] But none of these changes is captured adequately by Schmitt's
overstylized contrast between the noninterventionist liberal state of the
nineteenth century and the contemporary total state. Indeed, where laissez-
faire attitudes were strongest in the nineteenth century, government was
√ arguably most "societalized," often by business groups instrumentalizing
state authority in order to advance economic development.[67] From one
perspective, the real novelty in the early and the mid-twentieth century is
that the "societalization" of state power came to include interests locked
√ √ out of the political system of the nineteenth century, including labor unions
and interest groups representative of the socially and economically underprivileged. The character of "societalization" altered; pace Schmitt, we did
not move from a liberal state standing "above and beyond" society to one
in which society swallows up state authority.

The conceptual framework of the theory of the total state—especially
the murky idea of a fusion between state and society, predicated on the
incorrect view that state and society were principally "separate"—is too
underdetermined to accomplish the analytic tasks Schmitt expects of it.[68]
Here as well, Schmitt's vulnerability to an idiosyncratic variety of conceptual realism, in which the complex social and political patterns of a given
era are conveniently interpreted to give unmediated expression to the abstract claims of the dominant dogmas of the same period, rears its head.
Nineteenth-century political and economic reality never accorded neatly
with nineteenth-century liberal doctrine.

Of Schmitt's contemporaries, it was the increasingly isolated figure of
√ Hans Kelsen who best grasped the profound inadequacies underlying the
conceptual framework of the theory of the total state. In a scathing 1931

critique of Schmitt's ideas on the total state, Kelsen suggests that Schmitt's model of the total state is simply another example of the widespread tendency within contemporary political analysis to provide "long familiar facts with a new name."[69] Schmitt's argument that the total state represents a novel force on the political scene is undermined by the verity that many of its elements are common in history. Even states of classical antiquity and modern absolutism are "total states" in Schmitt's sense of the term. Just as it is ludicrous to argue that ambitious state intervention in society is a recent historical phenomenon, so, too, Kelsen declares, is it impossible to show that *no* meaningful distinction separates state and society in the contemporary regulatory-welfare state: "One need not be a defender of historical materialism in order to recognize that a state, based on a legal system guaranteeing the private ownership of the means of production and the private control of production and the distribution of goods," is hardly a "total state" intervening in *all* facets of private existence.[70] A political system that continues to preserve capitalist private property can hardly be described as one in which state and society constitute a seamless web. At least at one juncture, Kelsen points out, Schmitt himself implicitly concedes as much. Schmitt expressly defines "pluralism" as that setting where competing "social," "non-state" interests parasitically colonize the state "without ceasing to be purely social (non-state) bodies."[71] Implicitly, Schmitt thereby presupposes the continued existence of "purely social" interests within the total state. But how can Schmitt consistently do so while simultaneously arguing that the total state rests on a fusion of state and society?[72]

Schmitt tends to suggest that nineteenth-century conceptions of a division between state and society have lost *any significance whatsoever* in the twentieth century, whereas for Kelsen the meaning of the state/society divide has simply been *altered*. The fact that contemporary reality hardly conforms to early liberal ideology hardly demonstrates the anachronistic character of the underlying idea of a state/society divide.[73] Kelsen then relies on this general claim to develop a specific criticism of Schmitt's political theory. For the latter, the fusion of state and society simultaneously implies that the distinction between parliament and the executive has lost any real meaning; as we saw earlier, the dualism of "legislative state" vs. "executive state" in traditional liberalism rests, in Schmitt's theory, on the more fundamental dualism of "society versus the state." For Kelsen, however, the contrast between parliament and the executive has hardly become altogether insignificant in character, though the legislative-executive nexus has obviously changed in many respects since the nineteenth century. The indisputable fact that this nexus no longer takes the form of a face-off between popular political and social interests within parliament and an executive branch dominated by aristocratic and monarchical forces hardly proves that present conflicts between an elected legislature and the contemporary (popular) executive no longer serve a meaningful function. Alluding to the fateful battles between the executive and parliament during Weimar Germany in the early 1930s, Kelsen points out that it hardly requires great insight to acknowledge that the achievement of a proper relationship between the parliament and the executive remains of vital importance for those committed to democratic ideals of freedom and equality.[74]

Regrettably, Kelsen's refreshingly skeptical discussion of the theory of the total state seems to have been pretty much ignored during the final years of the Weimar Republic. Like Schmitt, most of Germany's overwhelmingly antidemocratic political and legal theorists were already occupied with a different task by the end of 1931 and early 1932: providing an ideological justification for an authoritarian system that would replace Weimar's "weak" democratic welfare state.

In the following chapter, we take a closer look at the central role played by Schmitt in the quest to establish a National Socialist alternative to liberal democracy.

5

AFTER LEGAL INDETERMINACY?

Soon after joining the Nazi Party on May 1, 1933, Carl Schmitt was rewarded with a prestigious professorship in Berlin, the editorship of Germany's major legal publication, *Die deutsche Juristen-Zeitung*, a leading post in the Nazi professors' guild, and the position of State Councilor [*Staatsrat*] to Prussia. Most important perhaps, Schmitt's National Socialist period was his most prolific. Between 1933 and 1936 alone, Schmitt authored four books, as well as over fifty essays for both academic and political journals. Waxing enthusiastic over Adolf Hitler and his struggle to "liberate" Germany from liberalism and Marxism, Schmitt repeatedly offers effusive praise for the emerging National Socialist legal order and the "national revolution" that made it possible.

Most shocking of all, Schmitt's writings from this period are filled with crude anti-Semitic diatribes. In an essay penned for the Nazi *Westdeutscher Beobachter* in March 1933, Schmitt praises the Nazi quest for racial and ethnic homogeneity [*Gleichartigkeit*], commenting that the ethnically and racially alien [*Fremdgeartete*] should cease their "dangerous" attempts to undermine the ongoing racial "awakening" of the German *Volk*. Echoing hardline Nazi "law and order" rhetoric, Schmitt simultaneously accuses "alien" elements of transforming the legal code into a defense of the rights of criminals.[1] In another piece in the same newspaper, intellectuals forced to flee Germany, including Albert Einstein, are described as racially alien elements who never belonged to the German *Volk* in the first place. In this vein, Schmitt disputes the view that Heinrich Heine deserves to be described as a German author.[2] In 1934, "normativistic" legalism is attributed to Judaism: because Jews lacked their own country and state, they allegedly generated the failed formalistic liberal attempt to limit political power by means of cogent general norms.[3] Jews purportedly polluted indigenous modes of authentic German legal thinking, once free of the ills of legal formalism. In 1935, Schmitt describes the Nuremberg racial laws as the foundations of a new German "constitution of freedom" [*eine Verfassung der Freiheit*].[4] Elsewhere he praises the Nazi quest to make anti-Semitism the core of the Nazi alternative to bankrupt (essentially Jewish) legal liberalism, commenting that the Nazis are right to try to protect "German blood."[5]

In 1936 Schmitt played a major role in staging one of National Socialist jurisprudence's most horrible exercises in anti-Semitism, the infamous conference on "German Jurisprudence in Struggle Against the Jewish Spirit."[6] In a statement shocking in part because it merely summarizes the underlying tenor of many of his writings from the Nazi period, Schmitt declares:

> The relationship of the Jew to our intellectual work [in the field of law] is a parasitic, tactical, trader's one. Through his gift for trade he often has a sharp sense for the genuine. . . . That is his instinct as parasite and genuine tradesman. But just as little as the gift for art is shown by the Jewish art dealer's ability to discover a genuine Rembrandt quicker than a German art historian, so little is a gift for legal science shown by his ability to recognize with greater speed good authors and good theories.[7]

Scholars continue to debate the significance of Schmitt's endorsement of National Socialism. In the English-language literature, Schmitt's anti-Semitic outbursts are still widely described as the mere "lip-service" of a traditional authoritarian, respectful of some important features of the rule of law, and basically hostile to the core of Nazi doctrine.[8] In part because Schmitt's Nazi-era writings remain for the most part untranslated, this view has gained a certain amount of popularity in American and English scholarly circles. The more sophisticated recent German-language scholarship on Schmitt better acknowledges his real enthusiasm for National Socialism. Much of this literature, however, is so concerned with the biographical details of Schmitt's life during this period that it unduly downplays Schmitt's theoretical aspirations and agenda. These authors are able to tell us what Schmitt had for breakfast on any given day between 1933 and 1945, and they seem amazingly confident of their ability to recount his most intimate thoughts on any of a broad array of topics. Yet they have surprisingly little to say about the theoretical roots of Schmitt's contributions to an identifiably National Socialist legal order, despite the fact that this was Schmitt's main undertaking during the Nazi period. Nor do they seem to see his racist and anti-Semitic outbursts as much more than a personal concession to the Nazi power-holders.[9]

Both here and in chapter 6, I pursue an alternative interpretative path. Schmitt's embrace of National Socialism was far more than an expression of political opportunism, though Schmitt's vanity and careerism undoubtedly did play a role in his fateful decision to join ranks with National Socialism in 1933. Focusing in this chapter on Schmitt's writings between 1933 and 1936, I suggest that Schmitt's marriage to Nazism stems *immanently* from core elements of his jurisprudence. As we have seen, for Schmitt the central problem of modern legal theory is the enigma of legal indeterminacy, according to which legal norms inevitably fail to provide meaningful guidance to legal decision makers. Schmitt sides with the Nazis because he sees them as offering a real chance for developing a novel legal order able to "solve" the dilemma of legal indeterminacy. Most shocking of all, he endorses the most terrible features of National Socialism—most importantly, its radical anti-Semitism—because he sees precisely these elements as indispensable to the task of constructing an alternative legal system capable of guaranteeing the determinacy allegedly missing from formalistic modes of liberal law. In the process, I hope to help overcome the divide between those who emphasize Schmitt's purportedly traditional legalist credentials and those who focus on his enthusiasm for the Nazi destruction of the rule of law. In my view, there is no question that Schmitt in the 1930s is concerned with reconceiving the foundations of legal determinacy; for this reason, Schmitt's writings from the Nazi period occasionally *appear* faithful to some traditional legal notions. But essential to Schmitt's idiosyncratic quest to reconceive the possibility of legal determinacy is an open endorsement of dystopian National Socialist visions of a racially and ethnically homogeneous "folk community" [*Volkgemeinschaft*]. In the final analysis, Schmitt's revised concept of legal determinacy breaks dramatically with the most humane elements of modern jurisprudence. His alternative to "normativistic" legal thinking is an intellectual and political fraud.

This interpretation should also help shed light on the complicated question of *continuity and discontinuity* within Schmitt's theory. In my view, Schmitt's Nazi-era reflections build directly on his Weimar-era ideas about the impossibility of the liberal quest to bind judicial and administrative actors to legal norms. As a Nazi activist, Schmitt reiterates the view stated in the early 1912 *Law and Judgment* that legal regularity still might be preserved by means of establishing a rank of homogeneous judges. There can be no question, however, that this idea, left relatively undeveloped in Schmitt's early legal writings, takes on a far more prominent place during the 1930s. Schmitt's Nazism represents an attempt to develop his earlier (relatively cautious) suggestion that homogeneity within the state apparatus might overcome the crisis of legal indeterminacy. In the final analysis, Schmitt's enthusiasm for Nazism stems significantly from the fact that he conceived of it as an opportunity to "test" and *embellish* an element of his early jurisprudence. But like any attempt to put theory into practice, it also demanded that the theoretical notion at hand, the demand for homogeneity within the judiciary, gain in clarity and precision. For Schmitt in the 1930s, Nazi anti-Semitism provided just this conceptual "improvement" over the relatively inchoate and vague notion of a homogeneous judiciary suggested by *Law and Judgment.*

After turning to Schmitt's ideas on the pervasiveness of legal indeterminacy (I), I explain why Schmitt (wrongly) believed that the National Socialist legal system could overcome legal indeterminacy and secure a novel form of postliberal legal determinacy (II). I then discuss the failings of Schmitt's reconceptualization of legal determinacy (III), as well as its broader contemporary implications (IV). The problem of legal indeterminacy continues to excite the interest of many jurists. Schmitt's Nazi-era contribution to the debate on legal indeterminacy may contain some important lessons for contemporary legal theory.

I

In earlier chapters I have tried to show that Schmitt's reflections on legal indeterminacy are central to every facet of his political and legal thought: his account of judicial and administrative action, his critique of liberal parliamentarism and constitutionalism, his disturbing analysis of the modern interventionist "total" state, and his open endorsement of a plebiscitary dictatorship during Weimar's final years. For the purposes of this chapter, it is important to recall two ways in which Schmitt's Weimar writings underscored the (alleged) bankruptcy of the traditional liberal preference for a binding and relatively determinate legal order able to provide effective direction to those who apply and interpret the law.

First, Schmitt argued early on that every legal interpretation inevitably includes an unpredictable "pure decision" that cannot be unambiguously justified by reference to the legal norm at hand: "Every legal thought brings a legal idea, which in its purity can never become reality, into another aggregate condition and adds an element that cannot be derived either from the content of the legal idea or from the content of a general positive legal norm that is to be applied."[10] By failing to take the independent dynamics of legal decision making seriously, liberal jurisprudence allegedly succumbs to a crude "normativism" that falsely downplays the role of legally unregulated acts of power within legal interpretation. Liberalism tends to favor a model of legal decision making in which legal interpretation tends to become nothing but an act of mechanical *subsumption*. As we saw in chapter 1, for Schmitt this error is most egregious in classical liberal authors like Montesquieu. Yet modern liberals—most notably, Schmitt's main intellectual rival, Hans Kelsen—supposedly succumb to some version of it as well.[11]

Second, Schmitt noted that even liberal democratic polities increasingly rely on legal forms incompatible with the traditional preference for relatively clear, general norms. Wherever the interventionist "total" state entails intensive regulation of the economy and ambitious forms of social policy, the significance of classical general legal norms within the legal order is dramatically reduced. The proliferation of vague clauses and principles ("in good faith," "in the public interest") within contemporary law, driven primarily by the inexorable expansion of state action in the modern capitalist economy, merely exacerbates the underlying weaknesses of traditional liberal conceptions of judicial decision making: vague clauses often allow those who apply and interpret the law to act in distinct and potentially inconsistent ways. In addition, administrative decrees and individual measures, by means of which substantial and often poorly regulated discretionary power is handed over to the executive, increasingly seem to become part and parcel of the everyday operations of the legal system. In Schmitt's prognosis, this trend suggests that classical attempts to distinguish clearly between the state of legal normalcy and the state of emergency have failed.[12] When Schmitt in 1922 bluntly declared that "[a]ll law is situational law," he was making much more than an abstract legal philosophical observation about the relationship between legal normalcy and the crisis situation.[13] From another perspective, he was merely offering an empirical *chronicle* of the decline of the liberal vision of a neatly codified system of cogent general norms capable of providing real guidance to legal decision makers.

In 1933, Schmitt's comments on the problem of legal indeterminacy take on especially drastic proportions. Whereas at least some of his previous writings on the problem of judicial decision making could be taken as implying that a *relative* indeterminacy, long downplayed by formalistic liberal jurists, characterizes the legal system, Schmitt's position now approaches what contemporary North American jurists today commonly describe as the *radical indeterminacy thesis*. In this view, "decisions officials make about the meaning of rules amount to creating meaning for the rules when there is none to begin with," and all legal cases are "hard cases."[14] In every legal situation, any conceivable result can be justified by the legal materials at hand. According to the radical indeterminacy thesis, "[a] competent adjudication can square a decision in favor of either side in any given lawsuit with the existing body of legal rules."[15] In Schmittian terminology, legal and administrative decision making is nothing but an autonomous "power decision" effectively unregulated by the legal materials at hand. The quest to bind officials to the legal norm is a silly formalistic liberal farce. Law is always a (normatively unregulated) decision.

Seeking to downplay the controversial character of this position, Schmitt introduces his version of the radical indeterminacy thesis by claiming that even those long under the magical spell of liberal normativism have begun openly to acknowledge its fraudulent analytical core. He attributes his own insight about the basic failings of liberal jurisprudence to a conversation—according to Schmitt, "one of the greatest experiences and meetings which drove me as a jurist to National Socialism" (!)—with an unnamed "world-famous, wise and experienced seventy-year-old American jurist," who allegedly commented to Schmitt that "today we are experiencing the bankruptcy of all *idées générales*."[16] The universalism of legal liberalism is dead. For Schmitt, indisputable evidence for this death is the utter failure of clarity and generality in law to guarantee the predictability and determinacy that liberals long promised that it could secure. Even the Americans, long mesmerized by the illusions of the liberal rule of law, have been forced to take note of liberal jurisprudence's funeral announcement.

In a 1934 essay, Schmitt argues that the liberal preference for cogent general legal norms inevitably reduces the legal order to a situation of "chaos" and "anarchy" unable to provide a minimal measure of legal predictability.[17] General legal norms merely function as a normativistic "mask" for the reality of radical indeterminacy because even the clearest general norm is unable to provide any help to legal decision makers. Legal categories possessing real generality are, by definition, unlikely to speak to the concrete details of the case at hand. Schmitt is surely aware that he is hardly the first legal thinker to acknowledge that some tension between general rules and particular cases is probably unavoidable; liberal jurists themselves long have acknowledged this problem. But Schmitt believes that liberals obscure the depth of the dilemma at hand. In particular, ambitious dreams of a codified set of abstract categories and rules badly exacerbate the tension between rules and individual cases. By demanding that the legal code consist of rules and categories having an ever more general and abstract character, liberalism seeks a legal code profoundly alien from the real-life demands of everyday legal experience. In short, liberals strive for a legal code unlikely to speak to the needs of the legal decision maker struggling with the concrete details of everyday life, thereby creating an excessively artificial and probably even fictional legal universe inevitably having highly open-ended implications for the judge and administrator.[18]

In this account, the inherent artificiality of liberal law simultaneously stems from the fact that the traditional liberal preference for *fixed* or *codified* law heightens the gap between the legal code and the concrete tasks faced by judges and administrators. Schmitt recalls another widely acknowledged limitation of liberal general law, namely the fact that statutes always represent a potentially static "fixation" of a legislative act that, by necessity, occurs before a judicial or administrative actor applies the statute. Once again, Schmitt claims that this failing has more serious consequences than liberals concede. Although liberal law by nature is "oriented towards the past" [*vergangenheitsbezogen*], the dictates of modern social and economic life demand a legal system conducive to a future-oriented *steering* of complex, ever-changing economic and social scenarios. Developing his earlier Weimar-era reflections on the challenges posed by the interventionist state to the rule of law, Schmitt in the mid-1930s argues that the liberal insistence on fixed laws, possessing stability and some degree of permanence, fundamentally conflicts with the dictates of modern state activity. Although emphatically emphasizing his hostility to Marxist conceptions of a planned economy, Schmitt asserts the necessity of a postliberal legal order possessing novel legal instruments able to coordinate a wide range of economic activities far better than the blunt and unduly static instrument of fixed, general law. Writing in 1935, Schmitt asserts that no better example of the "hostility to planning" [*Planfeindlichkeit*] inherent in liberal legalism can be identified than the American Supreme Court's recent attack on the New Deal.

In his interpretation, Franklin Delano Roosevelt's opponents on the Court are absolutely right to see the open-ended, highly discretionary, situation-specific elements of New Deal legislation as inconsistent with the fundamental principles of liberal jurisprudence. They are utterly mistaken, however, in their failure to acknowledge the necessity of such postliberal legal forms in the era of the modern interventionist state.[19] In this analysis, pervasive legal indeterminacy is a natural by-product of modern forms of state "steering."[20] The unavoidability of deformalized law simply demonstrates the anachronistic nature of liberal legalism.

Schmitt also undertakes to make modern pluralism responsible for the deeply indeterminate character of all law. In *State, Movement, Folk* (1933), Schmitt writes that

> [w]e have already reached the point in legal theory and practice where we quite seriously have to ask the epistemological question of to what extent a word or concept of the legislator can really bind those who have to apply the law at all. We have experienced that every word and concept immediately become controversial, unsure, indeterminate, and pliable when in a fluctuating situation different spirits [*Geister*] and interests try to make use of them.[21]

Radical indeterminacy characterizes even the most cogent legal concepts because indeterminacy derives, first and foremost, from the reality of radically distinct "spirits and interests" that inevitably try to make the law serve altogether different ends. In an implicit criticism of Max Weber, Schmitt questions Weber's faith that a minimal degree of legal determinacy is still possible in a disenchanted world characterized by an awesome array of competing gods. For Schmitt, even the relatively modest "rational legality" endorsed by Weber is necessarily a sham when jurists possessing the authority to interpret and apply the law pursue diametrically opposed moral and political agendas. In a modern pluralistic universe, legal determinacy is simply unachievable, because the demise of a widely shared, homogeneous worldview means that those who interpret even the most crystal-clear legal concept will do so in different ways.[22]

In an especially portentous line of inquiry, *State, Movement, Folk* goes on to offer an unambiguously racist gloss on the nature of modern pluralism. Schmitt here focuses on what he describes as the "existential" determinants of legal interpretation:

[i]t is an epistemological verity that only those are capable of seeing the facts [of the case] the right way, listening to statements rightly, understanding words correctly and evaluating impressions of persons and events rightly, if they are participants in a racially determined type [*artbestimmten Weise*] of legal community to which they existentially belong.[23]

The racially and ethnically "alien" are purportedly incapable of interpreting German law in a manner consistent with ethnic Germans. In what undoubtedly belongs among the most astonishing reworkings of a classical liberal argument in our century, Schmitt reminds the reader of Montesquieu's famous description of the judge as merely "*la bouche qui prononce les paroles de la loi.*" Yet Schmitt claims that this early statement of liberal hostility to judicial discretion now necessarily must be reconstructed in light of the widely accepted "epistemological verity" that different ethnic groups possess fundamentally distinct cultural and biological characteristics.[24] In contrast to our naive universalistic Enlightenment forefathers, Schmitt comments that those of us rightly more "sensitive" to the implications of ethnic difference "now see . . . the difference of the different mouths, which pronounce seemingly similar words and sentences differently. We notice how they 'pronounce' the same words so differently."[25] For Schmitt, ethnically based variations in the "mouths" that "pronounce" the law are a major source of the crisis of legal indeterminacy. Because the "existential determination" of legal decision making no longer rests on a common ethnic and intellectual basis, legal interpretation today inevitably is open-ended and fundamentally indeterminate.

How are we to interpret Schmitt's defense here of the "existential determination" of legal interpretation? As soon will be evident, Schmitt himself quickly proceeds to use this argument in order to justify National Socialist ethnic cleansing.[26] Nonetheless, many commentators rely on biographical evidence—for example, Schmitt's (purportedly) good ties to German Jews during the Weimar period[27]—in order to downplay Schmitt's overtly racist and anti-Semitic arguments. At the same time, more recent biographical research documents that Schmitt threw himself into a rather suspect literature on the difficulties of Jewish assimilation during this period, as well as the possibility that Schmitt's private life even before the National Socialist takeover exhibited the knee-jerk anti-Semitic prejudices common to those of his generation and his social and religious background.[28] Such evidence *might* imply that for Schmitt National Socialism simply served to legitimize an open, public expression of a series of deeply rooted anti-Semitic prejudices.[29] Nevertheless, the more important point is that the results of biographical research on Schmitt are likely to remain highly open-ended in character; it is too much to expect any biographer to be able to tell us exactly what Schmitt "really" was thinking when he chose to ally himself with National Socialism.[30]

In my view, this situation leaves those hoping to get to the roots of Schmitt's National Socialist writings with only one option: to take Schmitt's legal argumentation seriously. When we do so, Schmitt's contributions from the National Socialist period exhibit a terrible—yet undeniably systematic—logic.

II

In the shadow of the Nazi seizure of power, Carl Schmitt struggles to provide an answer to the enigma of legal indeterminacy. Clearly unsatisfied with the more dramatic implications of the radical indeterminacy thesis, Schmitt posits a postliberal conception of legal determinacy that builds directly on core features of National Socialism.

At first glance, Schmitt's most important work in legal theory from the mid-1930s, *On Three Types of Jurisprudential Thinking* (1934), seems to buttress the view of those who hope to emphasize Schmitt's Catholicism.[31] Developing a theory of what he describes as "concrete-order legal thinking" as an alternative both to liberal normativism and a "decisionism" in which an unregulated act of power, an "empty decision," is taken to be the core of legal experience, Schmitt here openly concedes his debt to the institutionalism of Catholic theorists M. Hauriou and G. Renard.[32] In fact, the opening section of *On Three Types of Jurisprudential Thinking* describes the "Aristotelian-Thomist natural law of the medieval period" as a forerunner to Schmitt's own concrete-order thinking.[33] Despite Schmitt's express homage here to some strands of twentieth-century Catholicism, it would nonetheless be misleading to ignore the crucial ways in which Schmitt breaks radically with Catholic varieties of legal institutionalism. Schmitt's own comment that he prefers the term "concrete-order thinking" in order to prevent any possible confusion with Catholic jurisprudence deserves to be taken seriously.[34] Never hesitating to describe the Nazi destruction of the liberal rule of law as a perfect expression of concrete-order thinking,

Schmitt's differences vis-à-vis Catholic institutionalism become clear in those sections of the study where Schmitt unabashedly endorses the most troubling aspects of the emerging National Socialist legal order. The Nazi labor law reforms of 1934, which reclassified employees as "disciples" [*Gefolgschaft*] while stripping them of basic workplace protections, is described by Schmitt as the clearest possible real-life expression of concrete-order thinking, while the introduction of the concept of the legally unregulated "Leader" [*Führer*] into the core of German public law garners Schmitt's enthusiastic endorsement.[35] For Schmitt, concrete-order thinking requires nothing less than the supremacy of the National Socialist movement in relation both to the traditional state apparatus and the German *Volk*.[36] Schmitt also links concrete-order thinking to anti-Semitism. Universalistic liberal normativism is taken to be a "typically Jewish" mode of legal analysis. For Schmitt, those who acknowledge the basic truths of concrete-order thinking purportedly grasp that every ethnic group has a system of law particular to its special attributes. Concrete-order thinking thereby demands nothing less than that ethnic Germans free themselves from "alien" legal and intellectual influences, most importantly, from "Jewish" conceptions of the rule of law emphasizing the importance of formal protections and procedures.[37]

For our purposes here, the concrete-order theory as developed by Schmitt between 1933 and 1936 is revealing for two main reasons. First, it represents the perfect theoretical expression of Schmitt's hostility to liberal conceptions of a system of codified, general law. Its underlying insight is that society needs to be conceived as a series of variegated communities or "orders" having highly specific needs resistant to codification by general legal norms or concepts. For Schmitt, it is inappropriate to apply a liberal model of the legal system, in which law supposedly is modeled on a set of calculable traffic regulations, to complex, situation-specific institutions such as the family or the workplace. The core experiences of these concrete orders, allegedly best captured by old-fashioned terms such as faith, discipline, and honor, simply cannot be subsumed under any set of general norms.[38] Even liberal concepts of state sovereignty need to be jettisoned in favor of the idea of a concrete "folk community," whose immanent dynamics unerringly conflict with the normativistic aspirations of liberal jurisprudence.[39] Quite consistently, Schmitt describes the proliferation of vague, open-ended standards, as well as the widespread tendency in contemporary law to blur the distinction between general and situation-specific, individual law, as empirical evidence that legal development *everywhere* increasingly approximates the theoretical tenets of concrete-order thinking. The fact that National Socialism embraces the trend toward open-ended, situation-specific law more systematically than liberal democracy simply proves for Schmitt that Nazism represents a quintessentially modern legal system, "a state for the twentieth century," better attuned to the exigencies of contemporary legal development.[40] The logical conclusion of the ongoing conflation of legislative and administrative power is nothing less than a "Leader State" [*Führerstaat*] in which the Leader possesses unlimited legislative and administrative authority.[41] Whereas liberal democratic polities continue to pretend that clear general norms are the best way of legally regulating complex activities, Nazism heroically "crosses the Rubicon" by systematically abandoning even the most meager remnants of this illusion.[42] In short, the theory of concrete orders rests on the assumption that the liberal quest for determinate, general law and formalistic modes of legal decision making is inherently flawed. For Schmitt, the ills of this quest must be attributed to the impossibility of the liberal attempt to gain some measure of legal determinacy *by means of the cogency and generality of the legal norm.*

Second, the theory of concrete orders points the way toward Schmitt's quest to articulate a postliberal conception of legal determinacy while building explicitly on his analysis of the irrepressible indeterminacy of liberal general law. *On Three Types of Jurisprudential Thinking* clearly shirks from one possible implication of the author's endorsement of the radical indeterminacy thesis. The radical indeterminacy thesis *might* imply that we need to conceive any act of legal interpretation as nothing but an altogether willful "decision not based on reason and discussion and not justifying itself . . . an absolute decision created out of nothingness."[43] In short, one could simply opt to celebrate the fact that legal interpretation inevitably consists of a series of expressions of more or less arbitrary, legally unharnessed power. But Schmitt now adamantly criticizes precisely this possibility, warning that decisionism "runs the risk of missing the stable content" in law.[44] A rigorous decisionist legal theory reduces law to a potentially inconsistent series of power decisions, thus proving unable to secure even a modicum of legal determinacy. A consistent decisionism would simply exacerbate the ills of (indeterminate) liberal legalism, making a virtue out of liberalism's most telling jurisprudential vice.[45]

Many have interpreted this argument as evidence of a momentous break within Schmitt's thinking: whereas his Weimar writings at times offer ✓ a decisionist reading of law like that now criticized by him, his National Socialist writings underline the dangers of decisionism.[46] Elements of the story recounted earlier in this book might seem to support this interpretation. I have also argued that the moment of judicial decision problematized in Schmitt's early legal writings "explodes" within Schmitt's late Weimar theory, ultimately shattering the normative restraints that Schmitt initially placed on it. Schmitt's celebration of the "norm-less" decision culminates in the embrace of an alternative to Weimar that Schmitt himself in 1932 describes as a dictatorship.[47] Nonetheless, it would be a mistake to take this as evidence of a basic discontinuity within Schmitt's thinking. First, during the Nazi period, Schmitt *continues* to emphasize the willful, arbitrary character of *liberal* law; within the confines of liberalism, judicial and adminis- ✓ trative action is unavoidably irregular and inconsistent. Of course, this line of argumentation is perfectly consistent with his Weimar reflections. Second, even Schmitt's early Weimar writings on judicial and administrative activity suggest, even though with great caution and questionable success, ✓ that willfulness within law could be overcome by extranormative features of the legal system, that is, by means of a homogeneous judiciary. What we have here is a shift in emphasis, but no inconsistency. In the context of the defeat of Weimar liberal democracy by the Nazis, it makes perfect sense for Schmitt to turn to the *constructive* task of developing a postliberal alternative to a system of liberal law that, in his view, is unavoidably plagued by willfulness. By the same token, when Germany was still liberal democratic, it was appropriate to emphasize the *deconstructive* side of his agenda, namely the critique of liberal jurisprudence. In that context, the celebration of the irrepressibility of the arbitrary decision within (liberal) law not surprisingly occupied the foreground of Schmitt's reflections. But even Schmitt's Weimar oeuvre contained both critical and constructive moments. The real difference is that the constructive side of this agenda now gains dramatically in significance. But even this shift within Schmitt's theory makes sense only within the context of its underlying continuities.

More astute commentators argue that it would be best to take his attempt here to criticize decisionism with a grain of salt. For these critics, concrete-order thinking itself is simply an "ideology" masking the reality of a National Socialist legal system that is fundamentally decisionist in character.[48] To the extent that Schmitt's apparent critique of decisionism during the Nazi period obscures fundamental continuities within his thinking, this criticism is legitimate. Nonetheless, National Socialist law was clearly *not* decisionist if decisionism means that judges and administrators can freely interpret and apply the law in *any* way they happen to consider appropriate at any given moment; Nazi-era judges were *not* free to decide in ways incompatible with National Socialist ideology. Although I take the characterization of Schmitt's Nazi-era theory as decisionist as an understandable attempt to capture how Schmitt makes a mockery of even a minimally acceptable conception of law, it remains crucial that we carefully trace the underlying logic of Schmitt's quest to reconceive the possibility of a novel form of legal determinacy. Only by doing so can we begin to understand why Schmitt's theory proved so useful to the Nazis. An authentic decisionist model of legal interpretation, in which legal actors are free to act *against* National Socialist principles as well as *in favor* of them, would not have been as helpful to the Nazis as Schmitt's own.

Of course, *State, Movement, Folk* intimated one possible path for salvaging a legal system relatively determinate and predictable in character: if a central source of legal indeterminacy lies in the heterogeneous character of those who interpret and apply the law, then the establishment of homogeneity within the ranks of German jurisprudence might go at least some way toward making legal predictability a real possibility. Although it is hopeless to expect much from a reform of the legal code, a radical reconstitution of jurists themselves [*Juristenreform*] might counteract some of the dangers at hand. In Schmitt's own words:

> [t]here is only one path [to legal determinacy]; the National Socialist state
> has decisively followed this path, and Roland Freisler captured its essence
> with the greatest clarity with the demand "Reform of the Jurists Instead
> of Reform of the Law." If there is still to be an independent judiciary
> despite the fact that a mechanical and automatic binding of the judge to
> a preexisting set of codified norms is no longer possible, then everything
> depends on the nature and makeup of our judges and administrators.[49]

In my reading of Schmitt's writings from this period, his enthusiastic engagement for National Socialism can be directly traced to this eerily straightforward set of axioms. Because of Schmitt's overtly ethnicist gloss in *State, Movement, Folk* on the sources of modern pluralism, only one solution is left here for beginning to reestablish some measure of legal determinacy: an ethnically homogeneous caste of judicial experts dedicated to an equally homogeneous worldview. In this fashion, the imperatives of Schmitt's legal theory in the mid-1930s come to intersect neatly with National Socialist racism and anti-Semitism. Just as the demand for ethnic and racial homogeneity [*Artgleichheit*] constitutes a core element of National Socialism, so, too, does Schmitt's attempt to formulate an alternative to liberal normativism require an ethnically and racially homogeneous estate of jurists.[50]

In fact, it is precisely the task of establishing an ethnically and methodologically homogeneous estate [*Stand*] of legal practitioners that takes on absolute primacy both for Schmitt the legal theorist and Schmitt the Nazi functionary in the 1930s. For immanent jurisprudential reasons, Schmitt enthusiastically endorses the Nazi quest to guarantee ethnic and racial homogeneity within Germany.[51] Not surprisingly, he pays special attention to the implications of this quest for German jurisprudence: Schmitt repeatedly proclaims that the creation of ethnic homogeneity is the *only* way Germany can hope to achieve a relatively determinate and predictable system of law. As a leader of the Nazi law professors' guild, Schmitt in this period emphasizes the implications of this position for the reform of legal education as well. He not only endorses the purging of racially "alien" faculty members, but also quite consistently endorses Nazi book burnings and calls for the ethnic cleansing of university libraries and reading lists.[52] At times Schmitt seems to suggest that the mere fact of ethnic homogeneity suffices to establish a "spiritually" homogeneous jurisprudence. More commonly, his polemics from this period imply that ethnic homogeneity *in conjunction* with an explicitly National Socialist legal education and training alone can create a homogeneous caste of future jurists likely to interpret and apply necessarily indeterminate legal clauses in a consistent manner. Ethnic homogeneity, it seems, is a necessary but not a sufficient condition of a determinate system of legal decision making. Thus, homogeneity needs to be complemented with a system of education able to keep aspiring judges and lawyers free from the taint of ethnically "alien" intellectual influences. In this spirit, Schmitt openly praises the Nazi destruction of intellectual pluralism and academic freedom in Germany's once impressive legal faculties, while simultaneously demanding that faculty members intent on guaranteeing that Nazism avoid the ills of normativism make absolutely sure that the basic verities of National Socialism are drummed into the minds of aspiring lawyers and judges.[53] Although conceding that the reconstruction of German jurisprudence along such ambitious lines is unlikely to be achieved within a few years, Schmitt never hesitates to praise the ruthless manner with which National Socialism has already begun to cleanse Germany of ethnically alien elements and the liberal normativism allegedly so popular among them.

Might the quest for alternative forms of homogeneity within German law just as easily have followed from Schmitt's quest to establish a postliberal form of legal determinacy? Did Schmitt's project require the embrace of the most horrible features of National Socialism? As mentioned above, Schmitt before 1933 sympathized with non-Nazi variants of right-wing authoritarianism. At the same time, it is unclear what other forms of homogeneity, given the basic contours of Schmitt's theory, might more effectively have played the role taken by nightmarish Nazi anti-Semitism. Schmitt was obviously hostile to left-wing attempts to establish social or class homogeneity. Even during the Weimar period, he noted that radical nationalism constituted the most authentic "political" force in our century.[54] Of course, radical nationalism need not take on racist or anti-Semitic features. Yet in light of Schmitt's profound hostility to modern universalistic conceptions of human equality, it is easy to see why he so quickly made Nazi anti-Semitism constitutive of his political and legal theory. Nazism surely broke in a drastic fashion with modern universalism; in this respect, Nazism was more consistent and rigorous than even Mussolini's Italy. In my view, this is why Schmitt ultimately considered Nazism superior to its numerous authoritarian competitors on the world scene in the 1930s: only the Nazis systematically abandoned the moldy *idées générales* that, in Schmitt's view, so long had exercised a detrimental influence on modern legal thought and practice. Of course, the relationship between political theory and praxis is always complex. Yet given the flawed structure of Schmitt's theory, his embrace of Nazism represented a logical choice.

No less revealing are Schmitt's contributions to a series of crucial debates within National Socialist jurisprudence during the first five years of the new regime. In an important recent essay, Peter Caldwell challenges the myth that Schmitt's theoretical position within National Socialist jurisprudence was consistently more moderate than that of rivals, such as Otto Koellreutter, who embraced Nazism well before Schmitt.[55] For our purposes here, especially striking is the manner in which Schmitt's attempt to construct an identifiably National Socialist conception of legal interpretation rests on the twin pillars of the programmatic agenda described above: Schmitt considers the formalist liberal quest to gain determinacy by means of clear general norms doomed, but he simultaneously hopes that some measure of determinacy might be achieved by a reconstitution of the ranks of the German legal profession. By systematically developing this line of argumentation, Schmitt offers a brand of jurisprudence particularly well suited to the political needs of the National Socialist leadership.

German jurists in 1933 were immediately confronted with the imposing problem of how to interpret legal statutes predating the Nazi takeover, many of which stemmed from Germany's first experiment in republican government, the Weimar Republic. Indeed, because the Nazis tarried awhile before instituting their own explicitly National Socialist laws, the question of how pre-Nazi-era statutes were to be interpreted by administrators and judges remained of central significance for much of the Nazi period. The fact that the overwhelming majority of jurists faced with the task of applying and interpreting such laws had been trained in pre–National Socialist conceptions of legal interpretation simply exacerbated the problem at hand from the perspective of Germany's new power holders. In the simplest terms, two alternatives seem to have presented themselves: one could try to bind judges tightly to preexisting statutes by insisting that judges continue to employ relatively traditional formalistic decision-making devices, *or* one could argue that National Socialist judges had no obligation to enforce laws predating the "national revolution" of 1933. Conveniently, the former position might reassure traditional elites, influential in the courts and administration during the regime's early years, that National Socialism was less frightfully subversive than its more militant representatives implied. At the same time, this option risked binding judges and administrators to laws that were utterly incompatible with National Socialist aspirations. In contrast, embracing the latter position might nicely serve Nazi policy aims, yet it risked legitimizing a freewheeling "activist" judiciary that might feel empowered to act, willy-nilly, in opposition to National Socialism. In light of the relative methodological heterogeneity of German jurists in the immediate aftermath of Hitler's takeover, this second option implied obvious political risks for National Socialism.

Relying on his theoretical reflections on the question of legal indeterminacy, Schmitt formulates an ingenious solution to this enigma. First, he argues against simply discarding the idea of a binding system of law altogether. Clearly worried by the specter of activist judges hostile to National Socialism, Schmitt insists, contrary to the second possibility just described, that judicial action always requires *some* basis in the law. Judges should *not* be allowed to act *ex nihilo*; they must be able to ground their actions in *some* legal act.[56] But this assertion hardly leads Schmitt to embrace the competing view that judges are bound to pursue traditional modes of judicial interpretation when faced with statutes predating the Nazi period. According to Schmitt, this first view presupposes an anachronistic liberal view of legal determinacy. Refashioning familiar arguments, Schmitt cleverly asserts that those who support traditional views of legal determinacy badly obscure the fact that no legal text can provide real guidance to decision makers. In this view, the interpretation of any legal text is ultimately determined by the particular "spirit" inhering, as he put it in his gloss on Montesquieu in *State, Movement, Folk*, in the "different mouths" that " 'pronounce' the same words so differently." Thus it is mistaken to claim that preexisting legal statutes necessarily conflict with National Socialism; such a view presupposes a degree of determinacy necessarily missing from the legal materials at hand. Those appealing to the text of pre-1933 laws in order to challenge National Socialism are simply juxtaposing their own (anti-Nazi) ethnic and intellectual "spirit" to the "spirit" of National Socialism. For Schmitt, they cannot legitimately claim to speak even in the name of those legal texts that seem overtly anti-Nazi in character.[57]

In this account, the very attempt to formulate the problem at hand as a choice between "judicial discretion" and "the binding of the judge to the statute" is incorrect in light of its implicit dependence on certain liberal legal illusions. In a pivotal but generally overlooked 1936 essay, Schmitt describes the manner in which traditional modes of legal interpretation in Germany tended to emphasize the semantic structure of the legal norm as a way of avoiding the problem of undertaking to resolve conflicts between the heterogeneous interests that played a role in the legislative history of the statute. Forced to grapple with the incompetence of the liberal legislature, jurists emphasized the coherence and relative autonomy of the statute vis-à-vis the irrationality of parliamentary politics. Faced with the unenviable task of trying to determine legislative intent in a pluralistic political world in which it was virtually impossible to do so, Schmitt concedes that it made some sense for pre-Nazi jurists to pursue a kind of interpretative literalism according to which "the statute is always more clever than the lawmaker."[58] But Nazi judges have no reason, even *if* it were possible to do so in the first place, to privilege the text of the statute over the task of ascertaining the underlying "spirit" of the legal order as a whole. The crisis of parliamentarism has been resolved by the Nazis; thus, jurists now should abandon their literal and formalistic interpretative devices. In contrast to the inept and pluralistic character of liberal parliamentary politics, Schmitt argues, National Socialism represents a coherent worldview, as sketched out in the Nazi Party Program as well as in a series of statements of legislative intent that function as helpful guides for judges and administrators trying to ascertain the basic principles of Nazi law. In this qualitatively different political context, there is no longer any pressing reason why the legal text should be favored vis-à-vis interpretations that may seem to depart from the semantic structure of the legal text. In the homogeneous ethnic and political universe of National Socialism, a central rationale behind interpretive literalism no longer obtains.[59]

For Schmitt after 1933, the first, indispensable step toward legal determinacy is clear enough: *all* laws must be interpreted in accordance with the coherent ethnic and intellectual "spirit" of National Socialism. For this reason, the creation of a judiciary exemplifying that same ethnic and ideological spirit is absolutely pivotal; "alien" ethnic groups will never feel at home in a concrete order not of their "kind" [*Art*]. In the (relatively limited) case of a judge's applying a piece of explicitly National Socialist legislation, it may even appear at first glance that the judge or administrator is simply engaging in a traditional mechanical application of the statute.[60] Nonetheless, the real force at work even in this scenario is the question of the spirit interpreting and applying the law. Schmitt concedes that vague, open-ended clauses easily lend themselves to an interpretation in accordance with the basic principles of National Socialism. But even seemingly clear pre-Nazi statutes quite legitimately can be interpreted in accordance with National Socialism: the ethnic predispositions and spiritual commitments of the juridical decision maker, and not the semantic attributes of the legal text, unavoidably are the truly decisive factors in legal interpretation. In this account, "[t]he binding [of the judge] rests on his adaptation [*Einfügung*] to an order of the folk resting on ethnic and racial homogeneity."[61] Only an estate of jurists intimately bred and trained in the particular legal mores and modes of thinking of the German folk is likely to interpret the law in a manner consistent with other legal practitioners who participate in the same shared ethnic community or concrete order.

For the National Socialist leadership in the years immediately after the demise of Weimar, Schmitt's argumentation here must have seemed heaven-sent. His position demands judicial compliance to National Socialist ideology while simultaneously countering the risky specter of forms of judicial activism *inimical* to Nazi ideology. Schmitt pays lip service to classical ideas of a "judge bound to law," thereby assuaging the fears of relatively traditional jurists potentially alienated by the radical antilegalist features of National Socialism, while in reality legitimizing a dramatic loosening of traditional forms of legal binding. This view makes *every* element of German law potentially subordinate to Nazi policy aims, *without requiring potentially time-consuming changes in the legal code*. Not surprisingly, Schmitt's ideas here were eagerly embraced by some Nazi leaders, and his model of legal interpretation exercised a real influence on National Socialist legal thinking throughout this period.[62]

Far more clearly than many of his colleagues, Schmitt presciently grasped that National Socialism was fundamentally hostile to *any* system of traditionally conceived binding law, even one fundamentally anti-Semitic in character. More resolutely than even those jurists whose pre-1933 Nazi credentials were far more weighty than his own, Schmitt appreciated that the establishment of an altogether novel, identifiably National Socialist legal code was at best unnecessary for the Nazi leadership, and at worst a potential impediment likely to be exploited by legal traditionalists who might use it in order to limit the awesome power of the Nazi power elite. Indeed, a constant theme in Schmitt's writings in this period is the ever-lurking danger of those who speak in the name of the "rule of law" [*Rechtsstaat*] while, in effect, trying to squash the National Socialist quest to construct what for Schmitt represents a superior, historically unprecedented system of legal determinacy via "the reform of jurists."[63] For Schmitt, the mushy and misleading concept of the rule of law is best discarded. He tends to consider the term "Leader State" [*Führerstaat*] a better description of National Socialism. Although National Socialism allegedly seeks legal determinacy and some measure of predictability, Schmitt repeatedly insists, its rendition of them differs qualitatively from that of its historical predecessors.[64]

In this account, those in favor of the establishment of a new expressly National Socialist legal code continue to pray at the altar of the formalist "empty fiction" of a loophole-free system of airtight, binding legal norms. He reminds those who disparage what may initially appear to be mere minor changes or amendments to the existing German legal code that even such alterations can function effectively to bring about profound and potentially revolutionary changes in the legal system.[65] In fact, Schmitt considers the National Socialist seizure of power a perfect example of this jurisprudential verity.[66] For Schmitt, those who insist on establishing a new

Nazi legal code simply fail to appreciate the intellectual and political novelty of the emerging National Socialist legal system. The judge in the Leader State is bound to the law, but this law has a different internal structure from that of the law of other constitutional systems; hence, judicial bindedness means something fundamentally new.[67] Because the judge partakes of the same ethnic community and folk spirit as the supreme lawmaker, the judge can legitimately veer, when necessary, from the express letter of the law in order to make sure that the will of the supreme Leader is respected in the individual case at hand. In this view, the judge is an assistant and even a colleague [*Mitarbeiter*] of the Leader, because both partake of a shared ethnic and spiritual background and thus are "bound" together by something far more profound than the semantic structure of the legal text.[68] Only because the establishment of racial and ethnic homogeneity makes a binding of this sort possible, can National Socialism permit judges to interpret legal texts in what may wrongly *appear*, from the vantage point of a more traditional jurisprudential perspective, to be a discretionary or even arbitrary manner.

For this reason, Schmitt often criticizes the claim that National Socialism is a *dictatorship*. Given the obvious brutality of the Nazi regime, it is easy to chalk this shockingly apologetic view up to Schmitt's opportunism. But here as well, much more than opportunism is at work. However apologetic and misleading, Schmitt's claim does capture something important about Nazism: National Socialism did in fact break dramatically with traditional forms of arbitrary government like those traditionally criticized by liberals who defended the ideal of the rule of law. Nazism was much more radical in its assault on minimal features of the rule of law than even the meanest "despotism" described by authors such as Locke and Montesquieu.

Because of the existence of a shared ethnic basis between the Leader and the judge, for Schmitt their relationship cannot be described as dictatorial in character. Similarly, the relationship between the German *Volk* and Leader rests on a shared "existential" basis and thus is hardly arbitrary or dictatorial in nature. In contrast, Schmitt considers the rule of the English in India dictatorial: there, one ethnic and racial group exercises power over a distinct racial group.[69] As we saw earlier in this study, during the Weimar period Schmitt often pointed to an "elective affinity" between dictatorship and legal indeterminacy: in light of the unavoidability of open-ended, arbitrary law, an executive-based dictatorship seemed the best answer to the legal imperatives of this epoch. It is easy to see, given the conceptual structure of Schmitt's theoretical framework, why the embrace of Nazism followed so smoothly for Schmitt in 1933: because National Socialism potentially "solves" the problem of legal indeterminacy, it also offers an opportunity for overcoming the theoretical and practical problems of dictatorship. Nazism can resolve the crisis of legal indeterminacy; by implication, it simultaneously suggests the possibility of a postliberal authoritarian state fundamentally distinct from traditional forms of dictatorship. In this respect as well, for Schmitt Nazism represents a revolutionary intellectual and political advance over the worn-out categories and practices of traditional political thought and practice, and hence a "state for the twentieth century."

Schmitt's view of the relationship between the Leader and judge might appear to represent an attempt to improve the stature of the judge by justifying a measure of judicial independence in relation to the Nazi leadership. But for Schmitt, judges are by no means thereby invested with unlimited discretionary privileges *in relation to the National Socialist spirit of the legal code as a whole*. No judicial action incompatible with the mores and spiritual currents of National Socialism is to be tolerated. Moreover, for Schmitt that spirit is coherently and consistently defined by the Nazi leadership and, most importantly, Hitler. Schmitt goes so far as to proclaim that Nazi law is sure to be far more determinant and predictable than law *ever* was within liberal democracy. Notwithstanding the Nazi abandonment of liberal concepts of legal determinacy, Schmitt proudly declares, National Socialism possesses more legal integrity than *any* competing legal system in the world.[70] Whereas liberal democracy continues to stumble along the worn-out path of normativistic liberalism, Nazism alone undertakes the quintessentially modern task of guaranteeing legal determinacy by means of "the reform of jurists."

III

In 1936, segments of the SS, allied with a number of Schmitt's most jealous rivals in the legal academy, succeeded in forcing Schmitt to give up a number of his posts. Schmitt's defenders have repeatedly exaggerated the depth of the blows experienced by Schmitt. The fact of the matter is that Schmitt continued to exercise a substantial impact on Nazi legal thinking; in chapter 6 we examine his turn to the politically explosive field of international law in 1937 and 1938. Nonetheless, there is no question that Schmitt's temporary political defeat in 1936 at least momentarily limited his impact on the ongoing construction of a National Socialist legal order.[71]

In light of the story told above, there is a certain irony to Schmitt's political troubles in 1936. After arguing vehemently that only the ethnic cleansing of the German judiciary could help provide a new form of binding, determinate law, Schmitt himself now comes face to face with the most obvious failing of his position: ethnic homogeneity is unlikely to go far in assuring jurisprudential consistency or agreement.[72] In 1936, even those "existentially" homogeneous colleagues who shared Schmitt's enthusiasm for National Socialism *disagreed* so heatedly with Schmitt about the proper contours of a National Socialist legal order that they willingly expended a great deal of political capital in order to do serious political damage to Schmitt. National Socialism did its best to exterminate the specter of what John Rawls terms "the fact of pluralism." But even its awesome power proved unable to guarantee Nazism complete victory in its struggle against the basic contours of a modern pluralistic intellectual universe. Although it would be silly to chalk up disagreement among Nazi lawyers as a victory for modern pluralism, it would be no less problematic to miss the ways in which continuing disagreement even among hard-core Nazi jurists suggests the inherent fragility of Schmitt's claim that a shared "existential determination" of judicial decision making could contribute to a novel postliberal form of legal determinacy. Schmitt's hope that ethnic cleansing might help secure legal determinacy ultimately proved more fantastic than even the most overstated liberal "empty fiction" of an airtight legal code free of loopholes, in which the judge is nothing more than "*la bouche qui prononce les paroles de la loi.*"

Nonetheless, judicial decisions in Nazi Germany did prove basically consistent with the "spirit" of National Socialism.[73] Yet this consistency was guaranteed, first and foremost, by institutional and political mechanisms. As Otto Kirchheimer, German-Jewish émigré and one-time left-wing aficionado of Schmitt's jurisprudence, observed in a prescient 1941 discussion of Nazi law:

> the [Nazi] judge, like any other administrative official, is accountable for the contents of his decision. Where the relentless pressure of the party through channels like the *Schwarze Korps* should prove of no avail . . . new organizational statutes provide ample facilities for discharging or

transferring a recalcitrant judge. The judiciary is entitled to have and to express opinions of its own only in those cases where it does not act as a kind of common executive organ to the combined ruling classes.[74]

In the final analysis, the most important feature of Schmitt's works between 1933 and 1936 is that they contributed systematically to precisely this subordination of the judiciary to the Nazi power elite. In this sense, Schmitt's writings did help guarantee some elements of a special form of legal determinacy. Yet this legal determinacy had nothing to do with earlier liberal conceptions of determinate law, nor can its relative "success" in guaranteeing a measure of consistency in legal action be traced to the (mythical) binding power of common ethnic roots.

As Kirchheimer notes, for classical liberalism the rationality of law stemmed from its predictable character, which meant that

> contending individuals and groups, though they are never sure which of the many possible interpretations of their behavior will prevail in any given case, usually could confine their actions within such limits that these could not be said to contradict openly the wording of the law and the procedural requirements of the established courts and agencies.[75]

In traditional liberalism, legal rationality rested in part on the existence of relatively determinate, universally applicable rules "which could be referred to by the ruling and the ruled alike and which thus might restrict the arbitrariness of administrative practice."[76] For Kirchheimer, Nazi law is also "rational," yet this rationality takes an altogether different form from that of liberalism: "Rationality here means only that the whole apparatus of law and law-enforcing is made exclusively serviceable to those who rule."[77] In this legal manifestation of what Kirchheimer describes as a form of truncated *technical* rationality, what counts is that legal decision makers provide a legal veneer for the political preferences of the ruling elite. In this caricature of traditional conceptions of legal determinacy, determinacy simply means that legal decisions cohere as closely as possible to the needs of the Nazi power elite. In Kirchheimer's account, this postliberal form of legal determinacy represents an unprecedented attempt to introduce "the industrial methods of taylorism . . . into the realm of statecraft in order to get the most precise answer to the question" of how the preferences of privileged party, state, and economic elites can be put automatically into effect.[78]

There is no question that Schmitt contributed to the achievement of some elements of this form of legal "determinacy" in Germany during the 1930s. By demanding the cleansing of elements potentially hostile to National Socialism and the destruction of any real legal and constitutional limits on the Nazi leadership, Schmitt surely played an important role in making sure that those who interpreted and applied the law served the wishes of the National Socialist elite.[79] Although Schmitt's theorizing too often obscures the harsh realities of National Socialist law, at times his own categories inadvertently unmask Nazi legal ideology. By repeatedly emphasizing the notion that the judge is a colleague or "assistant" to the omnipotent Leader, for example, Schmitt comes quite close to an express acknowledgment of one of the most troubling facets of National Socialist law: both in Schmitt's theory and in National Socialist reality, the judge inevitably becomes a mere administrative accessory of the National Socialist leadership.

IV

Let me conclude with a brief comment on the possible significance of Schmitt's National Socialist legal theory for contemporary North American jurisprudence.

Today it is once again a commonplace among some jurists that a profound and unavoidable indeterminacy necessarily characterizes the legal system. In the words of critical legal scholar Mark Kelman: "*All* rules will contain within them deeply embedded, structural premises that clearly enable decision makers to resolve particular controversies in opposite ways. . . . [A]ll law seems simultaneously either to demand or at least allow internally contradictory steps."[80] Notwithstanding traditional liberal aspirations for a binding and relatively determinate set of legal norms, law turns out to contain an irrepressible *arbitrariness*. Legal categories are simply "empty vessels" filled by acts of power that force meaning into them. In this view, *all* cases are "hard cases."

In contrast to most current proponents of the radical indeterminacy thesis, however, Schmitt was ultimately unsatisfied with simply deconstructing the liberal rule of law. As this chapter tried to demonstrate, Schmitt additionally undertook the reconstructive task of formulating a postliberal conception of legal determinacy, in which core features of the radical indeterminacy thesis nonetheless continue to function as an analytic presupposition for an alternative understanding of legal interpretation.

I suspect that some contemporary radical jurists are likely to consider Schmitt's attempt to salvage legal determinacy as ultimately inconsistent with his initial acceptance of the radical indeterminacy thesis. They often *celebrate* the irrepressible (decisionistic) arbitrariness allegedly at the core of liberal law in order, like Schmitt, to deconstruct it; they seem less interested in the task of sketching out a postliberal corrective to the legal status quo. From their perspective, Schmitt's attempt to establish legal determinacy by means of ethnic homogeneity might represent a particularly revealing example of the profound evils inherent in the anachronistic quest for legal determinacy. For those who accept this interpretation, Schmitt's Nazi-era writings will simply confirm the advantages of a rigorous version of the radical indeterminacy thesis, according to which *any* attempt to buttress the "myth" of legal determinacy is doomed to fail.

Of course, that position is problematic on its own terms: as Schmitt suggested during the Weimar period, those who accept the radical indeterminacy thesis arguably may need to abandon the most defensible features of the liberal democratic state as well. In contrast to some voices today endorsing the ongoing dismantling of the rule of law, Schmitt's thinking on this matter may at least be more consistent and systematic. Legal nihilism and liberal democracy hardly make good bedfellows.

But another interpretation of Schmitt's National Socialist theory is possible as well. In this alternative line of inquiry, Schmitt merely takes some tendencies within radical jurisprudence a step further than their contemporary practitioners have done thus far. Rather than resting satisfied with the ambiguous implications of the radical indeterminacy thesis, Schmitt tackles the hard questions often ignored by contemporary radical jurists, despite the fact that they follow logically from the radical indeterminacy thesis: what exactly should replace the liberal rule of law and its emphasis on relatively determinate rules? What type of legal order is possible in the shadows of the indeterminacy thesis? What form should a postliberal legal system take in light of the inherent indeterminacy of liberal law? The fact that Schmitt offers an ominous totalitarian antidote to the crisis of legal indeterminacy may suggest that the reconstructive task at hand is likely to prove more difficult than some contemporary defenders of the radical indeterminacy thesis concede. Like Schmitt, at least some of them seem bent on purging legal theory of even the most minimal elements of the liberal legal tradition. Enlightenment-bashing has become an academic growth industry within some segments of the American legal academy.[81] One of the most important unintended achievements of Schmitt's theory is that it systematically outlines the basic contours of an alternative legal model that welds antiliberalism to the radical indeterminacy thesis.

There is, of course, an underlying logic to Schmitt's frightening argument: if legal determinacy cannot be achieved at all by means of traditional legal materials, then the attempt to establish homogeneous judges does acquire a certain amount of plausibility. Given the conditions of modern pluralism, however, there can be no question that this project is a recipe for political disaster. Schmitt's embrace of the "cleansing" of the judiciary—indeed, of the political community as a whole—is surely one conceivable result of the total abandonment of the liberal concept of binding legal norms.

One influential line of argumentation within contemporary radical jurisprudence asserts that every modern legal system represents a patchwork of competing and fundamentally inconsistent moral and political ideals. For this reason, the quest to assure legal determinacy by appealing to a coherent set of moral or political principles seen as embedded within the legal system fails; the undeterminacy thesis, as defended by Dworkin and others, necessarily stumbles, since the ideals immanent within modern law are as incapable of providing a determinate answer to hard cases as are legal rules or statutes.[82] Schmitt would have agreed with the basic outlines of this diagnosis. His answer to it was to eliminate moral and political pluralism and thereby salvage legal determinacy.

The case of Carl Schmitt clearly contradicts the naive assumption shared by some jurists today "that liberating those who wield legal power from the 'mistaken' belief that legal doctrine constrains their actions will have progressive effects."[83] In Germany at midcentury, the "liberation" of state officials from binding legal norms hardly generated "progressive" results. On the contrary, it directly paved the way for Nazi terror, World War II, and the Holocaust.

6

INDETERMINACY AND
INTERNATIONAL LAW

For those of us skeptical of Carl Schmitt's normative and political aspirations, Schmitt's writings on international law pose a special challenge. International law remains one of the least developed areas of modern law. Its norms are open-ended and vague, enforcement mechanisms limited in character, and employment subject to the opportunistic whims of great powers that generally see it as little more than a handy political weapon. More than any other area of the law, international law is vulnerable to fundamental criticism. Not surprisingly, Schmitt occasionally succeeded in identifying the underlying inconsistencies of liberal international law, particularly in its interwar rendition, and his Weimar-era writings at times formulated a perceptive analysis of the League of Nations and modern forms of imperialism. Of particular importance here is Schmitt's early fascination with the sources of the U.S. hegemony in Central and South America, as well as his discussion of the increasingly decisive role of the United States in the European arena after World War I (I, II).

Yet Schmitt ultimately relied on precisely this critique of liberal international law to offer what surely constitutes one of his most terrible contributions in a long and often sordid intellectual career: a defense of National Socialist imperialism during the late 1930s and 1940s. This phase of Schmitt's theory not only demonstrates his support for National Socialism well into the 1940s, but also builds incontestably on core features of his Weimar critique of international law. Even in the Weimar period, Schmitt revealed a clear sympathy for forms of imperialist domination that, in his view, had successfully pierced the hypocrisies of liberal legalism. In the years following Hitler's seizure of power in 1933, Schmitt came to believe that Germany finally possessed a real chance to enter the elite club of great powers. Most provocative of all, Schmitt argued that the Nazis should learn from their main rival in the international arena: the example of American imperialism in Central and South America allegedly offered an excellent starting point for justifying German hegemony in Europe. Schmitt's writings after 1938 thus primarily focused on the task of defending what he described as the German "greater region" [*Grossraum*], purportedly modeled on the lessons of American political and economic domination in the New World (III, IV).

Unfortunately for Schmitt, his attempt to turn the enigmas of American foreign policy against contemporary liberal aspirations for a binding system of international law fails. Schmitt repeatedly thematizes the Achilles' heel of contemporary international law—the fact that the great powers often manipulate its open-ended, indeterminate features—in order to deconstruct and undermine it. But his argument can be read, against the grain, as an appeal to get rid of this Achilles' heel. Although Schmitt accurately describes many of the ills of American foreign policy, he cannot legitimately claim to build his critique of liberal international law on the experience of American imperialism. In this part of his theory as well, Schmitt conveniently distorts the history of the liberal past in order to discredit the unfulfilled agenda of the rule of law (V).[1]

I

In a fascinating yet long-forgotten monograph on the Allied occupation of the Rhineland region of Germany after World War I, the political theorist Ernst Fraenkel demonstrates that Allied policy toward the defeated Germans was one that explosively combined "political cynicism and legal idealism." Appealing to an ambitious Wilsonian liberalism resting on a virtually "unlimited belief in the force of law," the victorious Allies established a system of highly discretionary martial rule that in reality had little to do with the ambitious ideals of Western liberal jurisprudence.[2] Notwithstanding the endorsement of the Allied occupation by the newly established League of Nations, the occupying powers in fact considered themselves "entitled to do whatever they considered proper in their own interests," and thus a system of arbitrary situational law, suited to the ever-changing political needs of the French, British, and American occupation forces, characterized the Allied exercise of power in one of Germany's most important regions.³ In Fraenkel's interpretation, the enormous gap between liberal legal ideals, together with the sad reality of legal arbitrariness in the Rhineland, was one of the sources of the assault on liberal democracy in Weimar Germany. For a sizable number of Germans directly under the hegemony of Allied rule, Wilsonian liberalism's dream of extending the rule of law to the international arena understandably looked like nothing more than a rhetorical cover for a mean exercise of brute power. To Germans living outside the occupied territories as well, the significance of Allied hypocrisy seemed equally self-evident. Horror stories from the Allied occupation played a central role in the political propaganda of all the major parties, but especially those on the nationalist authoritarian right. Owing in part to the hypocrisy of Allied rule, this propaganda often proved highly effective.

Schmitt's writings from the 1920s easily allow us to guess at the impact this experience must have had on the young legal scholar, who clearly identified emotionally with the western and overwhelmingly Catholic section of Germany subject to Allied rule. As an instructor at the University of Bonn (between 1921 and 1928), Schmitt was provided with what amounted to a daily initiation into one of the more unfortunate moments in the history of the international order between the world wars. Predictably, many of Schmitt's writings from this period tackle manifestations of the gap between "political cynicism and legal idealism" chronicled by Fraenkel. Even if we endorse normative and political standpoints antithetical to Schmitt's own, there is no question that some of Schmitt's criticisms are legitimate.⁴ Nonetheless, we risk trivializing Schmitt's Weimar intellectual and political agenda if we simply read him as chiefly preoccupied, like so many of his countrymen on both the right and the left, with overcoming the local ills of the Allied treatment of post–World War I Germany. The power—indeed, the explosiveness—of Schmitt's reflections here stems from his success in translating commonplace criticisms of the Versailles Treaty and the League of Nations into a full-fledged assault on the intellectual core of the liberal quest in the twentieth century to include the international arena within the scope of a system of general, binding legal norms.

For Schmitt, allied domination of Germany is nothing but a particular version of a specifically modern form of imperialism, practiced most astutely by the United States, in which liberal international law generates a new and unprecedented system of domination more oppressive than any previous form of colonial domination. Liberals in the twentieth century espouse a universalistic ideal of self-determination, in which all peoples are granted the right to develop legally equal, independent sovereign states. Thus, direct forms of colonial domination are now basically anachronistic in character; in the twentieth century, direct territorial annexation becomes the exception to the rule. Schmitt considers this normative model a paradigmatic case of liberal hypocrisy. In reality, liberals today undermine state sovereignty by subjecting the vast majority of states to a tiny group of Leviathans, whose hegemony is all the more secure because liberal international law renders it invisible. The liberal ideal of the universal equality of all states now chiefly functions as a mask for novel forms of political and economic exploitation. In a similar vein, liberals dream of regulating political relations between independent states in accordance with a set of general norms and courts capable of applying those norms. Just as earlier liberal theorists sought to replace the state of nature within the domestic arena with a systematic rule of law, so, too, do modern liberals aspire to overcome the state of nature between nations by subjecting international conflicts to a rational and universally binding system of enforceable legal norms. But in Schmitt's view, the proliferation of liberal legal devices on the international scene merely provides a new set of weapons for those states, the great powers, that are best situated to exploit them. The quest for codified law on the international scene is bound to fail. In this view, international law is unavoidably and inherently a highly partisan system of "political justice." The League of Nations is at most a League of the Great Powers.

Here as well, the problem of legal indeterminacy plays a central role in Schmitt's theoretical reflections. As discussed in previous chapters, Schmitt emphasizes the basically indeterminate character of liberal law in order to discredit the rule of law. He relies on the same method in order to attack liberal conceptions of international law. Because the core of liberal international law, like its domestic corollary, is inherently open-ended in nature, the idea of a binding international rule of law is necessarily an illusion, albeit a potentially dangerous illusion suited to the needs of those political interests best capable of exploiting the radical indeterminacy of law. In the international arena as well, liberal rhetoric about the rule of law simply serves as an ideological front for a system of law that is fundamentally decisionistic. The real question is always who will best prove able to take advantage of the decisionist essence of liberal international law: as far as the "decisive concepts of international law" are concerned, "the primary and most important question is not (the always easily disputable and dubious) content of the norm, but rather the question of *quis judicabit?*"⁵ Because international law is unlikely to bind members of the international community even in the most modest fashion, it is imperative that those hoping to make sense of its operations figure out which political actors are most likely to manipulate legal norms and determine their content. An empirical analysis of political power, not legal hermeneutics, thus should make up the core of the study of international law. Even in the 1920s, Schmitt suggests that given the ascent of the United States, the Americans are most likely to "decide" the content of international law, and thus gain most from its proliferation.

Schmitt systematically develops this position in his polemic against the Allied occupation of the Rhineland, but it immediately becomes crucial to his broader assault on liberal international law. Although the Rhineland occupation is endorsed by the League of Nations and the Wilsonian liberalism on which it rests, in reality the Allies rely on vague legal clauses in order to exercise extensive forms of discretionary power in Germany. The Versailles Treaty left the extent of reparations undefined; sanctions were so broadly defined that the Allies have been able to justify virtually any action by reference to them; the investigative powers granted the Allies (in order to prevent German rearmament) allow for unlimited invasions of privacy; the powers of the occupying forces are so badly defined that arbitrary rule has now become the status quo in the occupied zone.⁶ Of course, none of this is coincidental. Vague clauses are preferred by the biggest boys on the international block because they are best situated to exploit them. Open-ended legal clauses are even more common in the international arena than in the domestic setting because the great powers have sought to oppose the establishment of statutes that might be taken as requiring some limitations on their sovereignty. In crucial moments, every great power knows that it needs to remain the sovereign judge in those cases affecting its political interests. For Schmitt, the League of Nations has left this state of affairs fundamentally unaltered, notwithstanding its claims to the contrary.⁷

Most hypocritical of all, the reality of Allied arbitrariness in postwar Germany is veiled by the political rhetoric of humanitarian liberalism. In Schmitt's assessment, the League of Nations is fundamentally committed to the territorial status quo in central Europe. Because it would be utopian to expect the League to try to overcome the self-evident misadventures of the Allies in postwar Germany, the League and Allied mistreatment of Germany are inextricably intertwined.⁸ Allied injustice is justified by reference to Wilsonian liberalism and its belief that the League represents a peace-loving tool in the employ of "universal humanity." This easy alliance between universalistic liberalism and the League's policies generates a convenient ideological offshoot for the Allies: if the Allied occupation is ultimately an act of "universal humanity," then even modest criticisms of the occupation forces, let alone the League itself, can easily be branded "inhumane." Liberal universalism in international law thereby rests on an exclusionary logic by which those opposed to practices committed under its auspices are described as acting against "humanity." Those challenging Allied injustice quickly become "criminal" opponents of international law, whereas even a violent exercise of power under the auspices of international law represents a "legal" contribution to the humanitarian-ethical pursuit of universal peace, a mere "police" action in which international law is simply "executed." This is the main reason why Schmitt considers liberalism the most fundamental source of the "discriminatory concept of war," according to which wars undertaken under the auspices of international law increasingly are no longer even described as wars, while wars in opposition to international law (and the territorial status quo ensconced in its norms) are pictured as criminal acts of a lawless inhumanity. Liberal states use international law to mask their own acts of violence as expressions of legality, while discriminating against their opponents by describing their actions as criminal and inhumane. Notwithstanding the claim of international law to seek universal peace, for Schmitt it is therefore destined to generate wars more horrible than those hitherto known to modern history. Those challenging the international liberal legal system immediately become the "criminal" enemy of all mankind. Thus, "[t]he Geneva League of Nations does not eliminate the possibility of wars. . . . It introduces new possibilities for wars, permits wars to take place, sanctions coalition wars, and by legitimizing and even sanctioning certain wars it sweeps away many obstacles to war."[9]

For Schmitt, the quest to use international law to resolve stormy political conflicts like those concerning the Rhineland rests on a politically absurd assumption, namely, the fundamental normalcy of the territorial status quo of post–World War I central Europe. Life-and-death political conflicts cannot be effectively solved by liberal legal devices. "Normal" legal rules are inappropriate in a situation of crisis or abnormalcy. In this spirit, early modern political theorists long recognized that the rule of law was a poor device for regulating the most fundamental political conflicts. They pictured relations between different states as representing an international "state of nature" qualitatively distinct from the "rule of law" sought within the domestic arena. In Schmitt's view, something akin to this state of nature still characterizes international politics. Although for Schmitt the idea of the state of nature is conceptually problematic, it gives expression to a crucial political verity: political communities in the international arena inevitably confront adversaries who "must be repulsed or fought in order to preserve one's own form of existence."[10] Of course, liberals may pretend otherwise, emphasizing the "potential" of the League for overcoming the irrational character of international relations, but for Schmitt it would be naive to confuse such aspirations with the reality of contemporary politics.[11] Because Germany's interests are still fundamentally opposed to those of the Western Allies, the attempt to regulate relations between Germany and her international competitors by peaceful legal means not only is bound to fail, but also represents a bad-faith effort on the part of Western liberalism to veil its fundamentally anti-German political agenda in the deceptively attractive language of international law.

Foreshadowing post-1945 Realist theorists of international relations, Schmitt repeatedly argues that the recourse to typically liberal forms of legal conflict resolution (for example, international tribunals) necessarily rests on a fiction—the existence of a functioning international political community in which existential, life-and-death political conflicts have been resolved. But no such community exists, either between Germany and her Western rivals or within the international community as a whole. The League of Nations is at best capable of coordinating "conferences" that perform some useful functions, but otherwise is unlikely to act as an effective decision-making body, given the fact that it lacks the homogeneity essential, in Schmitt's theory, to any successful political entity: "The differences in culture, race, and religion must lead to tensions" within the League of Nations that are unlikely to be effectively resolved in light of their fundamental political character.[12] "The real possibility of killing" haunts such conflicts, and "[t]hese can neither be decided by a previously determined general norm nor by the judgement of a disinterested and therefore neutral party."[13] In a telling metaphor, Schmitt concludes that the League rests on the ill-fated endeavor to create friendship between "lions" (that is, the great powers) and "mice" (second-class powers).[14] At best, judicial devices may function to mask these conflicts. More likely, the lions will simply employ them as one weapon in their struggle to wipe out the mice.

The gist of this argument is that legalistic liberals falsely believe that they can formalize—that is, subject to formal law—life-and-death political divisions between unavoidably heterogeneous, antagonistic political entities incapable of being formalized. The obvious vagueness of so much of international law turns out to make up only the tip of the iceberg. Even if it *were* possible to codify international law, this measure would hardly overcome the main problem at hand. After all, lions and mice are sure to differ about the interpretation of even those legal terms that seem unambiguous and clear-cut in nature. *All* legal concepts, and not just those obviously open-ended in character, are "easily disputable and dubious" in the international arena. Radical indeterminacy is at the very core of international law; it is not simply a problem resulting from vague and deformalized standards.[15] Admittedly, Schmitt's Weimar writings do focus on semantically ambiguous, open-ended legal standards as the most obvious source of indeterminacy in international law. Nonetheless, it would be a mistake to read Schmitt as suggesting that a system of formal, codified law could free itself from the specter of radical indeterminacy. *All* forms of liberal law are necessarly plagued by the problem of radical indeterminacy.

The Allied treatment of Germany is of more than local significance in another respect as well. In Schmitt's eyes, it provides an example of how the indeterminacy of liberal law allows liberalism, despite its lip service to the ideal of universal self-determination, to make the modern sovereign state a hollow shell of its former self. Pace modern liberal rhetoric about the legal equality of all sovereign states, in reality an ever-smaller number of political giants dominate international affairs. Although deeply hostile to legal positivism and its most impressive contemporary advocate, Hans Kelsen, Schmitt does admit that positivist theories of sovereignty contain an empirical half-truth about contemporary political reality: their hostility to traditional conceptions of state sovereignty corresponds to the very real decline in effective sovereignty among second-class states forced to live in the shadow of a relatively small group of massive sovereign "lions."[16] In this part of Schmitt's story, modern liberalism has abandoned any real interest in annexing territories or engaging in unmediated forms of direct political domination, chiefly because modern liberals have been forced to acknowledge the potential political costs of traditional forms of colonial domination.[17] Liberalism has simply found more effective instruments of control.

Most importantly, contemporary liberal states make ample use of what Schmitt considers the most creative American innovation in modern international law, the nonintervention treaty.[18] Fascinated by the United States' repeated use of the nonintervention treaty in its relations with Central and South American neighbors, Schmitt considers two of its features decisive. First, the promise of nonintervention nominally rests on a formal recognition of the sovereignty of the weaker state. Second, the treaty in fact makes a mockery of the idea of sovereignty by tying it to a series of typically open-ended, vague legal conditions that Central and South American countries (such as Cuba, Nicaragua, and Haiti) are supposed to meet. The nonintervention treaty is *in fact* an intervention treaty because the United States maintains the right to intervene if certain conditions—"public order," the "protection of life, liberty and property," "continued respect for international treaties"—are not upheld. Of course, the obvious vagueness of these conditions provides impressive leeway for extensive American intervention in the domestic and foreign affairs of a weaker power. Because of the de facto military and economic superiority of the United States in the new world, the United States in most cases unilaterally applies the ambiguous clauses at hand: "In the case of all of these nonintervention agreements it is important to note that due to the indeterminacy of their concepts the hegemonic power decides at its discretion and thereby places the political existence of the controlled state in its own hands."[19]

Schmitt delights in noting that the example of the nonintervention treaty illustrates his more general jurisprudential insight that "the exception is more interesting than the rule."[20] Not the main body of the general norms of the nonintervention treaty, but rather its declaration of a series of exceptions to the rules of nonintervention allows us to make sense of the real state of affairs between the United States and the political "mice" living in its shadow. The United States has long made generous use of such exceptional clauses, and military interventions resting on them—which, as Schmitt emphasizes, are often undertaken for the sake of protecting American property—have defined much of the contours of Latin American history.

Yet the nonintervention treaty is only one of the many weapons of modern American imperialism. According to Schmitt, the United States is well on the way (by 1932) to becoming the world's dominant power, chiefly because it best understands the political potentialities of the emerging system of international law. Schmitt's Weimar writings constantly make use of a terse phrase that he thinks allows him to capture the idiosyncrasies of American imperialism: "officially absent, but effectively present." In

Central and South America, American power is invisible to the extent that the United States recognizes the sovereignty of smaller powers. In fact, the United States is the dominant force in the region, owing in part to its skillful manipulation of the exceptions outlined in the nonintervention treaties. In addition, the Monroe Doctrine, whose elastic clauses similarly provide the United States with vast discretionary power in the Americas, plays a crucial role in guaranteeing the de facto hegemony of the United States.[21] Schmitt marvels at the fact that "this Monroe Doctrine is a very general, very broad 'doctrine,' which provides grounds for altogether contrary forms of action. . . . What actually makes up the concrete substance of this multilayered, ever-changing, highly transformable Monroe Doctrine is decided by the United States alone. Only the United States determines what the Monroe Doctrine means in the concrete case."[22] In an analogous fashion, the liberal League of Nations simply ignores the most worrisome form of American power in Europe, American economic penetration of the European economy, despite the obvious importance that American economic muscle possesses for the fate of European civilization. Whereas the League strives to illegalize traditional forms of military expansionism and conquest, it does absolutely nothing to oppose the increasing economic penetration and domination of much of Western Europe by the United States. From the perspective of the League, the most important form of American power on the continent is "invisible," but only because the liberal ideology at the core of the League is blind to the political potentialities of capitalist economic power.[23]

Schmitt tries to get maximum mileage out of the fact that Article 21 of the League of Nations, which declared that the League and the Monroe Doctrine were compatible, seems to rest on an endorsement of the Monroe Doctrine. Once again, the exception—in this case, a seemingly obscure element of postwar international law—purportedly proves more interesting than the rule.[24] The United States of course never formally joined the League but, for Schmitt, remains its dominant force. In this sphere as well, the Americans have proven brilliant at exercising "officially absent, but factually present" power. By accepting the main tenets of the Monroe Doctrine, the League allegedly hands over de facto political sovereignty in the Americas to the United States, which exploits the open-ended clauses of the Monroe Doctrine in order to intervene willy-nilly in the political and economic affairs of its neighbors. In this interpretation, the League's recognition of the legitimacy of the Monroe Doctrine means that the League effectively excludes meaningful European involvement in the Americas. At the same time, many of the Latin and South American states in which the United States exercises de facto hegemonic power are themselves active members of the League. Schmitt claims that their votes often played a decisive role in determining the outcome of crucial League resolutions about European affairs.[25] But if the United States is the de facto sovereign in much of the Americas, and if the substantial impact of the American states in the League is really nothing but a veiled exercise of power by the United States, then one is compelled to conclude that the United States is the "officially absent" but effectively decisive power within the League. The United States tolerates no European intervention within its American "empire," while simultaneously playing an active role in shaping the affairs of those European countries excluded from participation in the affairs of the Americas.[26]

Schmitt goes so far as to speculate that the 1928 Kellogg Pact potentially represents a starting point for transforming the Monroe Doctrine into a worldwide affair, according to which the United States would come to exercise hegemonic power on the global scale as it long has within the Americas.[27] Here as well, Schmitt underlines the problem of legal indeterminacy in order to pursue this surprising line of argument. Although promising to illegalize war, the Kellogg Pact in fact bans only wars that are an "instrument of national policy," in other words, traditional wars of national conquest. By no means does it intend to prevent military action under the auspices of "international politics," that is, wars engaged in for the sake of "universal humanity" according to liberal international law. Thus, the Kellogg Pact simply gives expression to the "discriminatory concept of war" that allegedly can function only to privilege the military adventures of liberal states over their rivals. Which liberal state is likely to determine the question of *quis judicabit?* in the case of the Kellogg Treaty? Who is best positioned to exploit its ambiguities? For Schmitt, the answer is obvious, in light of the fact that the economic, military, and political power of the United States is increasingly unmatched in the twentieth century. Just as the United States uses the open-ended clauses of the Monroe Doctrine in the Americas, Schmitt posits, so, too, can we be sure that it soon will rely on the Kellogg Pact to decide single-handedly when a war is defined as an instrument of international peace, a peaceful instrument for the maintenance of order and security, or when it is nothing but an act of barbarism undertaken against humanity.[28] For Schmitt, the United States is sure to describe its own wars, however bestial in character, as legal instruments having a humanitarian character, while describing its rivals' as criminal acts engaged in by the enemies of humankind.

II

Schmitt's Weimar-era critique of liberal international law in the interwar years undoubtedly captures some of its fundamental weaknesses. Those familiar with the Realist literature in international relations theory can rightly point to many striking parallels between Schmitt and the ideas of sophisticated critics of liberal international law like E. H. Carr and Hans Morgenthau; later I directly address the intellectual nexus between Schmitt and the American Realists.[29] By the same token, it would be a mistake to let Schmitt off the hook too easily even where his analysis seems most impressive.

Schmitt provides a powerful warning about the potential dangers of new forms of imperialism that wrap themselves in the mantle of liberal universalism. Unjustified wars surely have been waged in the name of "universal humanity" in our century, and Schmitt provides his reader with a heightened sense of the real dangers of military power when employed by a self-righteous political and economic liberalism.[30] At the same time, it is unclear exactly how Schmitt's frontal attack on novel forms of liberal political and economic domination is consistent with his polemics against modern universalism. For example, Schmitt repeatedly expresses outrage at the potential barbarism of new forms of liberal war making. But why is this a problem in the first place unless Schmitt himself implicitly shares at least some typically modern, universalistic concerns about the basic equality and value of all human life? Schmitt is no closet liberal. But is it merely a coincidence that Schmitt's outraged attack on the violence of modern liberal wars occasionally proves oddly reminiscent of the very "humanitarian pacifism" which he so despises.[31] It is striking that the phenomena analyzed by Schmitt—for example, what historians have described as the "informal imperialism" practiced by the United States in parts of the Americas—have so often been successfully criticized within the intellectual parameters of a universalistic normative standpoint, namely, by liberals and Marxists just as disgusted as Schmitt with its obvious hypocrisies.[32] Yet liberal and Marxist analyses are more consistent in at least one respect. Why criticize the

United States' political and economic domination of Latin America unless we presuppose, at least on some minimal level, a basic moral respect for peoples subjected to foreign political and economic exploitation? Foreshadowing some currents of contemporary postmodern anti-universalism, Schmitt too often simply assumes that liberal universalism necessarily rests on an inherently exclusionary logic. In a revealing comment in *The Concept of the Political*, for example, he makes the liberal "discriminatory concept of war" culpable for the attempt to exterminate native Americans in North America.[33] But is liberal universalism the culprit here, and not a *fraudulent* universalism favoring the interests and perspectives of privileged white European settlers?

For those, like Schmitt, convinced of the inherent cultural and political imperialism of modern liberal universalistic ideals, such traditional concerns are sure to seem quaint and unconvincing. Without implicit recourse to them, however, it is unclear how Schmitt can ground what occasionally seems to represent the standpoint of his entire critique of liberal international law. At crucial junctures, Schmitt criticizes the liberal agenda in international relations by emphasizing that its imperialistic core denies Germany "the right to her own free, independent, and undivided existence."[34] Yet this argument counts implicitly on one of the core conceptions of modern international law, the legal equality of all independent, sovereign states. Yet precisely this typically modern conception of statehood, notwithstanding its obvious limitations today, borrows substantially from certain elements of modern universalism: just as early modern political thought pictured independent, free, and equal individuals within a "state of nature," in a similar fashion early modern international law attributed "personhood" to the early modern state, and the "person" of the state was then pictured as free and legally equal within the international arena. How can Schmitt legitimately rely on such notions in light of his heated polemics against modern universalism?

It is also difficult to avoid the conclusion that a certain conceptual dogmatism characterizes Schmitt's declaration that interstate relations in our century remain fundamentally unregulated in character, that is, that international affairs still take place in a scenario approximating the "state of nature." My intention is not to downplay the irrationalities of contemporary interstate relations. Still, Schmitt provides us with a stark and overly dramatized choice: *either* we accept the unavoidability of a "state of nature" between states (in which there is at best only an extremely limited place for international law), *or* we strive for a centralized "world-state," possessing homogeneity and thus capable of functioning effectively as a coherent political entity. Because Schmitt, like more recent Realist theorists, considers the latter option both unlikely and fundamentally unattractive, he ultimately leaves us with a bleak picture of international politics in which the "real possibility of physical killing" necessarily continues to play a central role.[35]

Yet many of the more impressive defenses of liberal international law, and institutions like the League of Nations and United Nations, provocatively suggest that this formulation of the task at hand is fundamentally inaccurate. Schmitt's conceptual dogmatism means that he fails adequately to engage such views fully. For example, Schmitt delights in mocking Kelsen's vision of an international legal order in which traditional conceptions of state sovereignty have become anachronistic, but he fails to acknowledge some of the subtleties of Kelsen's account of international law. At least at some junctures in his career, Kelsen clearly shared some of Schmitt's skepticism about the likelihood of an emerging world state. At the same time, Kelsen struggled to identify the possibility of "transitional stages" in legal development between the violence-ridden "state of nature" and a full-scale international system of legislation and judiciary. Drawing a series of fascinating parallels to legal evolution in the domestic arena, Kelsen in 1940 argued that contemporary international law needs to be described as a system of "primitive law" possessing many of the same attributes as relatively underdeveloped, decentralized systems of law. In this view, it is simply historically inaccurate to collapse the concept of law and the existence of a centralized lawmaker. Core elements of the former long functioned in many legal cultures without the latter, as the obvious example of customary law suggests. Even in an underdeveloped and incomplete system of international law lacking a central sovereign, Kelsen notes, sanctions do exist. In a manner akin to primitive systems of law familiar from the European past, the application of these sanctions tends to be decentralized (that is, it remains in the hands of individual states that maintain war-making powers) and relatively irregular in character. Nonetheless, it is wrong to believe that the absence of an international sovereign dooms us to a situation of utter lawlessness.[36]

Kelsen's theory is *not* the final word on the matter. Nonetheless, it is striking that so many of Schmitt's criticisms can be interpreted as attacks on elements of liberal international law that liberals themselves rightly have considered evidence of the *underdeveloped* character of existing international law. Liberals, of course, have long led the battle against vague and open-ended legal norms; Locke, for example, famously warned of the dangers of "indeterminate resolutions" in the law. From a classical liberal perspective, the persistence of such norms within international law could be taken simply as (obvious) evidence of its unfinished character.[37] In a similar vein, it is important to note that many international jurists have rightly questioned the "legal" status of the Monroe Doctrine, arguing that its elastic form and employment as an instrument of American imperialism meshes poorly with a defensible conception of the international legal system.[38] Conveniently, Schmitt simply dismisses concerns of this type; for him, the fact that the Americans rely on the Monroe Doctrine is evidence enough of its "legal" character.[39]

What of Schmitt's suggestion that radical indeterminacy is an inherent feature of international law, even when relatively clear-cut norms are at hand? Of course, this is a complex matter. Yet at least one element of Schmitt's own reflections suggests that such indeterminacy might be reduced. To the extent that Schmitt attributes legal indeterminacy to the existence of vast de facto inequalities between political "lions" and "mice," we might interpret his argument as a critique of a *superficial* form of liberal legalism that wrongly ignores the obvious problems posed by vast inequalities in the international arena. If the existence of "lions" and "mice" is one main source in the international arena of legal indeterminacy, then those of us committed to the extension of the rule of law to the international arena can draw a positive lesson from Schmitt's critique distinct from his own: our legalistic instincts can be satisfied only if we finally drive the "lions" from the international arena, in short, by reducing the de facto material, military, and political inequalities among states. In that case, Schmitt's theory reminds us of the basic soundness of the insight that the rule of law needs to take the form of what Schmitt's chief social democratic rival in Weimar, Herman Heller, described as the *social* rule of law.[40] In the international arena, just as in the sphere of domestic politics, the effective operation of the formalities of the rule of law requires a relatively substantial degree of factual equality.[41]

Does Schmitt propose an alternative to the liberal international order? Although occasionally nostalgic for the days of the Holy Alliance, Schmitt's Weimar writings never sketch out a clear alternative to the purported evils of "Geneva and Versailles." Nonetheless, his pre-1933 comments about the

Monroe Doctrine point clearly toward the makings of Schmitt's subsequent National Socialist theory of international law. In this area of Schmitt's thinking as well, his Nazi-era theorizing builds directly on his Weimar ideas about legal indeterminacy.

As we have seen, Schmitt considers the Monroe Doctrine an essential component of modern American imperialism. But his assessment of the Monroe Doctrine is by no means purely negative. On the contrary, Schmitt can barely restrain his enthusiasm for this "astonishing political achievement of the United States."[42] In 1932 he bluntly asserts that it would be wrongheaded to consider the Monroe Doctrine a form of mean-spirited, inferior "cleverness and Machiavellianism."[43] On the contrary, the Monroe Doctrine is of "world-historical significance," a perfect manifestation of a "real and great imperialism."[44] The Americans have taught the rest of the world that the essence of modern imperialism is the manipulation of elastic legal concepts for the sake of swallowing up small and medium-sized states whose sovereignty is unlikely to survive the rapid economic and technological transformations of our era; the possibility that Germany might join their ranks clearly worries Schmitt. The Americans have brilliantly employed the Monroe Doctrine to reveal the future face of international relations: the world is destined to be carved up into a small group of "huge complexes," encompassing entire continents or more, in which a single political entity exercises de facto sovereignty over its neighbors.[45] The United States' domination of the Americas represents the future of international relations everywhere. In part, this has been achieved because the vocabulary and categories of American liberalism have become hegemonic in much of the world: "A people is only conquered when it subjects itself to an alien vocabulary and alien concepts of law, particularly international law."[46] American political hegemony rests on an uncritical acceptance by the world community of a set of inherently imperialistic liberal categories.

Even in the Weimar period, for Schmitt the real question is which countries are likely to gain membership to the elite group of "huge complexes" destined to dominate the globe. Although pessimistic in 1932 that Germany would prove up to the task at hand, Schmitt's envious glance here at the American achievement already says a great deal about his underlying aspirations: "as a German" examining the Monroe Doctrine, Schmitt comments, "I can only have the feeling of being a beggar in rags talking about the riches and valuables of strangers."[47]

Within a few years of the Nazi takeover, Schmitt would argue that it was possible for Germany to trade in her beggar's rags for a share of imperial glory. To that episode in our story I now must turn.

III

Extensive scholarship on National Socialist theories of international law convincingly demonstrates that Nazi lawyers during the 1930s were faced with the impossible task of trying "to reconcile the irreconcilable."[48] On the one hand, political opportunism compelled recourse to many of the traditional categories of modern international law. Hitler's removal of Germany from the League of Nations, German rearmament, and the repossession of the Saar and Rhineland areas were justified, both in popular and academic discourse, by appealing to a relatively traditional conception of an international order consisting of equal, independent, and indivisible sovereign states: reliance on the traditional discourse of modern international law performed the vital function of easing legitimate fears outside Germany about Hitler's true intentions. If German remilitarization were simply an attempt to salvage a sovereignty acknowledged by many to have been unfairly undermined by the Versailles Treaty, what possibly could be so disagreeable about it?

At the same time, Nazi lawyers were supposed to rely on the foundations of the National Socialist *Weltanschauung* to construct an alternative to modern universalistic conceptions of international law. Accordingly, many of them rushed to embrace racist and anti-Semitic ideas in order to discredit liberal international law, just as their colleagues in the areas of public and civil law were busily debunking liberal formal law in the name of the "substantial" law of the German *Volksgemeinschaft*. This more radical strand in Nazi international law theory in the 1930s generally culminated in what John Herz early on perceptively characterized as a "pluralistic dissolution of uniform international law," in which general norms within international law were taken to be inconsistent with ethnic and racial difference.[49] Nazi racism and anti-Semitism meshed poorly with the more traditional features of Nazi legal discourse: notions of racial and ethnic inequality, for example, clearly conflicted with the conception of the formal equality of all states, just as they clashed with liberal concepts of formal equality within public or civil law. Predictably, Nazi international law from the 1930s proved tension-ridden and inconsistent. Too often, the blatant racism and anti-

Semitism of Nazi international law doctrine threatened to undermine its politically opportune traditionalist moments, for such traditional features often relied, if only implicitly, on modern universalistic moral and political ideals.

Carl Schmitt's contributions to a theory of Nazi international law between 1933 and 1938 exhibit precisely this intellectually enigmatic quest "to reconcile the irreconcilable." Like many of his colleagues, Schmitt appealed to traditional conceptions of state sovereignty in order to provide a justification for Hitler's main foreign policy moves during the 1930s, and Schmitt missed no opportunity to praise Hitler and his guidance of National Socialist foreign policy.[50] Simultaneously, the "pluralistic dissolution of uniform international law" unavoidably occupies a central place in Schmitt's reflections as a result of his enthusiastic endorsement of Nazi racism and anti-Semitism.

In *National Socialism and International Law* (1934), Schmitt polemicizes against universalistic models of international law by demanding an alternative that would rest unambiguously on the Nazi view that there are different racial "types" [*Arten*] of human beings and thus different "types" of human communities.[51] Schmitt's ethnicist arguments here serve the same purposes they perform in his parallel reflections on public and private law from this period. *National Socialism and International Law* criticizes "reactionary" and "nihilist" juriprudential views, according to which the radical indeterminacy of international liberal law renders *any* system of interstate legal relations worthless.[52] For Schmitt, those emphasizing the radical indeterminacy of liberal law correctly perceive that formalistic liberal legalism generates nothing but legal "chaos," but they risk condoning this sad state of affairs by failing to appreciate the possibility of a postliberal legal paradigm able to overcome the crisis of legal indeterminacy.[53] As was discussed in chapter 5, Schmitt believed that legal indeterminacy could be counteracted by situating legal devices within an ethnically homogeneous community and an accompanying corps of jurists at home having its special "instincts" and trained in its particular modes of thought. From this perspective, indeterminacy within international law is chiefly a product of the liberal failure to recognize the dependence of an effective legal system on a common ethnic and racial "concrete order." Although the heterogeneous League of Nations inevitably suffers from the worst ills of legal indeterminacy, a regional alternative, resting on the ethnic and racial similarities of some European peoples, allegedly could guarantee a measure of legal deter-

minacy among a (select) group of European states: "An authentic League
of European peoples can only be successfully grounded by acknowledging
the problem of ethnic substance [*völkischen Substanz*] and by resting on the
national and ethnic relatedness [*nationale und völkischen Verwandschaft*] of
these European peoples" composing its membership.[54] Although he is conveniently vague about exactly *which* peoples are to constitute this new system, let alone which form its relations to ethnically distinct peoples is to
take, Schmitt in the mid-1930s is unambiguous about two points: the Soviet Union is not an authentically European power, and the "substance" of
this new system of regional law has to be determined by the Germans.[55]

Not surprisingly, Schmitt's formulations from this period are mired in
contradiction. He delights in declaring that the anti-universalistic character
of Nazi law renders it "non-imperialistic and nonaggressive," and thus a
dramatic intellectual and practical advance over both liberal law and Bolshevism, whose own universalistic features mean that it exhibits imperialistic qualities as well.[56] For Schmitt, the anti-imperialistic character of
German law is assured in part by its anti-Semitic and racist attributes: if
liberal universalism is inherently imperialistic, then the only answer to it
can take the form of a rigorous *anti-universalism* along the lines sketched out
by National Socialism. In this spirit, Schmitt praises German law because it
starts with the "fact" of ethnic difference and is merely concerned with the
"defensive" task of protecting "German blood" (!).[57] In contrast to liberalism, it thereby refuses to force one particular conception of humanity upon
its neighbors; liberal concepts of universal equality posit a basic sameness
among human beings, and liberalism hence lends itself to imperialism, as
exhibited by busybody liberal outrage at Germany's legitimate experimen-
tation in racial legislation. In this view, the anti-imperialistic character of
Nazi law manifests itself most clearly in the principle that "reciprocal respect" should characterize relations between distinct ethnic groups. Pace
liberalism, a belief in the existence of inherent ethnic differences hardly
necessitates imperialistic relations between distinct ethnic and racial groups.

But what exactly is the basis of this "reciprocal respect"? The reader
will search Schmitt's writings from this period in vain for an adequate
grounding for it. Contra Schmitt, the mere fact of ethnic difference hardly
provides an adequate justification for the suggestion that *all* ethnic groups
are worthy of respect; only some (modern, universalistic) conception of
basic human equality arguably is capable of justifying a position of this type.
What happens when a particular "folk" declares that its particular nature

requires it to dominate others? Schmitt has no answer to this question, in part because the great achievement of National Socialist law in his view lies precisely in the fact that it finally has freed Germany from the suffocating tentacles of modern universalism.

Schmitt's emphasis on the alleged anti-imperialism of National Socialist law corresponds to the underlying logic of his reflections from this period on modern war. Radicalizing his initial Weimar-era reflection on liberalism's "discriminatory concept of war," Schmitt now suggestively describes a Germany besieged by imperialistic powers that *already* have launched an attack on her territorial integrity. At precisely that historical juncture when Hitler's foreign policy took an increasingly expansionist tone, Schmitt provides a corresponding justification for Nazi belligerence.

Embellishing his earlier critique of the League of Nations, Schmitt again underlines the ways in which liberal international law blurs any meaningful distinction between war and peace. Intervention under the auspices of international law is a humanitarian "police action," even if it takes a bloody form, whereas relatively mild forms of nonviolent opposition to the League are criminalized: if a German military band in the occupied Rhineland plays a military hymn on a Sunday afternoon, Schmitt sarcastically comments, the indeterminate clauses of the Versailles Treaty allow the Allies to describe the action as a military "attack" on the League itself.[58] Schmitt now takes the additional step of arguing that this conceptual confusion in liberal international law corresponds to a real state of affairs in contemporary central Europe. Because Western liberals have relied on legal devices (the Versailles Treaty, the League of Nations, the Kellogg Pact) to mask their assault on German sovereignty, and because modern war making now clearly involves propagandistic and economic instruments (economic sanctions, for example) long employed against Germany, it is absurd to claim that the Allies succeeded in reestablishing "peace" in Germany after 1918.[59] The Allies have merely been employing more subtle (and effective) instruments of war making since 1918; Schmitt's analysis seems to suggest that World War I has yet (in 1937!) to come to a close. The villain here is Woodrow Wilson, whom Schmitt considers responsible for the hypocrisies of liberal international law and its "discriminatory concept of war."[60] And, at least after 1937 (when relations between Britain and Germany rapidly deteriorate), the British are described as the inventors of the horrors of modern total war. It is they who allegedly have been most consistent in criminalizing those who dare to question the hypocrisies of liberalism. According to Schmitt, peace-loving peoples have more to fear from English liberalism than from the German "total state" established by Hitler.[61]

But Germany is not simply under attack by Anglo-American liberalism and its dangerous universalistic, left-wing second cousin, Soviet Bolshevism. Even the purportedly neutral powers are now Germany's existential foes. In a series of writings in 1937 and 1938 on the problem of neutrality, Schmitt vehemently argues that genuine neutrality is simply inconsistent with participation in the League of Nations, or any of the other institutions of modern liberal international law, given their inherently imperialistic character. If the League of Nations is nothing but the latest weapon of the liberal "total war" undertaken for the sake of a fictional universal humanity, then neutrality is impossible within the confines of League membership. Although professing neutrality, even mild-mannered Switzerland thus has joined the ranks of Germany's foes through its membership in the League.[62]

By 1938 and 1939, Schmitt's message to his countrymen was plain enough: Nazi aggression in Europe represents nothing more than a *defensive*, anti-imperialistic battle, legitimately undertaken for the sake of protecting the "ethnic difference" of the Germans and "related" European peoples. Needless to say, this interpretation meshed neatly with that of the Nazi party leadership.

IV

On April 1, 1939, Schmitt gave a lecture on international law at the University of Kiel that immediately gained wide attention among both academics and the general public.[63] Major daily newspapers provided positive reports about Schmitt's comments, and Schmitt's ideas soon became the object of an intense debate among Nazi jurists.[64] As noted in chapter 5, Schmitt had experienced a political and intellectual setback at the hands of academic rivals and elements within the SS in 1936. Schmitt's 1939 lecture, which offered the outlines of a specifically National Socialist theory of what he described as the *Grossraum* (greater region), represented his revenge against his detractors. Once again, Schmitt was able to reestablish his reputation as one of Nazi Germany's leading jurists; once again, Schmitt was in the public eye. Schmitt's writings during this period reveal the depth of his commitment to National Socialism. Schmitt's post-1938 writings on international law are hardly the writings of an "unpolitical" intellectual scared by the specter of a German concentration camp.[65] Well into the 1940s, Schmitt enthusiastically contributed to the construction of a distinctly Nazi legal order because he firmly believed that only the Nazis could overcome the jurisprudential ills of modern liberalism.[66]

As previously discussed, Schmitt's Weimar-era reflections on American imperialism suffer from a fundamental tension. On the one hand, Schmitt considers the Americans culpable for many of the hypocrisies of contemporary liberal international law. On the other hand, Schmitt is clearly envious of the success of the Americans. Schmitt's late Nazi-era essays are primarily occupied with the task of overcoming this tension. In 1939 Schmitt again turns to the experience of American imperialism. But now he struggles to overcome the ambiguities of his previous account in order to make use of the American case as a justification for Nazi expansionism in Eastern and Central Europe. Schmitt's message in 1939 is a simple one: Germany can join the ranks of the world's great powers by developing her own version of the Monroe Doctrine. If the Nazis are to succeed in making sure that Germany joins the ranks of the handful of "huge complexes" destined to swallow up small and medium-sized states, they need to learn from the foreign policy successes of the greatest of the world's great powers, the United States.

Of course, this undertaking raises obvious problems for Schmitt in light of his previous emphasis on the *liberal* character of American imperialism. How are the Germans to emulate the Americans without succumbing to the (alleged) ills of legal liberalism? In order to answer this question, Schmitt now juxtaposes the "original" Monroe Doctrine to its subsequent imperialistic distortions. According to an argument repeated throughout this period in his career, the former assures American hegemony in the Americas but allegedly lacks most of the ills of modern forms of liberal imperialism. In contrast, the latter rest on an expansive universalistic liberalism and provide a justification for American capitalism and its unceasing quest for foreign markets. Whereas the late Monroe Doctrine (which Schmitt associates with the "big stick" policies of Theodore Roosevelt) offers nothing worth copying by the Nazis, elements of the "original" Monroe Doctrine present a positive model, though hardly one deserving of blind imitation.

First, the early Monroe Doctrine allegedly possesses a genuine political character, deriving from its acknowledgment of the life-or-death existential threat posed to the fledgling American republics by the monarchical, antidemocratic Holy Alliance. Second, it rests on a "political idea," namely, a militant commitment to a particular (liberal democratic) mode of political existence. Third (and probably most importantly within Schmitt's gloss), it was primarily a geopolitical principle, meaning for Schmitt that it insisted that "alien" (that is, European) powers had no legitimate place in the Americas.[67] As the most powerful American state, the United States necessarily monopolized the task of warding off alien powers. Revealingly, Schmitt not only considers this legitimate, but also tends to underline its (supposedly) defensive characteristics.

In this account, only at the end of the nineteenth century did the Americans mistakenly transform the Monroe Doctrine into an instrument of American economic domination and a legitimization for intervening, willy-nilly, in the affairs of extra-American powers. Although the Monroe Doctrine has always possessed liberal democratic elements, it was not until the end of the nineteenth century that the Americans *subordinated* the Monroe Doctrine's sensible geopolitical orientation to the missionary impulses of an expansionist, universalistic liberalism aimed at achieving an American-dominated capitalist free market and system of international law. Only at that juncture did the Monroe Doctrine's liberal universalistic moments reign supreme and American imperialism become a force to be reckoned with on the world scene. For Schmitt, Great Britain plays a central role in this transformation. By joining hands politically and spiritually with the British (for example, in World War I), the Americans ultimately inherited British dreams of a truly universal empire that would span the entire globe. Supposedly, the close ties of the United States to her chief liberal ally in Europe merely exacerbated the worst imperialistic tendencies of American liberalism.[68]

What form should a German Monroe Doctrine take? Most of Schmitt's writings from 1939 and the early 1940s try to answer this question. For obvious reasons, Schmitt repeatedly insists that the German rendition of the Monroe Doctrine needs to take the form of a creative reworking of the original. He clearly wants nothing to do with any of its liberal democratic features.

First, the Germans should build on the American insight that open-ended, elastic legal concepts are essential in the sphere of international politics. In contrast to the Americans, however, Schmitt situates these concepts within a "concrete order" of "specifically located, living with and next to each other and respecting each other" peoples [*Jede Ordnung sesshafter, mit-*

und nebeinander lebender, gegenseitig sich achtende Völker].[69] For Schmitt, a concrete order of this type must also exclude ethnically alien [*artfremde*] peoples; it seems that mutual respect is possible only among ethnically "related" peoples.[70] Even at this late stage in his Nazi career, Schmitt continues to hint at the possibility of developing a postliberal legal system by means of establishing a political community based on ethnic and racial "relatedness."[71]

Second, just as the Americans succeeded in developing a legal vocabulary appropriate to the particular needs of American liberal democracy, so, too, should the Germans formulate a legal theory resting on the special needs of the National Socialist *Volkgemeinschaft*. For this reason, Schmitt delights in relying on concepts and terms that lack any easy equivalent in other languages. By implication, only those in possession of authentic German "instincts" and mores are likely to understand them fully; Schmitt thereby builds on his claim from the mid-1930s that the ethnically derived "spirit" [*Geist*] of those who seek to interpret any given legal concept is always decisive. The key category of his theory is the complex term *Grossraum*, which literally means "great room" or "large space," but is often translated as "region" or "zone."[72] Most advantageous about this idiosyncratic German expression for Schmitt is that it illuminates the difference between his theory and traditional forms of "Jewish" liberal legalism. Embellishing familiar anti–Semitic arguments, Schmitt again argues that liberal jurisprudence was disproportionately influenced by cosmopolitan Jewish thinkers (in particular, Kelsen) who allegedly suffered from the lack of a "natural relationship to a concrete area of land."[73] The formalistic orientation of liberal legalism stems from the special needs of a people that has always lacked a territorially definable political "home" of its own. Whereas liberal jurisprudence thus absurdly tries to construct a system of universal international law valid for all places and all times, Schmitt argues that Nazi international law, in the spirit of the early Monroe Doctrine, must give a central place to the geographical and territorial situatedness of law. Allegedly, the term *Grossraum* best captures this regional or geographical facet of legal experience. In a similar vein, Schmitt insists on describing the dominant power within every *Grossraum* with the untranslatable *Reich*. Whereas expressions derived from the Latin *Imperium* allegedly connote assimilationist, "melting pot" [*Schmelztiegel*] aspirations alien to Nazi conceptions of ethnic homogeneity, Schmitt suggests, the German term *Reich* is free of such unwanted connotations.[74]

In short, *international* law in the literal sense of the term is impossible. At best, one can hope to achieve legal forms linking neighboring, "related" ethnic communities located in rough proximity to one another.[75] For Schmitt this insight implies the illegitimacy of legal intervention into any *Grossraum* by "alien" peoples located outside of it. In this fashion as well, the Monroe Doctrine is exemplary. Just as the United States long insisted that European powers should stay out of American affairs, so, too, should Europeans now insist that alien [*raumfremde*] powers—most importantly, the United States—mind their own business by avoiding involvement in European affairs. Schmitt thereby appeals to the Americans to respect their own foreign policy traditions by acknowledging the legitimacy of the emerging German Monroe Doctrine. Of course, Schmitt's timing here could not have been more opportune: he formulates this argument just as Nazi armies commence their drive for world conquest.[76]

Schmitt also argues that the German *Grossraum* theory, like the early Monroe Doctrine, needs to be guided by a distinct "political idea." But here the American example is only of minimal value. Schmitt bluntly declares that the early Monroe Doctrine's political commitments are now absurd, given the anachronistic character of liberal democracy in the face of modern economic and technological developments; Schmitt accepts the irrelevance of liberal democracy as self-evident.[77] The Germans should also employ the category of "freedom" in order to guarantee their hegemony in Europe. But they should advance a truly modern notion of what Schmitt now describes as "ethnic freedom" [*völkische Freiheit*]. In this view, National Socialism wages a heroic battle against assimilationist liberal ideals of citizenship by positing a political alternative capable of protecting the singularity and particularity of distinct ethnic groups. In Schmitt's argument here, the "liberty" to have one's ethnic and racial difference respected is a central goal of National Socialism.[78] For this reason, the Nazi *Grossraum* theory has an obvious existential foe: universal liberalism not only ignores the fundamental problem of ethnic difference, but also seeks a global community in which the need for distinct *Grossräume*, each possessing legal devices particular to its special ethnic character, is obscured.

Although acknowledging the supposed virtues of competing models of National Socialist international law, Schmitt continually implies that his model alone captures the essence of National Socialism.[79] At first glance, this may seem surprising. However problematic on its own terms, Schmitt's discourse of "respect" for ethnic difference seems distinct from cruder ideas of racial hierarchy advanced by rival Nazi ideologues. Yet precisely because Schmitt's argument here is more subtle than that of competing Nazi concepts of racial inequality, it potentially is all the more dangerous. Schmitt may have been a "better" Nazi than some of his rivals precisely because he offers a relatively sophisticated defense of National Socialist imperialism. His poison is so deadly precisely because it initially may not taste like poison.

First, Schmitt bluntly asserts that Jews in central and eastern Europe constitute an "alien" body.[80] They are undeserving of "ethnic freedom" in the first place. Second, he is notoriously vague when discussing which groups are "ethnically related" and thus rightful members of a *Grossraum* based on the principle of "ethnic freedom"; Schmitt himself is clearly primarily concerned with justifying Nazi intervention on behalf of ethnic German minorities in central and eastern Europe.[81] Despite the rhetoric of "ethnic freedom," it amounts in practical terms in his writings to nothing more than a defense of military intervention in the name of "saving" German minorities in Europe from the purported horrors of the "melting point" of ethnic assimilationism. (Of course, this was one of the most infamous justifications used by Hitler to dismantle the state system of central and eastern Europe; Schmitt's arguments here again neatly correspond to the political imperatives of Nazi foreign policy.) In light of the broader structure of his argument, none of this is a surprise. For Schmitt, the Germans are, in fact, a "superior" people in a vital sense of the term. Schmitt never hesitates to justify German predominance in the European *Grossraum* that he hoped the Nazis would achieve; supposedly, the Germans alone can establish a superior *Reich* capable of overseeing the "ethnic freedom" of subordinate peoples. As will shortly become evident, Schmitt believes that the era of the modern nation-state is rapidly coming to a close. Nonetheless, he still argues that some indispensable elements of modern statehood need to be preserved by political entities in order to avoid being decimated by their rivals. In particular, successful political communities need to develop impressive organizational and bureaucratic capacities in order to grapple with the dictates of an increasingly complex social and economic environment; of course, this was one of the main themes of his theory of the "total state" in the early 1930s. Just as the United States was long able to rely on its organizational superiority in the Americas to act as a "guardian" of its vision of (liberal) freedom, Schmitt suggests, so, too, should Germany now take advantage of its (purported) political and organizational talents to become guardian of its own vision of "ethnic freedom" in Europe.[82]

In a 1942 essay on the particularities of French legal culture, Schmitt asserts that different nationalities tend to possess different attributes and traits.[83] When read in light of Schmitt's emphasis on the purported superiority of German organizational capacities and suggestions that such differences are ethnically grounded,[84] his theoretical reflections ultimately risk becoming nothing more than a complicated way of declaring that Germans are now Europe's "natural" rulers. What evidence does Schmitt adduce for Germany's organizational superiority? As the German scholar Hasso Hofmann has commented, if "one asks for a positive justification for the German claim for political leadership [in Schmitt's theory], the findings are quite unsatisfying."[85] For Schmitt, Hitler's "successes" in the sphere of foreign policy seem to provide their own justification: German organizational superiority is demonstrated by means of German military and economic resurgence.[86] Interestingly, precisely where Schmitt's recourse to the early Monroe Doctrine potentially contradicts a main component of Nazi imperialism, namely, the German annexation of foreign territory, Schmitt sides with the Nazis. Recall Schmitt's emphasis in the Weimar period that the Monroe Doctrine acknowledged the formal sovereignty of Latin and South American states by refusing to engage in the open annexation of weaker states. In his Nazi-era attempt to build on the legacy of the Americans, Schmitt not only downplays this point, but also now openly argues that the idea of the legal equality of all sovereign states is nothing more than another moldy liberal myth worth discarding. Like the idea of the formal equality of all persons, the formal equality of all states is a silly fiction.[87]

Schmitt's concept of the *Grossraum* corresponds to the political needs of Nazi racial imperialism. But it simultaneously builds on a series of sociological half-truths about contemporary trends toward ever more centralized political and economic modes of organization. Schmitt's late Nazi writings repeat his claim from the Weimar period that most small and medium-sized states are now being systematically robbed of their sovereign status. Nowadays, the real players on the international arena consist of a handful of political giants. What drives this movement? Schmitt suggests that its sources are primarily economic and technological. Modern technology and contemporary economic organization have outstripped the nation-state, just as modern capitalism rendered the political decentralization of medieval and Renaissance Europe anachronistic. Existing political boundaries too often hinder the rational exploitation of economic and technological devices. Markets and economic networks are now supranational in character; radio allows political propaganda to reach the homes of foreigners living thousands of miles away from the voice of the broadcaster, while modern air warfare means that borders can be penetrated and foreign cities decimated within the blink of an eye. In this context, most existing state borders have little relation to the economic and technical possibilities of a world that seems to shrink in size daily, and modern nation-states are destined to be replaced by "greater regions"—in Schmitt's terminology, *Grossräume*—better attuned to the centralizing tendencies of our era and the "space revolution" [*Raumrevolution*] characteristic of it.[88]

Schmitt makes sure to distinguish his views from those of liberals who dream of an international market economy. In the language of contemporary social science, Schmitt endorses *regionalization*, but not *globalization*. That is, he envisions a world carved up into a handful of relatively separate political, legal, ethnic, and economic blocs, but he is deeply hostile to any idea of a truly global political and economic community.[89] His reasons for this preference are manifold, including, as noted, a hostility to ethnic "assimilation." But at least one consideration is primarily sociological: he believes that a truly globalized economy is unavoidably "chaotic" because it is inherently "hostile to planning" [*planfeindlich*].[90] As we saw in chapter 4, Schmitt is a proponent of a form of state interventionist capitalism. Yet he considers it unlikely that such intervention can prove effective if forced to tackle the problems of a truly global political economy. While regionalized political units larger than the contemporary nation-state can be "organized" economically and technologically quite well, a truly global political economy is likely to overwhelm existing organizational capacities. Thus, so much of Schmitt's seemingly anticapitalist rhetoric during this period turns out to be nothing but hostility to a *specific* form of competitive, free-market, laissez-faire capitalism, which in Schmitt's eyes is tied inextricably to the interests of Britain and the United States. Schmitt himself prefers an authoritarian mode of organized capitalism. But precisely because contemporary capitalism requires organization by political authorities, it makes most sense to conceive of the approaching global "order" as one consisting of a handful of competing regional *Grossräume*, but hardly a world state.

V

I have already tried to suggest that Schmitt's theory of the *Grossraum* meshed neatly with the aims of Nazi imperialism. Indeed, Schmitt himself actively sought to justify virtually every twist and turn in Nazi foreign policy by means of it. During 1939 and 1940, Schmitt employs the concept of the *Grossraum* in order to suggest the existence of a set of common interests between Nazism and the United States against Great Britain, to justify the Soviet-Nazi Pact, and to defend Japanese imperialism in the Pacific.[91] After the United States joins the Allied cause and Hitler invades the Soviet Union, it is then used to defend the Nazi war against both countries.[92] In light of our exegesis here, the enormous pliability of Schmitt's theory is hardly surprising. Schmitt hopes to formulate an elastic, open-ended set of concepts capable of guaranteeing German supremacy in Europe. As he noted during the Weimar period in his initial discussion of the Monroe Doctrine, *every "great imperialism" needs such concepts in order to justify situation-specific modes of political action required by the rapidly changing dictates of Realpolitik.*[93] Schmitt's intellectual "accomplishment" in the late 1930s and 1940s was that he developed a specifically National Socialist theory of international law that nonetheless provided the Nazis with plenty of room to engage in just those maneuvers required by an emerging imperialistic power. Schmitt offered a theory containing Nazi anti-Semitic elements, while making sure to avoid unduly circumventing the awesome discretionary powers required by the Nazi political leadership in its quest to conquer Europe.

In chapter 5, I criticized Schmitt's view that legal determinacy, even in the context of vague and open-ended norms, could be salvaged by establishing an ethnically homogeneous political community and "rank" of jurists. Schmitt's own manipulation of the *Grossraum* idea for the sake of defending virtually every Nazi foreign policy move underlines the bankrupt character of this agenda. In this theory, international law is reduced to a mask veiling the momentary dictates of racial imperialism. Schmitt accuses liberalism of suffering from a radical indeterminacy that renders legal experience chaotic and even arbitrary. His emphasis on the indeterminacy of liberal international law, though overstated, can hardly be dismissed out of hand; much international law does suffer from this ill. But Schmitt's own antidote to liberal jurisprudence hardly resolves the problem at hand. Here as well, the only "determinacy" achieved by Schmitt's alternative to liberalism is that guaranteed by the fact that he extends "the industrial methods of taylorism . . . into the realm of statecraft in order to get the most precise answer to the question of how the will of the political leadership can be put into practical effect as speedily as possible."[94] In Schmitt's legal theory, international law is systematically reduced to a direct and unmediated plaything of Nazi *Realpolitik*. The ills of existing liberal international law no doubt stem in part from the fact that its legal character too often is undermined by the need to make concessions to the great powers; the openended character of much international law derives from this source. But Schmitt's Nazi alternative simply makes a virtue out of this vice. His system of international law lacks any of the traditional virtues of liberal law—for example, the predictability that derives from the fact that public, general norms should apply to all members of the international community—for the sake of achieving a "determinacy" that consists in nothing but unmediated subservience to those who happen to exercise power most effectively in the international arena.

Can Schmitt legitimately claim to build on the legacy of the Monroe Doctrine? An impressive body of postwar German-language scholarship on Schmitt's theory of international law rightly argues that his recourse to American foreign policy represents a poor starting point for the theory of the *Grossraum*. Schmitt badly exaggerates the geopolitical facets of the early Monroe Doctrine. At least initially, the Monroe Doctrine was clearly a defensive measure undertaken against the *expansion* of European colonialism in the Americas, but it was long widely seen as consistent with *existing* European political and economic privileges on the American continents. European intervention in the American sphere was pervasive throughout the nineteenth century. In fact, the dominant power in South America until the end of the nineteenth century was probably Great Britain, not the United States. In contradistinction to Schmitt's *Grossraum* theory, American foreign policy during most of the nineteenth century hardly resisted *all* European intervention within its sphere, and the United States was not what Schmitt would have described as a dominant *Reich* within the Americas. Moreover, the early Monroe Doctrine was greeted warmly by the United States' sister republics in the Americas, in part because its liberal democratic ideals, at least initially, were more than an ideological cover for American political and economic hegemony. American states hoping to free themselves from colonial tutelage thus enthusiastically endorsed President Monroe's response to the Holy Alliance's ominous declaration of intent to strengthen counterrevolutionary forces in the Americas. During much of the nineteenth century, the Monroe Doctrine was also fundamentally universalistic, at least in the sense of resting on an Enlightenment-inspired belief in the superiority of liberal democratic legal and political forms. In the final analysis, it had little in common with Schmitt's *Grossraum* theory, let alone the Nazi butchery condoned by it.[95]

Nonetheless, Schmitt's exegesis is partly correct on one important point. At the end of the nineteenth century the Monroe Doctrine was reduced to a legal front for brutal forms of political and economic expansion. But Schmitt's analysis of the sources of this development is utterly wrongheaded. As we have seen, Schmitt attributes the imperialistic character of the "late" Monroe Doctrine in part to its embrace of universalistic liberal legal and political ideals. As a matter of fact, as interpreted by Theodore Roosevelt and defenders of American imperalism at the turn of the twentieth century, the Monroe Doctrine jettisoned the most defensible features of liberal universalism for Social Darwinism and crude concepts of racial inequality. Racial ideas, occasionally anticipating elements of those embraced by the Nazis and Schmitt in the 1930s and 1940s, took on a central role in American foreign policy precisely during that period that Schmitt accurately describes as imperialistic in character. Hannah Arendt was absolutely correct when she noted that "[i]f race thinking were a German invention, as it has sometimes been asserted, then 'German thinking' (whatever that might be) was victorious in many parts of the spiritual world long before the Nazis started their ill-fated attempt at world conquest." As Arendt rightly notes, "[racism] has been the powerful ideology of imperialistic policies since the turn of the century."[96] When Senator Albert J. Beveridge declared in 1900 that "God has made us adepts in government that we may administer government among savage and senile peoples," he was simply echoing sentiments then commonplace among America's ruling elite and her intellectual apologists.[97] One of the founders of American political science, John Burgess, argued at the end of the nineteenth century that only "Aryan peoples" possessed a talent for political order and organization, and thus the Americans (in Burgess's theory, an "Aryan" people, albeit one increasingly threatened by immigration from eastern and central Europe) could legitimately interpret the Monroe Doctrine as a call to gain political supremacy over the racially "inferior" masses composing much of the world's population.[98] Foreshadowing some components of Schmitt's theory, Burgess relied on the political myth of the inherent "political genius" of northern Europe; he then uses this myth to justify imperialism: "the temporary imposition of Teutonic order on unorganized, disorganized, or savage peoples for the sake of their own civilization and their incorporation in the world society" was justified in light of the fact that the "Teutons" represent the world's "great modern nation builders."[99] This racism was characteristically linked to a demand for "free markets" for American goods and capital, typically defended by means of the view that American capitalism had outgrown her national borders. To some extent anticipating Schmitt's view that modern economic and technological developments render the traditional nation-state anachronistic, American imperialism at the end of the nineteenth century rested on an explosive synthesis of expansionist capitalism and racism. It is no accident that it was during this period that direct territorial annexation (for example, Hawaii) was justified in part by appeal to the Monroe Doctrine, notwithstanding its manifest inconsistency with the spirit of President Monroe's original declaration.

Of course, Theodore Roosevelt was neither a fascist demagogue, nor was the American empire at century's end a Nazi *Grossraum*. The ills of American imperialism pale in comparison with the horrors of Nazi imperialism. The dangerous combination of racism and capitalism constitutive of modern imperialism has taken many different forms. As Arendt has shown in her classic *The Origins of Totalitarianism*, National Socialism built on elements of earlier varieties of imperialism, yet Nazism nonetheless represented a historical novelty. Patterns of thinking, institutions, and events essential to earlier forms of imperialism came to "reveal an altogether different meaning [within National Socialism] than what they stood for in the original context."[100] My point here simply is that Schmitt's gloss on the Monroe Doctrine conveniently obscures the manner in which the imperialism attributed to the "late" Monroe Doctrine anticipates some features of his *own Grossraum* theory. This blindspot is hardly surprising. If any period in the evolution of the Monroe Doctrine is reminiscent of Schmitt's *Grossraum* theory, it was that of the "late" Monroe Doctrine, when the liberal universalism despised by Schmitt took a backseat to the quest for profits and foreign plunder.

At many junctures during this study, I have suggested that Schmitt relies on historical myths in order to discredit his intellectual foes. He uses this ploy in his theory of the *Grossraum* as well. Schmitt's shocking defense of Nazi imperialism offers the clearest expression of its enormous political and intellectual dangers. In Schmitt's attack on liberal international law, historical fiction played a central role in preparing the way for the horrors of the Nazi war in Europe.

Epilogue to Part One

CARL SCHMITT IN THE AFTERMATH OF THE GERMAN CATASTROPHE

I n the first part of this study, I have tried to show that Carl Schmitt very early identified the central issue of twentieth-century legal theory, but that he wrongly believed that National Socialism offered the only real solution to it. Ultimately playing an important part in what Friedrich Meinecke famously described in 1946 as the "German catastrophe," Schmitt believed, well into the 1940s, that only Nazism offered an answer to the enigma of legal indeterminacy.

Did Schmitt revise his views following Germany's military defeat in 1945? Probably not. The overwhelming tone of Schmitt's postwar writings is fundamentally unrepentant. Schmitt's recently published diaries document the depth of his anti-Semitism well after the Nazi defeat.[1] Schmitt does occasionally critically comment on Hitler there, but his distaste for the emerging American-driven liberal hegemony in postwar Western Europe constitutes a more conspicuous component of his reflections.[2] Although free of the unrestrained anti-Semitic histrionics so pervasive in Schmitt's Nazi writings, his most important postwar contribution to legal theory, *The Nomos of the Earth in the International Law of the Jus Publicum Europaeum*, builds directly on the theory of the *Grossraum* discussed in chapter 6. Many of the basic arguments directed against "normativistic" Judaism in the Nazi period are now redirected against the United States.[3] His *The Situation of European Jurisprudence* (1950) similarly builds on Schmitt's ideas from the early and mid-1930s, especially the belief that a European "concrete order" might overcome the crisis of legal indeterminacy. The key argumentative shift is that Schmitt now leaves the *source* of postliberal legal determinacy undisclosed.[4] A short essay from the same year simply reiterates earlier criti-

175

cism of legal positivism in order to blame the rise of Nazism on Schmitt's liberal and democratic political and intellectual opponents.[5]

None of Schmitt's postwar writings suggests any regret or sense of responsibility on his part for the German catastrophe.[6] On the contrary, Schmitt clearly considered himself a victim not only of Nazism, but also of attempts to "reeducate" the Germans after the war.[7] Between 1945 and 1947, he spent more than a year in an American military jail (his American interrogators seem to have dismembered his personal library as well), and then Schmitt was banned from university teaching after the war. Throughout the remainder of his life, he clearly considered this punishment undeserved.

Schmitt was imprisoned because the Americans at first considered charging him at the Nuremberg Trials, before deciding to drop the matter because of the difficulty of linking Schmitt directly to Nazi atrocities. Ironically, Schmitt seems to have benefited from liberal jurisprudence's traditional preference for clarity and relative specificity in the definition of criminal acts. Yet General Lucius Clay hoped to punish the intellectual "masterminds" of Nazi Germany, and given Schmitt's prominent role among Germany's jurists, Schmitt was an obvious target.[8] In a series of exchanges with Robert Kempner, a German-Jewish refugee who played an important role in the American involvement in the Nuremberg Trials, Schmitt unequivocally denied any complicity in Nazism. Typically, his responses contain a number of (convenient) half-truths. Schmitt pointed out that his theory of the *Grossraum* was distinct from some competing Nazi theories of international law; he failed to mention that his own relatively complex ideas served his Nazi masters quite well. Schmitt also claimed that his *Grossraum* writings tend to avoid the crude Nazi discourse of "biological racism"; Schmitt conveniently forgot to note that his own theory of "ethnic freedom" [*völkische Freiheit*] corresponded neatly to Nazi foreign policy objectives, and certainly represented a form of ethnic and racial thinking containing terrible political implications. Moreover, Schmitt's conceptual framework for the *Grossraum* theory was always fundamentally anti-Semitic.[9]

Schmitt's defenders have long tried to exploit his suggestion at war's end that his status in the Nazi regime, at least after the 1936 feud with the SS, was akin to Benito Cereno's in Herman Melville's fascinating 1855 novella of that title. In Melville's story, slaves seize control of a Spanish slave ship and kill the captain and much of the crew. In his stead, they force, at risk of death, a surviving Spaniard, Benito Cereno, to "play" the role of captain in order to avoid detection when an American ship approaches the former slave ship. According to Schmitt's defenders, Schmitt, like Benito Cereno, had no real power among the Nazis after 1936. Germany, like the Spanish slave ship, had been seized by an irrational mob and a set of petty tyrants (Hitler and the Nazis). Akin to Cereno, Schmitt after 1936 was an ornament used by the regime, at the risk of harsh punishment, in order to gain a measure of intellectual respectability. Finally, Schmitt was "saved" by the Americans, who rightly squelched the political forces that threatened Schmitt's very existence.

Schmitt at one point does suggest an interpretation along these lines.[10] In light of our discussion of Schmitt's Nazi-era contributions here, however, there can be no question that it represents a desperate attempt at self-exculpation.

An alternative interpretation of Schmitt's highly ambivalent allusions to Benito Cereno is also possible. If I am not mistaken, this second reading is more in tune with the realities of Schmitt's Nazi-era activities.

When mentioning Benito Cereno in *Ex Captivitate Salus: Experiences from the Period 1945–47*, a book penned while imprisoned by the Americans, he was by no means thinking primarily of the role of intellectuals in Nazi Germany. In a revealing passage, he comments, "I am the last conscious representative of the *jus publicum Europaeum*, its last teacher and student in an existential sense, and I am experiencing its demise just as Benito Cereno experienced the journey of the pirate ship."[11] As we saw in chapter 6, Schmitt considered the United States responsible for destroying the traditional European system of interstate relations. In particular, Wilson's liberalism and its "discriminatory concept of war" allegedly undermined traditional European international law and generated the disorders of twentieth-century European politics; this is also one of the main themes of his postwar *The Nomos of the Earth in the International Law of the Jus Publicum Europaeum*, which Schmitt was probably working on when *Ex Captivitate Salus* was written. During the early 1940s, Schmitt also associated the United States with ethnic assimilationism. As we saw above, he believed that the Nazi quest for "ethnic freedom" offered a viable alternative to the liberal universalistic melting pot [*Schmelztiegel*]. When read in conjunction with Melville's story, Schmitt's comments, written within the walls of an American jail, take on fresh significance. Melville occasionally describes the slave ship in terms that could be read as anticipating Schmitt's own nightmares about liberal assimilationism. Melville makes a great deal of the racial composition of the ship, the *San Dominick*, repeatedly bringing attention to its mixed white, black, and "mulatto" crew: "the visitor was at once surrounded by a clamorous throng of whites and blacks, but the latter outnumbering the former more than could have been expected. . . . But, in one language, and as with one voice, all poured out a common tale of suffering."[12] Melville's description is clearly intended to fill his nineteenth-century North American reader with anxiety. The very name *San Dominick* is supposed to remind readers of the Jacobin-inspired slave rebellion of 1799 in Santo Domingo (Haiti).[13] Read in this light, Schmitt's employment of Melville is meant to describe Schmitt's experiences as a prisoner (both literally and metaphorically) of an ethnically and racially mixed *American* demos, now in control of the "ship" of European history. In this alternative reading, Schmitt is remarking critically, *not* about his place in the Nazi regime (which, in his view, tried unsuccessfully to counteract the American-led attack on the traditional European state system), but about his precarious status in an American-dominated Europe intent on pursuing a global, assimilationist economic and legal order. In Melville's story, the real captain of the rebel pirate ship, the tyrannical Babo, is described by Melville as an African who has "spent some years among the Spaniards."[14] In this respect as well, Schmitt's perception of his status in an American-dominated Germany parallels a crucial element of Melville's story. As his diaries reveal, Schmitt was obsessed during this period with the fear that American policy in postwar Germany was being significantly shaped by German-Jewish refugees who, in Schmitt's view, were returning to the continent to gain revenge against those, like Schmitt, who had led the courageous attack against "Jewish" normativism: "Precisely the assimilated Jew is the real enemy," Schmitt brutally comments in his diaries from after the war.[15] Reminiscent of the dangerous Babo in Melville's story, according to Schmitt, "assimilated" Jews now lead America's attack on Germany: "A very special master of the world, this poor Yankee, so fashionable with his ancient [*uralt*] Jews."[16]

Of course, Schmitt's reflections here are not only repulsive, but poorly informed as well. American policy in postwar Germany was chiefly determined by the imperatives of the Cold War, not by angry German Jews returning home to gain revenge on former Nazis.

The great irony of Schmitt's writings from the immediate postwar era is that his lifelong battle against formalistic legal liberalism now required him to defend some of the same legal devices that, just a few years earlier, he had denounced so ferociously. This predicament should come as no surprise to us: those threatened by the exercise of political power, rather than those who, like Schmitt during the Nazi period, engaged in its exercise, always have had the most to gain from the traditional formal protections provided by the rule of law. Facing the specter of Allied denazification, Schmitt immediately joined forces with those in Germany seeking a speedy conclusion to Allied "reeducation." Soon an outspoken defender of his old Nazi cronies' battle against Allied prosecution, Schmitt formulated a critique of the Nuremberg Trials in which he anticipated the main arguments employed against it in subsequent years by German conservatives.[17] Although Schmitt himself earlier viciously denounced the classical ideal of *nullum crimen, nulla poena sine lege* (no punishment without a preexisting statute),[18] he now appealed to the same principle in order to discredit the judicial prosecution of war criminals. A 1952 essay on Hobbes similiary criticizes retroactive lawmaking.[19] His postwar diaries speak critically of the use of vague, open-ended legal norms in the Nuremberg Trials, and a 1950 piece alludes appreciatively to Anglo-American conceptions of due process.[20] A 1949 newspaper article calls for a general amnesty for former Nazis.[21] Of course, during the Nazi period, Schmitt had enthusiastically praised the Nazi employment of vague, open-ended standards and had expressed no qualms about National Socialist forms of retroactive lawmaking.[22] National Socialism—Schmitt claimed—offered a world-historical solution to the inherent ills of "alien" Anglo-American liberal legal thought. In those days, Schmitt never said a word in favor of amnesty for those persecuted by the Nazis.

Having devoted his best years to trying to demonstrate the bankruptcy of liberal jurisprudence, Schmitt's postwar appeal to some elements of it necessarily rings hollow. In the face of the cautious (and ultimately limited) attempt by the Allies to denazify Germany, recourse to liberal jurisprudence proved opportune for Schmitt. But there is no textual evidence that his postwar experiences culminated in a fundamental revision of Schmitt's one-sided deconstruction of the liberal rule of law.

In contrast to Melville's Benito Cereno, who dies just after his liberation, Schmitt himself survived the "pirate ship" of the Federal Republic quite well: he reached the ripe old age of ninety-six. Although he was forbidden from teaching at German universities, and even though his most striking theoretical achievements were behind him, Schmitt continued to influence a sizable number of intellectuals in postwar West Germany.[23] As I hope to demonstrate in part 2 of this study, he also exercised a significant influence on postwar intellectual trends in the United States. The spirit of Carl Schmitt continues to haunt not only German courts and much German political discourse,[24] but political thinking in the United States as well.

Part Two

CARL SCHMITT IN AMERICA

7

CARL SCHMITT AND THE ORIGINS OF JOSEPH SCHUMPETER'S THEORY OF DEMOCRATIC ELITISM

I t is widely acknowledged that Joseph Schumpeter's democratic theory exercised tremendous influence on American political science immediately after World War II.[1] Less well known is that the genealogy of Schumpeter's "theory of democratic elitism" can be traced to a series of interwar debates in central Europe about the fate of parliamentary democracy. None other than Carl Schmitt, a colleague of Schumpeter's at the University of Bonn in the 1920s, played an important role in these debates. Schmitt was probably influenced by Schumpeter's initial contributions in the early 1920s to democratic theory. In turn, Schumpeter's classic *Capitalism, Socialism, and Democracy* (1942) can be read as an attempt to respond to Schmitt's own diagnosis of the crisis of parliamentarism.

I begin by describing a set of theoretical affinities between Schumpeter's and Schmitt's basic intellectual projects. Both authors respond to Max Weber's account of modern Western rationalism by suggesting that Weber downplays the role of *the irrational* within modern political and economic life. For both authors, *charismatic leadership* plays a far more important role in modernity than Weber ever acknowledges (I). I then turn to the specifics of Schumpeter's and Schmitt's dialogue on modern liberal democracy. Here as well, both authors are primarily concerned with the cultivation of an elite of charismatic leaders capable of circumventing the leveling winds of modern mass democracy. In order to counter the most problematic features of Schmitt's theory, Schumpeter struggles to show that a realistic, empirically minded analysis of modern liberal democracy need not culminate in a defense of dictatorship. By doing so, Schumpeter hopes to distinguish his own model of political competition from its fascist rivals (II, III). Nonetheless, Schumpeter's quest fails. Schumpeter's democratic theory ultimately remains mired in the same right-wing authoritarian intellectual milieu of which Schmitt was so much a part during the 1920s. In this fashion as well, the figure of Carl Schmitt continues to stalk contemporary North American political and legal theory (IV).

I

Schmitt was primarily a jurist, and Schumpeter an economist by training. Yet both were concerned during their long intellectual careers with the task of formulating a critical response to Weber's account of the distinctive traits of modern Western rationalism. Although many commentators on Schmitt and Schumpeter have acknowledged the central place of Weber in the writings of both authors, thus far none has noted their basic similarity in approach to Weber.

In the modern state, the advent of rationalism for Weber entails a system of tightly organized and cogently formulated general legal norms, in which "every concrete legal decision . . . [is] . . . the 'application' of an abstract legal proposition to a concrete 'fact situation' " according to a formal set of abstract legal propositions and logic.[2] In this view, judicial and administrative decision making are increasingly formalistic in character. For certain influential strands within modern jurisprudence, decision makers ideally were to be akin to "an automaton into which legal documents and fees are stuffed at the top in order that [they] may spill forth the verdict at the bottom along with the reasons, read mechanically from codified paragraphs."[3] Modern law can be described as rational for many reasons. Its systematic character rests on the (rational) scientific activity of legal experts, who play a crucial role in its emergence and cultivation. In addition, modern law's formal character corresponds to the needs of a *disenchanted* world, in which law necessarily has been robbed of any transcendent normative bearings; thus, it matches the needs of a social universe in which instrumental rationality has become predominant. Determinate and thus relatively predictable in character, modern rational law effectively facilitates the pursuit of private subjective interests and values, while simultaneously acknowledging that its own structure no longer can give expression to any universally acceptable moral ideas.

Schmitt's relationship to Weber is surely a complex one.[4] Schmitt accepts core elements of Weber's description of modernity as fundamentally rationalized and disenchanted in character. But it should now also be clear that so many of Schmitt's most important writings during the 1920s and 1930s represent an attempt to offer a critical response to Weber. First, Schmitt adamantly opposes the Weberian suggestion that modern law increasingly takes the form of a cogent legal code able to provide predictability and calculability; the core of Schmitt's legal theory during the 1920s and 1930s rests on the idea that legal trends that Weber clearly considered *irrational* and antimodern (for example, the proliferation of antiformal law, or the basic indeterminacy of judicial decision making) are pervasive within modern law. In addition, Schmitt defends a plebiscitary authoritarian alternative to modern liberal democracy. Dictatorship, not parliamentary democracy, is best suited to the imperatives of modern social and economic experience. In the process, Schmitt at times defends the possibility of what from Weber's perspective surely would have represented an enigmatic *reenchantment* of modernity: *Legality and Legitimacy*, for example, concludes with a call for a dictatorship based on charisma or perhaps "the authoritarian residues of a predemocratic era."[5] Of course, Weber himself occasionally toyed with the virtues of charismatic leadership in political essays immediately before his death in 1920.[6] Still, there is no question that Schmitt substantially radicalized this feature of Weber's political reflections. Weber hoped to overcome the deficiencies of modern parliamentarism by *supplementing* parliamentary government with mass-based plebiscitarianism, arguing that charismatic leaders provide a healthy corrective to highly bureaucratized modern representative bodies and political parties. In contrast, Schmitt opts to *supplant* parliamentarism with plebiscitary authoritarianism. For Schmitt, modernity's insidious egalitarian tendencies can be counteracted successfully *if* we achieve an authoritarian dictatorship dominated by leaders (allegedly) possessing a proven ability to engage in decisive political action.

Schumpeter's critical engagement with Weber's account of modern *economic rationalism* parallels Schmitt's response to Weber. Just as Schmitt underlines elements of modern experience that are irrational from Weber's perspective, Schumpeter suggests that Weber badly neglects the centrality of the charismatic economic entrepreneur, the heroic "leader" and driving force of modern capitalist development.[7] Parallel to Schmitt, Schumpeter hopes to defend charismatic leadership from the ultimately debilitating forces of modern rationalism, which in Schumpeter's account are destined to culminate in an ominous form of bureaucratic state socialism. In this view, the best protection against the ills of modern rationalism is a defense, albeit probably an ill-fated one, of the creative entrepreneur whose central attribute is the ability to engage in decisive, unforeseeable, and even "irrational" forms of economic action.

In Weber's theory of modern economic experience, core elements of modern capitalism provide a perfect expression of modern rationalism and its quest to render natural and social processes calculable. Just as modern law alone provides for optimal legal predictability, only in modern capitalism does "exact calculation" reign supreme in economic affairs. Characterized most fundamentally by a "systematic utilization of goods or personal service" in which "calculation underlies every single action of the partners," modern capitalism alone rests on highly developed forms of accounting and bookkeeping, formally free labor, and the separation of business from household activities, each of which facilitates the quest for predictable forms of economic activity able to secure optimal control over the natural world.[8] In this view, the modern capitalist entrepreneur is a sober, bourgeois type, expressive of a demanding "asceticism [that] was carried out of monastic cells into everyday life."[9] The discipline of the entrepreneur corresponds to the demands of a highly calculable and predictable economic universe in which increasingly "the technical and economic conditions of machine production . . . determine the lives of all the individuals who are born into this mechanism . . . with irresistible force."[10] Of course, in the *premodern* "capitalism[s] of promoters, speculators, concession hunters . . . above all, the capitalism especially concerned with exploiting wars," Weber acknowledges, entrepreneurial activity was "irrational" and adventurous, as entrepreneurs sought profit by means of risky and often reckless speculation, piracy, and even force.[11] But in *modern* capitalism, the entrepreneur allegedly trades in his more romantic traits for the self-possession of the contemporary businessman. Just as modern capitalism rests on the principle of exact calculation, so too does its leading figure, the modern entrepreneur, come to embody a disciplined, systematic and calculating ethos increasingly common among all strata of modern society.

Despite his emphasis on the rationalistic contours of modern capitalism, Weber never denies that some forms of modern socialism represent a possible extension of crucial elements of modern rationalism. By aspiring to deepen trends toward a "mechanized" and bureaucratized economic universe, socialism undoubtedly represents one possible outcome of the modern quest for predictability and calculability: "it is from . . . the discipline of the factory," the main institutional microcosm of the broader capitalist quest for efficiency, "that modern socialism has emerged."[12] Of course, Weber argues that state socialism is likely to culminate in a bureaucratic nightmare, perhaps even a "mechanized petrification" unprecedented in Western civilization. Yet this hostility serves only to reinforce his sense of the profoundly ambivalent character of modern rationalism. Having generated possibilities for individual liberty, rationalism potentially prepares the way for a state-dominated economy capable of satisfying basic economic needs in a regular and highly calculable fashion, but unlikely to provide even the most minimal possibilities for human autonomy.

Schumpeter's massive oeuvre builds, both explicitly and implicitly, on Weber's account of modern economic life. Schumpeter's writings are filled with descriptions of the "rationalizing" attributes of modern capitalism; in the pivotal *The Theory of Economic Development*, he explicitly attributes his use of this term to Weber.[13] Most importantly, he follows Weber closely in stressing the important place of modern capitalism in the emergence of a modern "rationalistic" civilization in which metaphysical, mystical, and romantic modes of thought are relegated to the sidelines and scientific "matter-of-fact" attitudes increasingly predominate. For Schumpeter, as for Weber, modern capitalism is "the propelling force of the rationalization of human behavior,"[14] facilitating the disenchantment of the modern world and a host of changes in human behavior and thought. Capitalist civilization is fundamentally antiheroic and utilitarian in character. Contra Karl Marx, it is also basically pacific; as Weber intimated, the modern capitalistic ethos of "exact calculation" is ultimately inconsistent with military and political adventurism.[15] Because "the same rationalization of the soul rubs off all the glamour of supra-empirical sanction from every species of class-wise rights," economic rationalism also inevitably fans the flames of modern mass democracy, inadvertently jeopardizing even minimal forms of political and economic privilege.[16] In this interpretation, capitalism need not fear the specter of the cataclysmic economic breakdown prophesied by Marxist theorists. Instead, immanent threats to capitalism derive from its own rationalistic culture, which for Schumpeter incessantly breeds radical egalitarian challenges to the legitimacy of forms of traditional political and capitalist inequality: Schumpeter repeatedly undertakes to demonstrate that intellectuals steeped in the culture of modern rationalism tend to give expression to anticapitalist views, thereby undermining the very institutional roots of the rationalistic culture of which they are so much a part. In a world in which a pervasive rationalism means that nothing can be sacred, even capitalism itself is likely to come under attack.[17]

Schumpeter goes even further than Weber in suggesting that state socialism rests on broader developmental tendencies constitutive of modern economic rationalism; here, economic rationalism leads *unavoidably* to an oppressive, perfectly rationalized state socialism.[18] Pace Mises and Hayek, socialism *is* economically feasible.[19] Even more importantly, it simply represents a deepening of present trends toward an economy dominated by huge bureaucratized firms in which leadership functions are exercised by a corps of highly trained technicians and specialists:

> the economic process tends to socialize *itself*—and also the human soul. By this we mean that the technological, organizational, commercial, administrative, and psychological prerequisites of socialism tend to be fulfilled more and more. Let us again visualize the state of things which looms in the future if that trend be projected. Business, excepting the agrarian sector, is controlled by a small number of bureaucratized corporations. Progress has slackened and become mechanized and planned. . . . Industrial property and management have become depersonalized— ownership having degenerated to stock and bond holdings, the executives having acquired habits of mind similar to those of civil servants. Capitalist motivation and standards have all but wilted away. The inference as to the transition to a socialist regime in such fullness of time is obvious.[20]

For Schumpeter, Marx was basically right to predict that small-scale competitive capitalism would inevitably be replaced by a "corporate capitalism" with a relatively small number of massive firms in which entrepreneurial functions themselves are rationalized. But Marx was wrong to see socialism as representing an altogether novel force in human history. On the contrary: socialism simply offers *more* of the instrumental rationality, mechanization, and bureaucratization so familiar to those already acquainted with the "iron cage" of rationalistic modern capitalist civilization. Socialism simply entails putting additional locks on the cage so as to eliminate any possibility of escape.

Although less hopeful than Weber about the prospects of capitalist civilization, Schumpeter nonetheless takes it upon himself to do battle with the socialist specter. In order to do so, however, Schumpeter introduces into the core of his economic theory a conception of the capitalist entrepreneur that is dramatically at odds with Weber's account of modern rationalism. In the process, his theoretical agenda approximates core features of Carl Schmitt's.

Whereas Weber tends to depict the modern capitalistic entrepreneur as an embodiment of the "sober" calculative ethos of modern capitalism, Schumpeter offers a more colorful portrayal of the entrepreneur. Indeed, a number of scholars have perceptively suggested that Schumpeter simply applies Weber's sociological category of charisma to his famous analysis of *economic* leadership in the capitalist firm.[21] Substantial textual evidence supports this interpretation. In Schumpeter's account, the entrepreneur is a heroic figure, capable of pursuing economic innovation by piercing the crust of worn-out commercial routines and introducing new forms of economic activity. The entrepreneur possesses a "will to conquer," a "joy of getting things done," resoluteness, vision, and a "sensation of power."[22] Without him, economic life would consist solely of a series of routinized "circular flows." Economic development would never occur, since no new goods, productive methods, sources of supply, forms of industrial organization, or markets would ever be introduced. It is *his* creative activity, not the changing currents of consumer demand, that for Schumpeter constitutes the fundamental phenomenon of economic development in modern capitalism. Consumers merely *respond* to the creative achievements of the entrepreneur. They no more determine entrepreneurship than, say, consumer demand "necessitated" innovations in computer technology in the 1960s or 1970s.

Moreover, the creative activity of the entrepreneur is badly captured by standard economic models of human rationality like those implicit in Weber's gloss on modern capitalism's ethos. Despite its centrality for modern economic life, modern social science has yet to develop tools appropriate for analyzing entrepreneurship.[23] In a provocative discussion of what we today would describe as the foundations of "rational choice theory," Schumpeter argues vehemently that many traditional conceptions of the "rational economic man" fail to capture the essence of entrepreneurship. In this view, the core of entrepreneurship consists in the ability to act in *novel* ways that often seem *irrational* from the perspective of preexisting forms of economic behavior. Existing models of rational action stumble here because

> [t]he nature of the innovation process, the drastic departure from existing routines, is inherently one that cannot be reduced to mere calculation, although subsequent imitation of the innovation, once accomplished, can be so reduced. Innovation is the creation of knowledge that cannot . . . be 'anticipated' by the theorist in a purely formal manner, as is done in the theory of decision making under uncertainty.[24]

Neoclassical conceptions of rational action correspond to an economic world of routine and the repetition of similar events. Yet they do a poor job of capturing forms of unprecedented and drastic shifts in behavior having highly unpredictable consequences. From the perspective of a model of rationality modeled on *calculation*, entrepreneurial activity seems utterly irrational.

For Schumpeter, the final tragedy of capitalism is its immanent subversion of the *differentia specifica* of capitalist development, the entrepreneur. Filled with nostalgic paeans to the disappearing entrepreneur of classical capitalism, Schumpeter's writings suggest that rationalization ultimately turns against precisely that figure so crucial to capitalism, the (irrational) charismatic entrepreneur.[25] Workers are not the only ones whose lives are remade under capitalism according to the dictates and rhythms of rationalization. The activities of the classical entrepreneur are similarly broken down into a distinct set of tasks, to be tackled by an array of specialized technicians, engineers, and managers.

> [R]ising specialization and mechanization, reaching right up to the leading functions, has thrown open positions at the top to men with purely technical qualifications that would, of themselves, be inadequate to the needs of family enterprise. A laboratory chemist, for example, may come to head a major chemical enterprise, even though he is not at all a business leader type.[26]

Yet this mechanization of entrepreneurship inevitably means the disappearance of those outstanding "leading personalities" [*Führerpersönlichkeiten*] who play a pivotal role in modern capitalism.[27] Economic innovation may still be possible in socialism. But it will no longer entail charismatic economic leaders forced to combine the tasks of management, investment, and risk-taking, as well as serving as an inspirational force capable of motivating and disciplining the workforce. For Schumpeter, the ethos of the modern technical specialist is simply incompatible with the "magic" of charismatic authority.

This strand in Schumpeter's account suggests some surprising thematic parallels with Schmitt's political and legal theory. While both authors hold crucial features of Weber's account of the modern condition in high regard, both ultimately move away from Weber's basically ambivalent assessment of modernity; Schmitt and Schumpeter are generally most interested in the negative facets of modern rationalism. While both thinkers do conjure up appealing images of an idealized liberal past, they do so only in order to present contemporary social and political development, conceived as a necessary offshoot of modern rationalism, in the worst possible light. Revealingly, both seek (irrational) figures allegedly capable of "saving" Western modernity from the excesses of rationalism. Schumpeter the social scientist tends to avoid express political proclamations. Nonetheless, a defense of the *differentia specifica* of modern capitalism, the creative, charismatic entrepreneur, clearly constitutes the underlying political agenda of many of his works.[28] For Schmitt, the defense of the creative, charismatic decision maker is similarly crucial to the formulation of a political and intellectual project attuned to the dictates of the twentieth century.[29] Schumpeter's economic "leader" and his Schmittian cousin possess a number of common traits. For Schmitt at crucial junctures, the mere capacity for resoluteness becomes the most important criterion of authentic political action. Analogously, Schumpeter embraces a conception of the entrepreneur in which possession of a "supranormal" will is arguably its most striking characteristic.[30] Both Schmitt and Schumpeter make it clear that not only the possession of charismatic capacities make effective leadership possible (for Schmitt, in the state; for Schumpeter, within the factory), but also such skills are possessed by only a tiny minority of human beings. Schmitt clearly doubts that most people possess the capacity for genuine political action, while Schumpeter similarly argues that the vast majority of human beings is incapable of even minimal economic innovation: "where the boundaries of routine stop, many people can go no further."[31] If humanity consisted solely of such inferior economic "types," no change—economic or otherwise—would occur. Reminiscent of great political and military leaders, economic leaders make up that small portion of humanity able to " 'lead' the means of production into new channels," generating development.[32] Not surprisingly, Schumpeter is as dismissive of social democratic models of worker self-management and economic democracy as Schmitt is of universalistic conceptions of popular sovereignty. Democratic conceptions of economic organization simply fail to do justice to the inevitability of an unequal distribution of economic "know-how." For Schumpeter, socialism is economically workable, but only in the form of highly bureaucratized "centralist socialism," based on substantial state ownership and central planning, in which a relatively small group of economic and political leaders oversees economic affairs.[33]

For both Schmitt and Schumpeter, "magic"—be it economic or political in character—is in short supply amid the conditions of modern disenchantment. The point, however, for both authors is to try to preserve certain forms of it. For Schmitt, this endeavour entails an assault on liberal democracy and the defense of dictatorship; for Schumpeter the economic theorist, it requires a defense of forms of capitalist production in which the entrepreneurial function has yet to be fully rationalized.

At times, Schumpeter can sound as militant in his defense of the charismatic economic leader, the private capitalist entrepreneur, as Schmitt in his defense of dictatorship. Yet Schumpeter is less hopeful than Schmitt about the fate of charismatic leadership in the modern world. Schmitt still believed, while embracing dictatorship in the early 1930s, that charismatic leadership can be successfully salvaged in modernity. In contrast, Schumpeter's economic theory ultimately offers a tragic vision, in which economic rationalism turns on capitalism and charismatic economic entrepreneurship while paving the way for socialism. Schumpeter's writings take on defensive and even resigned tones. At best, he hopes to slow the approaching socialist tide by defending the remaining vestiges of capitalist entrepreneurship where it still thrives.

II

In 1920 Schumpeter published a lengthy essay, "Socialist Possibilities For Today," in Germany's leading social science journal, the *Archiv für Sozialwissenschaft und Sozialpolitik*. Although ignored even by most Schumpeter aficionados today, the essay is surely one of his most important. Already the most famous non-Marxist economist in central Europe, Schumpeter had just finished a bout as a member of the new German Republic's Socialization Commission, and then an unsuccessful term as Finance Minister for Austria's first democratically elected government under the democratic socialist Karl Renner. In both positions, Schumpeter's position was a peculiar one. Although an outspoken right-wing critic of socialism, Schumpeter opted to work for governments committed to the socialization of the economy. Appointed to both posts primarily because of his economic expertise, Schumpeter's odd situation was quickly remarked upon by the press: one newspaper suggested that he possessed "three souls"—one conservative, one liberal, and one left-wing—a social democratic newspaper accused him of the most vile opportunism, and the satirist Karl Kraus noted sarcastically that Schumpeter had "more different views than were [even] necessary for his advancement."[34] Schumpeter himself quipped that he had chosen to work for socialists because "if somebody wants to commit suicide, it is a good thing if a doctor is present."[35]

Fortunately, Schumpeter's 1920 essay provides a more detailed explanation of his idiosyncratic political activities after World War I. Anticipating many of the basic economic arguments of the subsequent *Capitalism, Socialism, and Democracy*, Schumpeter insists on the inevitability of state socialism: the bureaucratization of the capitalist economy and undeniable trends towards concentration, the "technization" of the classic entrepreneur and his replacement by a corps of managers and trained technical experts, the growth of anticapitalist sentiment among the educated classes, and an ongoing transformation of private property tending to reduce the capitalist owner to a *rentier*, all point the way toward the likelihood of socialism. From this perspective, Schumpeter's apparent "embrace" of socialism after World War I simply amounted to an acknowledgment of the main structural forces at work in modern economic life. As Schumpeter never tired of repeating, the structural inevitability of socialism has no normative connotations. Despite his empirical predictions, Schumpeter himself always militantly opposed socialism.

Still, why is it appropriate for a conservative hostile to socialism to put his talents at the service of socialist politicians? Why not just lament the emergence of socialism while avoiding complicity in its alleged sins? Schumpeter's 1920 essay suggests an answer to this question. Schumpeter argues that the inevitability of socialism says nothing about the likely *time horizon* for its emergence. One of the main theses of "Socialist Possibilities For Today" is that socialization in many areas of the economy still remained premature after World War I. Although many trends indeed suggest the ongoing demise of capitalism, most of them are still relatively "unripened" in character.[36] As a political personage Schumpeter thus hoped to use his influence to discredit demands for socialization in those areas of the economy where the presuppositions of successful socialization—conveniently, Schumpeter's own discussion of these preconditions is quite ambiguous—remained unfulfilled. Where socialization seemed imminent and probably unavoidable, a principled conservative could still play a role in socialization by making sure that socialist proposals minimized possible threats to economic efficiency and individual freedom. As an advisor to socialist-dominated governments, Schumpeter hardly sought to subvert socialization from within. But he did hope that his political activities would allow him to minimize its potential ills.[37]

More important for our purposes here, Schumpeter's essay offers a disturbing account of the inevitable demise not only of capitalism, but also of representative democracy. Arguing that traditional liberal parliamentary institutions in contemporary Europe seem increasingly anachronistic even in those countries with rich liberal democratic traditions, Schumpeter describes many ways in which "the facts [of political life] discredit the official phraseology of our political life."[38] Reasonable deliberation has been jettisoned for a political universe dominated by bureaucratic mass parties akin to "psychotechnical machines" mobilizing support by means of appeals to unconscious irrational instincts; for Schumpeter, voters seem reminiscent of imprisoned Africans chained to slave ships over which they have no control; independent deliberative parliamentary representatives have been replaced by more or less obedient puppets, lacking even the bare time necessary to scrutinize legislative proposals; those pulling the strings are party bosses able to manipulate the meanest human instincts; parliament rarely exercises even a minimally critical function in relation to the executive. In short, parliament has lost its original meaning, its original techniques have failed, and its workings reveal themselves to be nothing but a farce.[39]

Schumpeter goes so far as to argue that the ongoing decay of liberal parliamentarism is an unavoidable consequence of modern mass democracy and the closely related striving for social equality.[40] Here again, the tragic overtones of Schumpeter's narrative are striking. Rationalistic capitalist civilization generates demands for political and social equality that unwittingly subverts the rationalistic ethos of liberal representative government. Both economic and political liberalism are characterized by an explosive dialectic, according to which they spawn mass political movements hostile to all forms of political and social hierarchy.

Appreciatively citing Georges Sorel's critique of liberal democracy, Schumpeter comments that all "leading individuals and classes" throughout history have rightly recognized that democratization entails "sinking in a swamp of mediocrity," and that democratic mediocrity is sure to undermine possibilities for effective political action.[41] Although enthralled by the (irrational) charisma of the capitalist entrepreneur, Schumpeter exhibits little sympathy for the emotionalism of modern mass democratic politics: mass democracy disfigures liberal parliamentarism, reducing its instruments to the inappropriate playthings of immature political and social actors inferior to those for whom they were originally intended. Democratization implies "chaos" and "disintegration,"[42] because it means giving the irrational and politically unfit masses unprecedented political power.

In this account, liberal parliamentarism was able to function effectively in the past only because it rested on a social consensus stemming from the fact that the poor and working classes lacked any say in parliamentary affairs. Of course, parliament was never perfectly homogeneous; Schumpeter acknowledges the relatively diverse sources of parliamentary representation even in nineteenth-century Europe. Nonetheless, parliamentary representatives in the nineteenth century—primarily from the bourgeoisie, the aristocracy, and the state bureaucracy—did share a relatively far-reaching set of common social interests which gave the liberal aspiration for "government by discussion" a real chance of succeeding, even if liberal theorists undoubtedly provided an overly idealized gloss on the realities of nineteenth-century parliamentarism.[43] Thus, liberal parliamentarism is bound to decay when political movements mobilizing the excluded pose a real challenge to the political and social status quo: "parliamentary deliberation about something that one group of parties refuses to accept under any circumstances loses any meaning."[44] In particular, when (irrational) democratic and socialist movements raise radical demands, parliament ceases to function effectively as a freewheeling, deliberative body. Utter political paralysis may result; in more fortunate polities, compromise between basically antagonistic social and political groupings becomes the modus vivendi of parliamentary government. In any event, the days of rationalistic parliamentarism have come to an end.[45]

"Creeping socialism," spawned by the entrance of the masses onto the political scene, hence inevitably facilitates the decay of parliamentary democracy. Not only is the movement toward socialism likely to destroy liberal democracy, but it is also difficult to imagine how socialism, once established, could coexist with liberal parliamentarism. In socialism, independent entrepreneurs would no longer guarantee the "discipline" in the workforce requisite for economic efficiency. Political authorities would now have to do so. For Schumpeter, traditional liberal institutions are unlikely to prove up to this task, and political authoritarianism and the militarization of work life thus are probably necessary for guaranteeing order in the workplace once the independent capitalist entrepreneur, the "leading personality" of the workplace, has been eliminated.[46] Schumpeter also claims that it is difficult to see what function parliamentary deliberation could possibly have in a socialist society. Since the most divisive political issues of our era, namely those concerned with economic divisions, have ostensibly been resolved, it is unclear why socialists would remain committed to the ideal of freewheeling debate, especially if worried about the specter of antisocialist groups making use of parliamentary institutions to incite opposition.[47]

Predictably, Schumpeter's bleak predictions ignited a minor controversy in the pages of the *Archiv für Sozialwissenschaft und Sozialpolitik*.[48] One of the German-speaking world's most famous economists, who until recently had been a relatively prominent public figure in Central Europe's new democracies, had done nothing less than proclaim the inevitable demise of liberal parliamentarism. Of course, many others in Central Europe during the same period—most prominently, Max Weber—had vividly described similar ailments in their analyses of modern liberal parliamentarism. But no scholar of Schumpeter's standing, and certainly none who had served in such prominent official capacities, had gone as far as Schumpeter in proclaiming the inevitability of parliamentary decay.[49] Schumpeter clearly hit a raw nerve. After all, he was implicitly suggesting that Central Europe's first and still relatively insecure experiments in liberal democracy had simply come too late, having missed the glory days of nineteenth-century parliamentarism before mass movements emerged to subvert parliamentary institutions. From this perspective, both the German and the Austrian experiments with parliamentary democracy were probably ill-fated experiments with a political form whose death knell was already sounding loud and clear throughout Western Europe.

Schumpeter's work on parliamentary decline was possibly one reason why he was named to a position on the relatively prestigious faculty at the University of Bonn in 1925. By the mid-1920s, the Bonn faculty had
 established itself as a center for scholarship on the problem of parliamentary

decay. One of Schumpeter's predecessors on the economics faculty, Moritz Julius Bonn, authored two important studies on parliamentary decay during the early 1920s dealing with many of the same issues as Schumpeter, while nonetheless shying away from Schumpeter's dramatic conclusions.[50] Like Schumpeter, M. J. Bonn believed that liberal parliamentarism was challenged by a series of novel social and economic developments; unlike Schumpeter, he was an unambiguous liberal democrat who militantly defended the underlying ideals of classical parliamentarism. The political scientist Erwin von Beckerath, whose brother was a colleague of Schumpeter's in the economics department,[51] was an expert on authoritarian attempts to resolve the crisis of parliamentarism. His 1927 *Wesen und Werden des faschistischen Staates*, a sympathetic account of Italian fascism, gained critical acclaim among right-wing circles.[52] Most important, Carl Schmitt—who was quite close to M. J. Bonn and surely acquainted with Beckerath—of course had also devoted a substantial amount of attention to the fate of parliamentarism in his *Crisis of Parliamentary Democracy* (1923). A relatively intense exchange seems to have taken place between the members of this unofficial circle. Schmitt and M. J. Bonn sparred both publicly and privately about the fate of parliamentary government,[53] and Schmitt would later write a relatively favorable view of Beckerath's book in which he took its author to task only for *downplaying* some of the strengths of Italian fascism as an alternative to liberal democracy.[54]

Not surprisingly, Schumpeter soon became familiar with those colleagues in Bonn who were preoccupied with the problems of parliamentary fragility. Archival documentation suggests that Schumpeter and Schmitt, who taught together at Bonn between 1925 and 1928, were personally acquainted.[55] Both were close in age (Schumpeter was born in 1883 and Schmitt in 1888), had similar antidemocratic political proclivities, and shared a Roman Catholic background. There is also evidence that Schmitt and Schumpeter swapped ideas, which is surely not surprising given the obvious overlap in interests. In a revealing 1948 letter to the German sociologist Helmut Schelsky, Schmitt reminisced about the "great pleasure" he gained from discussions with Schumpeter in Bonn during the 1920s, noting that he continued to gain personal satisfaction from Schumpeter's influence in postwar intellectual life in Europe and North America.[56] Schumpeter was also familiar with Schmitt's work. Schmitt published a number of short pieces, including one on democratic theory and the first (1927) version of his "Concept of the Political," in the *Archiv für Sozialwissenschaft und*

Sozialpolitik, on whose select editorial board Schumpeter served.[57] Archival materials suggest that in 1926 the journal put Schumpeter in charge of trying to encourage Schmitt to complete what later became the famous "Concept of the Political," and Schumpeter appears to praise Schmitt's reflections on "the political" in two revealing pieces of correspondence. In a letter from November 23, 1926, Schumpeter comments in a "personal vein" to Schmitt that "no other author" known to him possesses the same ability to address this "set of problems," and then in a postcard of September 8, 1927, from the vacation resort town of Baden-Baden, Schumpeter tells Schmitt that he "once again" found himself "admiring" Schmitt's "On the Concept of the Political."[58] The same journal also published a widely cited critical discussion of Schmitt's analysis of liberal parliamentarism by Richard Thoma, one of Germany's leading legal positivists.[59]

In turn, Schmitt was clearly familiar with Schumpeter's "Sociology of Imperialism," which he cited on a number of occasions in order to clarify his "concept of the political."[60] Although Schmitt's references to Schumpeter's theory of imperialism at first glance seem critical in nature, the German political theorist Ernst Fraenkel has plausibly suggested that Schmitt's "concept of the political," which legitimizes the attainment of power for its own sake within "a situation in which traditional values have lost their binding power and rational values are not acceptable," simply gives abstract theoretical expression to Schumpeter's conception of imperialism as resting on the "aimless quest for power."[61] For Schumpeter, "imperialism is the objectless disposition on the part of the state to unlimited forcible expansion."[62] According to Fraenkel, Schmitt offers a conception of politics conducive to the boundless expansionism characteristic of imperialism in this interpretation; Schmitt's concept of the political envisions nothing less than a corresponding *l'art pour l'art* in the political sphere.[63]

Schmitt was also acquainted with Schumpeter's ideas about parliamentary decline, and Schumpeter probably exercised some influence on Schmitt's *Crisis of Parliamentary Democracy*.[64] At the very least, the argumentative parallels between the two authors are striking. Of course, many of their contemporaries—Walter Lippmann in the United States, for example—were also chronicling the pathologies of mass politics during the 1920s. But few commentators on parliamentary fragility share as much as Schmitt and Schumpeter. Both openly take sides normatively with irrationalist and antidemocratic elite theorists, while simultaneously exuding a certain nostalgia for the lost world of rationalistic liberal parliamentarism.

Schumpeter makes use of Sorel in order to discredit universalistic liberal democratic conceptions of popular sovereignty, while Schmitt praises Sorel's "original historical and philosophical perceptions" and makes them a central component of his infamous assault on liberalism in *The Crisis of Parliamentary Democracy*.[65] (Schmitt later claimed credit for having introduced Sorel into academic political and legal theory in Germany.[66] As a matter of fact, Schumpeter beat him to it.) Like many other political observers at the same time, both authors emphasize the irrationalism of modern mass democratic politics, blaming the demise of deliberative politics on the entrance of popular movements, allegedly incapable of engaging in rational debate, into the parliamentary public sphere. But Schmitt and Schumpeter also rely on a similar sociological interpretation of the rise and fall of liberal parliamentarism. For Schmitt, as for Schumpeter, liberal parliamentarism was able to live up to the ambitious aspirations of classical liberal political thought only as long as political participation was limited to those with property and education [*Besitz und Bildung*]. Once mass-based political movements challenge the hegemony of the propertied classes by pursuing a left-wing anticapitalist agenda, liberal parliamentarism necessarily must die. Schmitt suggests that the collapse of the classical liberal state/society divide inevitably prepares the way for a "total state" in which deliberative parliamentarism is defunct; Schumpeter describes an irreversible "march into socialism," demonstrated in part by growing state activity in the capitalist economy and destined to destroy liberal parliamentarism. For both, the rise of social democracy and the modern interventionist welfare state inevitably undermines the foundations of liberal parliamentarism and prepares the groundwork for an authoritarian future.

III

Our discussion of Schumpeter's Bonn interlude places his enormously influential "theory of democratic elitism" in a new light. Of course, *Capitalism, Socialism, and Democracy* admits no intellectual debt to Carl Schmitt. To have done so in the United States in 1942 surely would have constituted scholarly suicide.[67] Nonetheless, it is difficult to avoid the suspicion that Schumpeter's argument was shaped by the irrationalist, authoritarian milieu in which Schmitt played such an important part in Germany in the 1920s and 1930s. Of course, Schmitt was not the only writer bashing liberal democracy from the far right after World War I; as we will see, Schumpeter himself was clearly influenced by the Italian economist and social philosopher Vilfredo Pareto. Nonetheless, affinities once again surface between Schumpeter's democratic theory in *Capitalism, Socialism, and Democracy* and Schmitt's writings from the 1920s and early 1930s. Schumpeter may not have "borrowed" his ideas directly from Schmitt, yet his intellectual exchange with Schmitt at Bonn at the very least helped cement Schumpeter's own antidemocratic proclivities.

Echoing Schmitt's conception of democratic homogeneity, Schumpeter here is hostile to universalistic conceptions of democracy and suggests that democracy can logically rest on exclusionary definitions of the populace based on race, ethnicity, or religion.[68] Like Schmitt, he argues that the border between democracy and authoritarianism is often blurry.[69] Schmitt insists that an authentic political theory must build on a pessimistic philosophical anthropology; *Capitalism, Socialism, and Democracy* does precisely this.[70] Schumpeter repeats his view that mass-based political decision making is inherently illogical and irrational, now adding that traditional liberal democratic conceptions of democracy constitute a political myth, in the Sorelian sense, employed by political minorities hoping to gain control over the masses.[71] Akin to the advertising techniques of the modern corporation, political propaganda and manipulation are essential facets of a political universe in which a plebiscitary appeal to the lower classes is necessary for the exercise of power.[72] Schumpeter even seems to embrace a decisionism reminiscent of Schmitt's: "rifts on questions of principle . . . cannot be reconciled by rational argument because ultimate values—our conceptions of what life and society should be—are beyond the range of mere logic."[73] For Schumpeter, as for Schmitt, fundamental political and moral choices ultimately rest on expressions of the (irrational) will. In contrast to Weber, neither author says much about how to ameliorate the worrisome implications of this vision.[74]

Schumpeter's alternative to traditional democratic "phraseology" similarly approximates elements of Schmitt's plebiscitary alternative to parliamentary democracy. *Capitalism, Socialism, and Democracy* simply presupposes the conclusion of the earlier "Socialist Possibilities for Today" that classical liberal parliamentarism is dead, and thus "the wishes of the members of a parliament are not the ultimate data of the process that produces government."[75] For both Schumpeter and Schmitt, government is inevitably executive-dominated. Thus, the main task of contemporary political theory is to guarantee the possibility of rule by effective elites that are able to demonstrate authentic leadership capacities. In this spirit, Schumpeter demands that we reverse the traditional view of the relationship between electorate and leadership "and make the deciding of issues by the electorate secondary to the election of the men who are to do the deciding."[76] Like Schmitt, Schumpeter allows for substantial possibilities for elite mass manipulation, openly conceding that the "[m]anufactured [popular] Will is no longer outside the theory, an aberration for the absence of which we piously pray; it enters on the ground floor as it should."[77] For Schmitt, "the people cannot counsel, deliberate, or discuss. It cannot govern or administer, nor can it posit norms; it can only sanction by its 'yes' the draft norms presented to it. Nor, above all, can it place a question, but only answer by 'yes' or 'no' the question put to it."[78] Democracy only means that the people have the opportunity of accepting or refusing the *proposals* of their rulers. In a slight modification of this thesis, Schumpeter concludes that "[d]emocracy means only that the people have the opportunity of accepting or refusing the *men* who are to rule them."[79]

Nonetheless, Schumpeter does try to distance himself from some of the most troublesome implications of Schmitt's plebiscitary model. Even before his National Socialist interlude, Schmitt was notoriously vague about exactly how plebiscitary leadership is to be chosen by the electorate. Characteristically, he only refers in the passage just quoted to the people's right to say "yes" or "no" to *questions* posed to it, thereby failing to specify the mechanisms by which the electorate can guarantee that leaders invested with the substantial authority of defining and formulating such questions do so in a manner relatively compatible with the popular will.[80] As I noted earlier in this study, Otto Kirchheimer was right on the mark when he observed that

> [f]or Carl Schmitt . . . the democratic character of the plebiscite consists purely in an unorganized answer which the people, characterized as a mass, gives to a question which may be posed only by an authority whose existence is assumed. Structure and accountability of this authority are unknown.[81]

For Schumpeter, the somewhat distinct conception of democracy as involving the electorate's power to say "yes" or "no" to its *leaders* necessarily entails acknowledging the central place of "free competition among would-be leaders for the vote of the electorate."[82] This political competition is sure to be imperfect; as noted, Schumpeter's model tolerates substantial elite manipulation of the electorate.[83] Still, Schumpeter's introduction of this idea of elite competition does represent a noteworthy conceptual innovation in relation to Schmitt. Writing from the safe shores of North America at the outbreak of World War II, Schumpeter uses it to ward off the more ominous implications of the antidemocratic *Parlamentarismus-kritik*—so evident in Schmitt's embrace of National Socialism—which he and Schmitt had practiced so well in the 1920s. In Schumpeter's model, the concept of free competition allegedly requires the endorsement of certain residues of classical liberalism. Even if political competition among elites is necessarily imperfect in character, Schumpeter claims that it continues to presuppose some (unspecified) minimum of basic political liberties.[84] Although openly dismissive of traditional liberal political thought, the concept of the "free vote" is not altogether lacking in substance here. Leaders face restraints—*some* chance of being dumped in favor of someone else— even if they are likely to be occupied with the task of "manufacturing" consent most of the time.

Here, full-fledged dictatorship is characterized by the permanent *monopolization* of political power by an elite group and the abrogation of even the most minimal possibility of elite competition.[85] National Socialism certainly was a dictatorship in this sense of the term. For Schumpeter, his former colleague Schmitt's embrace of it hence was certainly inconsistent with the "democratic method." Schmitt's diagnosis of the ailments of liberal democracy was basically correct, but a distinct prognosis is possible, or at least *Capitalism, Socialism, and Democracy* suggests as much.

Capitalism, Socialism, and Democracy vaguely attributes the sources of the pivotal concept of elite competition to modern economic theory. But if we move beyond the narrow horizons of Schumpeter's well-known 1942 monograph and take a closer look at Schumpeter's many other writings, we can easily trace it to Vilfredo Pareto, whom Schumpeter greatly admired.[86] Schumpeter helped introduce the teaching of Pareto's economic theory into the German-speaking world, and Pareto's influence is apparent in a number of Schumpeter's most important writings.[87] Pareto's impact on Schumpeter's democratic theory is undeniable: Schumpeter's concept of elite competition is substantially inspired by Pareto's emphasis on the virtues of elite circulation. Like Schumpeter, Pareto synthesized a profound skepticism for popular decision making with a fervent commitment to market capitalism, emphasizing the irrationality of the vast majority of humanity and the resulting absurdity of egalitarian democratic ideals. For Pareto, popular self-government is an oxymoron, and rule by a tiny elite inevitable. The nature of this elite depends on the particular functional imperatives of the social and political order in question. In a society of thieves, for example, the capacity to steal successfully would determine social and political rank. Although obviously sharing considerable common ground with Schmitt, Pareto's position is distinct from Schmitt's in one important way: Pareto insists that the cultivation of a truly capable set of leaders presupposed what he described as the *circulation des élites*. Even though the possession of those traits essential to the basic operation of a particular social and political system constitutes the original source of the privileged status of every ruling elite, every dominant elite tends to ossify by sealing itself off from the lower strata. As Schumpeter accurately paraphrases in his often flattering gloss on Pareto:

> there is in the lowest strata a tendency to accumulate superior ability that is prevented from rising, and in the topmost stratum . . . a tendency to disaccumulate energy through disuse—with resulting tension and ultimate replacement of the ruling minority by another ruling minority that is drawn from the superior elements in the *couches inférieurs*. This *circulation des élites* does not affect the principle that it is always *some* minority which rules . . . though it does produce [mythical] equalitarian philosophies or slogans in the course of the struggles that ensue.[88]

For Pareto, some political and social systems hinder the rise of "superior" materials from the lower stratum. Thus, not only are they prone to instability, but their leadership is also likely to grow decrepit. In contrast, those providing a well-oiled mechanism for elite circulation not only permit the regeneration of political and social leadership, but also are relatively safe from the specter of violent upheaval.

Significantly, Pareto believed that the circulation of elites was relatively high in modern democracy, which he otherwise described in terms as unflattering as those used by Schmitt and Schumpeter.[89] By building on this element of Pareto's alternative brand of irrationalist political theory, *Capitalism, Socialism, and Democracy* offers a clever response to Schmitt. Employing Pareto's insight, Schumpeter suggests that only a system providing some modicum of circulation among political elites is likely to assure the effective, charismatic political leadership desired by Schmitt; as Pareto taught, leadership is likely to ossify if unchallenged. Pace Schmitt, Schumpeter thus claims that one of the advantages of the competition between elites at the heart of his "democratic method" is that those who succeed in gaining power are likely to possess real skills in "the handling of men. And, as a broad rule at least, the ability to win a position of political leadership will be associated with a certain amount of personal force and also other aptitudes that will come in usefully in a prime minister's workshop."[90] Schumpeter seems doubtful that charismatic leadership is likely to be generated by any political system. But *if* it is to surface, it is most likely to do so where political leaders compete for the "free vote." According to Schumpeter, only his model of elite circulation, not Schmitt's openly fascist brand of plebiscitary authoritarianism, is likely to generate forceful, authentic leadership.

IV

Is Schumpeter successful in formulating an alternative to Schmitt's political theory? In my view, it would surely do an injustice to Schumpeter to ignore the obvious differences between his "democratic method" and Schmitt's views.[91] Even with all of its widely noted failings, Schumpeter offers a vision normatively and institutionally superior to Schmitt's.[92] In particular, Schumpeter's expectation that his approach is likely to assure the preservation of some basic civil and political rights makes it more appealing than Schmitt's. By the same token, it is difficult to overlook the possibility that Schmitt simply presents a more *consistent* theoretical expression of a series of worrisome basic assumptions shared by both authors.[93] If one accepts the presuppositions of the bleak philosophical anthropology shared by Schumpeter and Schmitt (as well as Pareto and Sorel), why side with Schumpeter's theory of democratic elitism over its adamantly authoritarian right-wing cousins? If the overwhelming mass of humanity is incapable of engaging even in minimally reasonable forms of political debate, why not follow Schmitt and deny them basic political and civil rights? Significantly, Pareto himself seems to have endorsed Mussolini's fascism in his final years, to some extent because he grasped that the *circulation des élites* hardly *necessitated* democratic techniques. For Pareto, contemporary "plutocratic democracies" seem increasingly prone to instability, in part because a politically and an economically dominant bourgeoisie faces "an intensification of the sentiments of hatred for the 'haves' " among the politically and socially underprivileged.[94] Might not an authoritarian alternative to contemporary liberal democracy prove more effective at guaranteeing the cultivation of "leadership materials" among the socially and political underprivileged and a superior system of elite circulation? By the early 1920s, Pareto probably thought so.[95]

In short, the main justification for Schumpeter's democratic method ultimately rests on its claim to provide capable and effective elite circulation. But this is surely an insufficient basis for justifying even the rather pale version of liberal democracy envisioned by Schumpeter; authoritarian political systems have often done quite well at making sure that ruling strata are recruited from the "ruled classes."[96] In the final analysis, Schumpeter defends the preservation of a minimum of civil and political rights because he sees them as necessary for elite circulation, for "free competition" among would-be leaders. It is by no means self-evident, however, that elite competition in this sense requires the protection of even the most elementary universal civil and political rights.

In a long-forgotten 1929 discussion of right-wing intellectual trends in early twentieth-century European thought, Hermann Heller made a similar observation about the intellectual relationship between Pareto and Schmitt's fascist political theory: for Heller, Pareto's position is distinct from Schmitt's, yet Schmitt's theory nonetheless represents a logical offshoot of Pareto's antidemocratic irrationalism. Since Heller's comments about Pareto's relationship to Schmitt can be applied to Schumpeter as well, it is worth quoting them at length:

> For Pareto, every political theory and political ideal, from Plato to Comte and Marx, is merely bad metaphysics, and every ideology is simply an instrument of struggle in the *bellum omnium contra omnes*. . . . Since these fictions are still necessary for the domestification of the human "beast," according to Pareto they can still provide the basis for a technology of state power . . . as part of a neo-Machiavellian political theory for a disillusioned bourgeois society. But if all political and legal thinking is simply the expression of a highly particular historical and social situation, if there is no set of common meanings shared between different generations, classes, parties, and nations, then there is no basis for debate or rational action . . . [t]hen indeed the basic category of the political is [Schmitt's] friend/enemy distinction, in which emphasis is placed on the

necessity of exterminating the existentially "other" during the case of conflict. Then the point of politics and of all history is the naked struggle for power, and those engaged in this struggle merely need to acknowledge which ideology is most effective at the present time in order to gain power in the eternal and ultimately meaningless circulation of elites.[97]

For Schumpeter as well, even the most minimal talk of the common good is hogwash, classical democratic political theory is bad metaphysics, elite rule is unavoidable, and "rifts on question of principle . . . cannot be reconciled by rational argument."[98] What then can save the logic of Schumpeter's own "disillusioned bourgeois" theory from the fate of Pareto's? Like Pareto, Schumpeter suggests that democratic "phraseology" is merely a myth employed by elites aspiring for power in the eternal competition for leadership positions. Can we be certain that Schumpeter's own "democratic method" is not just another myth in the employ of aspiring elites in the "naked struggle for power"—against defenders, perhaps, of the processes of political and social democratization so despised by Schumpeter?[99]

Schumpeter's theory *is* a rival to Schmitt's. This is a friendly rivalry, however, resting on mutual respect and an extensive set of shared intellectual assumptions. Schumpeter's theory is hardly fascistic. Yet Schumpeter may be only a few steps away from Schmitt's path.

To Schumpeter's credit, he never took the final steps toward embracing Schmitt's openly fascist political existentialism. Amid the bloody cataclysms of midcentury Central Europe, this was no mean achievement for a theorist with Schumpeter's antidemocratic background. Still, this hardly frees us today from the task of recalling the intellectual nexus between Schmitt and one of the major intellectual forces in postwar American political science. However unpleasant, scholarship will now have to examine the alarming possibility that authoritarian right-wing political theory exercised a subterranean influence, via Schumpeter, on this discipline. From one perspective, Schumpeter's "democratic elitism" simply reformulated an onerous tradition of Central European authoritarianism in order to make it more palatable to an American audience. Whitewashed of its more openly antidemocratic rhetorical flourishes, Schumpeter's contribution to this tradition proved an attractive starting point for historically and philosophically naive political scientists seeking an "empirical" alternative to the classics of normative democratic theory.

In what surely belongs among the great intellectual paradoxes of our times, many American political scientists, in the immediate aftermath of the victory over National Socialism in 1945, embraced a tradition of political thought that was complicit in the antidemocratic sins of twentieth-century European political theory and practice.

8

THE UNHOLY ALLIANCE OF CARL
SCHMITT AND FRIEDRICH A. HAYEK

C arl Schmitt's impact on contemporary free-market conservativism is even more substantial than his influence on democratic theory in postwar political science. Notwithstanding the fact that Friedrich A. Hayek repeatedly acknowledged his intellectual debts to Schmitt, and even though a number of central features of Hayek's legal and political argumentation parallel Carl Schmitt's theorizing, Schmitt's impact on Hayekian liberalism has been effectively ignored.[1] In this chapter, I would like to provide a corrective to this oversight by demonstrating the existence of significant structural ties between Schmitt's analysis of legal decay in the modern interventionist state, one of the central themes of Schmitt's writings from the late 1920s and early 1930s, and Hayek's influential postwar account of a "road to serfdom," whose way he believes has been marked out by the rise of the welfare state and the alleged disintegration of the liberal rule of law. Although many differences undoubtedly separate Schmitt and Hayek, Hayek nonetheless builds on key elements of Schmitt's theoretical assault on the Weimar left. Moreover, Hayek ultimately proves unable to avoid the troubling political implications of Schmitt's earlier attack on the democratic welfare state. Just as the logic of Schmitt's argumentation leads him to embrace an authoritarian alternative to Weimar, Hayek's reworking of Schmitt ultimately encourages him to endorse a set of institutional proposals having dubious liberal democratic credentials.

Over the course of the last fifteen years, countless political analysts have argued that the free-market attempt to restructure capitalist democracy bodes poorly for democratic politics. Although this study obviously can make only a modest contribution to that debate, it does seem to me that the "unholy alliance" of Carl Schmitt and Friedrich Hayek does raise difficult questions for those committed to the widely held belief that neo-liberal economics and liberal democracy are simply two sides of the same coin. Authoritarianism and capitalism have coexisted quite well in this century. A close examination of the intellectual relationship between Schmitt and Hayek helps explain why.

I

Let us try to recall for a moment an all but forgotten juncture in early twentieth-century German history. It is 1926: even though the Weimar Republic is enjoying a brief moment of relative stability, memories of political and economic disorder are still very much alive in the minds of German citizens. Although Weimar's founding document—authored by impressive jurists and statesmen like Friedrich Naumann and Hugo Preuss, but nonetheless in many ways a tension-laden product of the explosive political situation of war-weary, postrevolutionary Germany—promises substantial social and economic reforms, the Constitution's ambitious social democratic agenda remains unfulfilled thus far.[2] In order to remedy this failing, Weimar Communists (KPD) and Social Democrats (SPD) join forces and make use of the Weimar Constitution's relatively generous possibilities for direct democracy by proposing a referendum demanding the expropriation of royal property. The Kaiser was forced to flee Germany during the revolution of 1918, but the status of substantial monarchical properties, even at this relatively advanced juncture in the history of the Weimar Republic, remains unclear. The referendum has great symbolic significance. For democrats and leftists, a victory would represent a sign that Weimar has finally succeeded in smashing one of the pillars of the old order. In the eyes of those sympathetic to monarchical property claims, the referendum suggests all the potential dangers of mass-based democratic politics.

Although well over fourteen million voters support the expropriation of princely property, the left, as so often in 1920s and early 1930s Germany, is ultimately defeated at the polls. Conservative publicists and intellectuals—not the least of whom is Carl Schmitt, then an ambitious young jurist at the University of Bonn with a growing reputation—play a significant role in this defeat. His *Judicial Independence, Equality Before the Law, and the Protection of Private Property According to the Weimar Constitution* (1926) offers a scathing critique of the left's quest to expropriate royal property. This

work depends on an interpretation of the classics of modern liberal jurisprudence in order to formulate a dramatic contrast between *general legal
norms and individual legal commands or measures* explicitly directed at particular
objects and persons. In Schmitt's 1926 account, only general law satisfies
the conditions of the ideal of the liberal rule of law [*Rechtsstaat*], respects
the ideal of equality before the law, and guarantees judicial independence.
The generality of the legal norm represents the very core of liberal legalism,
for legal equality "in the face of an individual measure is logically inconceivable."[3] Legislative action that approximates the form of an individual
command inevitably blurs any meaningful distinction between judicial and
administrative decision making: when law is directed at a particular individual or object, judicial action no longer differs qualitatively from inherently
discretionary, situation-specific modes of administrative activity, and the
idea of an independent judiciary is thereby robbed of any substance. When
subject to an individual legal act, the judge becomes superfluous and the
idea of a judge "bound to the law" thus a farce. Although Schmitt's pivotal
book devotes surprisingly little energy to a clarification of the exact nature
of the crucial distinction between general and individual legal action, he
believes that he can categorize the left's attempt to expropriate royal property as an individual measure and thus demonstrate its ominous implications. If the legislator can "divorce some particular married couple, seize
control of any single newspaper, close down a single association, [or] arrest
unpopular persons," political tyranny results.[4] Hence, the Weimar left's
attempt to expropriate monarchical properties constitutes an act of "revolutionary violence." Such action may be necessary during the emergency
situation or a dire political crisis, but it lacks legitimacy in a period of
relative political normalcy.

Our exegesis of Schmitt's legal theory in part 1 of this study places
Schmitt's comments here in the appropriate context. Throughout the Weimar period, Schmitt was on principle a critic of liberal jurisprudence. Indeed, his recourse here to elements of the liberal rule of law is purely
strategic. At many junctures in the 1926 study, it indeed becomes clear that
Schmitt merely means to suggest that as long as the Weimar constitutional
system is committed to legal liberalism, it must endorse a traditional model
of the rule of law and, by necessity, conflict with the left's attempt to
undertake individual legal measures against royal property.[5] By no means
should we read Schmitt's employment of traditional strands of liberal legalism as an expression of a genuine sympathy for the liberal rule of law. As

was shown in part 1, Schmitt deconstructed that ideal well before publication of his 1926 pamphlet. Schmitt in 1926 merely speaks as a constitutional lawyer intent on informing his countrymen that if they aspire to take the liberal features of the Weimar Constitution seriously, they necessarily must oppose left-wing legal acts as inconsistent with the idea of general law.

Core elements of Schmitt's subsequent Weimar-era analysis of legal evolution in the era of the democratic interventionist state are anticipated by Schmitt's deceptively simple set of arguments from 1926. Very much in the shadow of this early study, Schmitt's interpretation of the ideal of the liberal rule of law plays a crucial role in his battle against Weimar's failed quest to establish the outlines of the modern democratic welfare state. Schmitt cleverly transforms the traditional ideals of liberal legalism into a weapon against Germany's first attempt to secure a stable liberal democracy. In chapter 3, I note that Schmitt occasionally relies on traditionalist legal liberal ideals *in order to subvert legal liberalism.* This is precisely the strategy taken here in his reflections on the rule of law and the welfare state.

Schmitt's peculiar and highly selective appropriation of traditional liberal democratic definitions of the legal norm—in his 1926 study, some of his comments seem to imply that general law is incompatible with virtually *any* form of state intervention in social and economic affairs![6]—represents another example of his tendency to rely on caricatures of early liberal political thought in order to disgrace contemporary aspirations for democratization. His view of general law blatantly distorts the complexity of traditional conceptions of it. Schmitt writes that "where only one individual *or several individuals* [emphasis added] should be affected [by a legal act], one can no longer speak of equality" before the law.[7] Is the proviso that a legal act cannot be directed at "several individuals" meant to eliminate the possibility of *any* form of more or less specialized legislation? Unfortunately, the reader will look in vain to Schmitt's writings from the late 1920s and early 1930s for an adequately precise conception of the generality of law. Too often, Schmitt seems to prefer to leave the reader with a set of (unexplicated and often rather murky) quotes from classical liberal political theory. This strategy is hardly surprising: Schmitt is interested in discrediting legal liberalism, not offering a defense of it by reformulating its intellectual foundations. In the *Constitutional Theory* (1928), where Schmitt provides his most extensive discussion of his view of general law, he writes that the principle of equality before the law means that legal "dispensations and privileges, regardless of what form they take," are unacceptable.[8] This rather open-ended definition of the generality of law clearly allows him to attack even the most cautious attempts at characteristically modern forms of social and economic regulation, which undoubtedly require *differentiated and specialized* forms of legislation (focused on specific objects and groups of individuals). If any form of particular or specialized legislation potentially constitutes a tyrannical act of revolutionary violence, the democratic welfare state will have to be depicted in nightmarish terms.

Indeed, Schmitt's writings from Weimar's final years—most importantly, *The Guardian of the Constitution* (1931) and *Legality and Legitimacy* (1932)—are filled with nasty polemics directed against Weimar Germany's so-called "pluralist party state," which, in effect, was Weimar's precocious version of the democratic welfare state, and against its dependence on abandoning nineteenth-century liberalism's (alleged) distinction between state and society. Although numerous commentators have since pointed to the exceedingly modest character of the Weimar welfare state,[9] Schmitt offers a terrifying portrait of Weimar's experiments with the instruments of interventionist politics. As we discussed in chapter 4, Schmitt argues that powerful organized interest groups colonize the Weimar governmental apparatus to such an extent that the German regime is no longer capable of standing above and beyond antagonistic, organized political and social constituencies and resolving conflicts among them. In Schmitt's at times downright apocalyptic account, the emerging welfare state entangles government in a multitude of social and economic spheres. But this entanglement simply results in a crippling of the state's autonomous decision-making capacities; the welfare state no longer allows government to serve as an effective arbitrator among competing interest groups. The "pluralist party state" fails to "distinguish between friend and foe."[10] The emergence of the democratic interventionist state threatens to plunge contemporary politics into a potentially explosive political crisis in which an "ethics of civil war" may be needed to guide political action. The integrity and coherence of the governmental decision-making apparatus are undermined so drastically that constitutionalism in the modern welfare state increasingly amounts to little but an attempt to reach a fragile "peace treaty" among hostile agglomerations of social and political power.[11]

Schmitt's own chief intellectual foe, legal positivism, purportedly facilitates this process in two main ways. First, legal positivists like Kelsen challenge traditional views of state sovereignty in favor of a view of modern democratic government that emphasizes its socially heterogeneous and compromise-oriented character. For Schmitt, positivists endorse precisely that parceling out of state decision-making authority to competing interest groups whose perils Weimar so dramatically illustrates. They encourage profoundly divisive structural tendencies in the democratic welfare state that suggest that its inherent logic is that of the emergency situation.[12] Second, they abandon the classical emphasis on the *semantic* generality of the legal norm in exchange for a view emphasizing the statute's democratic *origins* in a series of parliamentary procedures, thereby legitimizing the subjection of political life to modes of individual, case-oriented legislation that may constitute, as Schmitt had noted in 1926, acts of revolutionary violence.[13] By means of a remarkable intellectual sleight of hand, Schmitt then can depict precisely those voices who fought to the end to defend Weimar—in particular, positivists like Kelsen, sympathetic to the emergence of the democratic welfare state—as revolutionaries bent on debilitating the "substantial kernel" of the Weimar constitutional order.

But Schmitt's original 1926 account contains two further implications as well. Both are rigorously sketched out in his writings from the early 1930s. Although Schmitt repeatedly blames social democrats and their jurist friends for having brought Germany to the brink of political collapse, his *Judicial Independence, Equality Before the Law, and the Protection of Private Property According to the Weimar Constitution* still leaves open the possibility that the abandonment of liberal general law may be justified amid a serious political crisis. Even in 1926, Schmitt conceded that a crisis could require an emergency dictatorship ready to abandon so-called normativistic liberal law in favor of individual measures and commands.[14] In the face of the left's attempt to construct the democratic welfare state—as we have seen, for Schmitt this trend constitutes an implicit revolutionary threat—*just such an emergency regime is what Schmitt now proposes*. With the emergence of executive-based quasi-authoritarian regimes (under Heinrich Brüning and then Franz von Papen) in Germany in 1930,[15] Schmitt outlines a disturbing defense of a plebiscitary dictatorial system guided by precisely those individual measures and commands whose dangers he had seemed to warn his German readers about just a few years earlier. By means of an idiosyncratic reworking of the classical liberal democratic aspiration to distinguish general (parliamentary) laws from individual (executive) decrees, Schmitt provides a justification for a discretionary emergency dictatorship, in his view absolutely necessary if the inept, inefficient and politically perilous "pluralist party state" is to be replaced by a system superior to it. As Peter Gowan has similarly noted, Schmitt hoped to jettison the democratic Weimar welfare state for an authoritarian alternative, a new type of interventionist state that would succeed in divesting itself of burdensome "welfare obligations, [and] commitments to protecting [the] social rights" of subordinate social constituencies.[16] According to Schmitt, the "quantitative total state"—a weak, social-democratic inspired interventionist state—should be replaced by a "qualitative total state"—an alternative brand of interventionism, but one that guarantees authentic state sovereignty while simultaneously managing to provide substantial autonomy to owners of private capital.[17] Despite his railings against social-democratic forms of state activity, Schmitt explicitly argues that an "economic-financial state of emergency" necessitates far-reaching forms of governmental activity in society. Economic affairs and conflicts have become so central to modern politics that Schmitt believes that a careless attempt to disengage the state from social and economic affairs would simply exacerbate social and political tensions and further deepen the crisis of state sovereignty in Germany. But if virtually *any* attempt to undertake state intervention in social and economic life implies a frontal attack on the rule of law-ideal, it would seem that the interventionist state necessitates nothing less than the *complete* abandonment of the liberal rule of law. In other words, interventionist policies require a full-fledged system of arbitrary rule, and governmental social and economic regulation inevitably contains an arbitrary, decisionist legal core.

In *Legality and Legitimacy* Schmitt expressly sketches out the final implications of this line of argumentation. As we saw earlier, there Schmitt concedes that the "the administrative state which manifests itself in the praxis of 'measures' "—by which he means the interventionist state—"is more likely to be appropriate to a 'dictatorship' " than to classical liberal democracy. If the contemporary interventionist state requires discarding general law (and if, furthermore, the interventionist state is absolutely essential to contemporary politics), then the modern interventionist state will have to take the form of an executive-centered dictatorship. Arbitrary government is unavoidable in the era of interventionist politics.[18]

Ultimately, Schmitt's peculiar restatement of the liberal concept of general law thus leads him to pursue an unambiguously illiberal and anti-democratic agenda. It also permits him to vary his argumentation so as to accord with the ever-changing political imperatives of the battle against Weimar liberals and leftists. At first, Schmitt instrumentally employs his definition of general law in a *defensive* manner against attempts by the left to undertake novel forms of state intervention in the capitalist economy. But when Weimar's liberal and left-wing defenders lose political ground, Schmitt then can rely on his interpretation of the liberal legal statute in order to *justify* the establishment of an openly authoritarian, belligerently bourgeois interventionist state.

Would it not be better simply to abandon interventionist politics altogether? Could one try to recapture a classical liberal state/society scenario? Schmitt himself had often recalled, in surprisingly flattering terms, the world of early liberalism in his writings. So why not go back to it?

This is precisely Hayek's answer to the paradoxes of contemporary interventionist politics—which Hayek sees Schmitt as having quite accurately described. Schmitt, however, considers any attempt to return to early liberalism disingenuous. As he comments in *The Guardian of the Constitution*, in the contemporary political universe the demand for "nonintervention becomes a utopia, even a self-contradiction. For nonintervention would mean . . . nothing more than intervention on behalf of those who happen to be most powerful and most irresponsible."[19] For Schmitt, the real question is *who* intervenes, and *whose* interests are to be served by intervention. In his view, substantial state activity is necessary. In contrast to social democratic forms of intervention, Schmitt's own "qualitative total state" allegedly need not infringe unfairly on the privileged position of private capital.

II

Let us now try to return to a second moment in contemporary history. It is 1944. World War II has discredited much of the political right, and the left seems poised for a series of impressive political victories. Once again, the specter of expropriation rears its head. Many on the left consider nationalization a legitimate instrument of progressive public policy, and even some conservatives openly advocate the expropriation of select forms of private property. A young émigré scholar from Austria, Friedrich A. Hayek, responds with a polemic destined to become something of a political bestseller in the postwar world.[20] Addressed "to the socialists of all parties," Hayek's *The Road to Serfdom* dramatically argues that the emerging democratic welfare state is destined to undermine the rule of law and the legal predictability and certainty guaranteed by it.[21] For those familiar with Weimar-era legal debates, much of Hayek's account is surprisingly unoriginal. His own intellectual socialization, as he seems to concede on several occasions, took place in the shadow of the Weimar debates.

Inadequately sensitive to the fundamentally instrumental character of Schmitt's occasional recourse to legal liberalism, Hayek seems to parallel Schmitt's analysis in a number of respects.[22] First, Hayek relies on a dramatic contrast between *general law* and *individual commands or measures*, and his definition of general law is exceedingly open-ended: reminiscent of Schmitt, Hayek states that the rule of law requires that statutes not refer to the "wants and needs of particular people."[23] Although Hayek claims to derive this view from classical liberal political thought, he provides little real textual support for this view in *The Road to Serfdom*; as a matter of fact, classical concepts of general law are more complicated than Hayek suggests.[24] Second, Hayek argues that the growth of state intervention in the economy culminates in a "total state." Of course, Schmitt had introduced this term into German political thought in 1930 when describing the same phenomenon, in which the classical liberal state/society distinction allegedly loses any real significance, and Hayek expressly cites Schmitt's statement in *The Guardian of the Constitution* that the "*neutral* state of the liberal nineteenth century [is being transformed into] the *total* state in which state and society are identical."[25] Most importantly, Hayek seems to endorse Schmitt's central thesis. For Hayek, as for Schmitt, the emerging welfare state *necessitates* arbitrary forms of situation-oriented legal action, and it inevitably cripples parliamentary authority. The mere fusion of state and society, manifested most unambiguously in the contemporary democratic welfare state, unavoidably generates arbitrary government. Hayek shares Schmitt's view that the logic of the interventionist state corresponds most closely to a plebiscitary dictatorship, in "which the head of government is from time to time confirmed in his position by popular vote, but where he has all the powers at his command to make certain that the vote will go in the direction he desires."[26] In Schmitt's categories, the interventionist state is decisionist to the core, and a mass-based plebiscitary dictatorship is best suited to the imperatives of a legal universe destined to take on increasingly decisionist characteristics.

Whereas Schmitt endorses trends toward an authoritarian mass-based dictatorship, Hayek believes that we need to avoid the errors of the Germans: "it is Germany whose fate we are in some danger of repeating."[27] Thus, Hayek opts for a radical curtailing of the welfare state and a return to the "neutral state of the liberal nineteenth century." Allegedly, we can avoid the "road to serfdom," by taking the road back to that historical period when the purported fusion of state and society had yet to occur.

Although *The Road to Serfdom* refers to Schmitt on a number of occasions, Hayek's comments there are misleading. He criticizes Schmitt's Nazi-era polemics, while conveniently ignoring the extent to which his own account of legal decay in the administrative state parallels the idiosyncrasies of Schmitt's argumentation. In subsequent years, however, Hayek is far less reticent about acknowledging his debts to Schmitt. In *The Constitution of Liberty* (1960), which builds on the basic argument of *The Road to Serfdom*, Hayek introduces his definition of general law—which Hayek, like Schmitt, considers the centerpiece not only of the rule of law-ideal, but also of liberalism itself[28]—by citing Schmitt's major Weimar-era studies and commenting that "the conduct of Carl Schmitt under the Hitler regime does not alter the fact that, of the modern German writings on the subject, his are still among the most learned and perceptive."[29] Though Hayek refers to a number of additional sources for his definition of law, he seems to attribute a special place to Schmitt, whom he considers the most impressive opponent of Weimar legal positivism and its disastrous quest (for Hayek, as for Schmitt) to blur the distinction between general law and individual commands and measures. Indeed, Hayek's 1960 study can be interpreted as an attempt to struggle with the limits of Schmitt's problematic definition of the generality of law. At many junctures, Hayek seems to follow Schmitt in suggesting that legal generality is incompatible with any form of legal differentiation or specification whatsoever.[30] But in *The Constitution of Liberty* he appears to recognize the limits of the extreme character of this view. Now he admits that general law is consistent with legal specialization, as long as no individual person or object is *explicitly* named, and a particular legal category is acceptable both to those who fall under it and those who fall outside it.[31] Soon Hayek appears to throw his hands into the air in desperation: he admits that "no entirely satisfactory criterion has been found that would always tell us what kind of classification" is compatible with the ideal of general law.[32] This concession is truly astonishing, given the centrality of the concept of general law to his entire project. Even scholars sympathetic to Hayek's political agenda have emphasized the ambiguity of his definition of general law, and some have even gone so far as to deem it incoherent.[33] But such commentators ignore the manner in which Hayek's open-ended definition of general law allows him, in a manner once again similar to the twists and turns of Schmitt's analysis of legal decay in the welfare state, to rely on what initially seems to be a constant in his theory (the centrality of general law) so as to accord with the immediate imperatives of the political struggle against defenders of the welfare state. Hayek undoubtedly remains hostile to the interventionist welfare state throughout his intellectual career; this is inevitable given his view of the decisionist character of legal action when state and society have fused and the welfare state begins to emerge. But the *intensity* of this hostility clearly shifts. In his 1976 Preface to *The Road to Serfdom*, Hayek himself admits that he had not freed himself adequately in 1944 from "interventionist superstitions,"[34] and his final study, the three-volume *Law, Legislation, and Liberty* (written in the 1970s, amidst immense dissatisfaction with the welfare state and growing neoconservative political strength) is far more belligerent in its antiwelfare state polemics than *The Road to Serfdom*, which was written at a moment of broad sympathy for traditional left-wing economic policies. Because some versions of Hayek's definition of general law suggest that virtually any form of state intervention is incompatible with general law, whereas others provide at least some room for welfare state-type activities, this ambiguity is probably inevitable. Hayek's reliance on Schmitt generates a number of strikingly "decisionistic" elements within the core of his own project.

Still, Hayek's hostility to discretionary tendencies in the contemporary interventionist state hardly makes him a Schmittian. Even if Hayek's account parallels important elements of Schmitt's, it still differs from Schmitt's in many ways. It would be well, for example, to recall Hayek's idiosyncratic attempt to ground the rule of law in a brand of epistemological skepticism that sees rule-based action as an effective way for human beings to compensate for the ultimately limited nature of rationality.[35] And are not Hayek's political intentions, as noted above, clearly distinct from Schmitt's? If so, why should it matter if Hayek borrows from Schmitt?

The relationship between Hayek and Schmitt is more intimate, however, than I have been able to describe thus far. In his final works, Hayek openly endorses the core of Schmitt's critique of the so-called "pluralist party state." Moreover, he is quite honest about this: because the tendency toward legal decay in the interventionist state "has been most explicitly seen" by Schmitt, Hayek writes in *Studies in Philosophy, Politics, and Economics*, he believes that he can use Schmitt's detailed analysis of the democratic welfare state in order to criticize it.[36] Although Schmitt "regularly came down on what to me appears both morally and intellectually the wrong side," Hayek notes subsequently in *Law, Legislation, and Liberty*, the flawed character of the contemporary democratic welfare state "was very clearly seen by the extraordinary German student of politics, Carl Schmitt, who in the 1920s probably understood the character of the developing form of [interventionist] government better than most people."[37] Hayek's 1970s restatement of Schmitt's critique of the Weimar welfare state culminates in a series of institutional proposals having rather disturbing and even authoritarian implications. Having chosen to play by the rules of Schmitt's intellectual universe, Hayek proves unable to escape from all of its dangers.

In *Law, Legislation, and Liberty*, Hayek once again criticizes the tendency to abandon an emphasis on law's semantic generality in favor of a view emphasizing law's democratic origins in the legislative process. Again he attributes this fatal error to legal positivism and, most importantly, to Hans Kelsen. But now Hayek takes an additional step. He argues that the disintegration of general law generates a situation in which governmental authority is handed over to competing organized interests. When general law is abandoned, traditional liberal democratic institutions undergo a dramatic functional transformation. Open debate and political exchange within parliament are replaced by bargaining among bureaucratic parties more concerned with having their narrow interests represented than with engaging in liberal dialogue with their political opponents. Parties become amalgams of special interests aiming to have their (particularistic) desires achieved by particular or individual laws. Legislatures are so busy providing special favors to interest groups, and their activity is no longer distinct enough from that of administrators, that they no longer have time even for meaningful political deliberation.[38] When government is permitted to issue measures and commands, it makes sense for legislators to appeal to privileged, particularistic interest blocs; allegedly, this danger is reduced when legislators are allowed only to issue general rules and, thus, commit themselves solely to policies embodying the common good. Because contemporary liberal democracy has betrayed the traditional concept of general law, a "para-government has grown up, consisting of trade associations, trade unions and professional associations, designed primarily to divert as much as possible of the stream of governmental favour to their members."[39] Since the legislature is no longer limited by the requirements of legal generality, it is nominally omnipotent. But in fact it "becomes as a result of unlimited powers exceedingly weak, the playball of all the separate interests it has to satisfy."[40] The overall account of the contemporary welfare state here is very much like Schmitt's: supporters of the welfare state and their legal positivist allies ignore the virtues of legal generality, thus paving the way for the fusion of state and society and a "quantitative total state" that intervenes in a multitude of social spheres and seems all-powerful, but in fact is robbed of any real decision-making authority.

What then is Hayek's answer to the quagmires of contemporary interventionist politics? In the final volume of *Law, Legislation, and Liberty*, he concludes that we need institutional reforms that recapture the gist of classical attempts to distinguish clearly between legislative and governmental (or administrative) activities. Legislation should be limited to general rules, whereas government should be subordinate to legislation and "act on concrete matters, the allocation of particular means to particular purposes."[41] Because the activities of existing legislatures have come to differ little from what classical liberal thought would have considered situation-specific, relatively discretionary administrative activities, the contemporary legislature should be subordinated to a new upper house, that alone could make sure that proper legislative functions are performed, most importantly, lawmaking guided by genuine political exchange and taking the form only of general rules. Because "probity, wisdom, and judgement" are required of Hayek's ideal deliberative legislators, most appropriate would be an "an assembly of men and women elected at a relatively mature age for fairly long periods, such as fifteen years, so that they would not be concerned about being re-elected."[42]

Hayek's proposed legislature, which "should not be very numerous" and would consist of representatives "between their forty-fifth and sixtieth years," would be chosen in a manner altogether different from present legislatures. Since "it would seem wise to rely on the old experience that a man's contemporaries are his fairest judges," government would "ask each group of people of the same age once in their lives" to elect the legislature.[43] Making voting a one-time act should encourage "probity" among citizens as well, and thus help immunize them from the perils of special interest politics.

Two features of Hayek's curious institutional proposal are of special significance for us here. First, a real conceptual tension manifests itself in Hayek's political model, and it probably stems from his implicit dependence on Schmitt. Repeatedly, Hayek in *Law, Legislation, and Liberty* argues that "governmental" activities are unavoidably discretionary. This point is consistent with his endorsement of Schmitt's thesis that state intervention in social and economic affairs tends to require a decisionistic legal form.[44] But how then would it be possible to subordinate or regulate these activities in accordance with general legislative norms? If they are truly decisionistic—and thus a profound threat to freedom—it would seem that Hayek would probably have to exclude this possibility. By definition, decisionist state activity cannot be regulated in accordance with classical liberal legal norms. Hayek's dilemma looks something like this: *either* interventionist activities are genuinely decisionist and thus cannot be effectively subjected to "normativistic" general rules, *or* they may not be all that decisionist after all, and thus need not imply that the welfare state has already taken significant strides down the "road to serfdom." Unfortunately, Hayek sometimes wants to have it both ways. He wants to warn people of the inevitable perils of growing state activity *and* to claim, at least implicitly, that state activity may not be all that worrisome since it potentially could be regulated in accordance with general law.[45]

Second, one needs to ask whether Hayek's model deserves to be considered compatible with the basic ideals of modern liberal democracy. Liberal democracy has taken relatively distinct institutional forms in modern history. This fact should suggest that liberal democratic ideals are compatible with a rich diversity of institutional mechanisms. Could Hayek's proposals here pass some hypothetical test or standard that we might come up with for determining whether a particular set of institutions can still be deemed liberal democratic? To be sure, his model would result in a vast reduction in existing possibilities for democratic participation, and a sizable number even of the rather apathetic citizens found in contemporary liberal democracy would probably see them as constituting a substantial rollback of some of their most basic democratic rights. If we were to answer this question in the negative, it might further suggest that Hayek's reliance on Schmitt has proven rather costly. For then we could interpret Hayek's argument as an implicit concession to Schmitt's view that the "pluralist party state" ultimately can be transformed effectively only by authoritarian means. As noted above, Schmitt openly endorsed aspirations to free the interventionist state from social policy-based obligations to subordinate social groups, and he advocated a new form of interventionist politics, but one allegedly distinct from its Weimar predecessor in part because of its guarantees of autonomy to the owners of private capital. Despite undeniable differences between Hayek and Schmitt on this issue,[46] there is more than a faint echo of Schmitt's project in Hayek's argument: the concluding chapter of *Law, Legislation, and Liberty* ends with a call for a "dethronement of politics"—specifically, a dramatic reduction of state activity, which Hayek sees as overwhelmingly *social democratic* in character, in private capitalism. Although it would be unfair to Hayek to obscure the real differences between his rather peculiar political model and Schmitt's preference for a plebiscitary dictatorship,[47] Hayek is ultimately less distant from Schmitt than Hayek claims. Hayek is legitimately disturbed by Schmitt's model of a plebiscitary dictatorship in which questions are posed from above by an authority unaccountable to effective public control. Yet his own institutional vision is hardly altogether free of the authoritarianism evident in Schmitt's proposals.

Given Hayek's acceptance of so much of Schmitt's unflattering portrayal of the contemporary democratic welfare state, how could this be otherwise? Let me restate the underlying enigma noted in chapter 4: if we believe that the decision-making authority of contemporary government is crippled by characteristically welfare state-type organized interests, and if such interest blocs possess a genuinely popular basis in substantial portions of the citizenry[48] (for example, labor unions in parts of western Europe), does it not then make sense for some would-be reformer to demand a curtailment of traditional democratic mechanisms and rights? How else might the state be effectively cleansed of the influence of groups representing public employees, senior citizens, labor, or any of a diversity of other interests potentially hostile to an aggressive bourgeois economic agenda? Moreover, if the current situation is as apocalyptic as Schmitt and Hayek claim, dramatic action would seem absolutely imperative today. If the welfare state necessarily means, as Schmitt hinted in 1930, that its inhabitants are in a situation of civil war, then it is perfectly logical for critics of the welfare state to respond with an emergency dictatorship of their own.

III

To its credit, Schmitt's theory at least indirectly acknowledges that a full-fledged assault on the democratic welfare state today may very well find itself forced to revert to authoritarian political means. Hayek never explicitly endorses this view. Nonetheless, his peculiar brand of neoliberalism ultimately illustrates Schmitt's point. Notwithstanding Hayek's anxieties about the growth of discretionary state authority in our century, he seems to have surprisingly few qualms about defending a rather troubling political alternative to contemporary liberal democracy. Why? Like Schmitt, Hayek ultimately sees the interventionist welfare state as a genuine revolutionary threat to a political universe dominated by those with "property and education" [*Besitz und Bildung*]. Given the welfare state's purportedly revolutionary character, both theorists are ready to unleash a disturbing array of political instruments against it.

An analysis of the unholy alliance of Carl Schmitt and Friedrich Hayek potentially does more than provide an exegetical explanation for the sources of the more problematic political components of Hayek's market-oriented neoliberalism. In my view, it potentially offers a fruitful starting point for understanding the elective affinity between free-market economics and authoritarian politics that has become so common in the contemporary political universe. The unholy alliance of Schmitt and Hayek suggests that there is certainly more than one possible "road to serfdom" open to us today. In our times, the most tempting of such roads may very well be prepared by those who claim to represent liberal ideals, but in fact caricature and thereby rob those ideals of anything worth defending.

9

ANOTHER HIDDEN DIALOGUE—CARL SCHMITT AND HANS MORGENTHAU

In a series of autobiographical reflections published shortly before his death in 1980, Hans Morgenthau abruptly claimed that one of Carl Schmitt's most influential works, *The Concept of the Political*, borrowed substantially from Morgenthau's early Weimar writings in international law. Given its sensational character, Morgenthau's own retelling of this story deserves to be quoted in detail.

After conceding that Schmitt's work briefly influenced him as a young scholar, Morgenthau asserts that

> [i]t was with this man of immense—and intellectually well-deserved—prestige that I came into fleeting contact at the beginning of my academic career. In 1927 Schmitt had published a short book called *The Concept of the Political* that had a sensational impact upon German political thinking. I conceived of my doctor's thesis partly as a reply to that book although . . . the final title did not show it. But Schmitt recognized it immediately for what it was and wrote me a very complimentary letter, one of the very few I received on the publication of this, my first book. I was understandably overjoyed and asked Schmitt for an interview.[1]

Morgenthau then recounts that he visited Schmitt, only to encounter a "cold, contrived, dishonest" careerist more interested in staging "a public relations production" for one of his colleagues, Karl Bilfinger, than engaging in a serious intellectual exchange with an obscure young scholar.[2] In light of his personal experiences with Schmitt, Morgenthau notes that he was hardly surprised by the depth of Schmitt's subsequent enthusiasm for National Socialism. "No German political thinker of the interwar period

225

was more amply endowed with intellectual ability, but it is doubtful whether any surpassed him in lack of principle and servility to his Nazi masters."[3] According to Morgenthau, during the Nazi period Schmitt aspired to become nothing less than the "Streicher of the legal profession."[4]

Yet Morgenthau's story hardly ends there: "Schmitt paid me still a further compliment. He changed the second [1932] edition of his *Concept of the Political* in the light of the new propositions of my thesis without lifting the veil of anonymity from their author."[5] In short, Morgenthau suggests that one of the central texts of twentieth-century right-wing authoritarianism, Schmitt's *Concept of the Political*, integrates the insights of a young German-Jewish scholar forced to emigrate in 1933. This young scholar went on to a spectacular academic career, becoming one of America's most prominent political scientists and an intellectual driving force behind the Realist school of international relations.

Does the textual evidence suppport Morgenthau's claim? What exactly is the relation between Morgenthau's political thinking and "that brilliant, inventive scholar" whose character flaws so disgusted Morgenthau?[6]

I

A veritable academic growth industry surrounds Schmitt's *The Concept of the Political*.[7] Most recently, the Munich political theorist Heinrich Meier has offered an account of the evolution of Schmitt's thinking on "the concept of the political," carefully tracing the differences between the various (1927, 1932, and 1933) versions of what arguably constitutes Schmitt's most influential book. Although Meier in my view overstates the theological features of Schmitt's thinking, there is no question that we should be grateful for the light he sheds on the "hidden dialogue" that took place between Leo Strauss and Carl Schmitt in the early 1930s. In Meier's account, substantial differences between the 1932 and the 1933 versions of Schmitt's *Concept of the Political* can be attributed to Strauss's insightful 1932 critique of Schmitt's work.[8] Even though Schmitt long failed to acknowledge his intellectual debt to Strauss, Meier shows that Strauss clearly played a role in the formulation of Schmitt's "concept of the political."

Meier also observes that many elements of Strauss' post-Weimar oeuvre can be fruitfully interpreted as an attempt to respond to the problematic aspects of Schmitt's political and legal theory. Unfortunately, Meier's reading of Schmitt as a theological thinker probably leads him to understate the manner in which Strauss tried to distinguish himself from Schmitt. For those familiar both with Strauss's *Natural Right and History* and Schmitt's work, it is hard to avoid the conclusion that the decisionism criticized so forcefully in Strauss's most famous book bears a striking resemblance to core elements of Schmitt's political theory.[9] For Strauss, the fact that Schmitt's decisionism remained within "the horizons of liberalism" demonstrates unequivocally that the only answer to the pathologies of Western modernity lies in a return to classic natural right. In some contrast to Strauss himself, Meier is dismissive of those who focus on the decisionist features of Schmitt's theory. Because Meier obfuscates the deep irrationalist strands within Schmitt's theory, he downplays the manner in which Strauss's antimodernism can be read as a frontal attack on the (for Strauss, inherently modernist) decisionism embodied by Schmitt.[10] Although Schmitt and Strauss shared some common views—Meier notes that both were hostile to liberal democratic aspirations for a "world state"—ultimately Strauss was chiefly concerned with providing a *critical* rejoinder to Schmitt.

For our purposes here, a second weakness within Meier's learned study is of greater immediate significance. Because Meier is primarily concerned with chronicling Strauss's impact on Schmitt, he also clouds the fact that the truly important shifts in the basic argumentation of "the concept of the political" occurred between 1927 and 1932, *not* 1932 and 1933. Whereas the 1933 version of *Concept of the Political* did include some changes probably encouraged by Strauss's 1932 essay,[11] far more *fundamental* shifts in Schmitt's thinking can be identified between the 1927 and 1932 versions.[12] Moreover, those shifts in argumentation can be attributed to the influence of the young Morgenthau, who published an astute discussion of the "concept of the political" in a long-forgotten 1929 treatise on international law. As was later the case with Strauss as well, Schmitt never acknowledged Morgenthau's impact on his political theory. Particularly during the Nazi period, Schmitt was disinclined to concede his intellectual debt to Jewish scholars, especially those, like the young Morgenthau, associated with the democratic left.[13] Nonetheless, there was not only a second "hidden dialogue" between Morgenthau and Schmitt, but also this second dialogue, in my view, was ultimately more decisive for the constitution of Schmitt's "concept of the political" than Schmitt's dialogue with Strauss.

Although he fails to acknowledge its proper significance, even Meier is forced to take note of the striking differences between the 1927 "Concept of the Political" and the 1932 book with the same title. Meier rightly notes that Schmitt initially engaged in a rhetoric of "pure politics."[14] That is, Schmitt in 1927 described politics as constituting a distinct and independent value sphere existing *alongside* competing value spheres of morality, aesthetics, and economics. In this line of argumentation, politics is fundamentally distinct from economic, moral, and aesthetic activities. Its basic rules—in Schmitt's terminology, its criteria—are structurally distinct as well. Morality concerns the problem of good and bad, aesthetics is occupied with the contrast between the beautiful and the ugly, and economics with profitability and unprofitability, while politics concerns the contrast of friend and foe. The criterion of friend/foe refers to an altogether distinct category of objects from that of those captured by the criteria of "good versus evil" or "profitable versus unprofitable." For Schmitt in 1927, the political sphere was autonomous and distinct in exactly the same manner that other spheres of activity are.[15]

One can legitimately reach the conclusion that Schmitt in 1927 was hoping to build on Max Weber's famous account of the disenchantment of modern society, according to which distinct "life" or "value spheres," operating according to independent and autonomous logics, liberate themselves from all-encompassing religious worldviews. In Weber's famous lectures on "Science as a Vocation" and "Politics as a Vocation," which Schmitt reportedly attended in Munich at the end of World War I, a similar attempt to distinguish political activity from alternative value spheres organized according to distinct internal logics can already be detected.[16] Schmitt aspired to sketch out the details of a political complement to Weber's analysis of modernity, in which the autonomy of the political sphere had been implicitly acknowledged but hardly developed with sufficient refinement.[17] Meier downplays this intellectual context because it meshes poorly with his emphasis on religious motifs within Schmitt's thought. In my alternative (and more conventional) reading, the clear delineation of the value sphere of politics from morality within both Weber and Schmitt should be taken as an acknowledgment of the fundamentally disenchanted character of modern political existence: the very starting point of Schmitt's "concept of the political" is Weber's diagnosis of the *Entzauberung* of Western modernity. At the very least, this reading allows us to make sense of why Schmitt ultimately had no qualms whatsoever about abandoning religiously inspired normative ideals that long had played a major role in Western moral and political thought. Schmitt not only is dismissive of even minimal ideals of basic human equality (deriving in part from the intellectual legacy of Christianity), but also delights in the exercise of "brute power" in a manner inconsistent with even the most authoritarian strands of Christian political thought.[18]

Meier correctly notes that in the 1932 *Concept of the Political* the "conception of [independent] domains is replaced by a model of intensity."[19] Whereas the 1927 version of the text describes politics as fundamentally separate from other forms of activity, Schmitt in 1932 instead emphasizes that politics can spring up in a host of distinct arenas of human existence. Though the original 1927 essay occasionally seems to concede the oddity of the attempt to delineate politics clearly from other spheres of human activity, given the fact that political conflicts seem to relate inextricably to moral, economic, and even aesthetic differences,[20] only in 1932 does Schmitt unambiguously acknowledge the inappropriateness of the attempt to conceptualize politics as something basically unrelated to other forms of human activity. Schmitt grasps that "*everything* is potentially political," and he notes that politics can emerge in every domain of human existence.[21] In the 1932 *Concept of the Political*, politics is still described as an independent domain, but Schmitt clarifies his original statement by adding that this is so neither in "the same or analogous" manner as other spheres of activity, nor "in the sense of having its own separate object" [*nicht im Sinne einen eigenen neuen Sachgebietes*].[22] Politics no longer refers to a pregiven set of objects or concerns, but instead to "the most extreme degree of intensity of a bond or a separation, of an association or a disassociation."[23] A moral, an economic, or an aesthetic difference becomes political when it gains an especially intense character, so that in the extreme case violent conflicts are imminent. Political conflicts are those denoting the most extreme degree of intensity in struggles between opposed constellations of friends and foes, *not* those focussing on an a priori set of objects or concerns.

Meier's exclusive interest in the Schmitt-Strauss nexus does not allow him to decipher the sources of this decisive argumentative shift. An examination of Morgenthau's *The International Judicial System: Its Essence and Its Limits* (1929) helps us fill that gap. Focusing on the limitations of the international judicial system, Morgenthau in this early study not only thematizes many of the fundamental problems of international law that long fascinated Schmitt, but also devotes a substantial section of it to elaborating Morgenthau's own attempt to formulate a "concept of the political."[24] In 1929, Morgenthau was an assistant to Hugo Sinzheimer, a prominent Social

Democrat and an architect of significant Weimar social and labor legislation. Notwithstanding intense political disagreements between Schmitt and the young socialists attracted to Sinzheimer, Schmitt was acquainted with the younger lawyers who moved in Sinzheimer's circle at the University of Frankfurt. A number of them, including Franz Neumann and Ernst Fraenkel, were similarly engaged in the task of offering a critical response to Schmitt.[25] Although Schmitt's name appears only in the footnotes to Morgenthau's study, it is clear that Morgenthau in fact did intend his "doctor's thesis partly as a reply" to the 1927 version of "the concept of the political."[26] Morgenthau's dissertation challenges the idea that politics can be associated with a delimitable set of objects or concerns. In short, Morgenthau directly tackled Schmitt's 1927 model of a "pure politics." For his part, Schmitt seems to have grasped the significance of Morgenthau's dissertation for his own work. Although no copies of the personal correspondence described by Morgenthau have been located, annotated copies of Morgenthau's first book were found in Schmitt's personal library at his death.[27]

In the context of international law, Morgenthau observes in 1929, even seemingly noncontroversial matters (for example, internationally certified labor agreements, or intellectual property rights), often regulated with relative ease by means of international legal agreements, can suddenly take on a potentially violent character. Morgenthau concedes that some objects within international law seem on the whole less likely to become controversial or prone to violence (for example, postal agreements) than others (armaments). Yet he rightly insists that in the history of international law even generally noncontroversial objects have on occasion become the site of intense conflicts between nation-states. Pointing the way to Schmitt's 1932 reformulation of "the concept of the political," Morgenthau asserts that "there are no questions at all that deserve to be described as 'political' for eternity, whose political character derives from their internal nature and the concept of the political. . . ."[28] The fact that one state in an international dispute describes a conflict as "political," whereas its opponents dispute the political character of the conflict at hand, suggests that the very attempt to distinguish between political and nonpolitical objects can take an eminently political form.[29] Politics can occur in any domain, and claims to the contrary are often politically motivated.

For the young Morgenthau, the concept of the political hence must be described instead as "a characteristic, quality, or coloration, which any substance can take on. . . ."[30] An object can gain this quality to a greater or lesser extent, just as a physical object can be more or less warm.[31] But what exactly is the nature of the attribute of "politics"? Morgenthau claims that an initial definition could legitimately assert that politics, at least in the international arena, concerns the preservation and pursuit of "the individuality of a state" in relation to other states.[32] Yet a definition along these lines is unlikely to prove helpful; Morgenthau notes that it would necessarily include a vast array of relatively noncontroversial matters in interstate relations that rarely become the subject of intense controversy. Thus, we need a more nuanced "concept of the political" that allows us to make sense of those conflicts between states that prove particularly troublesome. As an international lawyer, Morgenthau was primarily concerned with explaining why some political conflicts are unlikely to be effectively resolved by judicial devices. In 1929, he was still relatively hopeful about the prospects of an ambitious system of international courts. Nonetheless, Morgenthau believed that an international judicial system is likely to gain legitimacy only if it is possible to determine successfully *which* political conflicts are inappropriate objects of judicial scrutiny. From this perspective, few things are more dangerous to the success of international law than is the ill-conceived quest to use judicial devices to solve fundamental conflicts in which the very question of the political status quo—and the legal system that rests on it—is at stake. Contra Schmitt, the young Morgenthau was fascinated by the problem of the *limits* to international judicial mechanisms, not in order to discredit the liberal quest for international law, but because he hoped to secure and strengthen it. Unlike Schmitt, Morgenthau in 1929 was not indiscriminately dismissive of legal "normativities." Instead, he worried about the dangers of a superficial legalism that naively posits that any conceivable political conflict can be resolved by courts and judges.

In this context, Morgenthau introduces "the model of intensity" that was later to loom so large in Schmitt's 1932 *Concept of the Political*. Morgenthau argues that the "concept of the political" in the proper sense of the term refers exclusively to "the degree of intensity with which an object of interest to a state relates to the individuality of a state."[33] Political conflicts are those exhibiting an especially intense or passionate character; for this reason, they are refractory to peaceful legal settlement.[34] Within the sphere of interstate relations, "the specifically political quality is to be seen in the particularly close relation that rulers assert from time to time between the state and certain goods or values that they hold indispensable to its security or greatness."[35] Conflicts concerning such goods and values, whose specific characteristics obviously vary enormously, are political dynamite and thus unlikely to be resolved satisfactorily by judicial devices. In this sense of the term, a dispute can be more or less political (just as it can be more or less warm or cold); intensity is always a matter of degree. Morgenthau concedes that it is probably impossible to determine at precisely what juncture a conflict can be described as political. The fact that political conflicts are by definition "passionate" makes it difficult to come up with a set of rational criteria or standards according to which one might unambiguously "measure" the political character of a particular conflict. Intense political experience means that it tends to elude every attempt to subsume it under determinate, general concepts like those typically employed by either the lawyer or the scientist.[36] Nonetheless, it remains possible to characterize political conflicts as having a "high" degree of intensity, even if it is necessarily difficult to determine exactly how high that degree of intensity must be if a conflict is legitimately to be described as political.

Of course, Morgenthau's argument at this stage might fairly be described as tautological: explosive political conflicts are those possessing substantial intensity. But *why* do some conflicts become intense or explosive in the first place? Schmitt's subsequent answer to this question rests chiefly on philosophical anthropology. Schmitt in 1932 defends a tradition of "realistic" political thinkers (Niccolò Machiavelli, Thomas Hobbes, J. G. Fichte, Joseph de Maistre, Donoso Cortes, G. W. F. Hegel) by asserting that their depiction of human beings as essentially aggressive and conflictual is more accurate than the naive and purportedly antipolitical model of human nature found in liberal and democratic authors like John Locke or Thomas Paine, who allegedly dispute the inherent "evilness" of man. In this view, the inevitability of intense, life-threatening political conflicts is always preprogrammed into the structure of human nature.[37] Politics is bloody because human beings are fundamentally bloodthirsty. For Meier, this strand within Schmitt's thinking provides unambiguous evidence of Schmitt's theological aspiration to ground political theory in a picture of a "fallen" humanity driven out of the Garden of Eden. Supposedly, Schmitt's political theory relies directly on the theological assumption of original sin.[38] When developing this argument, Schmitt indeed does refer to some theorists of the authoritarian Catholic right. By the same token, Meier's reading conveniently obscures the fact that Schmitt here repeatedly appealed to authors (for example, Machiavelli and Hobbes) who strove for a secularized, "realistic" picture of human nature and sought to *limit* the role of the church in secular affairs. If this *is* political theology, it is a strange one indeed: some of the most influential high priests of Schmitt's political theology were precisely those political thinkers who played a pivotal role in the secularization of modern political life.

At one juncture, Morgenthau in 1929 similarly hints at the possibility that the intensity of political life derives in part from "drives" constitutive of human nature;[39] Morgenthau's subsequent American writings develop this line of inquiry in much greater depth. But in 1929 Morgenthau primarily offers a legal-sociological explanation for intense political conflict. Only this distinct strand in Morgenthau's thinking allows us to make sense of the *fundamental* differences separating him from Carl Schmitt.

Meier points out that in the 1927 version "Schmitt speaks of 'war' seventy-seven times in the thirty-three paragraphs of his essay. The term 'civil war' does not occur once."[40] One might legitimately read Schmitt in 1927 as "reducing the political to foreign affairs."[41] The political becomes manifest when a "real possibility of killing" the foe occurs, and the foe is probably a foreigner, "the other, the stranger" [*der Andere, der Fremde*].[42] Foreign affairs, it seems, is the primary site of authentic politics. In 1932, "the concept of the political" then encompasses explosive domestic political conflicts as well as foreign wars. In part because of Schmitt's belated acknowledgment of the ubiquity of politics (recall that politics can *emerge* in any sphere of human affairs), Schmitt in 1932 expressly refers to the possibility of *civil war* and the existence of an "internal enemy." At home as well as abroad, conflicts can take on an intense political form in which the "possibility of killing" becomes imminent. For Schmitt in 1932, the possibility of civil war is as crucial for understanding the political as the specter of a foreign war.[43]

The distinction between civil and foreign war is a pivotal element of Morgenthau's 1929 comments. Conceivably, Schmitt's 1932 terminological reformulations on this issue can be attributed to Morgenthau as well. On one level, Morgenthau's original argument indeed foreshadows Schmitt's 1932 reflections. According to the fundamental principles of the "model of intensity" conception of the political formulated by Morgenthau, there is no reason to assume an a priori difference between domestic and foreign politics: "domestic and foreign politics constitute realms that are not essentially distinct," since conflicts in both realms obviously can become highly passionate.[44] At the same time, Morgenthau's 1929 account goes much further than Schmitt's in trying to explain why intense, potentially violent conflicts are more common in the international arena than in the sphere of domestic politics. Unlike Schmitt, Morgenthau in 1929 understands that philosophical anthropology hardly suffices as an explanation for why international conflicts are generally more explosive than domestic ones. Even if we accept a pessimistic model of human nature, it fails to demonstrate why some conflicts tend to become "existentially" intense while others do not.

Morgenthau argues that in the domestic arena the intensity of conflict is minimized in part because the political system generally provides an "elastic" framework for responding to changes in the configuration of political conflict. Legal norms can be altered in response to changing political needs; intense political struggles are typically resolved by means of peaceful institutional mechanisms whose legitimacy is acknowledged by all affected parties. The "system of norms" (that is, domestic legislative and judicial devices) generally succeed in providing an outlet for political conflict. In Morgenthau's 1929 terminology, the "system of norms" in the domestic arena is sufficiently "dynamic," which is another way of saying that it can adapt effectively to changes in the de facto structure of political conflict. Of course, this adaptation does not always happen. When "the system of norms" fails to respond effectively to the ever-changing structure of political conflict, civil war or revolution may result. Static and inflexible legislative and judicial instruments also potentially generate political violence in the domestic arena.[45]

For Morgenthau, such explosions are the exception in the domestic arena. But they constitute the rule in international politics. The fundamental failing of the existing system of international law is its static nature. International law codifies the international political status quo, while failing to provide adequate norm-based mechanisms with which interested parties could readjust international law so as better to correspond to the facts of political life: "The development of international law stopped at precisely that juncture where the most fundamental function of a legal system commences."[46] Existing international legal norms "freeze" the political constellation that existed when they were formulated and rendered valid. Yet either norms by means of which international law itself could be effectively altered are missing, or their enforcement depends on great powers likely to have a vested interest in the maintenance of the status quo. Morgenthau in 1929 clearly had one of the failings of the League of Nations in mind—the fact that its amendment procedures made it virtually impossible for defeated powers (like the Germans) to reshuffle the basic rules of the international system. Yet his argument is broader in scope. In the final analysis, the problem at hand is that the legal status quo in the international arena remains reminiscent of that "primitive, undeveloped" moment in human existence when conflicts between individuals themselves were ultimately resolved by violence because human communities had yet to develop flexible "systems of norms" capable of responding to shifts in power on the domestic level.[47]

Why then Morgenthau's simultaneous skepticism in *The International Judicial System: Its Essence and Its Limits* about ambitious attempts to extend the scope of international courts? Might not a dramatically expanded role for courts provide exactly that "dynamic" legal system allegedly missing from the international arena? In the domestic arena, courts obviously constitute one feature of a flexible "system of norms" essential to the task of minimizing the threat of violence.

The young Morgenthau's implicit endorsement of legal formalism probably led him to insist on a relatively limited role for courts in the international arena. In this view, courts are most effective when they avoid fundamental political conflicts and limit themselves to applying, in as non-discretionary a manner as possible, clearly formulated rules. Courts are intrinsically conservative institutions best suited to the task of providing legal expression to the political status quo; courts are likely to perform poorly when allocated the task of fundamentally reshuffling the basic structure of political power.[48] Even within the confines of a stable nation-state, courts deal poorly with political questions concerning the basic distribution of power: it would be naive, for example, to think that the question of slavery within the United States could have been resolved successfully by the Supreme Court. In this view, the chronic error of many liberal international lawyers is that they downplay the fact that an international legal system inevitably needs institutions, such as parliament on the domestic scene, that are suited to the task of undertaking fundamental shifts in political power. International lawyers rush to grant powers to international courts that they would rightly deny their judicial corollaries on the domestic scene.[49]

Morgenthau openly concedes the basic verity of Schmitt's observation that much international law remains profoundly indeterminate in character. Like Schmitt, he even considers the Monroe Doctrine a paradigmatic example of an open-ended clause exploited by a great power for the sake of gaining political hegemony over its neighbors.[50] In clear contrast to Schmitt, however, Morgenthau takes the pervasiveness of such standards as evidence of the underdeveloped status of the international political system: vague norms provide a pseudolegal mask for intense and stormy conflicts unlikely to be effectively resolved by judicial devices. Such norms exhibit few of the virtues of legality (generality, prospectiveness, stability, and clarity) because they address intense political conflicts that explode the confines of formal law. For Morgenthau, the existence of such conflicts calls out for the establishment of a more ambitious "dynamic" system of determinate international legal norms able to offer a vehicle for the expression of fundamental shifts in the distribution of power. Indeterminate norms are hardly intrinsic to international law. Instead, they point to the necessity of establishing a reformed international legal order capable of grappling with the changing exigencies of political conflict.[51]

Although his 1932 *Concept of the Political* thus is likely to have been shaped by Morgenthau, Schmitt never publicly responded to Morgenthau's sociological reinterpretation of the "concept of the political." It is possible, however, to discern the outlines of his likely response. Schmitt probably would have answered Morgenthau by asserting that it was simply naive to believe that the international order could be successfully reformed. As discussed in chapter 6, for Schmitt liberal aspirations to extend the scope of international law represent a hypocritical quest to extend American imperialism; for Schmitt, this quest is likely to deepen political conflict and to increase the likelihood of violent wars. In contrast, Morgenthau in 1929 hints at the possibility that fundamental reforms of the international legal system might be possible. He asserts that it would be intellectually narrow-minded to declare that it is a priori impossible for the human community to develop more effective forms of international conflict resolution. Dramatic changes have already occurred in the history of humanity's struggle to rely on norm-based devices to tame the specter of violence, and there is no intellectually honest reason for excluding the possibility of further improvements.[52] From this perspective, Schmitt's static view of the international order simply reproduces the worst ills of the unsatisfying international legal status quo.

What of Schmitt's complementary claim that the movement toward an international political community, if it *were* somehow to succeed, would merely rob human experience of its political character? As Schmitt comments in 1932, "[a] world in which the possibility of war is utterly eliminated, a completely pacified globe, would be a world without the distinction of friend and enemy and hence a world without politics."[53] According to Meier, Schmitt's hostility to the world-state also manifests itself in Strauss's writings: "Leo Strauss knows himself to be in agreement with Carl Schmitt in disapproving of a world-state, in rejecting the illusory security of a status quo of comfort and ease, in holding in low esteem a world of mere entertainment and the mere capacity to be interesting."[54]

Morgenthau's 1929 study also perceptively suggests why this shared picture of the liberal dream of a strengthened international community is a caricature. Morgenthau refuses to disparage conflict and competition over a vast array of social goods (including money and professions) for detracting from the "seriousness" of human life; the modern attempt to funnel conflict into peaceful channels is worthy of our respect, and Morgenthau seems skeptical of the claim that universal "comfort and ease" would be such a terrible thing. More importantly, even within the relatively secure confines of the modern nation-state where violence is the exception and not the rule, politics has hardly disappeared. Conflicts *always* risk taking a passionate form. Even a hypothetical "world-state" would necessarily be ridden with political conflict. What the modern nation-state *has* achieved is a certain capacity for minimizing the intensity of political conflict within its borders so as to prevent conflict, in most cases, from taking a violent form. The quest to strengthen international law hardly entails an attempt to flee from the harsh realities of political life. Yet a strengthened international legal system might offer a way to minimize the more destructive and violent facets of politics that so long have plagued humanity. Intense political activity will always be with us. But intensity need not mean incessant bloodshed.[55]

II

In the autumn of 1933, the twenty-eight-year-old Hans Morgenthau found himself "retired" as a result of the ethnic cleansing pursued by Carl Schmitt and the Nazis.[56] He would spend most of the next five years on the run.

Morgenthau taught briefly at the University of Geneva, where he faced hostile colleagues and anti-Semitic harassment by visiting German students. In 1935, he made his way to the University of Madrid in the fledgling Spanish Republic. Franco's victory put an end to any hopes of permanent residency there. Nor did the United States greet the refugee with open arms; the elderly Morgenthau later recounted depressing tales of the anti-Semitism he encountered from American immigration authorities. For a German Jew who had once aspired to contribute to the strengthening of international law, the rise of Nazism and war in Europe resulted in immeasurable personal, political, and intellectual turmoil.[57] A witness both to the demise of Weimar and the Spanish Civil War, the Morgenthau who arrived in New York in 1937 was a considerably more skeptical man than the Morgenthau who in 1929 had demanded a global rule of law. That skepticism would shape his critical reflections on liberal visions of an international legal and political order throughout the remainder of his long intellectual career.

Not surprisingly in light of Schmitt's prominence during the Nazi period, Morgenthau continued his intense intellectual engagement with the German theorist. Most importantly, in 1933 Morgenthau authored an incisive critique of Schmitt's *Concept of the Political* that Schmitt neither acknowledged nor answered. As part of a broader French-language study building directly on his 1929 reflections, Morgenthau scrutinizes Schmitt's "concept of the political" in order to demonstrate its intellectual and political bankruptcy. Of course, it is easy to understand why Morgenthau was so concerned in 1933 with distancing his own ideas from Schmitt's. Schmitt had borrowed directly from Morgenthau's work; Morgenthau's surprising accusation that Schmitt had effectively plagiarized from his doctoral thesis sufaces for the first time in his 1933 *La Notion du politique et la théorie des différends internationaux*.[58] Morgenthau very much needed to prove the superiority of his own "concept of the political" in the face of the Nazi Schmitt's appropriation of some of his core insights.

Morgenthau's 1933 critical reflections again focus on the ambiguities of Schmitt's claim that we need to envision politics as an autonomous value sphere distinct from the competing value spheres of morality, aesthetics, and economics. Morgenthau first unpacks Schmitt's crucial unstated conceptual assumptions by noting that Schmitt's model of a set of distinct value spheres rests implicitly on two distinct oppositions or contrasts [*Gegensätze*]. First, each individual value sphere is contrasted to competing value spheres (thus, politics is different from economics, morals, and aesthetics). Each sphere is different *in relation* to other spheres, and thus one can reasonably speak of the "political" as different from the "nonpolitical" (morals, aesthetics, and economics), or the "moral" as different from the "nonmoral" (politics, aesthetics, economics). Second, Schmitt's model simultaneously identifies a contrast or opposition *within* each value sphere. Hence, morality is occupied with the criterion of bad versus good, whereas aesthetics concerns the distinction between beautiful and ugly. According to Morgenthau, these two different forms of opposition are *collapsed* within Schmitt's argument. The reason for this conflation is that Schmitt simply assumed that the second type of contrast allows us to explain the first. That is, politics is different from economics because the former rests on the distinction between friend and foe, whereas the latter concerns the conflict between profitability and unprofitability. This conceptual move also initially seems to make sense since the second set of oppositions (for example, good versus bad, or beautiful versus ugly) might be seen as following directly from the first set of distinctions (morality versus the nonmoral, or the aesthetic versus the nonaesthetic).[59]

Why this conceptual hairsplitting? Morgenthau believes that the initial set of distinctions possesses some plausibility. Politics is *different* from morality, economics, and aesthetics, though not in the manner posited by Schmitt. Building on his 1929 comments, Morgenthau again hopes to prove that politics refers to those conflicts, regardless of the specific (moral, aesthetic, or economic) material with which they are concerned, which take on a particularly *intense* form. Yet there is no distinct set of predetermined objects intrinsically political in character; Morgenthau explicitly notes that political conflicts can emerge in arenas as distinct as the household and the workplace.[60] For Morgenthau, any attempt to gain additional mileage from the idea of differentiated value spheres is bound to fail. Here as well, Morgenthau argues that the reason certain conflicts gain in intensity are psychological and sociological. Thus, he expressly describes Schmitt's "concept of the political" as bad "metaphysics," accusing Schmitt of obscuring the empirical roots of intense political conflict.[61] In this updated version of his critique of Schmitt, the authoritarian German theorist goes wrong by defining the criterion of the political sphere by means of the contrast between friend and foe. For Morgenthau, the reduction of politics to the criterion of friend and foe is conceptually arbitrary. The criterion of friend versus foe fails to capture the distinct characteristics of political life, and Schmitt is wrong to believe that the model of politics as intensity, which the Nazi theorist clearly had taken from Morgenthau, could be unproblematically welded to the friend/foe distinction. In short, Schmitt's friend/foe model of politics fails to do justice to Morgenthau's (empirically minded) interpretation of politics as intensity.

Morgenthau observes that in the cases of morality, aesthetics, and economics, each of the internal distinctions described by Schmitt is nothing more than a tautological redescription of the basic "value" constitutive of the sphere at hand. In the case of morality, for example, the criterion of evil versus good is just another way of saying that the value sphere of morality is occupied with the problem of either possessing or exercising morality (goodness) or a *lack* of morality (evil). Similar tautologies can be located in Schmitt's description of aesthetics and economics: the value sphere of aesthetics concerns the possession of aesthetic merit (beauty) or the lack thereof (ugliness), while economics ultimately concerns the possession or lack of economic merit (profitability or unprofitability). Because of this tautological structure, *other* derivations could easily be surmised. Within the contours of Schmitt's argument, for example, one might legitimately declare that the criterion of economics consists in the contrast between "utility" and "harmfulness" [*l'utile et le nuisible*].[62]

Yet immanent flaws plague Schmitt's supposedly analogous derivation of the *political* criterion of friend versus foe. Morgenthau noted that this opposition by no means provides a self-evident expression to the contrast between the "political" and the "nonpolitical" or, alternately, the possession of "political value" in contrast to the "lack of political value."[63] Why not, for example, conclude that the criterion of politics lies in the distinction between "the active exercise of sovereign power" versus "the passive acceptance of sovereign power"?[64] Would that not offer a superior redescription of the idea that something either possesses or lacks political value or significance? It certainly accords better with everyday intuitions associating political skill with the active employment of sovereign power, and a lack of political savvy with the passive acceptance of political power. The point for Morgenthau is that the distinction between friend and foe hardly possesses the same logical plausibility as the criteria attributed by Schmitt to the competing value spheres of morality, aesthetics, and economics. At least those criteria represent tautological deductions, even if it is true that other deductions might be acceptable as well. Yet it is unclear why the friend/foe distinction follows systematically at all from the quest to delineate the value sphere of politics from competing value spheres.[65]

La Notion du politique then speculates that there might be another way of salvaging Schmitt's argument. Perhaps the distinction between friend and foe is chiefly a *concretization* and *personalization* of the attempt to give expression to the contrast between "the political" and "nonpolitical." Maybe the friend/foe distinction is intended to be located at a more specialized level of conceptualization than, for example, the criteria of good/bad or beautiful/ugly. After all, one could easily come up with a more concrete set of categories embodying the criteria allegedly constitutive of each value sphere of human existence. For example, we could restate the criterion of good/bad in terms of personal attributes, like "saint and sinner," or the economic criterion of profitability/unprofitability with the qualities of "frugality" and "spendthriftiness." Each of these redescriptions of the original criterion restates the original contrast in terms of personal attributes that represent legitimate *intensifications* of the original contrast (saintliness is an extreme form of goodness, while spendthriftiness is an extreme form of bad economics).[66]

Can the friend/foe distinction be saved by reinterpreting it in this light? For Morgenthau, the answer has to be "no." Recalling our implicit everyday usage of these terms, Morgenthau notes that a "foe" can either possess political significance or lack it. The same is true of a "friend." It is by no means self-evident that we can concretize and personalize the idea that someone possesses political significance or value simply by relying on the term "friend," or restate the idea of someone's being of little or no political value in terms of "enmity." Here as well, the underlying conceptual logic of Schmitt's project generates conclusions distinct from Schmitt's own. A systematic attempt to restate Schmitt's conception of politics as an autonomous value sphere legitimately might produce the contrast between "the great statesman" versus "the apathetic petit-bourgeois": the former represents a personal embodiment of political attributes, whereas the latter lacks those attributes.[67] Even within the conceptual confines of Schmitt's own system, the interpretation of friend/foe as a mere concretization of the distinction between "politically significant" and "politically insignificant" or "without political value" fails. For Schmitt, the foe represents a life-or-death threat to a particular community of homogeneous "friends"; the Schmittian foe can hardly be said to lack political significance. By the same token, the Schmittian "friend" probably refers to those with whom one is allied in a life-or-death struggle against an "alien" foe; relations between and among "friends" in Schmitt's sense may very well be *less* politically meaningful or significant than those between friends and foes.

According to Morgenthau in 1933, the categories of friendship and enmity refer to *dispositions* with which we regard the goals and aspirations of other individuals and groups. Friendship and enmity can occur in many realms of human existence. Morgenthau's point is that the categories of friend and foe fail to capture the essence of political experience. One can be a "friend of beautiful poetry" or an "enemy of religion." The categories of friend/foe are fundamentally neutral in respect to the value spheres making up human existence because they refer to whether or not a particular agent (or group of agents) favors the realization of some set of goals (for example, beautiful poetry) or opposes them.[68]

Of course, one can speak of *political* friends and foes: a political party can be a "friend of socialism" or an "enemy of China." But this is not the same meaning of the terms "friend/foe" as employed by Schmitt. It refers to the disposition possessed by actors in relation to the goals of other actors; it hardly captures what is distinct about politics vis-à-vis economics, morality, and aesthetics.[69] For Morgenthau, Schmitt's suggestion, implicit in his interpretation of the idea of politics as a distinct value sphere, that the friend/foe distinction corresponds to the conceptual contrast between the "politically significant" and "politically insignificant," is misleading. When we declare that the censorship of a particular newspaper is "politically without value" or "without significance" we are *not* saying that it is an act "in opposition to politics" or lacking in political value *altogether*, akin to the manner in which we might describe a heinous act of violence as being fundamentally "bad" and thus lacking in moral "value."[70] Instead, we are acknowledging that *from a particular political perspective*—for example, the defenders of China—that an act of censorship lacks merit, perhaps is even counterproductive. From this conceptual angle as well, the categories of friend/foe are *not* analogous to those of good/evil, beautiful/ugly, or profitable/unprofitable. For Morgenthau in 1933, the lesson of his abstruse reflections was plain enough: even if we accept some of Schmitt's own crucial initial assumptions, Schmitt's friend/foe distinction fails to capture the core of political existence.

III

In light of Morgenthau's perceptive early criticisms of Schmitt's "concept of the political," how are we to explain his 1979 reference to Schmitt's "originality and brilliance," particularly in "the new aspects of international law"?[71] Precisely because Morgenthau was so disgusted by Schmitt's character and disagreed so fundamentally with his political theory, his praise for the "brilliant, inventive" Schmitt cries out for an explanation.

Morgenthau's American writings lend themselves to one possible interpretation of the émigré scholar's praise for Schmitt's intellectual ability: notwithstanding Morgenthau's profound disagreements with Schmitt, he simultaneously agreed with Schmitt about a great deal. In the first section of this chapter, I noted that Morgenthau's Weimar writings differed from Schmitt's in two important respects. First, Morgenthau expressed hopefulness that a durable system of binding international law might be established. Second, his rendition of the "concept of the political" deemphasized Schmitt's pessimistic philosophical anthropology. On both these points, Morgenthau's position arguably grew *closer* to Schmitt's by the early 1940s. Morgenthau's mature reflections on the authentically political character of pessimistic views of human nature parallel Schmitt's similar reflections from the 1932 *Concept of the Political*,[72] and Morgenthau similarly comes to share Schmitt's profound skepticism about ambitious liberal models of international law. Whereas the young Morgenthau had hoped that a "dynamic" system of law might someday replace the static international legal status quo, by 1940 he doubts that international law will ever be able to take a form better attuned to the dynamics of political change:

> Any fundamental change of the social forces underlying a system of international law of necessity induces the prospective beneficiaries of the change to try to bring about a corresponding change of the legal rules, whereas the beneficiaries of the legal *status quo* will resist any change of the old order. Here a competitive contest for power will determine the victorious social forces, and the change of the existing legal order will be decided, not through a legal procedure provided for by this same legal order, but through a conflagration of conflicting social forces which challenge the legal order as a whole.[73]

The idea of an international system of codified law is problematic as well. Given the ubiquity of intense political tension within the international realm, Morgenthau emphasized after 1937, international law is sure to be plagued by a high degree of open-endedness and indeterminacy.[74] Legal formalism is unlikely to succeed in remaking the international arena in its own image.

Morgenthau's Realist theory parallels Schmitt on many points. Reminiscent of Schmitt, the mature Morgenthau repeatedly expresses a profound nostalgia for the structure of the European state system *before* legalistic liberal ideas became pervasive in thinking about international politics in the twentieth century. Traditional diplomacy and the balance of power allegedly proved relatively effective at minimizing international tension from the early modern to the end of the nineteenth century.[75] Like Schmitt, Morgenthau praises one of the main intellectual driving forces behind the traditional modern state system, Thomas Hobbes.[76] Again like Schmitt, he considers European colonialism an important outlet for political conflicts; European competition within the periphery allegedly functioned to reduce political violence *within* Europe itself.[77] Both authors also underline the illiberal and undemocratic elements of the traditional state system in order to explain its relative success in what Schmitt described as the "taming of war" [*Hegung des Krieges*].[78] For both, a world-historical cataclysm in modern international relations took place in the early twentieth century, when hypocritical Wilsonian liberalism generated a crude moralization of international politics. Although Morgenthau never openly makes use of Schmitt's notion of a "discriminatory concept of war," his analysis essentially follows the same line of argumentation. Waged under the banner of universal humanity, "liberal wars, far from fulfilling the liberal hopes [to end war], even brought about the very evils which they were supposed to destroy. Far from being the 'last wars,' they were only the forerunners and pioneers of wars more destructive and extensive" than those before them.[79] The ultimate source of the intensity of liberal war is that liberals condemn aristocratic and totalitarian wars: "When, on the other hand, the use of arms is intended to bring the blessings of liberals to peoples not yet enjoying them or to protect them against despotic aggression, the just end may justify means otherwise condemned."[80] Like Schmitt, Morgenthau complements this account of the emergence of modern liberal imperialism with an analysis of the technological roots of modern "total war" and its sources in the "technicized" character of modern political thinking. At times, the details of Morgenthau's story eerily approximate the analysis of the *Raumrevolution* offered by Schmitt in the early 1940s.[81]

For both Schmitt and the mature Morgenthau, the congenital political hypocrisy of modern liberalism generates violence in the international arena. Much of Morgenthau's famous *Scientific Man vs. Power Politics* can easily be read as a popularized version of Schmitt's analysis of the antipolitical core of liberalism.[82] For Morgenthau, liberalism struggles to escape the imperatives of "the concept of the political" by favoring economistic, moralistic, scientific, and legalistic categories and modes of thought. Within liberalism, each of these competing realms of human activity promises universal harmony and peace. Yet the characteristic liberal attempt to suppress politics is unavoidably doomed; irrepressible political conflicts then simply take on economic, moral, scientific, and legal masks. The result is that liberals fail, often disastrously, to grapple seriously with the autonomous exigencies of political life. Concrete political conflicts of interest quickly become pseudoreligious crusades in which liberal states engage in violence while appealing to the fictions of international law or universal morality. Liberals inevitably are forced to engage in political action, but their instinctive hostility to "the political"—in Morgenthau's Americanized terminology, "power politics"[83]—makes them particularly slippery political opponents.

Morgenthau even endorses elements of Schmitt's portrayal of the distinct pathologies of American liberalism. The United States has often been a particularly unwieldy and reckless great power because of the legalistic and moralistic qualities of American liberalism. The history of American foreign policy is characterized by a dangerous dialectic of "interventionism and isolationism"; both Schmitt and Morgenthau struggle to explain how these two elements of American foreign policy are really two sides of the same coin. Both authors also emphasize the manner in which liberal rhetoric in American foreign policy functions alongside the de facto exercise of brute power by the United States, especially in Central and South America. Both consider the Monroe Doctrine a perfect exemplar of the manner in which the United States, notwithstanding its liberal ideology, has successfully engaged in traditional power politics.[84]

IV

So what exactly is the relationship between Schmitt and Morgenthau and the latter's enormously influential Realist theory of international relations? Would it be fair to describe Morgenthau as a closet Schmittian who simply tried to moderate the more extreme features of the work of the master?

Despite the numerous parallels between Morgenthau and Schmitt just recounted, we should resist any interpretation that overstates Morgenthau's debt to Schmitt. Morgenthau respected the *diagnostic* merits of Schmitt's critique of liberal international law. Furthermore, both theorists were proponents of a tradition of Realist thinking in international politics, defended forcefully in Western political philosophy by thinkers like Thucydides, Machiavelli, and Hobbes; even for those of us hostile to the basic structure of Realist theories of international relations, there is still much to be learned from it about the pathologies of an international system dominated by an elite group of great powers.[85] Yet the complex relationship between Schmitt and Morgenthau simultaneously suggests the necessity of distinguishing between different strands of Realist thinking.

Although admittedly crude, the distinction that I would like to introduce is best captured by the expressions "Realism of Peace" and "Realism of War." In an insightful essay on Hobbes, Hedley Bull has rightly emphasized the fundamentally *pacific* character of Hobbes's thinking on international politics. Although emphasizing the anarchical structure of interstate relations and their irrepressible explosiveness, Hobbes's message was "that we should seek peace," both within the domestic and international arena. For Hobbes, violence was both an ever-present danger *and* the most horrible of the many misfortunes that plague humanity. His is anything but a bellicose or militaristic political philosophy.[86] In dramatic contrast to modern irrationalists like Sorel, there is no attempt in Hobbes to conceive of political violence as a force that purges and cleanses humanity, ultimately demonstrating, as it did for Schmitt, the "seriousness of human existence."[87] Hobbes is a Realist of Peace.

Morgenthau is clearly indebted to the Realism of Peace. Morgenthau's criticism of the hysteria of the Cold War and American military involvement in Vietnam, his sober assessment of the human tragedies of political terror and war, and his prescient insight that atomic warfare requires us to rethink the traditional categories of international politics, suggest clearly that Morgenthau, like Hobbes, wants us to grapple seriously with the problem of political violence *so that we can minimize its evils*.[88] Nothing in Morgenthau's theory points to a positive normative evaluation of making war. His lifelong refusal to attribute moral value to the pursuit of power politics was hardly an expression of reckless immorality. On the contrary, it arguably represents a healthy reluctance toward justifying the horrors of modern war with moral ideals utterly inconsistent with the butcheries commonly engaged in by modern states.[89] Morgenthau's is surely not the last word in the political philosophy of international politics.[90] Yet any attempt to super-sede Realism will need to avoid all those dangers he describes so power-fully.

If the analysis offered in chapter 6 of this study is correct, Carl Schmitt surely belongs to the tradition of the Realism of War. His is a Realism interested in exposing the inconsistencies and contradictions of contempo-rary international law chiefly *in order to exacerbate and ultimately explode those contradictions.* The ills of liberal internationalism are thematized for the sake of preparing the way for an order of "greater regions" [*Grossräume*] destined to generate violence on a far greater scale than anything we have seen in the liberal age. The massive German-language literature on Schmitt's theory of international relations typically makes a great deal of Schmitt's nostalgia for an early modern European era allegedly characterized by less violence than the era of the liberal "discriminatory war." Yet this literature conveniently downplays the fact that Schmitt's nostalgia, in contrast to Morgenthau's, is intended to delegitimize contemporary liberalism in order to replace it with the *Grossräume* described in chapter 6. Schmitt never seeks a return to a Hobbesian era superior to the total wars of the twentieth century. For strategic reasons, he appeals to select features of Hobbes's philosophy of international relations in order to justify Nazi imperialism. As Morgenthau noted as early as 1941, the result of this version of antiliberalism is nothing less than the reduction of the idea of law to "technical rules of domina-tion."[91] Despite his own profound qualms about liberal international law, Morgenthau grasps that Schmitt's medicine is sure to kill the patient.

In his 1932 essay on Schmitt, Strauss anticipates the distinction be-tween Hobbes and Schmitt described here. Strauss rightly notes that Hobbes hopes to overcome the violence of the "state of nature," whereas "Schmitt restores the Hobbesian concept of the state of nature to a place of honor." For Hobbes, "the fact that the state of nature is the state of enmity of all against all is adduced so as to yield a motive for relinquishment of the state of nature. Against this negation of the state either of nature or of the political, Schmitt sets the affirmation of the political," which Schmitt describes in terms of Hobbes's state of nature.[92] Strauss, like Morgenthau, understands that Hobbes hoped to overcome the instability and violence of the state of nature, whereas Schmitt sees Hobbes's choice as an ill-fated quest to suppress the political.

If I am not mistaken, the fundamental differences separating Morgen-thau's Realism of Peace from Schmitt's Realism of War can be traced to their early dialogue on "the concept of the political" recounted earlier in this chapter. Recall that Schmitt insists on separating the distinct value spheres of morality and politics. Remember as well that Morgenthau accepts this differentiation—with one important qualification. For the young Morgenthau, it is wrong to see morality and politics as referring to distinct categories of objects. Schmitt's conceptual ambiguities suggest that human existence may be neatly carved into competing political, moral, economic, and aesthetic realms, each concerned with a separate set of objects. In contrast, Morgenthau seeks to capture the specificity of the political, *without* accepting Schmitt's odd view of human experience as consisting of separate political, moral, economic, and aesthetic objects.

In his American writings, Morgenthau revealingly attributes the same conceptual error to fascism and National Socialism. *Politics Among Nations* describes Hitler and Mussolini as embodying precisely the "pure politics" the young Morgenthau previously located in Schmitt's political theory. In this interpretation, Hitler and Mussolini *delight* in "the will to power and the struggle for power as elemental social facts," and they are rigorously political actors for the simple reason that they systematically rob political action of any moral quality.[93] Both dictators represent real-life expressions of the misconstrued quest to divide human existence into distinct and essentially unrelated forms of activity. *Scientific Man vs. Power Politics* similarly interprets the defeat of fascism in terms of the fact that "it did not understand the nature of man, who is not only an object of political manipulation but also a moral person endowed with resources which do not yield to manipulation."[94] In Morgenthau's view, "[a] man who was nothing but a 'political man' would be a beast, for he would be completely lacking in moral restraints."[95] From this perspective, fascism represents the practical realization of the idea of a pure politics unrestrained by morality, a form of power for power's own sake, in which political activities are seen as fundamentally unrelated to moral concerns.

Does not Schmitt's 1932 *Concept of the Political* move beyond the ambiguous model of distinct value spheres found in his original 1927 reflections on "the concept of the political"? Following Morgenthau, Schmitt certainly makes some amends on this point. But I think that one can still take Morgenthau's reflections on Mussolini and Hitler as a veiled criticism of Schmitt as well. The 1932 *Concept of the Political* declares bluntly that morality simply has no place within the sphere of political action: "Normative illusions" are inappropriate to authentic politics.[96] Even in the most sophisticated rendition of Schmitt's "concept of the political," the attempt to *rid* the political sphere of normative concerns remains central. As Morgenthau grasps early on, it is unclear whether morality or ethics can have much of a place *at all* within Schmitt's political and legal theory. Although Schmitt by 1932 recognizes some of the difficulties of conceiving politics as concerned with objects distinct from those of competing forms of human action, he never adequately frees himself from the problematic insistence that politics and morality are basically unrelated. This error may simply have been a vestige of Schmitt's original, highly problematic 1927 formulation of the idea of politics as a distinct value sphere. Whatever its conceptual sources, it ultimately proves fatal to Schmitt's theory.

In opposition to a reading of Schmitt along these lines, Meier cites Schmitt's reference in *Political Theology* to the "demanding" character of every moral decision.[97] For Meier, Schmitt is a closet theologian, well aware of the centrality of theology and morality to politics. But Meier's reading here simply explodes the confines of Schmitt's own words. Schmitt's reference to the "demanding moral decision" is hardly an acknowledgment of the complexities of moral and political action in the modern world. Meier conveniently forgets to mention that Schmitt immediately describes this decision as one "created out of nothingness" and thus unrelated to any universal moral system, religious or otherwise.[98] According to Meier, we need to read Schmitt's "affirmation of the political" as an "affirmation of the moral," in light of the fact that the endorsement of friend/foe politics ultimately represented a critique of the idea of a world-state and its implicit reliance in the sinful quest to try to transform man into god: Schmitt's critique of the world-state is primarily an attack on the Anti-Christ, and the "false religion of technicity."[99] Unfortunately, this interpretation meshes poorly with Schmitt's voluntary excommunication from the Catholic Church in 1926, his express statements of hostility to Catholicism, and his enthusiastic embrace of the Nationalist Socialist regime during the 1930s and 1940s.[100] The ills of the world-state are hardly primarily moral or religious for Schmitt; its chief danger is that it would mean the demise of existential friend/foe conflicts, which Schmitt expressly describes as fundamentally unrelated to "normativistic" discord. In my view, this attempt to read Schmitt as a theologian not only misconstrues core elements of his political and legal theory, but also does a disservice to the more humane voices within modern Catholicism, for whom Schmitt's irrationalist ethical and political views were and are always anathema.

Morgenthau as well would surely have expressed skepticism about recent attempts to transform Schmitt into a religiously minded philosopher. On precisely the crucial question of the relation of politics to morals, Morgenthau's political theory differs importantly from Schmitt's. The rules of politics and morality are basically distinct; Morgenthau and Schmitt agree on this point. But for Morgenthau, this hardly justifies Schmitt's profound hostility to political actors who take moral concerns absolutely seriously. Unfortunately, Morgenthau's heated polemics about the dangers of *moralism* within foreign policy lead many to miss this point. In this view, moralism can prove dangerous within the political realm. Echoing Weber's vision of an "ethic of responsibility," Morgenthau demands of political actors that they grapple seriously with the many paradoxes of political action, particularly the fact that noble intentions often culminate in political and moral evils.[101] As Weber famously argued in the aftermath of World War I, a naive moral do-goodism can prove both politically and morally counterproductive. Morgenthau's hostility to the basically apolitical moralism of so much liberal foreign policy can legitimately be read as an application of the core intuitions of Weber's ethic of responsibility to the international arena. In contrast to Schmitt, for Morgenthau, the "defense of the autonomy of the political sphere against its subversion by other modes of thought does not imply disregard for the existence and importance of these other modes of thought. . . . Real man is a composite of 'economic man,' 'political man,' 'moral man,' 'religious man,' etc."[102] This fact means that even the political actor is obliged to respect competing standards, particularly those of the moral sphere. Because the distinct value spheres of human existence do not refer to different groups of predefined objects or issues, political conflicts are likely to have moral, economic, and aesthetic sides to them; the political actor is obliged to respect the rules of competing spheres that inevitably impact even on those decisions that seem most deeply political.[103] To pretend otherwise represents an irresponsible escape from the pluralistic structure of human life.[104]

From Morgenthau's perspective, human existence is inevitably tragic. Politics forces us to engage in actions unacceptable from a moral standpoint. Morality simultaneously demands of us that we avoid the evils of politics. Both liberalism and fascism obscure the "great tragic antinomies of human existence."[105] Liberal internationalists downplay the violence and brutality of so much political action by dreaming of a political future in which the harsh realities of power politics have been supplanted by international law and universal peace, whereas fascists like Schmitt celebrate "the lust for power" while simultaneously obscuring the rigorous demands of morality. Reminiscent of Weber, Morgenthau saw the conflict between politics and morality as tragic: "Its last resort, then, is the endeavor to choose, since evil there must be, among several possible actions the one that is least evil."[106] In the final analysis, "[n]either science nor ethics nor politics can resolve the conflict between politics and ethics into harmony."[107] One cannot escape political action within the ivory tower; man is by nature a political animal. Yet political action necessarily entails moral evil. At best we can hope to reach an uneasy modus vivendi between the competing demands of morality and politics by pursuing the least evil of all sound political choices.

For those of us who have yet to abandon the utopian dream of overcoming "the great tragic antinomies of human existence" by dramatically reducing the scope of violence in the international political arena, Morgenthau's political ethics inevitably seem cautious, probably even conservative. One might also raise legitimate questions about Morgenthau's success in distancing himself *sufficiently* from Schmitt; it is no accident that many of Morgenthau's critics have taken him as advocating a "pure politics" akin to that which he attributed to Schmitt and modern fascism.[108] Yet there can be no doubt that Morgenthau's theory, however flawed, represents an infinitely more honest and responsible answer to the quagmires of political and moral action in our times than Carl Schmitt's "concept of the political." Schmitt's contemporary defenders typically describe their master as "the Thomas Hobbes of the twentieth century." If any recent political thinker is worthy of this noble title, it would have to be Hans Morgenthau, not Carl Schmitt.

Conclusion

AFTER CARL SCHMITT?

Carl Schmitt's political and legal theory continues to gain in promi-nence within the English-speaking world. New translations and reis-sues of Schmitt's works appear at a steady rate, and a growing number of dissertations and monographs examine his ideas. The former left-wing journal *Telos* is now devoted to the propagation of Schmitt's theory.[1] Words of praise can be found for Schmitt within the pages of the conservative *National Review* as well.[2] Even "postmodern" political theorists are rushing to embrace Schmitt.[3] In a sure sign that Schmitt has "arrived" within the American academy, the editors of the *New York Review of Books* recently decided that the Schmitt renaissance warranted a lengthy discussion of his ideas.[4]

The novelty of the ongoing Schmitt renaissance should not be exag-gerated. As I have tried to document in part 2 of this study, Schmitt has long exercised a hidden influence on major figures within postwar political and legal thinking in North America. The main differences between this earlier Schmitt reception and the present one are probably twofold. First, writers like Schumpeter, Hayek, and Morgenthau forthrightly acknowl-edge Schmitt's National Socialist proclivities, whereas the more recent North American Schmitt reception has often been shockingly apologetic.[5] Second, the writers discussed in part 2 of this study offer creative and occa-sionally powerful critical reconstructions of Schmittian themes. Although their theories exhibit serious flaws in part because of their Schmittian back-drop, there can be no question that the contemporary Schmitt renaissance has failed to match the intellectual quality exhibited by Schumpeter, Hayek, and Morgenthau, let alone Neumann or Strauss, who similarly en-gaged with Schmitt's ideas and sought to respond to them.

Schmitt will continue to attract attention because he addressed not only the central concern of contemporary jurisprudence, the problem of legal indeterminacy, but a host of related issues of great importance to contemporary liberal democracy. Only by honestly acknowledging the diagnostic merits of his political and legal theory can we begin to understand why so many impressive intellectuals in our century grappled seriously with Schmitt's theory.[6] For the record, I do *not* think we should interpret the exchange described in part 2 of this study as simply another example of the fateful pathologies of modern German political and intellectual development, perhaps a paradigmatic case within intellectual history of the much-discussed German *Sonderweg*.[7] Much more than German exceptionalism is at work here. Schmitt spoke directly to some of the great dilemmas of our times, and to pretend that Schmitt's identification and analysis of those problems were idiosyncratically German (whatever that precisely means) obscures the depth of the problems faced by contemporary liberal democracy. Of course, Schmitt's resolution of each of these problems was ultimately disastrous, and he built on authoritarian, illiberal, and anti-Semitic traditions that obviously were well established within nineteenth- and early twentieth-century Germany. Yet Schmitt was by no means the only political or legal thinker in our century whose theory integrated the ugliest pathologies of Western modernity. He offered an especially fatal mix of these elements, but they can be located in many other writers and competing intellectual traditions.

The answer to antiformal trends within the legal system is not to abandon the rule of law. Parliamentary government and the public sphere are threatened in many ways; Schmitt's attack on them simply throws the baby out with the bathwater. The interventionist welfare state has often heightened administrative discretion and strengthened the executive branch, yet there is no reason to assume that we cannot effectively counteract such trends. Liberal international law is weak and is often applied hypocritically. But the answer to these ills is hardly to free the great powers from universal legal norms altogether. Schmitt diagnosed serious problems within existing liberal democracy, but at each juncture his own theoretical response exacerbated the problems at hand. His embrace of National Socialism vividly illustrates the dangers intrinsic to his own morally and intellectually bankrupt answers to the problems faced by liberal democracy in our century.

Schmitt's most important lesson to us, not surprisingly, concerns the primary target of his political and legal theory, the rule of law. No thinker in our century better illuminates the intellectual and political dangers of engaging in a one-sided deconstruction of the liberal idea that governmental action can be regulated according to clear, general norms and relatively formalistic modes of judicial action. By the same token, Schmitt was right to see that formalistic models of law often fail to accord with the legal and political realities of our century. Contemporary parliamentary lawmaking regularly falls short of the classical demand that like cases be treated alike by means of relatively cogent, stable norms; the regulatory and welfare states, as well as being indispensable, pose real challenges to liberal jurisprudence; the dream of an international order regulated by law generates dilemmas that go well beyond those concerning the establishment of the rule of law on the domestic scene. In the final analysis, the example of Carl Schmitt should leave us with a sense of the indispensable virtues of the rule of law, as well as legitimate unease about its status and empirical prospects today. Schmitt's attack on liberalism cries out for a defense of the rule of law that takes his (occasionally) provocative empirical observations seriously, while distancing itself from his own unjustified assault on liberalism's unfinished struggle against political insecurity and arbitrariness. Such a defense requires not only acknowledging the normative bankruptcy of Schmitt's ideas, but also demonstrating that the rule of law can operate effectively in a political and social environment that poses myriad challenges to it.

The twentieth century has been one of exceptional political brutality. It would be naive and presumptuous to believe that we could ever adequately compensate its millions of victims. Maybe, however, we can use the example of the crown jurist of National Socialism, Carl Schmitt, to help make sure that the next century avoids the worst horrors of the last.

NOTES

INTRODUCTION: WHY CARL SCHMITT?

1. Two important recent studies break with this pattern: Renato Cristi, *Carl Schmitt and Authoritarian Liberalism* (Cardiff: University of Wales, 1998) and John P. McCormick, *Carl Schmitt's Critique of Liberalism: Against Politics as Technology* (New York: Cambridge University Press, 1997). Also, see the essays collected in David Dyzenhaus, ed., *Law as Politics: Carl Schmitt's Critique of Liberalism* (Durham, N.C.: Duke University Press, 1998). My differences in relation to these works will be developed during the course of the exegesis that follows.

2. An impressive body of German-language literature on Schmitt does make Schmitt's critique of liberal jurisprudence central to an analysis of his theory: Hasso Hofmann, *Legitimität gegen Legalität. Der Weg der politischen Philosophie Carl Schmitts* (Berlin: Luchterhand, 1964); Matthias Kaufmann, *Recht ohne Regel? Die philosophischen Prinzipien in Carl Schmitts Staats- und Rechtslehre* (Freiburg, Breisgau: Karl Alber, 1988); Ingeborg Maus, *Bürgerliche Rechtstheorie und Faschismus: Zur sozialen Funktion und aktuellen Wirkung der Theorie Carl Schmitts* (Munich: Wilhelm Fink, 1980) and Peter Schneider, *Ausnahmezustand und Norm: Eine Studie zur Rechtslehre von Carl Schmitt* (Stuttgart: Deutsche Verlagsanstalt, 1957). Two excellent recent English-language discussions of Weimar political and legal thought also fall into this category: Peter C. Caldwell, *Popular Sovereignty and the Crisis of German Constitutional Law: The Theory and Practice of Weimar Constitutionalism* (Durham, N.C.: Duke University Press, 1997); David Dyzenhaus, *Legality and Legitimacy: Carl Schmitt, Hans Kelsen and Hermann Heller in Weimar* (Oxford: Clarendon Press, 1997).

3. The result has been a tendency to write about Schmitt from the perspective of his own postwar account of his experiences under the Nazis. Not surprisingly, studies of this type tend to be highly apologetic. Joseph Bendersky, *Carl Schmitt: Theorist for the Reich* (Princeton, N.J.: Princeton University Press, 1983) and George Schwab, *The Challenge of the Exception: An Introduction to the Political Ideas of Carl Schmitt between 1921 and 1936*, 2nd ed. (Westport, Conn.: Greenwood Press, 1989). I discuss the apologetic contours of these studies in my "Carl Schmitt and the Nazis," *German Politics & Society* no. 23 (Summer 1991): 71–79. The apologetic strand in North American Schmitt scholarship has been ably countered by

Richard Wolin in "Carl Schmitt, Political Existentialism, and the Total State," *Theory and Society* 19, no. 4 (August 1990): 389–416; and "Carl Schmitt—The Conservative Revolutionary: Habitus and the Aesthetics of Horror," *Political Theory* 20, no. 3 (August 1992): 424–47.

4. I depend here primarily on the reliable account by Manfred Wiegandt, "The Alleged Accountability of the Academic: A Biographical Sketch of Carl Schmitt," *Cardozo Law Review* 16 (1995): 1569–98.

5. For this reason, I focus here on this period in Schmitt's long career.

6. Schmitt's *Habilitation* was entitled *The Value of the State and the Significance of the Individual* [*Der Wert des Staates und die Bedeutung des Einzelnen*] (Tübingen: Mohr, 1914). I discuss this text at length in chapter 1. The *Habilitation* is a sort of second dissertation. Even today, it functions as an instrument assuring that German academics generally come from relatively privileged backgrounds; the economic insecurity generated by a system in which a second dissertation is a prerequisite to a permanent academic position effectively discourages those with modest or nonacademic roots. I discuss Schmitt's writings from this period in depth in chapter 1.

7. In a study well received in Catholic circles in the 1920s, *Römischer Katholizismus und politische Form* [*Roman Catholicism and Political Form*] (Munich: Theatiner, 1925), Schmitt aspired to formulate and defend an identifiably Catholic conception of political representation. But in Schmitt's most important treatises after his excommunication in 1926, Catholic themes are nonexistent or at most peripheral. Some odd theological comments can also be found in his postwar diaries, but I remain unconvinced that one should rely on textual evidence of this sort rather than on his systematic writings in political and legal theory. It is true that Schmitt was fascinated by the problem of secularization, for example, in *Political Theology: Four Chapters on the Concept of Sovereignty* [1922], trans. George Schwab (Cambridge: MIT Press, 1988), yet this no more provides unambiguous evidence of the preponderance of religious concerns within Schmitt's theory than it would, say, of Max Weber's account of "disenchantment" [*Entzauberung*]. Catholicism surely influenced Schmitt, as did many other intellectual strains within his Germany. But an exaggerated exegetical emphasis on religious motifs tends necessarily toward the esoteric in light of the fact that Schmitt's major works were distinctly nonreligious in character. For an excellent account of Schmitt's ideas about secularization that rightly avoids overstating Schmitt's Catholicism, see Ilse Staff, "Zum Begriff der Politischen Theologie bei Carl Schmitt," in *Christentum und Modernes Recht*, ed. Gerhard Dilcher and Ilse Staff (Frankfurt a.m.: Suhrkamp, 1984): 182–208. Staff shows that Schmitt's theory at crucial junctures *conflicts* dramatically with the Christian belief in the equal value of every human being, as well as certain traditional Christian reservations about the use of violence within the political sphere (200–1, 204–5).

8. For recent discussions focusing on Schmitt's religious background, see Andreas Koenen, *Der Fall Carl Schmitt: Sein Aufstieg zum "Kronjuristen des Dritten Reiches"* (Darmstadt: Wissenschaftliche Buchgesellschaft, 1995) and Bernd Wacker,

ed., *Die eigentliche katholische Verschärfung. Konfession, Theologie und Politik im Werk Carl Schmitts* (Munich: Wilhelm Fink, 1994). The theoretically most sophisticated reading of Schmitt as a religious thinker is provided by Heinrich Meier of the University of Munich. I address Meier's interpretation in detail in chapter 9.

9. For a vivid discussion of this crucial moment in the history of Weimar and Schmitt's role in it, see David Dyzenhaus, "Legal Theory in the Collapse of Weimar: Contemporary Lessons?" *American Political Science Review* 91 (1997): 121–34.

10. Dirk van Laak, *Gespräche in der Sicherheit des Schweigens: Carl Schmitt in der politischen Geistesgeschichte der frühen Bundesrepublik* (Berlin: Akademie Verlag, 1993).

11. In this spirit, John Rawls comments that "if the precept of no crime without a law is violated, say by statutes being vague and imprecise, what we are at liberty to do is likewise vague and imprecise. The boundaries of our liberty are uncertain. And to the extent that this is so, liberty is restricted by a reasonable fear of its exercise" (*The Theory of Justice* [Cambridge, Mass.: Harvard University Press, 1971], 239–40).

12. For important recent discussions of the rule of law, see Joseph Raz, *The Authority of Law: Essays in Law and Morality* (Oxford: Clarendon Press, 1979), 210–29; Jeremy Waldron, "The Rule of Law in Contemporary Liberal Theory," *Ratio Juris* 2, no. 1 (1989): 79–96; Richard H. Fallon Jr., " 'The Rule of Law' as a Concept in Constitutional Discourse," *Columbia Law Review* 97, no. 1 (1997): 1–56, and Andrew Altman, *Critical Legal Studies: A Liberal Critique* (Princeton, N.J.: Princeton University Press, 1990), 9–12, 22–56. For a broader historical perspective on the evolution of the rule of law, see Franz L. Neumann, *The Rule of Law: Political Theory and the Legal System in Modern Society* (Leamington Spa, U.K.: Berg, 1986).

13. On the American case, see Theodore J. Lowi, *The End of Liberalism: The Second Republic of the United States*, 2nd ed. (New York: Norton, 1979) and Cass Sunstein, *After the Rights Revolution: Reconceiving the Regulatory State* (Cambridge, Mass.: Harvard University Press, 1990).

14. Raz, *The Authority of Law*, 217. Of course, this is a complicated issue; I cannot even begin to do justice to it here. My point is simply that conflicts are possible between the rule of law, as traditionally conceived, and certain forms of constitutional jurisprudence.

15. The following attempt to distinguish between different conceptions of legal indeterminacy is an elaboration and revision of Lawrence B. Solum's excellent reflections on this issue: "On the Indeterminacy Crisis: Critiquing Critical Dogma," *University of Chicago Law Review* 54, no. 2 (1987): 462–503; and "Indeterminacy," in *A Companion to Philosophy of Law and Legal Theory*, ed. Dennis Patterson (Oxford: Blackwell, 1996), 488–502.

16. In this vein, H. L. A. Hart famously argued that we should see the legal system as consisting of "a core of certainty and a penumbra of doubt when we are engaged in bringing particular situations under general rules" (*The Concept of Law* [Oxford: Clarendon Press, 1961], 119). In this view, rules contain both a core of settled meaning and a penumbra of relative indeterminacy.

17. Kenneth Culp Davis, *Discretionary Justice: A Preliminary Inquiry* (Baton Rouge: Louisiana State University Press, 1969).

18. For an example of this view, see Hans Kelsen, *The Pure Theory of Law* [*Die Reine Rechtslehre*], trans. Max Knight (Berkeley and Los Angeles: University of California, 1967), 351–52.

19. In accordance with this usage, subsequent references in this study to "formalism" refer to this model. Note, however, that formalism in the context of the limited indeterminacy thesis entails no necessary commitment to controversial attempts to defend a strict division of law from morality or politics. Some defenders of the limited indeterminacy thesis embrace such views (for example, Hans Kelsen); others do not. As Judith N. Shklar has noted, "[i]t is . . . one thing to favor the ideal of a *Rechtsstaat* above all ideological and religious pressures, and quite another to insist upon the conceptual necessity of treating law and morals as totally distinct entities" (*Legalism: Law, Morals, and Political Trials* [Cambridge: Harvard University Press, 1986], 43). The formalist position is much more subtle than many of its critics concede, who wrongly read it as entailing *perfect* determinacy in legal decision making. Contemporary critical literature on liberal jurisprudence is filled with crude caricatures of the formalist position (David Kairys, ed., *The Politics of Law: A Progressive Critique* [New York: Pantheon, 1982]). As will become evident, Carl Schmitt relied on such caricatures as well.

20. For a recent defense of this view, see Frederick Schauer, "Formalism," *Yale Law Review* 97 (1988): 509–48. By means of a reinterpretation of the Frankfurt School jurists Franz L. Neumann and Otto Kirchheimer, I have tried to defend a social democratic version of the *limited determinacy thesis* in my *Between the Norm and the Exception: The Frankfurt School and the Rule of Law* (Cambridge, Mass.: MIT Press, 1994). In the present study, I will *not* undertake to present a detailed conceptual defense of the limited indeterminacy thesis, in part because I think that others are already doing so with great effectiveness. My interest here lies chiefly in pointing to some of the perils of certain forms of antiformalism within legal theory and practice. In my view, those dangers are badly downplayed within the United States. Although it would be absurd to assert that all roads beyond legal formalism lead to Carl Schmitt, it is incumbent on those critical of traditional forms of liberal jurisprudence to grapple seriously with the dangers posed by Schmitt's fascist variety of antiformalism. I also think that formalists can learn something from Schmitt: few other theorists in this century have shown as clearly how the empirical reality of contemporary liberal democracy conflicts with formalist legal aspirations. Whereas Schmitt relies on this insight to discredit formalism, in my view it suggests instead the need for substantial political and social reforms. For some modest proposals along these lines, see William E. Scheuerman, "The Rule of Law and the Welfare State: Towards a New Synthesis," *Politics and Society* 22, no. 4 (1994): 195–213.

21. William W. Fischer III, Morton J. Horwitz, and Thomas A. Reed, eds., *American Legal Realism* (New York: Oxford University Press, 1993).

22. Richard A. Posner, *Overcoming Law* (Cambridge, Mass.: Harvard University Press, 1995), 18. The best overview of Posner's theory is Richard Posner,

The Problems of Jurisprudence (Cambridge, Mass.: Harvard University Press, 1990). I thematize Posner's antiformalism in my "Free Market Anti-Formalism: The Case of Richard Posner," *Ratio Juris* 12 (1999).

23. Ronald Dworkin, *Law's Empire* (Cambridge, Mass.: Harvard University Press, 1986), especially 225–32.

24. Put crudely, both Posner and Dworkin see those legal materials emphasized by proponents of the limited indeterminacy thesis as highly indeterminate, but hope to compensate for this indeterminacy by relying on certain suprapositive methods and ideals, namely classical liberal economics (Posner) and liberal political morality (Dworkin).

25. For the classic statement of this argument, see Duncan Kennedy, "Form and Substance in Private Law Adjudication," *Essays on Critical Legal Studies* (Cambridge, Mass.: Harvard Law Review, 1986). I am unconvinced that arguments of this type are as destructive of traditional liberal legal ideals as their proponents claim. Even Cass R. Sunstein, although hardly an ally of traditional formalist jurisprudence, rightly notes that "[p]eople can urge a 60-mile-per-hour speed limit, a prohibition on bringing elephants into restaurants, a ten-year maximum sentence for attempted rape, and much more without taking a stand on debates btween Kantians and utilitarians. . . . [R]ules sharply diminish the level of disagreement among people who are subject to them and among people who must interpret and apply them. When rules are in place, high-level theories need not be invoked in order for us to know what rules mean, and whether they are binding." Effective rules are often realizable even in the context of profound moral and political disagreement. Indeed, we often negotiate such disagreement by means of rule making: rules are a powerful instrument for facilitating social cooperation, given real-life restraints of time and energy that often prevent actors from resolving fundamental moral and political disagreements (*Legal Reasoning and Political Conflict* [New York: Oxford University Press, 1996], 110–11).

26. For a fine survey, see Altman, *Critical Legal Studies: A Liberal Critique*, 90–98. Altman rightly notes that CLS is a diverse and complex movement that cannot be easily summed up within a few sentences. Here I am simply referring to some (influential) lines of argumentation within CLS. On the relationship of Legal Realism to CLS, see Neil Duxbury, *Patterns of American Jurisprudence* (Oxford: Clarendon Press, 1995); and Andrew Altman, "Legal Realism, Critical Legal Studies, and Dworkin," *Philosophy and Public Affairs* 15, no. 3 (Summer 1986): 205–35.

27. I am *not* trying to engage in the game of guilt by association. Nor do I intend to suggest that those who embrace ideas that are occasionally reminiscent of Schmitt's have already set out on the disastrous road to fascism or National Socialism. Yet I do think it fruitful to rely on Schmitt to point to some potential argumentative weaknesses within contemporary debates about the rule of law. In my view, too many contemporary American legal theorists exhibit a profound blindness in reference to the theoretical significance of the experience of totalitarian law in this century. This weakness risks rendering American legal thought provincial and irrelevant, given that totalitarianism has been a very real and immediate problem

262   Notes: Introduction

for much of humanity in this century. I hope that this study can make a modest contribution to filling in that lacuna.

28. See Duncan Kennedy, "Legal Formality," *Journal of Legal Studies*, vol. 2 (1973): 351–83; and Roberto Mangabeira Unger, *Law in Modern Society: Toward a Criticism of Social Theory* (New York: Free Press, 1976), 221–22, 238–42. Although Unger has recently expressed some telling reservations about extreme versions of the radical indeterminacy thesis, his view of the formalist model of the rule of law as fundamentally fraudulent remains basically unchanged. In the spirit of his early writings, he also continues to express sympathy for a "case-by-case" system of law, but one free of the traditionalist features of Anglo-American common law (*What Should Legal Analysis Become?* [New York: Verso, 1996], 63–77, 113–22). In addition, some CLS authors have tentatively acknowledged the open-ended political implications of the radical indeterminacy thesis. For example, Mark Tushnet concedes that "[t]o say that indeterminacy means that disruption of the status quo becomes possible is not to say that disruption of the status quo in all its aspects is always desirable. . . . Nothing in the indeterminacy thesis asserts that disruption of everything is always desirable, or of course that disruption even of the unjust aspects is likely" ("Defending the Indeterminacy Thesis," *Quinnipiac Law Review* 16, no. 3 [1996]: 348). But even Tushnet ultimately views the task of clearing away the purported illusions of legal formalism as an important step toward greater political and social justice.

29. Ingo Müller, *Hitler's Justice: The Courts of the Third Reich*, trans. Deborah Lucas Schneider (Cambridge: Harvard University Press, 1991). In Weimar, conservative judges and civil servants usurped substantial decision-making authority in order to challenge even modest reforms initiated by the legislature. They typically employed antiformalist devices (and reactionary interpretations of open-ended legal standards) to undermine parliamentary laws and constitutional norms in conflict with their own antidemocratic and socially conservative agenda. Weimar is theoretically interesting because it represents an example of a "transitional" legal system in which emerging liberal and democratic principles exist along with deep antiliberal and antidemocratic currents. Notwithstanding its many idiosyncrasies, its legal experiences are relevant to many countries undertaking the transition from dictatorship to liberal democracy, where many of the preexisting principles of the legal system are likely to contain illiberal elements.

30. This is a complicated issue within both theories. Yet it is telling that both Dworkin and Posner tend to offer an unappealing portrayal of the legislature as dominated by irrational "special interests," which they then typically contrast to the superior rationality of judicial decision making. Within Dworkin's theory, the question at hand concerns the precise status of the requirement of "fit" within legal interpretation; in Posner's theory, it depends on the extent to which he is willing to condone judges who interpret ambiguous or open-ended legislation in accordance with free-market ideals.

31. Posner sees the common law as consistent with free-market ideals; Dworkin locates his interpretation of liberal political morality in many areas of American

law. Of course, even American legal culture is by no means uniformly liberal. It long has contained more than its own fair share of racism (Randall Kennedy, *Race, Crime, and the Law* [New York: Pantheon Books, 1997]).

32. The difficulties of what Dworkin describes as "wicked law" have been peripheral to his work (*Law's Empire*, 101–8). One of Dworkin's students, David Dyzenhaus, has gone much further in trying to tackle the difficulties that "wicked law" poses for antipositivist theory (*Hard Cases in Wicked Legal Systems: South African Law in the Perspective of Legal Philosophy* [Oxford: Clarendon Press, 1991]).

33. Posner, *Overcoming Law*, 404. Sunstein has similarly highlighted the anti-pluralistic implications of Dworkin and Posner (*Legal Reasoning and Political Conflict*, 48–53, 96–100).

34. On Schmitt and Hans Kelsen, see Caldwell, *Popular Sovereignty and the Crisis of German Constitutional Law*, 40–62, 85–119; and Dyzenhaus, *Legality and Legitimacy: Carl Schmitt, Hans Kelsen and Hermann Heller in Weimar*, 38–160. On Schmitt and the Frankfurt School jurists: Scheuerman, *Between the Norm and the Exception: The Frankfurt School and the Rule of Law*. The intellectual connection between Schmitt and Leo Strauss has garnered much attention. For a fine introduction, see Robert Howse, "From Legitimacy to Dictatorship—and Back Again: Leo Strauss's Critique of the Anti-Liberalism of Carl Schmitt," *Canadian Journal of Law and Jurisprudence* 10, no. 1 (1997): 77–104. I comment on the Schmitt–Strauss connection in chapter 9.

1. THE CRISIS OF LEGAL INDETERMINACY

1. Carl Schmitt, "Das Gesetz zur Behebung der Not von Volk und Reich," *Deutsche Juristen-Zeitung* 38, no. 7 (April 1, 1933): 455–58, which offers a ringing endorsement of the National Socialist Enabling Act of March 23, 1933. The Enabling Act invested Hitler with dictatorial powers. Also, see Carl Schmitt, "Das gute Recht der deutschen Revolution," *Westdeutscher Beobachter* 12, no. 108 (May 12, 1933): 1–2.

2. For the biographical details, see Cristi, *Carl Schmitt and Authoritarian Liberalism*, 25–33. Schmitt then wrote a commentary on the law he helped draft: Schmitt, *Das Reichsstatthaltergesetz* (Berlin: Carl Heymanns Verlag, 1933).

3. Carl Schmitt, *Staat, Bewegung, Volk: Die Dreigliederung der politischen Einheit* [*State, Movement, Folk*] (Hamburg: Hanseatische Verlagsanstalt, 1933).

4. Schmitt, *Staat, Bewegung, Volk*, 42–46. Also, see Carl Schmitt, *Fünf Leitsätze für die Rechtspraxis* (Berlin: Deutsche Rechts- und Wirtschaftswissenschaft Verlag, 1933), as well as Carl Schmitt, *Über die drei Arten des rechtswissenschaftlichen Denkens* [*On Three Types of Jurisprudential Thinking*] (Hamburg: Hanseatische Verlagsanstalt, 1934).

5. Schmitt, *Staat, Bewegung, Volk*, 43. All translations from German texts, unless otherwise stated, are the author's own.

6. Schmitt, *Staat, Bewegung, Volk*, 43–44.

7. Schmitt, *Staat, Bewegung, Volk*, 45.

8. In German, see the illuminating article by Lorenz Kiefer, "Begründung, Dezision und Politische Theologie: Zu den frühen Schriften von Carl Schmitt," *Archiv für Rechts- und Sozialphilosophie* 76 (1990): 479–99.

9. The phrase here is Max Weber's. In contrast to Schmitt, however, Weber hoped that a modest version of this ideal could be salvaged. Max Weber, *Economy and Society: An Outline of Interpretive Sociology*, vol. 1, ed. and trans. Guenther Roth and Claus Wittich (Berkeley: University of California, 1979), 979. For a fine survey of Weber's contributions to jurisprudence: Anthony Kronman, *Max Weber* (Stanford, Calif.: Stanford University Press, 1991).

10. Schmitt, *Staat, Bewegung, Volk*, 44–45. Schmitt refers disparagingly on many occasions to this famous passage in Montesquieu. Yet even Montesquieu's view of judicial action is more subtle than Schmitt lets on. Montesquieu notes that it is only in republics where "the very nature of the constitution requires the judge to follow the letter of the law." In a monarchy judges need to "investigate their spirit" only if laws are not explicit (Montesquieu, *The Spirit of the Laws*, trans. Thomas Nugent [New York: Hafner, 1949], 75). In fairness, Schmitt does seem to provide a more sympathetic reading of Montesquieu in his *Die Diktatur* [*Dictatorship*] (Munich and Leipzig: Duncker & Humblot, 1928), 109. For the most part, however, Montesquieu functions as a convenient bogeyman in Schmitt's assault on liberal jurisprudence.

11. Kelsen, *The Pure Theory of Law*, 349.

12. Carl Schmitt, *Gesetz und Urteil. Eine Untersuchung zum Problem der Rechtspraxis* [1912] [*Law and Judgment*] (Munich: C. H. Beck, 1968). There is the obligatory dismissive reference to Montesquieu (7). As one recent historian of legal theory has noted, *Begriffsjurisprudenz*, or the "jurisprudence of concepts," "imagined [that] it had constructed a seamless network of rules which answered all problems scientifically, and excluded all extraneous values." *Begriffsjurisprudenz* was criticized widely for its "excessively literal, and therefore often absurd and unjust adherence to the letter of the law" (J. M. Kelly, *A Short History of Western Legal Theory* [Oxford: Clarendon Press, 1992], 359–60). Within contemporary radical jurisprudence in the United States, it is similarly commonplace to caricature formalist juriprudence by reducing it to a crude, exaggerated variant of formalism. For a critical discussion of this move, see Solum, "On the Indeterminacy Crisis: Critiquing Critical Dogma," 475.

13. Schmitt, *Gesetz und Urteil*, 15.

14. See also Carl Schmitt, "Juritische Fiktionen," *Deutsche Juristen-Zeitung* 18, no. 2 (1913): 805, where the idea that the "will of the statute" can directly guide the judge is described as a fiction.

15. Schmitt, *Gesetz und Urteil*, 27.

16. Schmitt, *Gesetz und Urteil*, 27.

17. Schmitt, *Gesetz und Urteil*, 32.

18. The Free Law School emphasized the virtues of suprapositive legal materials as a basis for judicial decision making. Its conservative proponents favored appeals to a (vague) "feeling for the law" [*Rechtsgefühl*] while those in its camp

sympathetic to political and social reform sought an increased role for the empirical social sciences within the legal system. This second strand occasionally drew the Free Lawyers close to American jurists like Louis Brandeis and Benjamin N. Cardozo. Indeed, Cardozo was familiar with the German Free Law School: Benjamin N. Cardozo, *The Nature of the Judicial Process* [1921] (New Haven: Yale University Press, 1965), 16–18, 70. Contemporary political and legal theorists are most likely familiar with the Free Law School from Weber's polemic against it. Weber associates the Free Law School with troublesome antiformal trends in the law. Schmitt and Weber agree that the Free Law Movement initiates a series of theoretical innovations incompatible with traditional liberal concepts of norm-based legal decision making. Unlike Weber, Schmitt sides with the Free Law School, arguing that it is only *inadequately* radical in its intellectual assault on formalist jurisprudence. See Weber, *Economy and Society*, vol. 1, 882–95.

    19. Schmitt, *Gesetz und Urteil*, 20–21, 40–41.

    20. Schmitt, *Gesetz und Urteil*, 67.

    21. Schmitt, *Gesetz und Urteil*, 48–50. Schmitt tries to enlist Hegel as an ally by recalling the argument in *The Philosophy of Right* that "[d]etermination . . . imposes only a general limit within which variations are also possible. . . . It is impossible to determine by reason, or to decide by applying a determination derived from the concept, whether the just penalty for an offence is corporal punishment of forty lashes or thirty-nine, a fine of five dollars as distinct from four dollars and twenty-three groschen or less. . . . It is reason itself which recognizes that contingency, contradiction, and semblance have their sphere and right" (G. W. F. Hegel, *Elements of the Philosophy of Right*, ed. Allen Wood, trans. H. B. Nisbet [Cambridge: Cambridge University Press, 1991], para. 214). At least two key differences separate Schmitt and Hegel here: First, for Hegel such indeterminacy is a genuinely peripheral aspect of legal experience, in part because Hegel takes legal formalism seriously. Indeed, the view expressed in this passage fits easily under the rubric of the *limited indeterminacy thesis*. Second, this moment is never associated, as in many of Schmitt's writings, with a moment of irrational, normatively unregulated power or arbitrary willfulness. For these reasons, I find attempts to read Schmitt as a right-wing Hegelian unconvincing. In this vein, see Cristi, *Carl Schmitt and Authoritarian Liberalism*, 96–107. Hegel was many things, but hardly an antirationalist who tried to undermine the rule of law. Schmitt's theory arguably fits better philosophically into Nietzschean currents within early twentieth-century German thought. But since Schmitt showed no systematic interest in Nietzsche's legacy, I am not sure how much one should make of any intellectual connection between Nietzsche and Schmitt. For better or for worse, Schmitt's main interlocutors were his peers in legal theory (Hans Kelsen, Hermann Heller), social theorists like Weber, and classical political theorists with strong institutional interests (for example, Niccolo Machiavelli, Thomas Hobbes, and Montesquieu). My impression is that he was uninterested in much of what passed for academic philosophy in his day, as well as in thinkers, like Nietzsche, whose legal ideas were peripheral to their overall thinking. For an interesting attempt to read Schmitt in the context of

Nietzsche's legacy, see John McCormick, "Dangers of Mythologizing Technology and Politics: Nietzsche, Schmitt, and the Antichrist," *Philosophy and Social Criticism* 21 (1995): 55–92. For a discussion of similarities between Schmitt and Martin Heidegger, see Richard Wolin, *The Politics of Being: The Political Thought of Martin Heidegger* (New York: Columbia University Press, 1990), 28–40.

22. Schmitt, *Gesetz und Urteil*, 71.

23. Schmitt, *Gesetz und Urteil*, 71, 78–79.

24. Schmitt, *Gesetz und Urteil*, 86.

25. Schmitt, *Gesetz und Urteil*, 88. This model may be akin to the traditional English idea of a community of judges whose special training in the intricacies of the common law allegedly can provide for a measure of legal predictability. One would do well to recall, however, that a crucial element of this experience, as Weber argued, was that English common lawyers long constituted "a strong organized guild which, by corporate and economic interests, through a monopoly of the bench and a central position at the seat of the central courts," gained "a measure of power which neither king nor parliament" could ignore (Weber, *Economy and Society*, vol. 1, 794). If this comparison is a fair one, how then does Schmitt hope to guarantee a similar corporate spirit among modern expert jurists? As will be shown in chapter 5, he ultimately believed that ethnic and "spiritual" homogeneity alone could help guarantee this shared spirit. For Schmitt, legal determinacy requires the destruction of modern pluralism.

Like Weber in his discussion of the common law, some recent CLS scholars have also noted that the "sociological" composition of lawyers and the judiciary is essential for understanding why, despite deep indeterminacy at the level of legal norms and precedents, a high degree of legal predictability nonetheless may obtain within a legal system. On one level, the problem is that "[w]hat a well-socialized white male lawyer finds to be an unquestionably reasonable resolution of a legal claim may seem quite unreasonable to an Asian-American working class woman" (Tushnet, "Defending the Indeterminacy Thesis," 350, 352). Interestingly, Schmitt would have accepted this diagnosis. His answer to it, however, was to try to save legal determinacy by eliminating the pluralism at the roots of such differences.

26. This is probably the reason why Schmitt makes the odd claim that "juristic fictions" can perform a positive function in the legal process: "The fiction is a consciously arbitrary or false assumption [for example, the idea of a binding norm] that nonetheless advances knowledge and can produce valuable results" (Schmitt, "Juristische Fiktionen," 806).

27. It is noteworthy that the application of Schmitt's theory would surely have resulted in increased authority for the judiciary vis-à-vis the legislature, precisely at that juncture when Social Democracy in Germany had made substantial electoral gains. (In 1912, the SPD gained 34.8 percent of all votes cast in parliamentary elections; in 1887, the SPD had received a mere 10.1 percent.)

28. Schmitt, *Der Wert des Staates und die Bedeutung des Einzelnen*, 22. Schmitt seems to have a number of different legal theories in mind, including socialist theories that conceive of law as an instrument of a dominant social class. Some of

Schmitt's initial observations about the limits of power-realist views of law resemble the underlying argumentation of Alexander Passerin d'Entreves' classic *The Notion of the State: An Introduction to Political Theory* (Oxford: Oxford University Press, 1967).

29. Schmitt, *Der Wert des Staates und die Bedeutung des Einzelnen*, 29.

30. Notwithstanding Schmitt's subsequent hostility to Kelsen, Schmitt offers words of praise for Kelsen in this early work (Schmitt, *Der Wert des Staates und die Bedeutung des Einzelnen*, 30–31). Kelsen analogously argues that legal analysis should be clearly distinguished from empirical studies of power. In chapter 3 I argue that Kelsen posits a "pure theory of law" from which an empirical analysis of the concrete dynamics of state power has been purged, while Schmitt responds with a theory in which "pure power" plays a pivotal role and the place of (normative) legal restraints is drastically demoted.

31. Schmitt, *Der Wert des Staates und die Bedeutung des Einzelnen*, 30.

32. In a review article from this period, Schmitt argues that the widespread tendency within German legal theory to separate law's normative elements from its empirical components tends to fail: Schmitt, "Review of Julius Binder, *Rechtsbegriff und Rechtsidee: Bemerkungen zur Rechtsphilosophie Rudolf Stammlers*," *Kritische Vierteljahresschrift für Gesetzgebung und Rechtswissenschaft* 17, nos. 3–4 (1916): 431–41. This observation is probably one source of Schmitt's own attempt to move beyond the antinomy of law versus power.

33. Schmitt, *Der Wert des Staates und die Bedeutung des Einzelnen*, 79.

34. Enormous concentrations of political power were commonplace during World War I. But they did not necessarily take the form of the military dictatorship realized in Germany. Clinton Lawrence Rossiter, *Constitutional Dictatorship: Crisis Government in the Modern Democracies* [1948] (New York: Harcourt Brace Jovanovich, 1963), 104–17, 151–71, 240–55.

35. Carl Schmitt, "Diktatur und Belagerungszustand: Eine staatsrechtliche Studie" ["Dictatorship and the State of Siege"], *Zeitschrift für die gesamte Strafrechtswissenschaft* 38 (1917): 139.

36. Bendersky, *Carl Schmitt: Theorist for the Reich*, 19–20.

37. See also Carl Schmitt, "Die Einwirkungen des Kriegszustandes auf das ordentliche strafprozessuale Verfahren," *Zeitschrift für die gesamte Strafrechtswissenschaft* 38 (1917): 791.

38. Schmitt, "Diktatur und Belagerungszustand," 156–58. Marie Jean Antoine Condorcet is also associated here with Rousseau's failed quest to see administrative action as based on a "syllogistic" reading of the legislative norm (158).

39. Schmitt, "Diktatur und Belagerungszustand," 157.

40. Schmitt, "Diktatur und Belagerungszustand," 157.

41. Schmitt, "Diktatur und Belagerungszustand," 157.

42. Schmitt, "Diktatur und Belagerungszustand," 159–60.

43. Schmitt, *Die Diktatur*, viii. My discussion here focuses on that part of *Dictatorship* which first appeared in 1922; the 1928 edition included an amended discussion on the emergency powers of the Weimar President. Elements of Schmitt's

theory of dictatorship are also summarized in an encyclopedia article: Carl Schmitt, "Die Diktatur," *Staatslexikon*, ed. Hermann Sacher (Freiburg: Herder, 1926), 1447–53.

44. Schmitt, *Die Diktatur*, ix.

45. Schmitt, *Die Diktatur*, viii.

46. Carl Schmitt, *The Crisis of Parliamentary Democracy*, trans. Ellen Kennedy (Cambridge, Mass.: MIT Press, 1985), 33–50. The nexus between parliamentarism and the rule of law within Schmitt's theory is discussed in detail in chapter 2.

47. The concept of the "concrete exception" is intimately related to the idea of "indifference in reference to the content" of the law. For Schmitt, "[t]he exception is that which cannot be subsumed; it defies general codification, but it simultaneously reveals a specifically juristic element—the decision in absolute purity. The exception appears in its absolute form when a situation in which legal prescriptions can be valid must first be brought about" (Schmitt, *Political Theology*, 13).

48. Schmitt, *Political Theology*, 5.

49. Schmitt, *Political Theology*, 13. Again, the problem of legal indeterminacy here is considered to be of significance to more than a narrowly defined category of legal decision makers. It is seen as pointing to the fact that a rich diversity of political and legal actors inevitably subordinate "normativistic" law to exercises of pure power or pure willfulness.

50. Schmitt, *Political Theology*, 12.

51. Schmitt, *Political Theology*, 66. On the conceptual structure of Schmitt's "decisionism" and its relationship to similar strands in Martin Heidegger and Ernst Jünger, see Christian Graf von Krockow, *Die Entscheidung. Eine Untersuchung über Ernst Jünger, Carl Schmitt, Martin Heidegger* (Stuttgart: Ferdinand Enke, 1958).

52. Schmitt, *Political Theology*, 17.

53. Schmitt, *Political Theology*, 31.

54. Carl Schmitt, *The Concept of the Political*, trans. George Schwab (New Brunswick, N.J.: Rutgers University Press, 1976), 67.

55. John P. McCormick, "The Dilemmas of Dictatorship: Carl Schmitt and Constitutional Emergency Powers," *Canadian Journal of Law and Jurisprudence* X, no. 1 (January 1997): 172.

56. McCormick, "The Dilemmas of Dictatorship," 174.

57. Schmitt, *Gesetz und Urteil*, v.

58. Unger, *What Should Legal Analysis Become?*, 65.

59. Unger, *What Should Legal Analysis Become?*, 77.

60. Stanley Fish, *There's No Such Thing as Free Speech and It's a Good Thing, Too* (New York: Oxford University Press, 1994), esp. 141–79.

61. For a critical account of such strands within CLS, see Altman, *Critical Legal Studies: A Liberal Critique*, 90–98.

2. THE DECAY OF PARLIAMENTARISM

1. For a discussion of Schmitt's influence, see Ellen Kennedy, "Carl Schmitt's *Parlamentarismus* in Its Historical Context," in Schmitt, *The Crisis of Parliamentary*

Democracy, xiii–xlix. Unfortunately, Kennedy's critical comments are underdeveloped. For an account of Schmitt within the German context, see Kurt Kluxen, *Geschichte und Problematik des Parlamentarismus* (Frankfurt a.M.: Suhrkamp, 1983), 175–96. Insightful in this respect is also Ernst Fraenkel, *Deutschland und die westlichen Demokratien* (Frankfurt a.M.: Suhrkamp, 1991).

2. For one important recent exception: Michael J. Sandel, *Democracy's Discontent: America in Search of a Public Philosophy* (Cambridge, Mass.: Harvard University Press, 1996).

3. To claim that Schmitt was simply concerned with "destroying the purely mechanical approach to parliamentarism, namely, that any qualified majority may at any moment" restructure the constitution, profoundly understates Schmitt's hostility to parliamentary government (George Schwab, *The Challenge of the Exception*, 67–72). Bendersky similarly obscures Schmitt's hostility to liberal representative government (*Carl Schmitt: Theorist for the Reich*, 64–84). For another simplified account of Schmitt's ideas, see John Keane, *Democracy and Civil Society: On the Predicaments of European Socialism, the Prospects for Democracy, and the Problem of Controlling Social and Political Power* (London: Verso, 1988), 153–90. Keane's argument that Schmitt ignored premodern parliaments in his account of the rise and fall of liberal parliamentarism is irrelevant to the core of Schmitt's argument. In addition, Keane's suggestion that Schmitt denied the possibility of reforming parliament is inaccurate. Schmitt frequently concedes the possibility of tinkering with parliament so as to make sure that it might perform some more or less useful "socio-technical" functions; he just doubts that it could recapture its crucial, classical deliberative core. Inadequately critical of Schmitt are Richard Bellamy and Peter Baehr, "Carl Schmitt and the Contradictions of Liberal Democracy," *European Journal of Political Research* 23 (1993): 163–85. More reliable is Bernard Manin, *The Principles of Representative Government* (New York: Cambridge University Press, 1997), 193–235.

4. Schmitt, *The Crisis of Parliamentary Democracy*, 5. This is a reliable English translation of the 1926 edition of *Die geistesgeschichtliche Lage des heutigen Parlamentarismus* (Berlin: Duncker and Humblot, 1926); there was an earlier 1923 edition as well. As I discuss shortly, Schmitt develops his Weimar-era argument about modern parliamentarism in *Die Verfassungslehre* [*Constitutional Theory*] (Munich: Duncker and Humblot, 1928) and *Der Hüter der Verfassung* [*The Guardian of the Constitution*] (Tübingen: Mohr, 1931). He also broaches the topic in shorter essays in Carl Schmitt, *Positionen und Begriffe im Kampf mit Weimar-Genf-Versailles 1923–1939* [*Positions and Concepts in the Struggle Against Weimar-Geneva-Versailles*] (Hamburg: Hanseatische Verlagsanstalt, 1940); Carl Schmitt, *Verfassungsrechtliche Aufsätze aus den Jahren 1924–1954* (Berlin: Duncker and Humblot, 1973). Schmitt's critical analysis of political romanticism, developed during the same period, can also be fruitfully read as part of his critique of liberal rationalism. In *The Crisis of Parliamentary Democracy*, Schmitt emphasizes the similarities between the German Romantic notion of eternal discussion and the liberal ideal of the deliberative parliament, commenting that it is "confused" to see German Romanticism as conservative and antiliberal (36). In this view, Romanticism suffers from many of the same ills as

"indecisive" liberalism (Carl Schmitt, *Political Romanticism* [1925], trans. Guy Oakes [Cambridge, Mass.: MIT Press, 1986]).

5. Schmitt, *The Crisis of Parliamentary Democracy*, 35, 45–46.

6. Schmitt, *The Crisis of Parliamentary Democracy*, 34–36, 40–41, 45–47. This nuance is significant because Schmitt's most formidable contemporary critic, Hans Kelsen, accused him of endorsing an "absolutistic" view of political deliberation that, in Kelsen's view, was incompatible with the basic preconditions of a "disenchanted" (Weber) moral and political universe and a genuinely modern form of democracy. For Kelsen, a political theory that emphasizes "absolute truths" tends to have authoritarian implications, whereas a fallibilistic view of politics that acknowledges the "relative" quality of most political arguments alone provides room for a genuinely liberal, open process of political decision making (Hans Kelsen, *Das Problem des Parlamentarismus* [Vienna: Wilhelm Braumüller, 1926], especially 39–40). Although I am sympathetic toward Kelsen's critique, I am not sure that it fully captures the complexities of Schmitt's interpretation of liberal rationalism. In *The Crisis of Parliamentary Democracy*, Schmitt considers "relative" rationalism more important for parliamentarism than its "fanatical" or "absolutist" versions (Bentham, Condorcet) (Schmitt, *The Crisis of Parliamentary Democracy*, 38–39, 46).

7. Carl Schmitt, *Die Verfassungslehre*, 315.

8. Schmitt, *Die Verfassungslehre*, 310–16.

9. Schmitt, *The Crisis of Parliamentary Democracy*, 3.

10. Schmitt, *The Crisis of Parliamentary Democracy*, 42.

11. Schmitt, *The Crisis of Parliamentary Democracy*, 42. Schmitt is citing Junius Brutus' *Vindiciae contra Tyrannos* (1579) here.

12. Schmitt, *The Crisis of Parliamentary Democracy*, 45. In a perceptive critique, Ferdinand Tönnies argues against Schmitt that he tends to overstate this contrast. For Tönnies, classical models of the executive hardly excluded deliberation; by the same token, legislation was not associated with the quest for truth to the extent described by Schmitt. In short, in Schmitt's analysis, the rationalism of legislation is overstated and the potential rationalism of the executive understated (Ferdinand Tönnies, "Demokratie und Parlamentarismus," *Schmollers Jahrbuch für Gesetzgebung, Verwaltung und Volkswirtschaft im Deutschen Reich* 51 [1927], 8–11).

13. Condorcet, cited in Schmitt, *The Crisis of Parliamentary Democracy*, 44. See also Schmitt, "Diktatur und Belagerungszustand," where he levels the same accusation against Rousseau (158).

14. Schmitt, *The Crisis of Parliamentary Democracy*, 45–46. Although undeveloped, Schmitt's comments here are extremely interesting. American constitutional democracy certainly does give much more autonomy to the executive—and, for that matter, the judiciary—than crucial strands of continental Enlightenment rationalism would have considered appropriate. Unfortunately, Schmitt downplays the interesting implications of this suggestion. After all, it might be taken as evidence that influential strands within liberal political and legal theory certainly have tried to come to grips with the problem of the "exception" in law. But the implicit claim here is that American liberalism contains more "political" elements than its

European counterparts. In chapter 6, we examine Schmitt's discussion of American conceptions of international law, where he similarly emphasizes the political capacities of American liberals.

15. Schmitt, *The Crisis of Parliamentary Democracy*, 44–45.

16. Schmitt, *The Crisis of Parliamentary Democracy*, 49.

17. Schmitt, *The Crisis of Parliamentary Democracy*, 35.

18. Schmitt, *The Crisis of Parliamentary Democracy*, 30.

19. Schmitt, *The Crisis of Parliamentary Democracy*, 26–29. For a more detailed analysis of Schmitt's view of democracy and its relationship to the concepts of equality, homogeneity, and identity, see Schmitt, *Die Verfassungslehre*, especially 223–38, 276–82. In *Die Verfassungslehre* Schmitt argues for a basic contradiction between (the "political" idea of) democracy and ("anti-political," "normativistic") liberalism. For a helpful analysis of the conceptual issues at hand here, see Ulrich Preuss, "Der Zusammenhang von Demokratie und Gleichheit in der Verfassungstheorie Carl Schmitts," in *Gleichheit und Konservatismus*, ed. F. de Pauw (Zwolle, Belgium: W.E.J. Tjeenk Willink, 1985), 117–32.

20. Otto Kirchheimer and Nathan Leites perceptively argued early on that "identity" is both an empirical and normative category for Schmitt. It is tied to claims about what democracy *ought to be* and, furthermore, should contribute to an empirical analysis (and a critique) of contemporary democracy. On the empirical level, Schmitt believes that democracy ultimately cannot function without far-reaching "sameness" or homogeneity, but Kirchheimer rightly notes that Schmitt's emphasis on homogeneity is misleading and overstated: from multiethnic and multilingual Belgium to class-divided France and England, many relatively pluralistic, heterogeneous democracies have flourished. On the basis of the peculiarities of the deeply divided, crisis-torn Weimar Republic, Schmitt formulates a number of highly problematic empirical generalizations about twentieth-century mass democratic polities. Schmitt's normative claim is misleading insofar as it distorts the fact that democratic theorists long aspired to realize *both* freedom *and* equality, *both* collective autonomy *and* equality. Democracy was conceived of as collective self-determination, and not solely or even primarily (as Schmitt argues) as equality understood in terms of a far-reaching political homogeneity (Otto Kirchheimer and Nathan Leites, "Comments on Carl Schmitt's *Legality and Legitimacy*" [1933] in *The Rule of Law Under Siege: Selected Essays of Franz Neumann and Otto Kirchheimer*, ed. William E. Scheuerman [Berkeley: University of California, 1996], 64–68).

21. Schmitt, *The Crisis of Parliamentary Democracy*, 8–15. It is significant that Schmitt was formulating this part of the argument (in 1926) at the same time that he was beginning his work on the "concept of the political."

22. Carl Schmitt, "Der Begriff des Politischen," *Archiv für Sozialwissenschaft* 58, no. 1 (1927): 4. This essay will be examined in greater detail later on, particularly in our discussion of Hans Morgenthau. In 1932, Schmitt extended and reworked it into a book; where appropriate, I cite the English translation: Schmitt, *The Concept of the Political*, trans. George Schwab (New Brunswick, N.J.: Rutgers University Press, 1976).

23. Schmitt, "Der Begriff des Politischen," 6.
24. Schmitt, *Political Theology*, 66.
25. Schmitt, *The Crisis of Parliamentary Democracy*, 9.
26. Schmitt, *Die Verfassungslehre*, 209–10.
27. Schmitt, *Römischer Katholizismus und politische Form*, 29. Schmitt's early reflections on the concept of representation clearly contain authoritarian Catholic elements, but before long they took on nationalistic and fascistic hues. For a discussion of this development, see McCormick, *Carl Schmitt's Critique of Liberalism: Against Politics as Technology*, 157–205. Schmitt's peculiar views on representation do not fall easily under any of the common categorizations of representation developed within modern political theory. It sometimes seems closest to the medieval, even "mystical" model thematized by Hannah Fenichel Pitkin, *The Concept of Representation* (Berkeley: University of California Press, 1967), 241–42, 295.
28. For an early (1936) statement of this criticism, see Neumann, *The Rule of Law: Political Theory and the Legal System in Modern Society*, 26–27.
29. Elsewhere I have restated some of these traditional criticisms of Schmitt's "concept of the political" in "Modernist anti-Modernism: Carl Schmitt's Concept of the Political," *Philosophy and Social Criticism* 19, no. 2 (1993): 79–98. It is no accident that Leo Strauss was so concerned about the potential dangers of this element of Weber's thinking in light of his familiarity with the ills of Schmitt's decisionism. See Leo Strauss, "Comments on Carl Schmitt's *Der Begriff des Politischen*" (his commentary on the 1932 version of Schmitt's study on the concept of the political), reprinted in Schmitt, *The Concept of the Political*, 81–105; and more generally, Leo Strauss, *Natural Right and History* [1953] (Chicago: University of Chicago, 1965).
30. Schmitt, *The Crisis of Parliamentary Democracy*, 6; Schmitt, *Die Verfassungslehre*, 319.
31. James Bryce, *Modern Democracies* (New York: Macmillan, 1921).
32. Charles Maier, *Recasting Bourgeois Europe: Stabilization in France, Germany and Italy in the Decade after World War I* (Princeton, N.J.: Princeton University Press, 1975). For just a few examples of the massive contemporary literature on parliamentary decay, see Suzanne Berger, "Politics and Anti-Politics in Western Europe," *Daedalus* 108, no. 1 (Winter 1979): 46–47; Bernard Manin, *The Principles of Representative Government*, which confirms many of Schmitt's arguments, 202–18; Claus Offe, *Contradictions of the Welfare State*, ed. John Keane (Cambridge, Mass.: MIT Press, 1984), esp. 166–167; and Gianfranco Poggi, *The State: Its Nature, Development, and Prospects* (Stanford, Calif.: Stanford University Press, 1990), 128–44. Even more telling are the recent empirical studies on parliaments in western Europe, Japan, and the United States in Ezra Suleiman, ed., *Parliaments and Parliamentarians in Democratic Politics* (New York: Holmes and Meier, 1986). Despite the cautious tone of the contributions in this volume, many of them can be read as supporting a number of features of Schmitt's unflattering portrayal of contemporary parliaments. This is also true of a recent German anthology on parliamentary institutions: Kurt Kluxen, ed., *Parlamentarismus* (Königstein: Verlag Anton Hain, 1980).

Much of the empirical literature argues that the relatively powerful United States Congress, especially because of the tenuous nature of party ties in the United States, provides something of an exception to these broad trends. Interestingly, Schmitt never explicitly discusses the United States Congress in his works; perhaps doing so would have forced him to reconsider some of his more dramatic assertions about parliamentary decay. Perhaps, though, one should avoid emphasizing the exceptional qualities of the American case. As Theodore Lowi has powerfully argued in *The End of Liberalism*, the American Congress has similarly abandoned many of its traditional lawmaking functions.

33. For a critical survey of some of these debates, Bernhard Peters, *Rationalität, Recht und Gesellschaft* (Frankfurt a.M.: Suhrkamp, 1991), especially 51–93.

34. Schmitt, *The Crisis of Parliamentary Democracy*, 1.

35. Schmitt, *Die Verfassungslehre*, 310.

36. Schmitt, *Die Verfassungslehre*, 310–11.

37. Schmitt, *Die Verfassungslehre*, 307–8. Weber and Kelsen developed defenses of liberal parliamentary practice, but they did so while breaking with traditional liberalism's grounding in moral universalism. Both were value-skeptics who believed that "disenchantment" [*Entzauberung*] rendered traditional ("substantive") moral defenses of parliamentarism anachronistic.

38. Schmitt bluntly asserts that "property is no [personal] quality that can be represented." Wealth, it seems, is incapable of representation in the Schmittian sense. For this reason, liberal parliamentarism is self-destructive. From the outset, parliament is seen as a means for protecting economic interests; when this agenda gains the upper hand in relation to the representation of *Bildung*, parliament increasingly is reduced to an economic clearinghouse, allegedly unable to fulfill minimal political functions. The tendency to undertake the functions of economic coordination behind closed doors (for example, in secret committee meetings, or in corporatist sessions closed to the public) exacerbates this trend. While representation should provide a visible, public form, parliament takes on an increasingly private, even secretive form: "The representative character of parliament and the deputy collapses. As a result, parliament is no longer the place where political decisions are made" (Schmitt, *Die Verfassungslehre*, 311–12, 319).

39. Schmitt, *Die Verfassungslehre*, 313.

40. Schmitt, *Die Verfassungslehre*, 312–14, 322–23. A pithy version of Schmitt's sociology of parliamentarism is also presented in Carl Schmitt, "Der bürgerliche Rechtsstaat," *Die Schildgenossen* 8 (1928): 127–33.

41. Otto Kirchheimer, "Constitutional Reaction in 1932" (1932) in *Politics, Law, and Social Change: Selected Essays of Otto Kirchheimer*, eds. Frederic S. Burin and Kurt L. Shell (New York: Columbia University Press, 1969), 78.

42. This is one of the central arguments of Schmitt's subsequent *Legalität und Legitimität* [*Legality and Legitimacy*] (Munich: Duncker and Humblot, 1932), esp. 30–40.

43. See Carl Schmitt, *Unabhängigkeit der Richter, Gleichheit vor dem Gesetz und Gewährleistung des Privateigentums nach der Weimarer Verfassung* [*Judicial Independence,*

Equality Before the Law, and the Protection of Private Property According to the Weimar Constitution] (Berlin: de Gruyter, 1926), where he attacks the nongeneral legal form of the Weimar left's referendum in favor of expropriating royal property.

44. This aspect of Schmitt's argument is developed in depth in *Der Hüter der Verfassung*, especially 71–95. We examine it in greater depth in chapter 4.

45. Schmitt, *Die Verfassungslehre*, 319.

46. For a summary of the substantial empirical literature on legislative composition, see Gerhard Loewenberg and Samuel C. Patterson, *Comparing Legislatures* (Boston: Little, Brown, 1979), 68–78. In France, representatives with working-class or lower-middle-class backgrounds never have exceeded 35 percent of the overall total. In Great Britain, the majority even of Labor MPs since 1945 no longer has a traditional working-class background. In contrast, the representation of "professional, managerial, and white collar" groups in European parliaments now exceeds in every case 50 percent (in the German Federal Republic over 80 percent; in the United Kingdom nearly 60 percent; in France about 65 percent). Lawyers, whom Schmitt mentions in *Die Verfassungslehre* as being the typical social carriers of deliberative parliamentary politics, make up large numbers of contemporary elected representatives in many polities (in the United States about 50 percent). Although the historical story is very complicated, substantial parliamentary representation prior to the twentieth century was pre-bourgeois in character. If any period in the history of parliamentarism deserves to be deemed "bourgeois," it may very well be our own rather than the mid-nineteenth century.

47. But even the German neo-Marxists who endorsed some version of this interpretation during the 1930s synthesized it with an analysis of the exceptional features of modern German history in order to explain the demise of Weimar Democracy. See, for example, Franz L. Neumann, *Behemoth: The Structure and Practice of National Socialism* [1942] (New York: Harper & Row, 1944), especially 3–34.

48. Lowi, *The End of Liberalism.*

49. Peters, *Rationalität, Recht, und Gesellschaft*, 51–93.

50. Recent commentators have ably contested Schmitt's interpretation of early nineteenth-century German concepts of parliamentarism. See Hans Boldt, "Parlamentarismustheorie. Bemerkungen zu ihrer Geschichte in Deutschland," *Der Staat* 19, no. 3 (1980): 407–10.

51. Schmitt, *Die Verfassungslehre*, 338. This claim is also repeated in Schmitt, "Der bürgerliche Rechtsstaat," 127.

52. For a helpful discussion of this, see Ernst Fraenkel, *Deutschland und die westlichen Demokratien*, 35–37.

53. Schmitt, *Die Verfassungslehre*, 326–30. On the social composition of the French parliament at the end of the 19th century, see Loewenberg and Patterson, *Comparing Legislatures*, 73. For a helpful survey of the development of French parliamentarism in the nineteenth and twentieth centuries: Francois Gogul, "Geschichte und Gegenwartsproblematik des französischen Parlamentarismus," in *Parlamentarismus*, ed. Kurt Kluxen.

54. Jean Cohen and Andrew Arato, *Civil Society and Political Theory* (Cam-

bridge, Mass.: MIT Press, 1992), 234 and more generally, 201–6, 231–41. Although their interpretation seems to ignore *Die Verfassungslehre* and thus, for example, underplays the complexities of Schmitt's reliance on the British case, Cohen and Arato offer the best account of Schmitt's analysis of parliamentary democracy available in English.

55. Schmitt, *Die Verfassungslehre*, 321. Schmitt's chronology could hence be read as leaving open the possibility of a parliamentary "window of excellence" between 1832 and 1850. Yet he never explicitly describes this period as a fulfillment of his vision of classical liberal parliamentarism.

56. Schmitt, *Die Verfassungslehre*, 324.

57. Kurt Kluxen, "Die Umformung des parlamentarischen Regierungssystems in Großbritannien beim Übergang zur Massendemokratie," in *Parlamentarismus*, ed. Kurt Kluxen, 120–30. For a criticism of romanticized accounts of eighteenth- and nineteenth-century English parliamentarism: Wolfgang Jäger, *Öffentlichkeit und Parlamentarismus* (Stuttgart: Kohlhammer, 1973), 17–28. Jäger's polemic is intended to criticize the young Habermas's somewhat idealized view of English liberal politics during the heyday of the "bourgeois public sphere" in *The Structural Transformation of the Public Sphere* (Cambridge, Mass.: MIT Press, 1989), but a number of its features provide a helpful corrective to an analogous tendency in Schmitt. Jäger also rightly criticizes the implicit assumption in Schmitt's account that nineteenth-century polities were vastly more faithful to important rule of law virtues than were their twentieth-century successors. Individual measures and open-ended law are hardly new; they were commonplace in the nineteenth century, despite significant efforts toward the codification of law. This is true of both common law and Continental legal systems. For an excellent discussion of the sad realities of the nineteenth-century Prussian *Rechtsstaat*, see Albrecht Funk, *Polizei und Rechtsstaat: Die Entwicklung des staatlichen Gewaltmonopols in Preussen 1848–1918* (Frankfurt a.M.: Campus, 1986).

58. Schmitt, *Die Verfassungslehre*, 324.

59. Schmitt, *Die Verfassungslehre*, 325.

60. In 1913 Schmitt wrote that the "fiction . . . is a path which humanity pursues thousands of times in all the sciences to reach the right aim by means of incorrect assumptions." Specifically, Schmitt is talking here of "juridical fictions," including Montesquieu's vision of a "mechanical" judge. Schmitt vaguely suggests that it is appropriate to make use of such "fictions" in order to make progress in the sciences. Is his idealized description of parliamentarism here meant to perform the function of such a fiction (Schmitt, "Juristische Fiktionen," 805)?

61. Schmitt, *The Crisis of Parliamentary Democracy*, 68.

62. Schmitt, *The Crisis of Parliamentary Democracy*, 68.

63. Schmitt, *The Crisis of Parliamentary Democracy*, 68.

64. A revealing example of this is Schmitt's *Unabhängigkeit der Richter, Gleichheit vor dem Gesetz und Gewährleistung des Privateigentums nach der Weimarer Verfassung*, where he describes the German left's rather modest attempt to socialize royal property as an act of revolutionary violence (14).

65. Schmitt, *The Crisis of Parliamentary Democracy*, 2–3.

66. Schmitt claims that with the demise of deliberative parliamentarism, "provisions concerning freedom of speech and immunity of representatives" lose their original grounding (3). Later, he extends this claim by arguing that with parliamentarism's demise "the *whole* system of freedom of speech, assembly, and the press, of public meetings, parliamentary privileges, is losing its rationale" (emphasis added) (Schmitt, *The Crisis of Parliamentary Democracy*, 49).

67. Cohen and Arato, *Civil Society and Political Theory*, 205.

68. But probably not in *all* of Schmitt's writings. In *The Guardian of the Constitution* (1931), Cohen and Arato's exegetical claim that for Schmitt "the principle of discussion belongs to the level of society" (Cohen and Arato, *Civil Society and Political Theory*, 203) is accurate. But Schmitt does not think that this requires him to reevaluate his hostile account of parliamentarism. Because the collapse of the traditional state/society divide and the concomitant emergence of the modern interventionist state allegedly undermine deliberative activities in society at large, Schmitt believes that he can continue his project of developing a one-sided attack on parliamentarism. In addition, Schmitt's view that deliberation is inherently antipolitical perhaps leads him to misconstrue the significance of the liberal ideal of government by discussion.

69. For a richer account of the classical liberal ideal of "government by discussion" than that provided by Schmitt, see Habermas, *The Structural Transformation of the Public Sphere*, especially 27–129. For the controversy surrounding Habermas's study, see Craig Calhoun, ed., *Habermas and the Public Sphere* (Cambridge, Mass.: MIT Press, 1992). I am less concerned with defending the detail of Habermas's model of the public sphere here than in recalling its success, contra Schmitt, in refusing to reduce the site of political deliberation to parliament. Habermas rightly criticizes Schmitt's simplistic conception of deliberative liberalism in his "The Horrors of Autonomy," in *The New Conservatism: Cultural Criticism and the Historians' Debate*, ed. and trans. Shierry Weber Nicholsen (Cambridge, Mass.: MIT Press, 1989), 128–39.

70. Many have emphasized these positive elements. For a recent statement of this view, see Jürgen Habermas, "Law and Morality," in *The Tanner Lectures on Human Values* 8 (1988), ed. Sterling M. McMurrin (Salt Lake City: University of Utah Press, 1988), 217–79.

3. THE CRITIQUE OF LIBERAL CONSTITUTIONALISM

1. For three recent discussions of this feature of Schmitt's theory, see Caldwell, *Popular Sovereignty and the Crisis of German Constitutional Law*, 85–119; Dyzenhaus, *Legality and Legitimacy: Carl Schmitt, Hans Kelsen, and Hermann Heller in Weimar*, 38–101; Rune Slagstad, "Liberal Constitutionalism and Its Critics: Carl Schmitt and Max Weber," in *Constitutionalism and Democracy*, ed. Jon Elster and Rune Slagstad (New York: Cambridge University Press, 1988). The German literature on Schmitt's constitutional theory is vast. For a helpful survey of it, see Rein-

hard Mehring, "Carl Schmitts Lehre von der Auflösung des Liberalismus. Das Sinngefüge der *Verfassungslehre* als historisches Urteil," *Zeitschrift für Politik* 38 (1991): 200–16.

2. Ulrich Preuss, "Der Begriff der Verfassung und ihre Beziehung zur Politik," in *Zum Begriff der Verfassung: Die Ordnung des Politischen*, ed. Ulrich Preuß (Frankfurt a.M.: Fischer Verlag, 1994), 10.

3. Leo Strauss, "Comments on Carl Schmitt's *Begriff des Politischen*," 105.

4. Schmitt, *Die Verfassungslehre*, 9. *Constitutional Theory* [*Die Verfassungslehre*] is the centerpiece of Schmitt's Weimar jurisprudence, thus my emphasis on it here. Schmitt's constitutional theory is also concisely summarized in "Der bürgerliche Rechtsstaat."

5. On the role of general law within classical liberalism, see Schmitt, *Die Verfassungslehre*, 138–57.

6. Carl Schmitt, "Review of Gerhard Anschütz, *Die Verfassung des deutschen Reiches vom 11. August 1919*," *Juristische Wochenschrift* 55 (1926): 2270–72. Anschütz was a leading legal positivist in Weimar.

7. For Schmitt's most important polemic against the left's preference for non-general law, see Schmitt, *Unabhängigkeit der Richter, Gleichheit vor dem Gesetz, und Gewährleistung des Privateigentums nach der Weimarer Verfassung*, 22–24, where the issue of judicial independence is scrutinized. Schmitt's views on the rule of law and the interventionist welfare state are analyzed in depth in chapter 4; his relationship to Hayek, in chapter 8.

8. Hans Kelsen, *Reine Rechtslehre* (Darmstadt: Scientia Verlag, 1985), 64.

9. Schmitt, *Die Verfassungslehre*, 9.

10. Schmitt, *Die Verfassungslehre*, 67. Although Kelsen is left unnamed, Schmitt is referring to Kelsen's democratic theory and its emphasis on the virtues of political compromise. Schmitt tends to caricature Kelsen. Schmitt's criticism here has some basis within Kelsen's thinking, however. In his democratic theory, Kelsen argues that ours is a "relativistic" age in which the belief in "absolute" moral truths necessarily has waned. Democracy is the best political form for modernity because it directly expresses the dictates of modern moral relativism. Basic liberal democratic mechanisms and procedures (free speech, minority protections) make sense only if the members of the political community accept the possibility that their moral and political views might turn out to be incorrect. If one believes in the absolute correctness of one's own views, there is no reason to accept liberal democratic procedures; then it is consistent to demand a monopoly on political power (Hans Kelsen, *Vom Wesen und Wert der Demokratie* [Tübingen: Mohr, 1929]). On this point, Kelsen proves a convenient target for Schmitt. In fact, not all legal positivists in Weimar shared Kelsen's problematic value relativism; See Ingeborg Maus, " 'Gesetzesbindung' der Justiz und die Struktur der nationalsozialistischen Rechtsnormen," in *Recht und Justiz im "Dritten Reich,"* ed. Ralf Dreier and Wolfgang Sellert (Frankfurt a.M.: Suhrkamp, 1989), 82–84.

11. Schmitt, *Die Verfassungslehre*, 11. But why does Schmitt accept the inevitability of the demise of natural law? In *The Concept of the Political* he endorses Weber's

278   *Notes: Chapter 3*

famous assertion that the political and moral "life spheres" are unavoidably distinct in modernity. In short, he accepts the basic accuracy of crucial features of Weber's picture of modern "disenchantment" [*Entzauberung*] (26–28). Schmitt, *The Concept of the Political*, 26–28. In his postwar diaries, Schmitt explicitly describes natural law as an anachronism (*Glossarium. Aufzeichnungen der Jahre 1947–1951*, ed. Eberhard Freiherr von Medem [Berlin: Duncker and Humblot, 1991], 50).

12. Schmitt, *Die Verfassungslehre*, 11–36.

13. In the discussion of basic rights developed in *Constitutional Theory*, private property possesses a privileged position, whereas "social rights" (for example, to a job), which had a prominent place within the Weimar Constitution, are for Schmitt at most rights in a limited, "relative" sense (*Die Verfassungslehre*, 163–70).

14. Schmitt, *Unabhängigkeit der Richter*. On the antisocialist impulses of Schmitt's theory, the best study remains Maus, *Bürgerliche Rechtstheorie und Faschismus: Zur sozialen Funktion und aktuellen Wirkung der Theorie Carl Schmitts*.

15. Schmitt's occasional strategic employment of classical liberal legal ideas misleads many of his readers. Renato Cristi, for example, believes that Schmitt in the late 1920s endorsed an "authoritarian liberalism" that respected crucial rule of law values. Cristi not only ignores Schmitt's deconstruction of the rule of law in his early jurisprudential writings, but also misses the fact that Schmitt pointedly refers to his ideas about legal indeterminacy even in those texts where he uses idealizations of early liberal positions in order to discredit contemporary liberalism (Cristi, *Carl Schmitt and Authoritarian Liberalism*, 126–45). See Schmitt's own 1931 reminder about his views on indeterminacy within judicial action in *Der Hüter der Verfassung*, 45–46.

16. Schmitt, *Die Verfassungslehre*, 8.

17. Schmitt, *Die Verfassungslehre*, 50.

18. Schmitt, *Concept of the Political*, 27. This passage might suggest a Hobbesian interest in demonstrating the primacy of power vis-à-vis law. Schmitt goes well beyond Hobbes, however. Schmitt repeatedly gives his interpretation of friend/foe politics radical nationalistic and ethnic connotations. As Ulrich Preuss has noted, Schmitt's "ethnicist" constitutional theory rests on a substitution of the ethnos for the demos: *das Volk* is conceived as an "ethnic and cultural oneness," with a "capacity to realize its otherness in relation both to others and the liberal-universalist category of mankind." I employ the term "ethnicist" in this study in accordance with Preuss's definition (Ulrich Preuss, "Constitutional Powermaking for the New Polity: Some Deliberations on the Relations Between Constituent Power and the Constitution," *Cardozo Law Review*, 14, nos. 3–4 [January 1993]: 649–50).

19. Schmitt, *Concept of the Political*, 27.

20. Schmitt, *Der Hüter der Verfassung*; for Kelsen's reply, see *Wer soll der Hüter der Verfassung sein?* (Berlin-Grünewald: W. Rothschild, 1931). For a learned discussion of the Schmitt/Kelsen exchange, see Stanley Paulson, "The Reich President and Weimar Constitutional Politics: Aspects of the Schmitt-Kelsen Dispute and the 'Guardian of the Constitution,'" paper presented at the Annual Meeting of the American Political Science Association, Chicago, September 1995.

21. Schmitt, *Political Theology*, 28.

22. Schmitt, *Die Verfassungslehre*, 87.

23. Schmitt, *Die Verfassungslehre*, 87.

24. For Schmitt, "when the power and authority of the constituent power, whose decision the constitution rests on, is recognized," a constitution is "legitimate." Power is then described as something "necessarily real," whereas authority implies "continuity" and tradition. Moreover, "[i]n every state, power and authority coexist and depend on each other" (*Die Verfassungslehre*, 75, 87). For an early criticism of this aspect of Schmitt's theory, see Erich Voegelin, "Die Verfassungslehre von Carl Schmitt," *Zeitschrift für öffentliches Recht* 11 (1931): 89–101. Voegelin endorses some of Schmitt's criticisms of Kelsen's legal positivism, but criticizes Schmitt's failure to integrate normative concerns into his analysis of the problem of legitimacy. Later I discuss the conceptual roots of this error.

25. Schmitt, *Die Verfassungslehre*, 20–36. As Franz L. Neumann notes, "Carl Schmitt, by adopting the American theory of the 'inherent limitations upon the amending power,' tried to distinguish between amending and violating modifications of the Constitution. He was of the opinion that amendments to the Constitution could not assail the 'Constitution as a basic decision' . . . The fundamental decisions regarding value preferences which the Constitution embodies, Schmitt thought, could not be modified even by the qualified parliamentary majority which [in Weimar] had the power to amend the Constitution" (*The Democratic and Authoritarian State: Essays in Poltical and Legal Theory* [Glencoe, Ill.: Free Press, 1957], 53–54).

26. Schmitt, *Die Verfassungslehre*, 56–60.

27. As I have argued elsewhere, Hannah Arendt criticizes precisely those elements of French revolutionary thought that Schmitt praises here. In her view, Absolutism contributed to the failings of the French Revolution, whereas the Americans were fortunate because they were spared the specter of Absolutism. For Schmitt, despite liberalism's hostility to Absolutism, liberal constitutionalism would lack minimal "political" elements unless it preserved something of the heritage of Absolutism. In contrast to Arendt, Schmitt dismisses the significance of the American constitutional tradition. Purportedly, the Americans lack a genuine constitutional theory. *The Federalist Papers* provide mere details about "practical organizational questions" (*Die Verfassungslehre*, 78–79). For Arendt's contrasting views, see her *On Revolution* (New York: Penguin Books, 1963). See also Scheuerman, "Revolutions and Constitutions: Hannah Arendt's Challenge to Carl Schmitt," *Canadian Journal of Law and Jurisprudence* 10, 1 (January 1997): 141–62.

28. Recall from chapter 2 that Schmitt accepts the unavoidability of *democratic* sovereignty in the modern world (*The Crisis of Parliamentary Democracy*, 22–32). But the principle of popular sovereignty is reformulated in an idiosyncratic authoritarian manner in Schmitt's theory.

29. Schmitt, *Political Theology*, 66. For a thoughtful criticism of Schmitt's use of Sieyes, see Stefan Breuer, "Nationalstaat und pouvoir constituant bei Sieyès und Schmitt," *Archiv für Rechts- und Sozialphilosophie* 70 (1984): 495–517.

30. Schmitt writes that "[a] people [*Volk*] must already exist as a political unity if it is to become the subject of constitution-making." He praises Sieyès's preference for the term "nation" over "people," arguing that it better captures the idea of a *Volk* capable of political action, in contrast to political entities not fully coherent in ethnic or cultural terms [*nur eine irgendwie ethnisch oder kulturell zusammengehörige . . . Verbindung von Menschen*] (*Die Verfassungslehre*, 61, 79). Schmitt also identifies the French Revolution as the birthplace of "national democracy," and comments that the presupposition of this type of democracy is national homogeneity (*Die Verfassungslehre*, 231). Although Schmitt here does leave open the possibility that homogeneity can take distinct forms, I believe that most textual evidence suggests that even during the 1920s he considered national or ethnic homogeneity most likely to guarantee political unity. See, for example, his comments on the "energy of nationalism" in *The Crisis of Parliamentary Democracy*, 74–75.

31. Schmitt, *Die Verfassungslehre*, 79; Schmitt, *Die Diktatur*, 140–43.

32. Schmitt, *Die Verfassungslehre*, 79.

33. Schmitt, *Die Verfassungslehre*, 77.

34. Richard Fuchs, "Carl Schmitts *Verfassungslehre*," *Juristische Wochenschrift* 60, nos. 23–24 (1931): 1661.

35. Rousseau, *The Social Contract*, Book 3, Chs. 12–13, in *Political Writings*, ed. and trans. Frederick Watkins (Madison: University of Wisconsin Press, 1986), 98–101.

36. Schmitt, *Die Verfassungslehre*, 315.

37. Schmitt, *Legalität und Legitimität*, 93.

38. Kirchheimer, "Constitutional Reaction in 1932," 78.

39. The Weimar legal positivist Richard Thoma made a similar point in a famous response to Schmitt's critique of parliamentarism. (Thoma, "On the Ideology of Parliamentarism," reprinted in Schmitt, *The Crisis of Parliamentary Democracy*, 81).

40. The relationship between democracy and constitutionalism remains a lively topic of dispute. See Stephen Holmes, "Gag Rules or the Politics of Omission," and "Precommitment and the Paradox of Democracy," in *Constitutionalism and Democracy*, 19–58, 195–240; Bruce Ackerman, *We the People*, vol. I (Cambridge, Mass.: Harvard University Press, 1991); Ulrich K. Preuss, *Constitutional Revolution: The Link Between Constitutionalism and Progress*, trans. Deborah Lucas Schneider (Atlantic Highlands, N.J.: Humanities Press, 1995).

41. The Weimar theorist Hermann Heller developed this observation in his brilliant but forgotten *Die Souveranität* (Berlin: de Gruyter, 1927). For excellent discussions of Heller's theory and its relationship to the ideas of Kelsen and Schmitt, see Wolfgang Schluchter, *Entscheidung für den sozialen Rechtstaat: Hermann Heller und die staatstheoretischen Diskussion in der Weimarer Republik* (Baden-Baden: Nomos, 1983), and Dyzenhaus, *Legality and Legitimacy: Carl Schmitt, Hans Kelsen and Hermann Heller in Weimar*.

42. On this debate, see Stanley Paulson, "Lon L. Fuller, Gustav Radbruch, and the 'Positivist Thesis,' " *Law and Philosophy* 13 (1994): 313–59; and Manfred

Walther, "Hat der juristische Positivismus die deutschen Juristen im 'Dritten Reich' wehrlos gemacht?," *Recht und Justiz im "Dritten Reich,"* ed. Ralf Dreier and Wolfgang Sellert, 323–54. In fact, antiformalistic modes of decision making played a pivotal role in the Weimar judiciary's alliance with authoritarianism.

43. For an interesting interpretation of Schmitt that focuses on his hostility to universalistic liberalism: Matthias Kaufmann, *Recht ohne Regel? Die philosophischen Prinzipien in Carl Schmitts Staats- und Rechtstheorie.*

44. Of course, modern liberalism offers a vision of the rule of law different from, say, Aquinas. My point is solely that Schmitt's conceptual paraphernalia prevents him from making distinctions of this sort. For a concise historical discussion of different models of the rule of law, see Judith N. Shklar, "Political Theory and the Rule of Law," in *The Rule of Law: Ideal or Ideology,* ed. Allan C. Hutchinson and Patrick Monahan (Toronto: Carswell, 1987), 1–17.

45. Schmitt, *Unabhängigkeit der Richter,* 23.

46. Schmitt, *Die Verfassungslehre,* 154. He then makes the peculiar comment that "equality [before the law] is only possible where minimally a majority of cases can be affected" (155). Occasionally he formulates a broader conception of general law as well: general law is incompatible with regulations affecting "several individuals" (*Unabhängigkeit der Richter,* 22).

47. The literature on Kelsen is massive. An excellent introduction can be found in Ralf Dreier, *Recht-Moral-Ideologie. Studien zur Rechtstheorie* (Frankfurt a.M.: Suhrkamp, 1981), 217–40. Dreier is important here because he concedes that Kelsen's insistence on a clean break between legal science, on the one hand, and ethics and sociology, on the other, is overstated, notwithstanding his clear sympathy for Kelsen and hostility toward Schmitt.

48. Schmitt, *Political Theology,* 21.

49. Schmitt considers "Kelsen's restatement of legal positivism . . . the fulfillment of the Enlightenment project which attempts to subject human interaction to an impersonal order of rules: the rule of law and not men" (David Dyzenhaus, " 'Now the Machine Runs Itself': Carl Schmitt on Hobbes and Kelsen," *Cardozo Law Review* 16, no. 1 [August 1994]: 10). In the process, Schmitt makes things too easy for himself. Kelsen clearly breaks radically with much of Enlightenment liberalism. Locke and Kant surely would have worried about Kant's value-relativism; one can imagine Montesquieu shaking his head in disbelief at Kelsen's view that an empirical analysis of political power has no rightful place within jurisprudence.

50. Schmitt, *Political Theology,* 21.

51. Liberal regimes have developed effective legal "normativities" for the regulation of crisis situations (Ernst Fraenkel, ed., *Der Staatsnotstand* [Berlin: Colloquium, 1964]). John McCormick makes too many concessions to Schmitt when he argues that liberalism has failed to deal adequately with the problem of the state of emergency. McCormick's endorsement of Schmitt on this point misses the extent to which functioning liberal democracies have developed institutional mechanisms able to contain emergency situations (McCormick, "The Dilemmas of Dictatorship: Carl Schmitt and Constitutional Emergency Powers").

52. Schmitt, *Die Verfassungslehre*, 9–10.
53. Schmitt, *Die Verfassungslehre*, 76. In *Political Theology*, where Kelsen looms large, Schmitt is even blunter on this point: Schmitt describes legal validity as deriving from a "pure decision not based on reason and not justifying itself, that is . . . an absolute decision created out of nothingness" (66). The adjective "pure" is revealing: Kelsen's "pure" system of normativity becomes Schmitt's "pure" act of empirical power.
54. Weber, *Economy and Society*, vol. I, 4.
55. Of course, even modern legal formalists (that is, proponents of the *limited determinacy thesis*) consider such traditional views overstated as well.
56. Schmitt, *Die Verfassungslehre*, 24–25.
57. Schmitt, *Die Verfassungslehre*, 253.
58. Jacques Derrida, "Declarations of Independence," trans. Tom Keenan and Tom Pepper, *New Political Science* 15 (1986): 10.
59. Bonnie Honig, "Declarations of Independence: Arendt and Derrida on the Problem of Founding a Republic," *American Political Science Review* 85 (1991): 106.
60. Derrida is familiar with Schmitt: see Jacques Derrida, "Force of Law: The 'Mystical Foundation of Authority,'" *Cardozo Law Review* 11 (1990): 981. For a more nuanced yet similarly critical discussion of Derrida in this context, see Seyla Benhabib, "Democracy and Difference: Reflections on the Metapolitics of Lyotard and Derrida," *Journal of Political Philosophy* 2, no. 1 (1994): 1–23.
61. Wolin, *The Politics of Being: The Political Thought of Martin Heidegger*, 30.
62. Robert Cover, "Violence and the Word," *Yale Law Journal* 95, no. 8 (July 1986): 1607.
63. Cover notes that he is "prepared to argue that all law which concerns property, its use and its protection, has a similarly violent base" ("Violence and the Word," 1607).
64. Cover, "Violence and the Word," 1608–9.
65. Cover, "Violence and the Word," 1621, 1628.
66. Austin Sarat and Thomas R. Kearns, "Making Peace with Violence: Robert Cover on Law and Legal Theory," in *Law's Violence*, ed. Austin Sarat and Thomas R. Kearns (Ann Arbor, Mich.: University of Michigan Press, 1992), 232.

4. THE TOTAL STATE

1. Michel Crozier, Samuel P. Huntington, and Joji Watanuki, *The Crisis of Democracy: Report on the Governability of Democracies to the Trilateral Commission* (New York: New York University Press, 1975), 13. The best critical discussion of this interpretation of contemporary democracy, which has played a pivotal role in neoconservative political practice over the course of the last twenty years, is Claus Offe, *Contradictions of the Welfare State*, ed. John Keane (Cambridge, Mass.: MIT Press, 1984), 65–87.
2. Crozier, Huntington, and Watanuki, *The Crisis of Democracy*, 47, 177.

3. A Hong Kong businessman, hostile to attempts to guarantee self-government there, captured one possible implication of this position quite nicely: "One man one vote would be the end of Hong Kong! Lots of welfare and high taxes!" Quoted in Ian Buruma, "Holding Out in Hong Kong," *New York Review of Books* 44, no. 10 (June 12, 1997): 56.

4. The classic study of Weimar social policy remains Ludwig Preller, *Sozialpolitik in der Weimarer Republik* (Stuttgart: Franz Mittelbach, 1949).

5. Schmitt concedes his own debt to Ernst Jünger, who in 1930 analyzed the "total mobilization" [*totale Mobilmachung*] of economic, political, and technological forces as central to modern war making. Like Schmitt, Jünger sees democratization as a central source of modern total mobilization (Jünger, "Die totale Mobilmachung," in Jünger, *Essays I: Betrachtungen zur Zeit* [Stuttgart: Ernst Klett Verlag, 1960], 123–47). Schmitt refers to Jünger in *Der Hüter der Verfassung*, 79. Much of this volume appeared as a series of shorter essays published in 1930 and 1931. It is the most important statement of Schmitt's *initial* conceptualization of the total state during the early 1930s. Schmitt then reformulated his theory of the total state in 1932 and 1933, *after* it was subjected to a barrage of criticisms that will be examined shortly (II).

6. Schmitt, *Der Hüter der Verfassung*, 73–91, where he provides the clearest account from the early 1930s of the nineteenth-century liberal state and its demise.

7. There is also a slight shift in emphasis here vis-à-vis the discussion of parliamentarism in *Constitutional Theory*. Rather than describing classical parliamentarism's short-lived political virtues as a weapon of the propertied and educated against the lower classes, he emphasizes the ways in which the democratization of parliament was challenged by monarchical and bureaucratic elites in the state executive. Here as well, however, Schmitt is vague about historical details: exactly when and where did a liberal state exist along the lines described here?

8. Schmitt, *Der Hüter der Verfassung*, 73. A similar observation has been made by Franz L. Neumann: "The liberal state has always been as strong as the political and social situation . . . demanded. It has conducted warfare and crushed strikes; with the help of strong navies it has protected its investments, with the help of strong armies it has defended and extended its boundaries, with the help of the police it has restored 'peace and order' " ("The Change in the Function of Law in Modern Society," in *The Rule of Law Under Siege: Selected Essays of Franz L. Neumann and Otto Kirchheimer*, ed. William E. Scheuerman, 101).

9. Schmitt, *Der Hüter der Verfassung*, 78–79. The "societalization" of the state is also a theme in Carl Schmitt, *Hugo Preuss: Sein Staatsbegriff und seine Stellung in der deutschen Staatslehre* (Tübingen: Mohr, 1930), where he similarly traces the transformation of the neutral liberal state into the interventionist welfare state (19–21). For Schmitt, the total state manifests itself most clearly in the emergence of the interventionist welfare state; Schmitt thus focuses on this element (and thus I do the same in my exegesis). But it is important to note that it is also characterized by a tendency to abandon state neutrality in the religious and cultural realms as well.

10. Schmitt, *Der Hüter der Verfassung*, 79.

11. Schmitt, *Der Hüter der Verfassung*, 81–82. For this reason I disagree with Cristi's view that Schmitt tried to synthesize the authoritarian state and free-market economics. As we will see, Schmitt indeed does hope to *limit* certain (characteristically social democratic) forms of state intervention. But he does insist on the need for an active state role within the capitalist economy. The model attributed by Cristi to Schmitt accords with the historical reality of Pinochet's Chile and other authoritarian right-wing dictorships. Yet Schmitt was less enamored of the classical liberal model of the "free market" than Cristi admits in *Carl Schmitt and Authoritarian Liberalism*.

12. Carl Schmitt, "The Age of Neutralizations and Depoliticizations" (1929), trans. John McCormick and Matthias Konzett, *Telos* 96 (Summer 1993): 119–30. This essay was included in the 1932 version of Schmitt's *Concept of the Political*. The accompanying introduction to the *Telos* translation by McCormick, "Introduction to Schmitt's 'The Age of Neutralizations and Depoliticizations' " (130–43) is essential reading on this element of Schmitt's theory. In an important recent study, McCormick sees Schmitt's critique of technology as constitutive of the core of Schmitt's critique of modernity: John McCormick, *Carl Schmitt's Critique of Liberalism: Against Politics as Technology* (New York: Cambridge University Press, 1997). My own reading is that Schmitt does occasionally invoke a critique of modern technology in order to lambaste liberalism. He also is more than willing, however, to endorse elements of modern technology when it suits his battle against liberalism. In his writings on international law in the 1930s and 1940s, for example, he argues that economic and technological progress necessitates the destruction of the existing system of liberal international law and its replacement by a new system dominated by mammoth regional political units [*Grossräume*]. Furthermore, Schmitt's Nazi theory systematically reduces law to a "technical" instrument of domination and manpulation; a truncated form of instrumental or technical rationality is allowed to run amok in crucial periods of Schmitt's development (see chapters 5 and 6). McCormick ignores these elements of Schmitt's theory because his discussion of Schmitt's National Socialist interlude is incomplete. Schmitt's main "foe" is liberalism and, specifically, the liberal rule of law; the critique of modern technology is an important secondary theme in his writings. Schmitt was *not*, as McCormick claims, "a critical theorist of sorts" in "close proximity" to the Frankfurt School (*Carl Schmitt's Critique of Liberalism*, 17). For better or worse, the Frankfurt School believed that contemporary society could be "superseded" by a superior socialist alternative that nonetheless would preserve the rationalistic achievements of liberalism. In contrast, Schmitt crudely sought to negate the universalistic and rationalistic impulses of liberalism. I criticize McCormick's study in detail in "Review of John McCormick," *European Journal of Philosophy* (December 1998): 376–78.

13. Schmitt, *Political Theology*, 66.

14. Schmitt, "The Age of Neutralizations and Depoliticizations," 138.

15. Schmitt, "The Age of Neutralizations and Depoliticizations," 138.

16. Schmitt uses the term "economic-technical" to describe his own era on a number of occasions, for example, in *Legalität und Legitimität*, 96.

17. Schmitt, "The Age of Neutralizations and Depoliticizations," 136.

18. Schmitt, "The Age of Neutralizations and Depoliticizations," 136. This assertion, which appears in many of Schmitt's writings from the early 1930s, poses an obvious problem for him. While Schmitt hopes to rely on the diagnosis of our times as an "economic-technical age" in order to justify the unavoidability of the total state, it remains unclear why the nineteenth century, to the extent that it also was an "economic age," required only limited forms of state intervention in the private realm. Ultimately, Schmitt's argument has to demonstrate that the relatively limited interventionist devices of nineteenth-century liberalism no longer suffice in face of the complex, deeply partisan character of contemporary economic life. Yet it is unclear that his speculative contribution to the philosophy of history allows him to distinguish clearly enough between different *moments* in the "economic age," that is, between the nineteenth-century liberal belief in economics as a neutralizing force, and our distinct twentieth-century acknowledgment of economics as a "central sphere." For this reason, Schmitt's two lines of inquiry about the origins of the total state need to be seen as complementary. His philosophical argument places his concrete political and economic observations within a broader historical context; at the same time, without the concrete political and economic account, his speculative argument is incomplete as an explanation of the rise of the total state.

19. Schmitt remarks on the modern character of state/society relations in Italy and the Soviet Union as early as 1929. Importantly, Schmitt's sympathies clearly lie with the fascist version of state interventionism, in contrast to its state socialist counterpart (Schmitt, "Wesen und Werden des faschistischen Staates," in *Positionen und Begriffe im Kampf mit Weimar-Genf-Versailles*, 111–12). Both fascism and Bolshevism are described as total states in *Der Hüter der Verfassung*, 84.

20. Schmitt, "The Age of Neutralizations and Depoliticizations," 141.

21. See Schmitt's contributions to *Verhandlungen des Siebten Deutschen Soziologentages vom 28 September bis 1 Oktober 1930 in Berlin*, ed. Deutsche Gesellschaft für Soziologie (Tübingen: Mohr, 1931), 56–59. Schmitt is right to suggest that new media technology raises difficult questions for *traditional* liberal conceptions of freedom of the press, in which freedom of the press is conceived as a *negative* liberty in which state nonintervention is of central significance. Whether the need for positive state action in the realm of communicative freedom demonstrates the anachronistic character of liberal conceptions of free speech, as Schmitt soon suggests, is clearly another matter altogether.

22. As Hans Boldt has noted, the Weimar executive after 1930 "did not try to find a majority in parliament at all, and the inability of Parliament to pass resolutions had been largely brought about by the government itself, which resolved the *Reichstag* again and again" ("Article 48 of the Weimar Constitution, Its Historical and Political Implications," in *German Democracy and the Triumph of Hitler: Essays in Recent German History*, ed. Anthony Nicholls and Erich Matthias [London: George Allen & Unwin, 1970], 93). Schmitt served as an advisor to the emergency presidential regimes that ruled Germany after 1930; his writings are consistent with

Boldt's description of the Weimar executive's ultimately catastrophic agenda. In light of the well-established fact that Schmitt defended many of the most radical anticonstitutional moves taken by these governments, it seems difficult in my view to see Schmitt as hoping to "save" Weimar. For Schmitt's role in the infamous coup against the Prussian state government in 1932, see Dyzenhaus, "Legal Theory in the Collapse of Weimar: Contemporary Lessons?" As I hope to show in the following pages, Schmitt sought a constitutional (counter)revolution, in which Weimar's basically liberal democratic core was to be replaced by a dictatorship. To use Schmitt's own terminology, this dictatorship was of a sovereign, not a commissarial type.

23. Schmitt, *Der Hüter der Verfassung*, 132–59.

24. Schmitt, "Die staatsrechtliche Bedeutung der Notverordnung" (1931), in *Verfassungsrechtliche Aufsätze aus den Jahren 1924–1954*, 244–45.

25. Schmitt, "Die staatsrechtliche Bedeutung der Notverordnung," 257–59.

26. This was how Hans Kelsen interpreted Schmitt's views in his *Wer soll der Hüter der Verfassung sein?* A closer look at Kelsen's perceptive critique of Schmitt's theory of the total state follows shortly.

27. Schmitt, *Der Hüter der Verfassung*, 115–31. Also, see Schmitt, "Staatsrechtliche Bedeutung der Notverordnung," 240–42, 247, 259. Schmitt's empirical account here does capture some of the more troubling trends in the legal systems of twentieth-century capitalist welfare states, but he fails to demonstrate the *inevitability* of such developments. Elsewhere I have tried to argue, pace Schmitt, that both a more generous welfare state *and* greater legal uniformity and predictability are achievable (Scheuerman, "The Rule of Law and the Welfare State: Towards a New Synthesis"). In my view, Schmitt's lesson for those of us committed both to a robust version of the rule of law *and* to more social and economic equality is the need to undertake far-reaching legal and social reforms.

28. Schmitt, "Staatsethik und pluralistischer Staat" (1930), reprinted in Schmitt, *Positionen und Begriffe im Kampf mit Weimar-Genf-Versailles*; also see Schmitt, *Der Hüter der Verfassung*, 87.

29. Carl Schmitt, "Staatsideologie und Staatsrealität in Deutschland und West-europa," *Deutsche Richterzeitung* 31, no. 7 (July 15, 1931): 271–72.

30. Cited in Roger Boesche, *The Strange Liberalism of Alexis de Tocqueville* (Ithaca, N.Y.: Cornell University Press, 1987), 251.

31. Otto Hintze, "Wesen und Wandlungen des modernen Staates" (1931), in Hintze, *Staat und Verfassung: Gesammelte Aufsätze zur allgemeinen Verfassungsgeschichte*, 2nd ed. (Göttingen: Vandenhoeck and Ruprecht, 1962), 473, 488–96.

32. Ernst-Rudolf Huber, "Verfassung und Verfassungswirklichkeit bei Carl Schmitt," *Blätter für deutsche Philosophie* 5 (1931–1932): 312.

33. Gerhard Leibholz, *Die Auflösung der liberalen Demokratie in Deutschland* (Munich and Leipzig: Duncker and Humblot, 1932), 67–70. On Leibholz, see the study by Manfred Wiegandt, *Norm und Wirklichkeit: Gerhard Leibholz (1901–1982): Leben, Werk und Richteramt* (Baden-Baden: Nomos, 1995).

34. Otto Koellreutter, "Volk und Staat in der Verfassungslehre: Zugleich eine

Auseinandersetzung mit der Verfassungslehre Carl Schmitt," *Zum Neubau der Verfassung*, ed. Fritz Berber (Berlin: Junker and Dunnhaupt, 1933).

35. Ernst Forsthoff, *Der totale Staat* (Hamburg: Hanseatische Verlagsanstalt, 1933).

36. See, for example, the detailed study on *Die Tat* by Klaus Fritsche, *Politische Romantik und Gegenrevolution: Fluchtwege in der Krise der bürgerlichen Gesellschaft: Das Beispiel des 'Tat' Kreises* (Frankfurt a.M.: Suhrkamp, 1973).

37. Franz Neumann, "Über die Voraussetzungen und den Rechtssbegriff einer Wirtschaftsverfassung" [1931], in Neumann, *Wirtschaft, Staat, Demokratie. Aufsätze 1930–1954*, ed. Alfons Söllner (Frankfurt a.M.: Suhrkamp, 1978), 82.

38. Heinz O. Ziegler, *Autoritärer Staat oder Totaler Staat* [*Authoritarian or Total State*] (Tübingen: Mohr, 1931). Ziegler's ideas exercised a substantial influence on Leibholz, Koellreutter, and even Forsthoff in their responses to Schmitt. I have been unable to find much biographical information about Ziegler. In his mammoth study of totalitarian political theory, the French writer Jean-Pierre Faye claims that Ziegler ended up fighting against the Nazis as part of the Royal Air Force (*Théorie du recit: Introduction aux langages totalitaires* [Paris: Collection Savoir Hermann, 1972], 72).

39. Ziegler, *Autoritärer oder Totaler Staat*, 16, 18, 19.

40. Ziegler, *Autoritärer oder Totaler Staat*, 20.

41. As will be evident shortly, this interpretation is wrong. Nonetheless, it is understandable in terms of Schmitt's proximity during this period to an idiosyncratic group of reactionary authors, centered around the journal *Die Tat*, whose critique of contemporary capitalism often employed populist, pseudosocialist rhetoric and categories. Like many on the left, *Die Tat* suggested that capitalism was in a serious crisis and required a "revolution"; in the spirit of Schmitt, this revolution was by no means intended as an attack on the basic privileges of capital. Schmitt publicly praised *Die Tat*, describing it as one of the best political journals available in Weimar's final years. Like its editors, he also sided with General Kurt von Schleicher in Weimar's final power feuds. See Fritsche, *Politische Romantik und Gegenrevolution*, especially 57.

42. Ziegler, *Autoritärer oder Totaler Staat*, 30–31.

43. Schmitt, *Legalität und Legitimität*, 93.

44. Schmitt, *Legalität und Legitimität*, 93.

45. Schmitt, *Legalität und Legitimität*, 92. Stephen Holmes similarly has emphasized the fundamentally antidemocratic quality of the Schmittian plebiscite (*The Anatomy of Antiliberalism* [Cambridge, Mass.: Harvard University Press, 1993], 49–50, 275–76).

46. In this model, "the plebiscite consists purely of an unorganized answer which the people, characterized as a mass, gives to a question which may be posed only by an authority whose existence is assumed. Structure and accountability of this authority is unknown" (Otto Kirchheimer, "Constitutional Reaction in 1932," 78). Clearly, a model of this type has nothing in common with the aspirations of the American founders, Tocqueville, or Mill. It is unclear to what extent, in Schmitt's model, the plebiscite can be said to "contain" the executive.

288   Notes: Chapter 4

47. Schmitt, *Legalität und Legitimität*, 94.

48. Schmitt, *Legalität und Legitimität*, 93–95.

49. Carl Schmitt, "Die Weiterentwicklung des totalen Staates in Deutschland" (1933), in Schmitt, *Verfassungsrechtliche Aufsätze aus den Jahren 1924–1954*, 362.

50. This element of Schmitt's argument was anticipated as early as 1930 in a revealing lecture presented to a prominent organization of German industrialists, the *Langnamverein*, when he called for a "rollback of the state [in the economy] to a natural and correct amount." Any attempt to counteract "unnatural" forms of state intervention, however, requires a "strong state." A minimal (liberal) state is unlikely to prove up to this task in our century. See Schmitt's (untitled) lecture in *Mitteilungen des Vereins zur Wahrung der gemeinsamen wirtschaftlichen Interessen in Rheinland und Westfalen*, ed. Max Schlenker (Düsseldorf: Matthias Strucken, 1930), 458–59. This lecture was important enough from Schmitt's perspective that he allowed for it to be reprinted, with some minor alterations, at least twice: Carl Schmitt, "Eine Warning vor falschen Fragestellungen," *Der Ring*, no. 48 (November 30, 1931): 344–45; "Zur politischen Situation Deutschlands," *Kunstwart* 44 (January 1931): 253–56. A translation is found in Cristi, *Carl Schmitt and Authoritarian Liberalism*, 212–33.

51. Carl Schmitt, "Starker Staat und gesunde Wirtschaft: Ein Vortrag vor Wirtschaftsführern," *Volk und Reich*, no. 2 (1933): 89–90; Schmitt, "Machtpositionen des modernen Staates" [1933], in Schmitt, *Verfassungsrechtliche Aufsätze aus den Jahren 1924–1954*, 371. It is striking that Schmitt juxtaposes his model of "economic self-administration" to social democratic conceptions of economic democracy, in which labor unions play an important role.

52. Schmitt, *Legalität und Legitimität*, 87, 96–98. The second part of the Weimar Constitution was a mixture of liberal, democratic, socialist, and traditional elements. It included not only basic liberal political and civil rights, but also social rights (to a job, for example) and special protections for the family and churches. Conveniently, Schmitt is somewhat ambiguous about which sections of it should be "cleansed." He is quite clear, however, that the liberal parliamentary devices outlined in the first part of the constitution are anachronistic.

53. Schmitt, "Der Staat des 20. Jahrhunderts," *Westdeutscher Beobachter*, 28 June 1933, 1–2.

54. Schmitt, *Staat, Bewegung, Volk. Die Dreigliederung der politischen Einheit*, 22–32.

55. Andreas Koenen, *Der Fall Carl Schmitts. Sein Aufstieg zum "Kronjuristen des Dritten Reiches,"* 411–12. Only later would Alfred Rosenberg and Rudolf Freisler, as well as Schmitt's rival within the legal academy, Otto Koellreutter, discredit the concept of the total state by accusing its leading theorist, Carl Schmitt, of failing to acknowledge adequately the Nazi conception of an ethnicist *Volk* and ignoring the central place of the National Socialist *political movement* in the emerging "new order." On this debate: Koenen, *Der Fall Carl Schmitts*, 517–23; and Peter Caldwell, "National Socialism and Constitutional Law: Carl Schmitt, Otto Koellreutter, and the Debate over the Nature of the Nazi State, 1933–1937," *Cardozo Law Review*

16 (1995): 399–427. More generally on Nazi political theory and its relationship to Nazi political reality, see Jane Caplan, "National Socialism and the Theory of the State," in *Reevaluating the Third Reich*, ed. Thomas Childers and Jane Caplan (New York: Holmes and Meier, 1993), 98–113.

In my view, Nazi critics were often inaccurate in their description of Schmitt's ideas. Alfred Rosenberg, for example, misses Schmitt's attempt to distinguish between the quantitative and the qualitative total state; he wrongly reads Schmitt as a traditional statist who favors bureaucratic intrusion in all realms of human life ("Totaler Staat?" *Völkischer Beobachter* 47, 9 [September 1, 1934]). In fact, *State, Movement, Folk* (1933) provides a reworked version of the theory of the total state in order to guarantee a prominent place for the purportedly "dynamic" National Socialist movement and a complementary racist conception of the *Volk*. As Franz L. Neumann has noted, this "tripartite theory" (in which the Nazi state, movement, and *Volk* constitute the pillars of the new order) was basically retained by the Nazis after 1933; only minor modifications were made (*Behemoth: The Structure and Practice of National Socialism, 1933–1944*, 66). Throughout the early and mid-1930s, Schmitt repeatedly emphasizes the limitations of traditional forms of authoritarianism in which rule is exercised by a bureaucratic elite lacking a "mass" plebiscitary basis. Schmitt was no *statist* in the manner attributed to him by his Nazi ideological rivals during the 1930s. As we will see in the next chapter, Schmitt also does far more than pay lip-service to the anti-Semitic elements of the Nazi conception of the *Volk*. He makes anti-Semitism a central element of his jurisprudence.

56. By the same token, the fact that leading Nazis abandoned the term hardly demonstrates Schmitt's anti-Nazi intentions!

57. Lutz-Arwed Bentin, *Johannes Popitz und Carl Schmitt: Zur wirtschaftlichen Theorie des totalen Staates in Deutschland* (Munich: Beck Verlag, 1972), 114–15.

58. On the political battles of this period, see Gotthard Jasper, *Die gescheiterte Zähmung. Wege zur Machtergreifung Hitlers 1930–1934* (Frankfurt a.M.: Suhrkamp, 1986).

59. This is not to deny that the Nazi state exhibited its own form of internal disorganization, planlessness, and administrative chaos. This is an important theme in much of the most interesting historical scholarship about the regime. See Peter Hüttenberger, "Nationalsozialistische Polykratie," *Geschichte und Gesellschaft* 2, no. 4 (1976): 417–32. The question of the polycratic nature of the Nazi state remains central to contemporary debates. See the essays collected in *Reevaluating the Third Reich*, ed. Thomas Childers and Jane Caplan.

60. Neumann, *Behemoth: The Structure and Practice of National Socialism, 1933–1944*, 251–364. Especially good on Nazi economic ideology is Avraham Barkai, *Das Wirtschaftssystem des Nationalsozialismus. Der historische und ideologische Hintergrund 1933–1936* (Cologne: Verlag Wissenbschaft und Politik, 1977).

61. Schmitt, "Machtpositionen des modernen Staates," in Schmitt, *Verfassungsrechtliche Aufsätze aus den Jahren 1924–1954*, 368–69.

62. Schmitt, "Machtpositionen des modernen Staates," 369–70.

63. As will be discussed in chapter 8, writers like Hayek do go quite a way down Schmitt's perilous authoritarian path.

64. Holmes, *The Anatomy of Antiliberalism*, 49. One should add that this is a version of soccer in which the "rules of the game" (that is, laws) are open-ended and ever-changing.

65. In the words of a leading scholar of American legal development: "By reputation, the nineteenth century was the high noon of *laissez-faire* . . . But when we actually burrow into the past, we unearth a much more complex reality." Substantial governmental regulation of the economy, *undertaken by states and municipalities*, occurred in the United States. For example, the development of railroads, perhaps the most important industrial innovation of the nineteenth century, was a product of joint state and private action; early American railroads (including the famous Pennsylvania Railroad) were mixed public and private enterprises. Even the "federal government was not totally passive," as evidenced by a number of massive development projects undertaken by Washington (Lawrence M. Friedman, *The History of American Law*, 2nd ed. [New York: Simon and Schuster, 1985], 177–78, 192–93).

66. Lawrence M. Friedman, *Total Justice* (New York: Russell Sage Foundation, 1985), 5. Friedman sees the final change listed here as essential to a quest for "total justice" that he considers constitutive of the modern welfare state.

67. Again, the United States, where the fragmentation of state power in the nineteenth century contributed to an extraordinary lack of state autonomy in relation to the business community, is probably the best example of this (Friedman, *A History of American Law*, 177–201).

68. Nonetheless, it has played a central role in German political thought in the twentieth century. Jean Cohen and Andrew Arato, *Civil Society and Political Theory*, 201–54. Reinhart Koselleck, for example, sees it as an important cause of the "global civil war," most clearly represented by the confrontation between the United States and Soviet Union, that allegedly has characterized the twentieth century (*Critique and Crisis: Enlightenment and the Pathogenesis of Modern Society* [Cambridge, Mass.: MIT Press, 1988]). On the ties between Schmitt and Koselleck, see Dirk van Laak, *Gespräche in der Sicherheit des Schweigens: Carl Schmitt in der politischen Geistesgeschichte der frühen Bundesrepublik*, 187–88, 224–26.

69. Kelsen, *Wer soll der Hüter der Verfassung sein?*, 32.

70. Kelsen, *Wer soll der Hüter der Verfassung sein?*, 33.

71. Schmitt, *Der Hüter der Verfassung*, 71.

72. Kelsen, *Wer soll der Hüter der Verfassung sein?*, 30–31.

73. Kelsen, *Wer soll der Hüter der Verfassung sein?*, 40.

74. Kelsen, *Wer soll der Hüter der Verfassung sein?*, 39–40.

5. AFTER LEGAL INDETERMINACY?

1. Schmitt, "Das gute Recht der deutschen Revolution," *Westdeutscher Beobachter*, 12 March 1933, 1–2. An important element of Nazi ideology was its "law and order" appeal. See Otto Kirchheimer, "Criminal Law in National Socialist Germany," in Scheuerman, ed., *The Rule of Law Under Siege*, 172–95.

2. Schmitt, "Die deutschen Intellektuellen," *Westdeutscher Beobachter*, 31 May 1933, 1–2.

3. Schmitt, "Nationalsozialistisches Rechtsdenken," *Deutsches Recht* 4, no. 10 (1934): 225–29.

4. Schmitt, "Die Verfassung der Freiheit," *Deutsche Juristen-Zeitung* 40, no. 19 (1935): 1133–36.

5. Schmitt, "Die nationalsozialistische Gesetzgebung und der Vorbehalt des '*ordre public*' im internationalen Privatrecht," *Zeitschrift für die Akademie des Deutschen Rechts* 3 (1936): 207, 208.

6. Schmitt, "Die deutsche Rechtswissenschaft im Kampf gegen den jü dischen Geist," *Deutsche Juristen-Zeitung* 41, no. 20 (1936): 1195–99.

7. Schmitt, cited and translated by Dyzenhaus, *Legality and Legitimacy: Carl Schmitt, Hans Kelsen and Hermann Heller in Weimar*, 99. A pamphlet could easily be filled with Schmitt's anti-Semitic outbursts from the 1930s and 1940s. When Schmitt proudly commented in 1936 that under his editorship the *Deutsche Juristen-Zeitung* played a leading role in trying to eliminate the "Jewish influence" over the "German spirit," he was not exaggerating ("Schlusswort des Herausgebers," *Deutsche Juristen-Zeitung* 41, no. 24 [1936]: 1454).

8. For examples of this approach, see Bendersky, *Carl Schmitt: Theorist for the Reich*, and Schwab, *The Challenge of the Exception*.

9. For an example of this burgeoning genre, see Paul Noack, *Carl Schmitt: Eine Biographie* (Berlin: Propyläen, 1993).

10. Schmitt, *Political Theology*, 30.

11. This (incorrect) interpretation of Kelsen is suggested in Schmitt, *Political Theology*, 14, 19, 28–35.

12. This trend has been anxiously thematized by other authors as well: Clinton L. Rossiter, *Constitutional Dictatorship: Crisis Government in the Modern Democracies*; and Jules Lobel, "Emergency Power and the Decline of Liberalism," *Yale Law Review* 98 (1989): 1385–1433.

13. Schmitt, *Political Theology*, 13.

14. Altman, *Critical Legal Studies: A Liberal Critique*, 91.

15. Solum, "On the Indeterminacy Crisis: Critiquing Critical Dogma," 462.

16. Schmitt, "Nationalsozialistisches Rechtsdenken," 225. Although I have been unable to find adequate archival confirmation for this view, some evidence suggests that the unnamed American jurist here may have been Roscoe Pound. During a controversial visit to Austria and Germany in 1934 that garnered extensive coverage in the American press, Pound insisted to reporters that evidence of brutality in central Europe had been greatly exaggerated. In addition, he dryly described Hitler as "a man who can bring them [the Central Europeans] freedom from agitating movements." According to one report, Pound met with faculty members at the University of Munich in 1934. In September of the same year, he was awarded an honorary degree from the law faculty of the University of Berlin, whose most prominent faculty member—and "leader" of the Nazi lawyers' guild—at that point was no other than Carl Schmitt. See Charles Beard, "Germany Up to Her Old

Tricks," *The New Republic* 80 (1934): 299; and David Wigdor, *Roscoe Pound—Philosopher of Law* (Westport, Conn.: Greenwood Press, 1974), 250–51. Of course, Pound's legal theory was fundamentally distinct from Schmitt's. Yet like Schmitt, Pound had long criticized formalistic legal thought. By the 1930s, however, Pound had become anxious about the implications of antiformalism for legal determinacy, soon taking on the role of an outspoken conservative political and methodological critic of Legal Realism and its more radical attacks on formalism. Interestingly, there is a certain parallel to Schmitt's development in the 1930s as well: Schmitt embraces antiformalism while nonetheless hoping to salvage the possibility of legal determinacy.

17. Schmitt, "Unsere geistige Gesamtlage und unsere juristische Aufgabe," *Zeitschrift der Akademie für deutsches Recht* 1 (1934): 12.

18. Schmitt, "Nationalsozialistisches Rechtsdenken," 227–28.

19. Schmitt, "Die Rechtswissenschaft im Führerstaat," *Zeitschrift der Akademie für Deutsches Recht* 2 (1935): 438–40. Liberal jurists have similarly noted that formal "[r]ules force the future into the categories of the past" within drawing Schmitt's antiliberal implications from this observation (Frederick Schauer, "Formalism," 542).

20. This extends throughout Schmitt's Nazi period. In an essay written in part during the early 1940s but first published in 1950, Schmitt similarly chronicles the inevitable decline of codified, general law and the proliferation of indeterminate forms of open-ended law. In the twentieth century, the liberal legislature is replaced by a "motorized lawmaker," which hands over vast delegations of authority to the executive in response to the enormous needs of ever-changing, situation-specific state action in the era of modern interventionist politics. Here as well, Schmitt sees the main source of this development in the unavoidability of the state's "steering of the economy" (Schmitt, *Die Lage der europäischen Rechtswissenschaft* [*The Situation of European Jurisprudence*] [Tübingen: Internationaler Universitätsverlag, 1950], 20–22).

21. Schmitt, *Staat, Bewegung, Volk*, 43. The German word *Geist* is difficult to translate; the closest English approximation is "spirit." But *Geist* takes on ethnic and racist connotations for Schmitt during the mid-1930s. This undertone comes out pointedly in a journalistic piece, where he comments that to partake of German "spirit" much more is required than mastery of the German language or academic credentials from a German university: one needs to belong to the (particularistic) German *Volk*. Thus, German Jews (such as Heine or Einstein) lack a proper German "spirit" (Schmitt, "Die deutschen Intellektuellen," 1–2).

22. In an analogous vein, contemporary CLS theorists argue that the fact that every modern legal system rests on a patchwork of inconsistent principles and ideals dooms the quest for legal determinacy. Indeterminacy is as profound at the level of the legal system's immanent principles and ideals as it is at the level of formal rules and precedents. The decisive difference here is that Schmitt then concludes that moral and political pluralism should be sacrificed for the sake of preserving legal determinacy. It goes without saying that CLS scholars disapprove of the racism and anti-Semitism evident within Schmitt's writings.

23. Schmitt, *Staat, Bewegung, Volk*, 45.

24. The word "biological" is Schmitt's own. This would seem to counter those who have insisted that Schmitt endorsed a traditional Catholic anti-Judaism but hardly radical Nazi anti-Semitism (*Staat, Bewegung, Volk*, 45). Schmitt can be read elsewhere as criticizing Italian fascism for "ignoring" the importance of racial difference. In comparing fascist and Nazi law, he notes that "the greatest difference" exists vis-à-vis the racial question and the relationship of the state to party. On both points, Nazism is superior in Schmitt's view (Schmitt, "Faschistische und national-sozialistische Rechtswissenschaft," *Deutsche Juristen-Zeitung* 41, no. 10 [1936]: 619–20).

25. Schmitt, *Staat, Bewegung, Volk*, 45. In an essay from the same year, Schmitt comments that "our liberal grandfathers and fathers" failed to understand the "existential" determination of all thought. Specifically, they missed that every *Volk* has basic instincts, styles of thought, and a "spirit" distinct to it (Schmitt, "Die deutschen Intellektuellen," 1–2).

26. Schmitt, "Das gute Recht der deutschen Revolution," 1; Schmitt, "Ein Jahr deutscher Politik," *Westdeutscher Beobachter*, 23 July 1933, 1.

27. Reference is typically made to Schmitt's dedication of his most important Weimar study, *Die Verfassungslehre*, to Dr. Fritz Eisler. Needless to say, the existence of such personal ties is no evidence of a lack of anti-Semitism.

28. Koenen, *Der Fall Carl Schmitt: Sein Aufstieg zum "Kronjuriten des Dritten Reiches,"* 315–16, 357–59, 372–73.

29. Raphael Gross, "Carl Schmitt und die Juden: Strukturen einer deutschen Rechtslehre," Ph.D. diss., University of Essen, 1997.

30. For an insightful critique of Schmitt's recent biographers, see Ingeborg Maus, "Die Bekenntnisse der Unpolitischen. Zur gegenwärtigen Carl Schmitt–Renaissance aus Anlass einer Biographie," *Frankfurter Rundschau*, 2 April 1994, ZB2.

31. The most detailed version of this interpretation is Koenen, *Der Fall Carl Schmitt.*

32. Schmitt, *Über die drei Arten des rechtswissenschaftlichen Denkens*, 54–55.

33. Schmitt, *Über die drei Arten*, 7.

34. Schmitt, *Über die drei Arten*, 57–58.

35. Schmitt, *Über die drei Arten*, 63–64.

36. This is the basic argument of Schmitt, *Staat, Bewegung, Volk*. Schmitt provides a prehistory of the Nazi "movement-dominated" state in *Staatsgefüge und Zusammenbruch des zweiten Reiches* (Hamburg: Hanseatische Verlagsanstalt, 1934). Schmitt's attempt to develop a tripartite political theory in which the National Socialist movement possesses supremacy garnered criticism from competing Nazi ideologues who worried that Schmitt's description of the "folk" as a nonpolitical entity unfairly downplayed the supposedly democratic character of National Socialism. On this debate, see Neumann, *Behemoth: The Structure and Practice of National Socialism*, 66.

37. Schmitt, "Nationalsozialistisches Rechtsdenken," 226. For Schmitt's asso-

ciation of "empty" formalistic elements of the rule of law with Judaism, see, for example, the reference to "Stahl-Jolson" in Carl Schmitt, "Der Rechtsstaat," *Nationalsozialistisches Handbuch für Recht und Gesetzgebung*, ed. Hans Frank (Munich: Zentralverlag der NSDAP, 1935), 6. Schmitt's anti-Semitic diatribes against Julius Stahl (originally Jolson) seem to have been his very own "contribution" to Nazi anti-Semitism. Stahl's name is dirtied in many of Schmitt's texts from this period.

38. Schmitt, *Über die drei Arten*, 52.

39. As chapter 6 will elaborate, this is a pivotal feature of Schmitt's analysis of international law.

40. This term is first introduced by Schmitt in "Der Staat des 20. Jahrhunderts," *Westdeutscher Beobachter*, 28 June 1933, 1. It becomes one of Schmitt's stock phrases during this period.

41. Schmitt, "Der Führer schützt das Recht" (1934), in Schmitt, *Positionen und Begriffe im Kampf mit Weimar-Genf-Versailles*, 199–204.

42. Schmitt, "Die Rechtswissenschaft im Führerstaat," 438–39. Ingeborg Maus correctly emphasizes the central place here of Schmitt's account of the decay of the classical liberal concept of general law (" 'Gesetzesbindung' der Justiz und die Struktur der nationalsozialistischen Rechtsnormen," in Dreier and Sellert, *Recht und Justiz im "Dritten Reich,"* 81–104).

43. Schmitt, *Political Theology*, 66.

44. Schmitt, "Preface to the Second Edition" (1934), *Political Theology*, 3. Schmitt is intent in this period on showing that National Socialist law, if built on the foundations sketched out by his theory, need not take an arbitrary [*willkürlich*] form. For a clear statement of this view, see Schmitt, "Nationalsozialismus und Rechtsstaat," *Juristische Wochenschrift* 63, nos. 12–13 (1934): 713–18. This aspiration is also summarized clearly by one of Schmitt's doctoral students in a book review of his mentor's work: Günter Krauss, "Review of Schmitt, *Staat, Bewegung, Volk*: Zu einer neuen Schrift von Carl Schmitt," *Deutsches Recht*, 4, no. 1 (1934): 24, where the possibility of legal determinacy is linked directly to racial and ethnic homogeneity.

45. This argumentative move possibly parallels shifts within Martin Heidegger's philosophy during the same period. As Richard Wolin shows in a lucid recent study, Heidegger endorsed a form of decisionism while, like Schmitt, ultimately undertaking to counteract extreme individualistic and voluntaristic readings of it. For Heidegger, this entailed incorporating the *Dasein* of *Being and Time* within the historical collective or community of National Socialism; for Schmitt, the quest to avoid a subjectivistic, even arbitrary model of law analogously encouraged him to endorse Nazi conceptions of a homogeneous ethnic and racial community (Wolin, *The Politics of Being: The Political Thought of Martin Heidegger*, especially 28–40, 53–66). From this perspective, Heidegger's brief 1933 letter to Schmitt, in which he thanks Schmitt for sending him a copy of *The Concept of the Political*, may represent more than a polite professional formality: during this period, both authors were intent on overcoming manifest dangers of decisionism by means of integrating National Socialist models of the community into the heart of their theories. Heideg-

ger's letter to Schmitt has been reprinted in *Telos*, no. 72 (1987): 132. Interestingly as well, Heidegger during the 1930s saw National Socialist Germany as representing a superior "third path" beyond the ills of Western liberalism and Eastern Bolshevism. In his view, both competing systems were fundamentally similar in many important respects: "From a metaphysical point of view, Russia and America are the same; the same dreary technological frenzy, the same unrestricted organization of the average man. . . . [And thus] the farthermost corner of the globe has been conquered by technology and opened to economic exploitation" (cited in Wolin, *The Politics of Being*, 103). Furthermore, Heidegger saw the Nazi experiment as being threatened unfairly by the imperialistic "pincers" of the United States and the Soviet Union; Germany was endangered by liberalism and socialism, and thus should lead the way in circumventing the annihilation of European culture. As we will see in chapter 6, this diagnosis is reproduced in Schmitt's writings in international law during the same period.

46. George Schwab, "Introduction," in Schmitt, *Political Theology*, xxv. Schwab comments that at the end of the Weimar period Schmitt "realized the limits of decisionism." Matters are complicated by the fact that Schmitt himself during this period occasionally emphasizes a "break" in his thinking, according to which decisionism is abandoned for "concrete order thinking." Of course, this was politically advantageous for Schmitt in 1933 and 1934: it allowed him to emphasize the "distinct" National Socialist character of his theory. In a different manner, this reading was also politically convenient for Schmitt's defenders after World War II, who hoped to salvage the "real" (that is, pre-Nazi) Schmitt by emphasizing a profound break between Schmitt's Weimar and Nazi periods.

47. Schmitt, *Legalität und Legitimität*, 87.

48. Neumann, "The Change in the Function of Law in Modern Society," in Scheuerman, ed., *The Rule of Law Under Siege*, 138.

49. Schmitt, *Staat, Bewegung, Volk*, 44. Schmitt's comments on common law systems are interesting in light of this argument. For Schmitt, common law systems suggest that legal determinacy is possible by means other than those prescribed by legal formalism and its characteristic emphasis on the virtues of a systematic legal code. In particular, England shows that determinacy is achievable by means of a homogeneous "rank" of jurists schooled in the special needs of the English "national community" (Schmitt, "Aufgabe und Notwendigkeit des deutschen Rechtsstandes," *Deutsches Recht* 6 [1936]: 185). At the same time, Schmitt considers Anglo-American common law inferior to his proposed German alternative. British and American common lawyers are allegedly infected by the naive "normativities" of universalistic liberalism and thus remain incompletely antiliberal in their thinking.

50. For a statement of the central place of ethnic homogeneity to Nazism, see Schmitt, "Ein Jahr nationalsozialistischer Verfassungsstaat," *Deutsches Recht*, 4, no. 2 (1934): 29; and Schmitt, "Das gute Recht der deutschen Revolution," 1, where Schmitt explicitly draws the connection between the core of Nazi ideology and his vision of Nazi law: "the underlying legal conception, permeating and buttressing

the whole legislative task that lies before us, can be captured by one word: homogeneity." Schmitt's legal theory thereby captures what arguably constitutes a core feature of National Socialism.

51. The most shocking is Schmitt, "Die Verfassung der Freiheit," where he argues that the Nuremberg racial laws should be interpreted as a guide informing judges and administrators how they are to interpret *all* elements of the German legal system. In this respect, they represent a preamble for German law as a whole, and thus a specifically National Socialist "constitution." In the same spirit, see Schmitt, "Die nationalsozialistische Gesetzgebung und der Vorbehalt des *'ordre public'* im internationalen Privatrecht," 206, 208.

52. Schmitt, "Die deutsche Rechtswissenschaft im Kampf gegen den jüdischen Geist," 1194–97; and Schmitt, "Die deutschen Intellektuellen," 1.

53. Schmitt, "Bericht über die Fachgruppe Hochschullehrer im BNSDJ," *Deutsches Recht* 4, no. 1 (1934): 17. My impression is that the biographical literature on Schmitt downplays the extent to which he envisioned himself as a "founding father" for a new generation of National Socialist jurists. Schmitt's didactic concerns come out clearly in a number of essays: Schmitt, "Über die neuen Aufgaben der Verfassungsgeschichte" (1936) in Schmitt, *Positionen und Begriffe im Kampf mit Weimar-Genf-Versailles*, 229–35; and Schmitt, "Review of Hans Gerber, *Auf dem Wege zum neuen Reich*," *Deutsche Juristen-Zeitung* 39, no. 23 (1934): 1474. The intensity of Schmitt's activities as a teacher in Berlin is documented in Christian Tilitzki, "Carl Schmitt—Staatsrechtlehrer in Berlin," *Siebente Etappe* (October 1991): 67–117.

54. Schmitt, *The Crisis of Parliamentary Democracy*, 75.

55. Caldwell, "National Socialism and Constitutional Law: Carl Schmitt, Otto Koellreutter, and the Debate over the Nazi State, 1933–1937."

56. Schmitt, "Neue Leitsätze für die Rechtspraxis," *Juristische Wochenschrift* 62, no. 50 (1933): 350–51; Schmitt "Nationalsozialismus und Rechtsstaat," 716. Consistent with his radical ideas about legal indeterminacy, Schmitt's concept of the binding of the decision maker to the law here is extremely minimal: it merely requires that the judge or administrator identify *some* basis within the legal system for his actions, even if that entails nothing more than an appeal to an open-ended standard such as "public morals" or "in good faith."

57. Schmitt, "Der Weg der deutschen Juristen," *Deutsche Juristen-Zeitung* 39, no. 11 (1934): 692–95.

58. Schmitt, "Aufgabe und Notwendigkeit des deutschen Rechtsstandes," 184. Also, see Schmitt, "Die geschichtliche Lage der deutschen Rechtswissenschaft," *Deutsche Juristen-Zeitung* 41, no. 1 (1936): 16.

59. Schmitt, "Aufgabe und Notwendigkeit des deutschen Rechtsstandes," 183–85. Of course, Nazi ideology was arguably less consistent than Schmitt asserts here. Perhaps this is why he is concerned during this period with highlighting what he takes to be its core element, namely, the pursuit of ethnic homogeneity [*Artgleichheit*]. In this way, he hopes to clarify the essential ideological and "spiritual" core of National Socialism, which legal actors then should refer to when deciding cases.

60. Schmitt, "Aufgabe und Notwendigkeit des deutschen Rechtsstandes," 184.

61. Schmitt, "Der Weg der deutschen Juristen," 698. In this vein, Schmitt writes that "legality within its most narrow confines" requires racial and ethnic homogeneity (Schmitt, "Der Neubau des Staates- und Verwaltungsrechts," in *Deutscher Juristentag 1933. Ansprachen und Fachvorträge*, ed. Rudolf Schraut [Berlin: Deutsche Rechts- und Wirtschaftswissenschaft Verlagsanstalt, 1934], 252).

62. Instead of waiting for new statutes, judges and administrators in Germany simply ignored the language of existing law whenever it conflicted with Nazi policy or ideology. In this way, rule of law protections were discarded first and foremost not by new legislation, but simply by antiformalistic judicial devices. For our purposes here, it is important to recognize that Schmitt offered an intelligent defense of such practices. On Schmitt as a major influence on Nazi law, see Bernd Rüthers, *Entartetes Recht: Rechtslehren und Kronjuristen im Dritten Reich* (Munich: DTV, 1994), 101–80.

63. Richard H. Weisberg's fascinating recent study of Vichy law might be taken as evidence that Schmitt's worries about a residual formalism were overstated. Even though French jurists during the Vichy period appear to have preserved more elements of a traditional legalistic approach than their colleagues on the other side of the Rhine, they nonetheless managed to play a crucial role in Vichy's most heinous crimes (*Vichy Law and the Holocaust in France* [New York: New York University Press, 1996]). More comparative research on the French, the German, and the Italian variants of fascist law is needed before this problem can be resolved. Studies of fascist law typically remain trapped within the intellectual confines of particular national legal traditions, despite the international character of fascist and Nazi movements at midcentury.

64. Schmitt, "Ein Jahr nationalsozialistischer Verfassungsstaat," 27; Schmitt, "Was bedeutet der Streit um den Rechtsstaat?" *Zeitschrift für die gesamte Staatswissenschaft* 95 (1935): 189–200; and Schmitt, "Einleitung," in Günther Krauss and Otto von Schweinichen, *Disputation über den Rechtsstaat* (Hamburg: Hanseatische Verlagsanstalt, 1935), 85.

65. Schmitt, "Kodifikation oder Novelle," *Deutsche Juristen-Zeitung* 40, nos. 15–16 (1935): 923–24.

66. Schmitt, *Staat, Bewegung, Volk*, 5–11; Schmitt, *Das Reichstatthaltergesetz*; Schmitt, "Das Staatsnotrecht im modernen Verfassungsleben," *Deutsche Richterzeitung* 25, nos. 8–9 (1933): 254–57; and Schmitt, "Das Gesetz zur Behebung der Not von Volk und Reich," 455–58.

67. Schmitt, "Kodifikation oder Novelle," 924.

68. Schmitt, "Kodifikation oder Novelle," 924–26; and Schmitt, "Aufgabe und Notwendigkeit des deutschen Rechtsstandes," 184–85. Of course, the same logic implies giving the *Führer* legally unlimited legislative and administrative powers.

69. Schmitt, "Der Neubau des Staates- und Verwaltungsrechts," in Schraut, ed., *Deutscher Juristentag 1933*, 250–51.

70. Schmitt, "Nationalsozialismus und Rechtsstaat," 716.

71. For a reliable account of this feud and the distortions of it by Schmitt's postwar followers, see Bernd Rüthers, *Carl Schmitt im Dritten Reich*, 2nd ed. (Munich: C.H. Beck, 1990), 81–108. Archival research also suggests that the threat to Schmitt during 1936 has been ridiculously exaggerated. For example, one of his presumed Nazi enemies, Reinhard Höhn, continued to serve with Schmitt as co-advisor on a host of dissertation and habilitation projects until the end of World War II at the University of Berlin (Tilitzki, "Carl Schmitt—Staatsrechtlehrer in Berlin," 38–39). Of course, academic co-advisors often squabble. Yet it is unlikely that Höhn and his buddies in the SS were intent on destroying Schmitt—physically, if necessary—if Höhn continued to cultivate professional ties with Schmitt well into the 1940s.

As we will see in chapter 6, after his feud with the SS in 1936, Schmitt hardly abandons the anti-Semitic ideas constitutive of his contributions to Nazi law after 1933. Schmitt's 1938 study on Hobbes, for example (Schmitt, *Der Leviathan in der Staatslehre des Thomas Hobbes* [*The Leviathan in the State Theory of Thomas Hobbes*] ([Cologne: Hohenheim, 1982]) is filled with anti-Semitic comments; Schmitt again offers a critique of the rule of law in which Jews are blamed for the "normativistic" legal tendencies allegedly inimical to the modern state. For a good survey of the anti-Semitic contours of Schmitt's interpretation of Hobbes, see Dyzenhaus, *Legality and Legitimacy in Weimar: Carl Schmitt, Hans Kelsen and Hermann Heller in Weimar*, 91–94. I see no textual evidence for Dyzenhaus's claim, however, that Schmitt in the Hobbes book hints at criticisms of the Nazi attack on the rule of law. The reason that Schmitt fails to offer a "celebration of Nazism as the restoration of the state" (92) is that by 1938 he had already begun to outline the core argument of his critique of international law: the nation-state is dead, destined to be replaced by continental "greater regions" [*Grossräume*] carving up the globe into distinct ethnic and economic-technological modes of organization.

72. In fact, anti-Semitism played an important role in some facets of the Nazi legal system, while in others its role was minimal (Ernst Fraenkel, *The Dual State* [New York: Oxford University Press, 1941]). The fact that Schmitt made so much of anti-Semitism arguably highlights the radicalism of his views within the Nazi debate.

73. Dreier and Sellert, eds., *Recht und Justiz im "Dritten Reich"*; Hubert Rottleuthner, ed., *Recht, Rechtsphilosophie und Nationalsozialismus*, *Archiv für Rechts- und Sozialphilosophie Beiheft 18* (Frankfurt a.M.: Fischer, 1978); Ilse Staff, ed., *Justiz im Dritten Reich* (Frankfurt a.M.: Fischer, 1978); and Michael Stolleis, *Recht im Unrecht. Studien zur Rechtsgeschichte des Nationalsozialismus* (Frankfurt a.M.: Suhrkamp, 1994).

74. Kirchheimer, "The Legal Order of National Socialism," in Kirchheimer, *Politics, Law and Social Change: Selected Essays of Otto Kirchheimer*, 102–3. A combination of enthusiasm for the regime and a set of informal and formal control mechanisms assured judicial compliance with National Socialism (Ralph Angermund, *Deutsche Richterschaft 1919–1945* [Frankfurt a.M.: Fischer, 1990]).

75. Kirchheimer, "The Legal Order of National Socialism," 99. This is an

interpretation of liberal jurisprudence according to which it rests on the *limited indeterminacy thesis*.

76. Kirchheimer, "The Legal Order of National Socialism," 99.

77. Kirchheimer, "The Legal Order of National Socialism," 99.

78. Kirchheimer, "The Legal Order of National Socialism," 100.

79. Nonetheless, it would be a mistake to overstate the extent to which the Nazis achieved even this perverse form of legal determinacy. In this chapter, I have tried to explain why that project was destined to fail. Well into the 1940s, the Nazi leadership worried about inconsistencies within judicial decision making (Heinz Boberach, ed., *Richterbriefe: Dokumete zur Beeinflussung der deutschen Rechtsprechung 1942–1944* [Boppard am Rhein: Harald Boldt, 1975]).

80. Kelman, *A Guide to Critical Legal Studies* (Cambridge, Mass.: Harvard University Press, 1987), 59–61, 258.

81. Examples of this genre can be found in Gary Minda, *Postmodern Legal Movements: Law and Jurisprudence at Century's End* (New York: New York University Press, 1995).

82. Roberto M. Unger, "The Critical Legal Studies Movement," *Harvard Law Review* 96 (1983): 571; Unger, *What Should Legal Analysis Become?*, 66–67.

83. Solum, "On the Indeterminacy Crisis: Critiquing Critical Dogma," 500.

6. INDETERMINACY AND INTERNATIONAL LAW

1. The English-language literature on this period of Schmitt's career is paltry. Gary Ulmen summarizes Schmitt's ideas, but his discussion is shockingly uncritical: Gary L. Ulmen, "American Imperialism and International Law: Carl Schmitt on the U.S. in World Affairs," *Telos* 72 (Summer 1987): 43–72. The German literature is vastly superior. See Lothar Gruchmann, *Nationalsozialistische Grossraumordnung. Die Konstruktion einer "deutschen Monroe-Doktrin"* (Stuttgart: Deutsche Verlagsanstalt, 1962); and Dan Diner, *Weltordnungen. Über Geschichte und Wirkung von Recht und Macht* (Frankfurt a.M.: Fischer, 1993), 77–124. Although written by a Nazi and thus suffering from some obvious problems, Ernst Rudolf Huber's " 'Positionen und Begriffe': Eine Auseinandersetzung mit Carl Schmitt," *Zeitschrift für die gesamte Staatswissenschaft* 101 (1941): 1–44, includes some insightful comments about Schmitt's critique of international law.

2. Ernst Fraenkel, *Military Occupation and the Rule of Law: Occupation Government in the Rhineland, 1918–1923* (New York: Oxford University Press, 1944), 4–5. As part of the Versailles agreement, the Saar and Rhineland regions were placed under the control of Allied-dominated commissions. Occupation of the Saar was to last fifteen years, and then a referendum was to decide whether it would become part of Germany or France; according to the original agreement, foreign troops were to occupy the Rhineland until 1935. Beyond the fact that the Versailles Treaty thereby robbed the Germans of control of two strategic economic and military regions, it also gave the Allies the potential to regulate and limit German military forces at large.

3. Fraenkel, *Military Occupation and the Rule of Law*, 194.

4. See, for example, his discussion of irregularities in electoral laws in the Saar (Schmitt, "Die Wahlordnung fuer das Saargebiet von 29. April 1920," *Niemeyers Zeitschrift für Internationales Recht* 34 [1925]: 415–20).

5. Schmitt, "Die politische Lage der entmilitarisierten Rheinland," *Abendland: Deutsche Monatshefte für europäische Kultur, Politik und Wirtschaft* 5, no. 10 (1929–1930): 308.

6. Schmitt, "Das Rheinland als Objekt internationaler Politik" (1925), 32; "Der Status Quo und der Friede" (1925), 35; "Völkerrechtliche Probleme im Rheingebiet" (1928), 99–100, all reprinted in Schmitt, *Positionen und Begriffe im Kampf mit Weimar-Genf-Versailles*.

7. Schmitt, *Die Kernfrage des Völkerbundes* (Berlin: Duemmlers Verlag, 1926), 10–11.

8. Schmitt, *Die Kernfrage des Völkerbundes*, 47–55. Schmitt argues that Article 19 of the League, which allows for the reconsideration of "conditions whose continuance might endanger the peace of the world," is effectively irrelevant given the power constellations found within the League.

9. The argument is stated most clearly in Schmitt, *Concept of the Political*, 56, but its elements are scattered throughout Schmitt's Weimar writings. It also plays an important role in his Nazi-era writings.

10. Schmitt, *The Concept of the Political*, 27.

11. Schmitt, *Die Kernfrage des Völkerbundes*, 4; and Schmitt, "Völkerrechtliche Probleme in Rheingebiet," 108. Schmitt's clearest defense of the idea that interstate relations approximate the "state of nature" described by early modern political thought is found in his 1938 study on Hobbes. There, Schmitt expresses a certain nostalgia for Hobbes's "nondiscriminatory concept of war," according to which the individual sovereign state alone is suited to the task of defining justice and providing for legality. Because the state of nature in which individual states are located is basically lawless, "there can be neither a legal war nor a legal peace" (between separate nations) (*Der Leviathan in der Staatslehre des Thomas Hobbes*, 76). Schmitt shows respect for Hobbes's view that this model alone is able to overcome the dangers, so obvious in Hobbes's time, of civil wars between competing religious groups, each of which claims a monopoly on religious and moral truth. From Schmitt's perspective, modern international law suffers from ills dangerously reminiscent of those described by Hobbes. By legitimizing a (fictional) system of international law, liberalism undermines state sovereignty, so pivotal in the Hobbesian view to political stability, and paves the way for new "holy wars" to be waged in the name of universal liberal ideals (*Der Leviathan in der Staatslehre des Thomas Hobbes*, 72–76). It is important to note that Schmitt's nostalgia for the Hobbesian model is qualified substantially by his view, to be discussed later in section IV, that the era of the modern sovereign nation-state is now coming to a close. In the twentieth century, we cannot realistically hope to recapture this era and the Hobbesian rules which defined it; at the same time, Schmitt finds reference to it useful in his battle against liberalism. In addition, part of Schmitt's argument here is

the empirical allusion that an international community based on Hobbesian principles is likely to prove more humane than one based on modern liberalism; lacking
the universalistic pathos of modern liberalism, it is unlikely to wage brutal wars in
the name of humanity. As Schmitt argues most clearly in a study published after
World War II, but clearly begun during the early 1940s, *Der Nomos der Erde im
Völkerrecht des Jus Publicum Europaeum* [*The Nomos of the Earth in the International Law
of the Jus Publicum Europaeum*] (Cologne: Greven Verlag, 1950), Wilsonian liberalism
thus represents an attack on what had been an unambiguously superior system of
international relations. There, neither the Kaiserreich nor Hitler's Germany is held
responsible for the German catastrophe and the collapse of international law in our
century. On the contrary, the disruptive force of Wilsonian liberalism allegedly
destroyed the Hobbesian conception of the "non-discriminatory war" and paved
the way for the horrors of our times. Wilson, not Hitler, launched World War II
(!). For timely contemporary criticisms of this line of argumentation, see Hans
Wehberg, "Universales oder Europäisches Völkerrecht?" *Die Friedens-Warte* 41, no.
4 (1941): 157–66, for a critical discussion of Schmitt's romanticized view of preslib-
eral international politics; Golo Mann, "Carl Schmitt und die schlechte Juristerei,"
Der Monat 5 (October 1952): 89–92, for a critical discussion of Schmitt's hostility
to Wilsonian liberalism.

12. Schmitt, *Die Kernfrage des Völkerbundes*, 19–20, 63–80. See also Schmitt,
Die Verfassungslehre, 376–37, as well as "Das Doppelgesicht des Genfer Völkerbundes" (1926), in Schmitt, *Positionen und Begriffe im Kampf mit Weimar-Genf-Versailles*,
41.

13. Schmitt, *The Concept of the Political*, 27.

14. Schmitt, *Die Kernfrage des Völkerbundes*, 68.

15. Hence Schmitt's statement that the most important legal concepts within
the international arena are *always* fundamentally controversial. In my reading, this is
more than one of Schmitt's many rhetorical flourishes; it should be taken absolutely
seriously as a jurisprudential claim (Schmitt, "Die politische Lage der entmilitarisierten Rheinland," 308). This is also the source of his repeated assertion that the
question of *quis judicabit?*, rather than the "normativities" of international law, needs
to be considered the centerpiece of international law.

16. Schmitt, *Die Kernfrage des Völkerbundes*, 10–11; and Schmitt, "Völkerrechtliche Probleme im Rheingebiet," 107. Kelsen again is Schmitt's main target here.
In many works, Kelsen argued for the primacy of international law vis-à-vis the
domestic legal system of each state. The internal norms of individual states must
conform to international law; in the case of a conflict, international law should
prevail. In Kelsen's theory, "municipal laws must always conform to international
law; in cases of conflict, the latter declares all domestic rules or acts contrary to it
to be illegal." See Antonio Cassese, *International Law in a Divided World* (Oxford:
Clarendon, 1986), 21; and Hans Kelsen, *Das Problem der Souveränität und die Theorie
des Völkerrechts* (Tübingen: Mohr, 1920). From Schmitt's perspective, Kelsen's theory represented an ideological justification for the worst hypocrisies of liberal international law. More recent empirically minded scholars have confirmed Schmitt's

anxieties about the declining significance of the idea of the legal equality of all states (Susan Strange, *The Retreat of the State: The Diffusion of Power in the World Economy* [Cambridge: Cambridge University Press, 1996], 13).

17. Schmitt, "Das Rheinland als Objekt internationaler Politik," 28–30. In this view, open annexation has proven too costly: the annexing powers often were seen as having a series of obligations—for example, guaranteeing basic legal and even political rights—to the peoples of annexed territories. Schmitt's argument here is also a challenge to Joseph Schumpeter's influential theory of imperialism, according to which modern capitalism is essentially pacific and nonimperialist in character. For Schumpeter, imperialism is an atavistic leftover from a precapitalist era. For Schmitt, Schumpeter's theory represents a "highly political denial of the political character of economic processes and concepts." That is, it is a characteristically liberal-economic attempt to mask the potential political qualities of economic power (Schmitt, "Völkerrechtliche Formen des modernen Imperialismus" [1932], in Schmitt, *Positionen und Begriffe im Kampf mit Weimar-Genf-Versailles*, 162). I take a closer look at the nexus between Schmitt and Schumpeter in chapter 7.

18. Schmitt, "Das Rheinland als Objekt internationaler Politik," 29; "Der Völkerbund und Europa," 91–92; "Völkerrechtliche Probleme im Rheingebiet," 106; and "Völkerrechtliche Formen des modernen Imperialismus" (1932), 169–72, all reprinted in *Positionen und Begriffe im Kampf mit Weimar-Genf-Versailles*.

19. Schmitt, "Das Rheinland als Objekt internationaler Politik," 29. For example, Article 3 of the Treaty of Havana (1901) reads that "the government of Cuba consents that the United States may exercise the right to intervene for the preservation of Cuban independence, the maintenance of a government adequate for the protection of life, liberty, and individual liberty." Relying on Article 3, the United States occupied Cuba between 1906 and 1909 (cited in Hans Morgenthau, *Politics Among Nations: The Struggle for Power and Peace* revised and enlarged ed. [Chicago: University of Chicago Press, 1954], 295–96).

20. Schmitt, *Political Theology*, 15. Exception or "optional clauses" certainly do play a major role in international law. Hans Morgenthau, *Politics Among Nations*, 263–66.

21. President Monroe's unilateral declaration of December 2, 1823, acknowledged the legitimacy of existing European colonies and dependencies within the Americas, while simultaneously proclaiming that "with governments who have declared their independence," attempts to suppress that independence would be interpreted as "manifestations of an unfriendly disposition towards the United States" (cited in Hans Morgenthau, *Politics Among Nations*, 39).

22. Schmitt, "Völkerrechtliche Formen des modernen Imperialismus," 166. Also on the Monroe Doctrine: see Schmitt, *Die Kernfrage des Völkerbundes*, 11, 20, 54, 72–73. The central place possessed by the Monroe Doctrine in modern international law in Schmitt's theory is evinced by the fact that he includes it in an edited collection of international law documents from 1930 (Carl Schmitt, ed., *Der Völkerbund und das politische Problem der Friedenssicherung* [Leipzig: Teubner, 1930]).

23. Schmitt, "Völkerrechtliche Formen des modernen Imperialismus," 162–63; Schmitt, *Concept of the Political*, 54–55, 78–79.

24. Article 21 was a concession to Woodrow Wilson, who argued—against Latin American opposition—that it was necessary if the United States Senate were to accept American membership in the League. The Senate never permitted U.S. membership in the League, but the League was left with an ambiguous statement about its relation to what, by the end of the nineteenth century, had come to serve as the main justification for American interventionism not only in the Americas, but in the Pacific region and Far East as well.

25. Schmitt counts eighteen American states, one-third of the League members, as de facto vassals of the United States. His favorite example of American influence is the vote on the 1931 German-Austrian Customs Union, in which Latin American votes proved pivotal. Obviously, his argument here is exaggerated. American influence in Brazil, for example, was relatively limited in contrast to its role in Cuba or Panama (Schmitt, "Völkerrechtliche Formen des modernen Imperialismus," 172).

26. On the United States and the League of Nations: see Schmitt, "Der Völkerbund und Europa," 91–92; and "Völkerrechtliche Formen des Imperialismus," 174–75.

27. The Kellogg Pact of August 27, 1928, condemned war as a means of national policy. Most members of the international community soon signed it, but the great powers insisted on certain reservation clauses. The United States declared the Monroe Doctrine consistent with it; Great Britain followed the American example by declaring a right "to defend regions of the world the welfare and integrity of which constitute a special and vital interest for our peace and safety."

28. Schmitt, "Völkerrechtliche Formen des modernen Imperialismus," 176–77.

29. E. H. Carr's *The Twenty Years' Crisis, 1919–1939: An Introduction to the Study of International Relations* (New York: Harper and Row, 1964) makes many claims reminiscent of Schmitt's. In contrast to the German author, however, Carr pointedly emphasizes that a Realist analysis of power in the international arena can hardly free itself altogether of moral concerns. In chapter 9, we examine Schmitt's influence on Hans Morgenthau.

30. In this vein, see Danilo Zolo's recent account of the Gulf War as the "first cosmopolitan war" waged with the full support of the liberal international legal order and the United Nations. As Zolo reminds us, "the Allies used a greater quantity of explosives in the forty-two days of 'Desert Storm' than were used in the whole of the Second World War." On the American side, 148 died; on the Iraqi side, the numbers are probably 220,000, including many civilians (Zolo, *Cosmopolis: Prospects for World Government* [Cambridge, Mass.: Polity Press, 1997], 24).

31. For example, see Schmitt, *Concept of the Political*, 48–49, where Schmitt declares that it "is a manifest fraud to condemn war as homicide and then demand of men that they wage war, kill and be killed, so that there never again will be war."

32. William Appelman Williams, *The Tragedy of American Diplomacy*, 2nd ed., revised and enlarged (New York: Dell, 1972), for example, similarly describes the idiosyncrasies of American "imperial anti-colonialism."

33. Schmitt, *Concept of the Political*, 55. The idea that liberal constitutionalism is inherently hostile to "difference" has experienced a revival of sorts in recent years. For a critical discussion: William E. Scheuerman, "Constitutionalism and Difference," *University of Toronto Law Journal* 14, no. 2 (1997): 263–80.

34. Schmitt, "Völkerrechtliche Probleme im Rheingebiet," 108.

35. "A world state which embraces the entire globe and all of humanity cannot exist. The political world is a pluriverse, not a universe" (Schmitt, *Concept of the Political*, 53).

36. Hans Kelsen, *Law and Peace in International Relations* (Cambridge, Mass.: Harvard University Press, 1948). One could also criticize Schmitt here from the perspective of recent empirical work on "international regimes" or "governance without government." This body of literature focuses on systems of shared norms and institutions within the international arena (for example, the World Trade Organization [WTO] whose rules are enforced by a complex coalition of individual states, but by no single sovereign in the classical sense of the term. Many scholars have suggested that this phenomenon has gained in importance in recent decades (James N. Rosenau and Ernst-Otto Czempiel, eds., *Governance without Government: Order and Change in World Politics* [Cambridge: Cambidge University Press, 1992]).

37. For a discussion of the proliferation of deformalized law in the international arena by one of Schmitt's contemporaries: Thomas Baty, "The Trend of International Law," *American Journal of International Law* 33 (1939): 653–64. I discuss the problems posed by antiformal trends within contemporary international economic law in William E. Scheuerman, "Economic Globalization and the Rule of Law," *Constellations* 6, no. 1 (1999). American international lawyers of a "critical" bent have become skeptical of the traditional liberal quest for codified law. Reminiscent of Schmitt, they thematize the pervasiveness of indeterminacy within international law in order to discredit liberal models of it. Unlike Schmitt, they seem oblivious to the possibility that the deconstruction of liberal international law raises profound problems for their progressive political preferences. For an overview of this discourse, see Nigel Purvis, "Critical Legal Studies in Public International Law," *Harvard International Law Journal* 32, no. 1 (1991): 81–127. For a sample, see David Kennedy, "A New Stream of International Law Scholarship," *Wisconsin International Law Journal* 7, no. 1 (1988): 1–49.

38. Lothar Gruchmann, *Nationalsozialistische Grossraumordnung. Die Konstruktion einer "deutschen Monroe-Doktrin,"* 146–47.

39. Schmitt, "Völkerrechtliche Formen des modernen Imperialismus," 167–68.

40. Hermann Heller, "Rechtsstaat oder Diktatur?" in Heller, *Gesammelte Schriften*, vol. II, ed. Christoph Müller (Tübingen: Mohr, 1992), 443–62.

41. Although often forgotten today, the United Nations rests on an unambiguous commitment to the establishment of greater social justice. For this reason, the United Nations at least acknowledges the centrality of linking the quest for international law to the struggle to counteract illegitimate de facto inequalities. For a recent attempt to build on this legacy, whose chief opponent in the international realm

often has been the United States, see David Held, *Democracy and the Global Order: From the Modern State to Cosmopolitan Governance* (Stanford, Calif.: Stanford University Press, 1995). In this spirit, Jürgen Habermas discusses the necessity of developing transnational forms of social policy in his "Jenseits des Nationalstaats? Bemerkungen zur Folgeproblemen der wirtschaftlichen Globalisierung?" in *Politik der Globalisierung*, ed. Ulrich Beck (Frankfurt a.m.: Suhrkamp, 1998), 67–84.

42. Schmitt, "Völkerrechtliche Formen des modernen Imperialismus," 178.

43. Schmitt, "Völkerrechtliche Formen des modernen Imperialismus," 179.

44. Schmitt, "Völkerrechtliche Formen des modernen Imperialismus," 169.

45. Schmitt, *Die Kernfrage des Völkerbundes*, 11; and Schmitt, "Völkerrechtliche Probleme im Rheingebiet," 107.

46. Schmitt, "Völkerrechtliche Formen des modernen Imperialismus," 179.

47. Schmitt, "Völkerrechtliche Formen des modernen Imperialismus," 179.

48. Joseph Florian and John Herz, "Bolshevist and National Socialist Doctrines of International Law," *Social Research* 7, no. 1 (1940): 6.

49. John Herz, "The National Socialist Doctrine of International Law and the Problems of International Organization," *Political Science Quarterly* 54, no. 4 (1939): 539. Herz also makes the underlying contradiction within National Socialist law described here the main theme of a superb monograph, written after he was forced to flee Germany: Eduard Bristler [John Herz], *Die Völkerrechtslehre des Nationalsozialismus* (Zurich: Europa, 1938). Much of the literature on Nazi international law confirms the conclusions of Herz's groundbreaking research in the 1930s. See Virginia L. Gott, "The National Socialist Theory of International Law," *American Journal of International Law* 32 (1938), especially 711–13; Detlev F. Vagts, "International Law in the Third Reich," *American Journal of International Law* 84 (1990): 661–700; and Rüdiger Wolfrum, "Nationalsozialismus und Völkerrecht," in *Recht und Rechtslehre im Nationalsozialismus*, ed. Franz Jürgen Säcker (Baden-Baden: Nomos, 1992), 89–101.

50. See Carl Schmitt, *Nationalsozialismus und Völkerrecht* (Berlin: Junker & Dunnhaupt, 1934), in which he demands that Germany be treated as an equal in the international community; and Schmitt, "Sowjet-Union and Genfer Völkerbund," *Völkerbund und Völkerrecht* 1, no. 5 (1934): 267, where he repeats the demand. Schmitt's writings from this period provide a virtually complete apologetic history of the main trends within Nazi foreign policy. Germany quit the League on October 14, 1933; Schmitt immediately endorsed this move in a front-page newspaper article, telling his readers that a vote for Hitler (on November 12, 1933) constitutes a vote for peace (Schmitt, Frieden oder Pazifismus?" *Berliner Börsen-Zeitung*, 11 November 1933, 1). Schmitt's 1934 publications similarly endorse this decision. In 1935, Hitler directed the press to describe the 1935 Soviet-French pact as an attack on the Locarno Pact, a collective security agreement of 1925 intended to relax tensions stemming from the occupation of the Rhineland (see Ludolf Herbst, *Das nationalsozialistische Deutschland 1933–1945* [Frankfurt a.M.: Suhrkamp, 1996], 144); Schmitt immediately jumped on the bandwagon with "Über die Innere Logik der Allgemeinpakte auf gegenseitigen Beistand" (1935), reprinted in Schmitt,

Positionen und Begriffe im Kampf mit Weimar-Genf-Versailles, 204–9, and a front-page article in Germany's leading legal journal, "Die Sprengung der Locarno-Gemeinschaft durch Einschaltung der Sowjets," *Deutsche Juristen-Zeitung* 41, no. 6 (1936): 337–41, where the Nazi position is defended. He praises Italian fascist atrocities in Ethiopia in "Die siebente Wandlung der Genfer Völkerbundes" (1936), in *Positionen und Begriffe im Kampf mit Weimar-Genf-Versailles*, 210–13. Immediately after the passing of the Nuremberg laws, Schmitt rushes to defend them in "Die nationalsozialistische Gesetzgebung und der Vorbehalt des 'ordre public' im Internationalen Privatrecht." His writings are also filled with polemics against the traditional legal idea of *pacta sunt servanda*, that is, the principle of the sanctity of treaties, precisely when Hitler was systematically dismantling Germany's treaty obligations to her neighbors.

51. Schmitt, *Nationalsozialismus und Völkerrecht*, 5, 7.

52. Schmitt, *Nationalsozialismus und Völkerrecht*, 15, 17.

53. Schmitt, *Nationalsozialismus und Völkerrecht*, 19.

54. Schmitt, "Die siebente Wandlung des Genfer Voelkerbundes," 213. This argument is repeated frequently. See also, Schmitt, "Über die Innere Logik der Allgemeinpakte auf gegenseitigen Beistand," 209, where he refers to the idea of a distinct "European community"; and "Sprengung der Locarno-Gemeinschaft durch Einschaltung der Sowjets," 339–40.

55. Schmitt, "Sprengung der Locarno-Gemeinschaft durch Einschaltung der Sowjets," 337–41; and Schmitt, *Nationalsozialismus und Völkerrecht* 28.

56. Soviet Marxism is universalistic in outlook and thus, for Schmitt, its legal conception is inherently imperialistic as well. Schmitt, "Die nationalsozialistische Gesetzgebung und der Vorbehalt des *'ordre public'* im Internationalen Privatrecht," especially 206, 211. The argument is repeated elsewhere, even after Schmitt's alleged break with National Socialism in 1936: see "Völkerrechtliche Neutralität und völkische Totalität" (1938), in Schmitt, *Positionen und Begriffe im Kampf mit Weimar-Genf-Versailles*, 257; and "Neutralität und Neutralisierungen" (1939), also in *Positionen und Begriffe im Kampf mit Weimar-Genf-Versailles*, 286.

57. Schmitt, "Die nationalsozialistische Gesetzgebung und der Vorbehalt des *'ordre public'* im Internationalen Privatrecht," 208.

58. Schmitt, *Nationalsozialismus und Völkerrecht*, 21. For the general argument, see Schmitt, *Die Wendung zum diskriminierenden Kriegsbegriff* (Munich: Duncker and Humblot 1938), especially 42–43.

59. Schmitt, "Über das Verhältnis der Begriffe Krieg und Frieden" (1938), in *Positionen und Begriffe mit Weimar-Genf-Versailles*, 247; also see, Schmitt, "'Inter pacem et bellum nihil medium,'" *Zeitschrift der Akademie für Deutsches Recht* 6 (1939): 595.

60. Schmitt, *Die Wendung zum diskriminierenden Kriegsbegriff*, 51–52. This argument is then developed in greater depth in *Der Nomos der Erde im Völkerrecht des Jus Publicum Europaeum*, 191–299.

61. Schmitt, "Totaler Feind, totaler Krieg, totaler Staat" (1937), in *Positionen und Begriffe im Kampf mit Weimar-Genf-Versailles*, 238, and Schmitt, *Land und Meer*.

Eine weltgeschichtliche Betrachtung [1942] (Stuttgart: Reclam, 1954), 5. Schmitt's anti-British arguments are summarized in Stephen Holmes, *The Anatomy of Antiliberalism* (Cambridge, Mass.: Harvard University Press, 1993), 53–57.

62. Schmitt, "Das neue Vae Neutris," reprinted in *Positionen und Begriffe im Kampf mit Weimar-Genf-Versailles*, 252–53; Schmitt, "Völkerrechtliche Neutralität und völkische Totalität" (1938), 257.

63. The lecture served as the basis for a number of articles and, most important, Schmitt's 1939 book, *Völkerrechtliche Grossraumordnung mit Interventionsverbot für raumfremde Mächte* (Berlin: Deutscher Rechtsverlag, 1939).

64. For example, Karl Heinz Bremer, "Völkerordung und Völkerrecht," *Münchner Neueste Nachrichten*, 26 April 1939, 4; "Das 'Reich' im Völkerrecht," *Frankfurter Zeitung*, 3 April 1939, 2; "Grossräumiges Denken: Prof. Carl Schmitt sprach in Kiel," *Deutsche Allgemeine Zeitung*, 4 April 1939, 7. On the reaction, see Bendersky, *Carl Schmitt: Theorist for the Reich*, 251–61. Lothar Gruchmann's monograph shows that Schmitt's writings were an important contribution to a broader Nazi attempt to appropriate the idea of the Monroe Doctrine for the sake of both keeping the United States out of the war between 1939 and 1941 and justifying Nazi imperialism. Hitler himself referred to the Monroe Doctrine in an important speech held on April 28, 1939, just a few weeks after Schmitt's lecture in Kiel gained national attention. Joachim Ribbentrop also made use of this discourse, and there is at least some evidence that the United States, if only for a brief moment, took it seriously during the summer of 1940 (Gruchmann, *Nationalsozialistische Grossraumordnung. Die Konstruktion einer "deutschen Monroe-Doktrin,"* 11–20). The question of whether Schmitt directly influenced Hitler's April speech is less important than the fact that Schmitt, once again, had managed to propel himself into the very center of debates within Nazi international law. Of course, Schmitt's timing could not have been more opportune: the outlines of the *Grossraum* theory were sketched out right before the Nazi invasion of Poland.

65. Bendersky, *Carl Schmitt: Theorist for the Reich*, 243–73.

66. This move also entails trying to overcome the antinomies found within Schmitt's writings in international law from 1933 to 1938. Schmitt now abandons traditional ideas (for example, the idea of the formal equality of all sovereign states) in favor of a full-fledged, National Socialist conception of international law.

67. Schmitt's contrast between the (good) "early" Monroe Doctrine and its (bad) "late" rendition is alluded to in many of Schmitt's texts from this period. It is formulated most clearly in *Völkerrechtliche Grossraumordnung mit Interventionsverbot für raumfremde Mächte*, 21–40; "Grossraum gegen Universalismus" (1939), in Schmitt, *Positionen und Begriffe im Kampf mit Weimar-Genf-Versailles*, 295–302; and Schmitt, "Die letzte globale Linie," in *Völker und Meere*, ed. Egmont Zechlin (Leipzig: Otto Harrassowitz, 1944), 342–49. The "early" Monroe Doctrine is also described positively in Schmitt, *Der Nomos der Erde im Völkerrecht*, 256–70.

68. Schmitt, *Völkerrechtliche Grossraumordnung mit Interventionsverbot*, 53–54; and Schmitt, "Die Raumrevolution," *Das Reich*, 29 September 1940, 3. (*Das Reich*, by the way, was edited by Josef Goebbels.) Carl Schmitt, *Land und Meer. Eine*

weltgeschichtliche Betrachtung, 59–60. Schmitt's account of English liberalism, whose universalistic attributes he somewhat crudely traces to the fact that England very early became a sea power, is also articulated in "Das Meer gegen das Land," *Das Reich*, 9 March 1941, 17–18; and "Beschleuniger wider Willen oder: Problematik der westlichen Hemisphäre," *Das Reich*, 19 April 1942, 3.

69. Schmitt, *Völkerrechtliche Grossraumordnung mit Interventionsverbot für raumfremde Mächte*, 7. *Sesshaft* can be translated roughly into "seated" or "situated." It is still common in German to describe Gypsies as lacking this attribute; Schmitt here also clearly intends it as a criticism of "cosmopolitan" Jews.

70. Schmitt, *Völkerrechtliche Grossraumordnung mit Interventionsverbot für raumfremde Mächte*, 64.

71. See, for example, Schmitt's comment that "norms and rules only gain their meaning and logic within the context of a concrete order" in "Die Auflösung der europäischen Ordnung im 'International Law' (1890–1939)," *Deutsche Rechtswissenschaft* 5 (1940): 277.

72. For example, the term *süddeutscher Raum* can be translated as "the region of southern Germany," or *Wirtschaftraum Hamburgs* as the "economic region of Hamburg."

73. Schmitt, *Völkerrechtliche Grossraumordnung mit Interventionsverbot für raumfremde Mächte*, 12–13. Raphael Gross has rightly noted that Schmitt's *Raum* terminology is fundamentally anti-Semitic in character: Raphael Gross, "Carl Schmitts 'Nomos' und die Juden," *Merkur* 47 (1993): 410–20. A similar argument has also been proffered by Wolfgang Palaver, "Carl Schmitt on *Nomos* and Space," *Telos* 106 (Winter 1996): 105–27. Not surprisingly in light of their anti-Semitic conceptual starting point, Schmitt's writings during this period continue to be splattered with anti-Semitic references. For example, see "Das 'Allgemeine Deutsche Staatsrecht' als Beispiel rechtswissenschaftlicher Systembildung," *Zeitschrift für die gesamte Staatswissenschaft* 100 (1940): 22, where he describes the German-Jewish jurist Otto Mayer as an example of how the "relatedness" of the French and Germans was "poisoned" by means of inappropriate Jewish "involvement" [*Einmischung*] in their affairs; and "Die Formung des französischen Geistes durch den Legisten," *Deutschland-Frankreich: Vierteljahresschrift des deutschen Instituts/Paris* 1 (1942), where he associates Judaism with zealotry (18) and talks of the "total lack of connections of the Jewish spirit to the German people" (24). In addition, it is difficult to overlook the anti-Semitic imagery employed by Schmitt in his account of modern liberal universalism. Both Anglo-Saxon liberalism and the Jews allegedly endorse a *raumlosen Universalismus* (territory-less universalism), and thus Schmitt considers it fitting to describe the British as encouraging an "exodus" of valuables and legal titles from Europe ("Das Meer gegen das Land," 17–18, and "Raum und Großraum im Völkerrecht," *Zeitschrift für Völkerrecht* 24 [1941]: 179). Nicholaus Sombart was intimate with Schmitt during this period and has persuasively documented the depth of Schmitt's anti-Semitism (*Jugend in Berlin, 1933–1942. Ein Bericht* [Frankfurt a.M.: Fischer, 1991], 249–76). Although I find Sombart's synthesis of psychoanalysis and feminism theoretically superficial, at least his study succeeds, in contrast

to much of the existing English-language literature, in documenting the depth of Schmitt's anti-Semitism (Sombart, *Die deutschen Männer und ihre Feinde: Carl Schmitt—ein deutsches Schicksal zwischen Männerbund und Matriarchatsmythos* [Frankfurt: Fischer, 1991], 261–94).

74. Schmitt, *Völkerrechtliche Raumordnung mit Interventionsverbot für raumfremde Mächte*, 71.

75. Schmitt is extremely vague when describing the likely form relations between distinct *Grossräume* should take ("Raum und Grossraum im Völkerrecht," 146, 177).

76. After the United States joins forces with the British, Schmitt criticizes the Americans for having joined the wrong side ("Beschleuniger wider Willen oder: Problematik des westlichen Hemisphäre," 3). This 1942 piece is also fascinating for the light it sheds on Schmitt's picture of the United States, which he describes as politically indecisive and socially divided, and thus incapable of establishing a coherent international order. Given its internal contradictions, the United States is most likely simply to export disorder to the rest of the world. Schmitt's comments here anticipate the picture of the United States presented in many sections of *Der Nomos der Erde im Völkerrecht*. Raphael Gross, in my view correctly, argues that many of Schmitt's anti-Semitic ideas are reformulated as anti-American ideas after World War II (Gross, "Carl Schmitts 'Nomos' und die Juden"). This tendency is already evident in Schmitt's writings from the early 1940s.

77. Schmitt, *Völkerrechtliche Grossraumordnung mit Interventionsverbot für raumfremde Mächte*, 36. Of course, this assertion could be taken as building on Schmitt's entire oeuvre, which was always concerned with demonstrating the bankruptcy of liberal democracy.

78. Schmitt, *Völkerrechtliche Grossraumordnung mit Interventionsverbot für raumfremde Mächte*, especially 63–65, 70–71; and Schmitt, "Die Raumrevolution," as well as "Raum und Großraum im Völkerrecht," 178, where he relies on the term *ethnic freedom* [*völkische Freiheit*]. In 1944, the *Grossraum* is described as aiming to protect the "historical, economic and spiritual substance and particularity" of any given people ("Die letzte globale Linie," 349). In his postwar writings, Schmitt continues to make use of the category of the *Grossraum*. But its racial and ethnic elements are downplayed in favor of economic and technological considerations. Of course, those features are part of the original analysis as well.

79. Schmitt, *Völkerrechtliche Grossraumordnung mit Interventionsverbot für raumfremde Mächte*, 15–16, where he praises competing National Socialist conceptions of a *Raum*-based international order (like that developed by Karl Haushofer), but argues that his model is ultimately superior. In a similar vein, see Schmitt, "Reich und Raum. Elemente eines neuen Völkerrechts," *Zeitschrift der Akademie für Deutsches Recht* 7, no. 13 (1940): 201–2; and Schmitt, "Raum und Großraum im Völkerrecht," 146, where he refers to the SS author Werner Best. Best criticized Schmitt's theory, accusing it of lacking sufficient Nazi credentials: Best, "Völkische Grossraumordnung," *Deutsches Recht*, 10, no. 25 (1940): 1006–7; "Nochmals: Völkische Grossraumordnung statt: 'Völkerrechtliche' Grossraumordnung," *Deutsches Recht*

11, no. 29 (1941): 1533–34. A careful reading of these essays suggests, however, that Schmitt's position and Best's are ultimately quite close. Schmitt makes use of the "folk" terminology (for example, in his concept of *völkische Freiheit*) as Best demands. Another rival, Reinhard Höhn, attacks Schmitt's theory of the *Grossraum* for failing to break adequately with a traditional legal formalism favoring "abstract" and "general" categories over "concrete" ones. At the same time, Höhn praises Schmitt for introducing the *Grossraum* terminology into Nazi legal thinking; Höhn comments that Schmitt performed a great "service" by making the problem of the *Grossraum* the centerpiece of debates among Nazi international lawyers (283). Although the essay's polemical tone could lead the reader to miss this point, Höhn chiefly hopes to refine and embellish Schmitt's theoretical innovations. There are some clear differences in tone and emphasis here, but Schmitt and Höhn clearly share a great deal as well (Höhn, "Grossraumordnung und völkisches Rechtsdenken," *Reich, Volksordnung, Lebensraum* 1, no. 1 [1941]: 256–88). For a fine discussion situating Schmitt's theory in the context of competing Nazi theories, see Dan Diner, *Weltordnungen. Über Geschichte und Wirkung von Recht und Macht*, 77–124.

Schmitt's apologists often refer to these refinements to suggest that Schmitt's view was distinct from that of the Nazis. (For example, Bendersky, *Carl Schmitt: Theorist of the Reich*, 252–55.) Two caveats are in order here. First, there was no single National Socialist theory of international law; Schmitt's theory was one among a number of competing Nazi models. The fact that Schmitt differs on occasion, for example, from Haushofer or Best hardly means that Schmitt's theory was not basically Nazi in character. There was never a single, homogeneous Nazi theory of international law—or, for that matter, much else. The relationship between ideology and political practice within National Socialism is simply more complicated than this view tends to suggest. Second, Schmitt himself implies that his theory of international law supersedes, in the Hegelian sense, competing Nazi models of international law. That is, his theory contains the "most developed" features of their insights while nonetheless answering questions that competing theories cannot. In my reading of Schmitt, this claim definitely needs to be taken seriously. The mere fact that his theory is more complex than that of his intellectual rivals hardly transforms Schmitt, as writers like Bendersky have suggested, into a principled anti-Nazi. Especially interesting on this score is a 1942 book by G.A. Walz, published by the Nazis themelves: much of this book borrows *directly* from Schmitt's writings! G.A. Walz, *Völkerrechtsordnung und Nationalsozialismus* (Munich: Zentralverlag der NSDAP, 1942). For an accessible English-language survey of competing *Raum* conceptions in Nazi international law by an American contemporary, see Charles Kruszewski, "Germany's *Lebensraum*," *American Political Science Review* 34 (1940): 964–75.

80. Schmitt, *Völkerrechtliche Grossraumordnung mit Interventionsverbot für raumfremde Mächte*, 64.

81. Schmitt, *Völkerrechtliche Grossraumordnung mit Interventionsverbot für raumfremde Mächte*, 55–66, where he criticizes universalistic models of minority protection in eastern Europe.

82. Schmitt, *Völkerrechtliche Grossraumordnung mit Interventionsverbot für raumfremde Mächte*, 77, 82–88.

83. Schmitt, "Die Formung des französischen Geistes durch die Legisten," where he comments that "one people [*Volk*] is especially musical, whereas another is technologically talented and educated," 2.

84. For example, he continues to subscribe to the idea that the Jews are an "alien" [*artfremd*] people possessing traits fundamentally distinct from those of the Germans.

85. Hofmann, *Legimität gegen Legalität: Der Weg der politischen Philosophie Carl Schmitts*, 220.

86. For examples of Schmitt's praise for Hitler's leadership during this period, see *Völkerrechtliche Grossraumordnung mit Interventionsverbot für raumfremde Mächte*, 87–88; also "Grossraum gegen Universalismus," 302, where Hitler is praised for trying to use the Monroe Doctrine against the Americans; and "Führung und Hegemonie," *Schmollers Jahrbuch für Gesetzgebung, Verwaltung und Volkswirtschaft im Deutschen Reich*, 63 (1939): 7–8, where Schmitt waxes enthusiastic about Hitler's leadership abilities.

87. Schmitt, *Völkerrechtliche Grossraumordnung mit Interventionsverbot für raumfremde Mächte*, 75–76, 82–83.

88. The economic and technological elements of the *Grossraum* theory are developed at many junctures: "Die Raumrevolution," 3; "Das Meer gegen das Land," 17–18; "Raum und Grossraum im Völkerrecht," 145–49; "Reich und Raum: Elemente eines neuen Völkerrrechts," 201–2. More generally on the demise of the modern nation-state, see "Staat als konkreter, an eine geschichtliche Epoche gebundenen Begriff" (1941), in Schmitt, *Verfassungsrechtliche Aufsätze aus den Jahren 1924–1954*, 375–85.

Clearly, this element of Schmitt's theory is hardly inherently fascistic. In a strikingly similar mode, contemporary analysts of "globalization" describe a "condensation of time and space" which is more than slightly reminiscent of what Schmitt described as the *Raumrevolution*. What *is*, obviously, troubling in Schmitt's theory is the beliefs that such trends are inconsistent with the rule of law and democratic government and that the "space revolution" justifies German political and economic domination of her neighbors. For a good survey of the ongoing debate on globalization, see Malcolm Waters, *Globalization* (New York: Routledge, 1995).

89. Linda Weiss persuasively argues that contemporary changes in the capitalist world economy suggest not a literal globalization of economic and political processes, but a regionalization ("The Myth of the Powerless State," *New Left Review* 225 [1997]: 3–27). In her view, we are witnessing the development of regional political and economic blocs (the EU, NAFTA, APEAC) in Europe, the Americas, and Asia, in which economic integration is deepened within distinct regions, but not necessarily across and between such regions. Within each region, Weiss argues, a single, dominant "catalytic" state plays a crucial role in deepening regional economic and political ties. To the extent that this interpretation is accurate, it is difficult to avoid acknowledging the *diagnostic* foresight of some elements of Schmitt's

Grossraum theory. As the prominent international lawyer Antonio Cassese has noted, trends toward political and economic regionalization pose difficulties for the liberal ideal of a truly *international* legal order (*International Law in a Divided World*, 411). Schmitt's theory clearly illuminates some of these dangers. Interesting in this context is also Samuel P. Huntington's best-selling *The Clash of Civilizations and the Remaking of World Order* (New York: Simon and Schuster, 1996). Huntington occasionally echoes Schmitt, notwithstanding the fact that he is a liberal democrat whose political preferences are obviously different from Schmitt's. For Huntington, as for Schmitt, the trend toward regionalization is irreversible. For both authors, each "greater region" (in Huntington's terminology, "civilization") rests on a political, economic, and cultural identity distinct from its competitors, and each "greater region" is likely to consist of a leading state and set of peripheral "concentric" states. Huntington not only shares Schmitt's skepticism about the prospects of international legal devices for the regulation of conflicts between distinct civilizations, but also similarly argues that liberal universalism is self-righteous and potentially disruptive within the international arena (for example, see 310). Reminiscent of Schmitt's call for the Americans to return to the nonimperialistic (read: nonuniversalistic) phase of the Monroe Doctrine, Huntington similarly wants the West (most importantly, the United States and Western Europe) to abandon its (Enlightenment) universalistic aspirations. Just as authoritarian Asian states have recently emphasized the virtues of indigenous "Asian values" in order to delegitimize international legal devices, so, too, should the "West" emphasize its own distinct, particular "values." Like Schmitt, Huntington is quite vague when describing how conflicts between civilizations are to be resolved; it is probably no accident that he concludes with a call for the West to maintain its military superiority (312). I am grateful to Nathan McCune of the University of Toronto for bringing the similarities between Schmitt and Huntington to my attention.

90. Schmitt, "Die Raumrevolution" 3; as well as the reference to the "chaos" of British liberal universalism in "Raum und Grossraum im Völkerrecht," 169.

91. In particular, see "Schmitt, "Grossraum gegen Universalismus," 295–302, and "Raum und Grossraum im Völkerrecht," 176.

92. This strategy is seen most clearly in Schmitt, "Beschleuniger wider Willen oder: Problematik der westlichen Hemisphäre," 3, and "Die letzte globale Linie," 347. In particular, the latter essay, probably written during the second half of 1943, underlines the depth of Schmitt's commitment to the National Socialist cause. Even at this late juncture in World War II, he accuses the United States of engaging in imperialism in Africa, the Near East, and Asia (348). German and Japanese military involvement in these parts of the world, it seems, was merely defensive in character. In light of this essay, it seems to me that Reinhard Mehring is wrong when he claims that Schmitt's writings correspond to Nazi foreign policy until 1942. I see no reason for excluding the likelihood that Schmitt's views coalesced with those of the Nazis until the end of World War II. See Reinhard Mehring, *Pathetisches Denken: Carl Schmitts Denkweg am Leitfaden Hegels: Katholische Grundstellung und antimarxistische Hegelstrategie* (Berlin: Duncker and Humblot, 1989), 165.

93. For a reliable discussion of how Schmitt's Nazi theory builds directly on his analysis of American imperialism, see Peter Schneider, *Ausnahmezustand und Norm: Eine Studie zur Rechtslehre von Carl Schmitt*, 224–26.

94. Otto Kirchheimer, "The Legal Order of National Socialism," 100.

95. Developing these arguments, and many others, in opposition to Schmitt's reinterpretation of the Monroe Doctrine is the important achievement of Gruchmann's *Nationalsozialistische Grossraumordnung. Die Konstruktion einer deutschen "Monroe-Doktrin."*

96. Arendt, *The Origins of Totalitarianism* (San Diego: Harcourt Brace Jovanovich, 1979), 158.

97. This rhetorical gem can be found in Morgenthau, *Politics Among Nations*, 44.

98. Burgess was an influential professor at Columbia University and founder of the *Political Science Quarterly*. See the excellent discussion by Hans-Ulrich Wehler, *Der Aufstieg des amerikanischen Imperialismus: Studien zur Entwicklung des Imperium Americanum 1865–1900* (Göttingen: Vandenhoeck and Ruprecht, 1974), 57.

99. John Burgess, cited in John G. Gunnell, *The Descent of Political Theory: The Genealogy of an American Vocation* (Chicago: University of Chicago Press, 1993), 49–50. Of course, the fact that Burgess sees imperialism as temporary distinguishes his views significantly from Schmitt's. At the same time, Burgess offers more than a restatement of John Stuart Mill's well-known defense of liberal colonialism. By the end of the century, race thinking came to play a central role in colonial and imperial thinking to an extent that was not the case in Mill's theory.

100. Seyla Benhabib, *The Reluctant Modernism of Hannah Arendt* (Thousand Oaks, Calif.: Sage Publications, 1996), 64.

EPILOGUE TO PART ONE: CARL SCHMITT IN THE AFTERMATH OF THE GERMAN CATASTROPHE

1. Schmitt, *Glossarium: Aufzeichnungen der Jahre 1947–51*, 18, 81, 154, 241, 255, 264.

2. Schmitt, *Glossarium: Aufzeichnungen der Jahre 1947–51*, 54, 117, 120–22, 186, 250, 264.

3. Raphael Gross, "Carl Schmitts 'Nomos' und die Juden."

4. Schmitt's, *Die Lage der europäischen Rechtswissenschaft* [*The Situation of European Jurisprudence*] recounts the story of the deformalization of law (described here as the "motorization" of the legislator), resulting chiefly from the "steering of the economy by the state" (20). As previously discussed, this diagnosis played an important role in his theory of the total state and his Nazi-era writings from the 1930s. Schmitt now alludes to common European legal traditions as a possible source of a postliberal form of legal determinacy. Yet it is unclear exactly what common traditions Schmitt has in mind.

5. Schmitt, "Das Problem der Legalität" (1950), in Schmitt, *Verfassungsrechtliche Aufsätze aus den Jahren 1924–1954*, 440–51.

314   *Notes: Epilogue to Part One*

6. In a letter of July 7, 1976 to the political theorist Ingeborg Maus, Schmitt continued to deny any responsibility for the rise of National Socialism: *"Ich habe Hitler nicht ermächtigt . . . und ich* [habe] *vor und nach* 1933 *seine Legitimierung und sogar Legalisierung von Weimar her in Frage gestellt."* ("I never empowered Hitler. . . . And both before and after 1933 I disputed his legitimacy and even legality from the perspective of Weimar.") I am grateful to Professor Maus for providing me with a copy of this letter.

7. This response was common among Germans after the war. See Josef Foschepath, "German Reaction to Defeat and Occupation," *West Germany Under Construction: Politics, Society & Culture in the Adenauer Era*, ed. Robert G. Moeller (Ann Arbor, Mich.: University of Michigan Press, 1997), 73–92.

8. Claus-Dietrich Wieland, "Carl Schmitt in Nürnberg" (1947), *1999: Zeitschrift für Sozialgeschichte des 20. und 21. Jahrhunderts* 2, no. 1 (1987): 96–122; Dirk van Laak, *Gespräche in der Sicherheit des Schweigens. Carl Schmitt in der politischen Geistesgeschichte der frühen Bundesrepublik*, 31–36. On the American prosecution of Nazi jurists, see Klaus Bästlein, "Der Nürnberger Juristenprozess und seine Rezeption in Deutschland," in *Das Nürnberger Juristen-Urteil von 1947*, ed. Lore Maria Peschel-Gutzeit (Baden-Baden: Nomos, 1996), 9–36.

9. "Interrogation of Carl Schmitt by Robert Kempner, I–II," *Telos* 72 (1987), especially 111, 115.

10. Schmitt, *Ex Captivitate Salus: Erfahrungen der Zeit 1945/47* (Cologne: Greven Verlag, 1950), 21–22.

11. Schmitt, *Ex Captivitate Salus: Erfahrungen der Zeit 1945/47*, 75.

12. Herman Melville, *Billy Budd, Sailor and Other Stories*, ed. Harold Beaver (New York: Penguin, 1970), 221. Schmitt is hardly the only political theorist to grasp the significance of Melville's "Benito Cereno." See John Schaar, "The Uses of Literature for the Study of Politics: The Case of Melville's 'Benito Cereno,' " in his *Legitimacy and the Modern State* (New Brunswick, N.J.: Transaction Books, 1981), 53–88.

13. See the editor's annotations in Melville, *Billy Budd, Sailor and Other Stories*, 449.

14. Melville, *Billy Budd, Sailor and Other Stories*, 290.

15. Schmitt, *Glossarium: Aufzeichnungen der Jahre 1947–51*, 18. Schmitt accuses the Jews of committing terror (!) against him (81); see also his nasty comments about those who fled Nazi Germany (252). Those who interrogated Schmitt (Kempner and Otto Flechtheimer) were of German-Jewish background.

16. Schmitt, *Glossarium: Aufzeichnungen der Jahre 1947–51*, 264.

17. See the recently published Carl Schmitt, *Das internationale Verbrechen des Angriffskriegs und der Grundsatz "nullum crimen nulla poena sin lege,"* ed. Helmut Quaritsch (Berlin: Duncker and Humblot, 1994). Written in the summer of 1945, this book was commissioned by a prominent German industrialist, Friedrich Flick, who sought to avoid prosecution by the Allies. The manuscript serves this function well. Schmitt now does concede that crimes were committed by the Nazi leadership. The purpose of this concession, however, is merely to limit Allied prosecution

to a tiny clique of political leaders; Schmitt's concern here is clearly with *minimizing* the scope of Allied denazification as much as possible. By no means should denazification extend to "ordinary business people." (Flick, by the way, was anything but that; he was one of Germany's leading industrialists before and after the German defeat in 1945.) Moreover, Schmitt argues against the view that the Germans had acted in opposition to international law in 1939 by invading Poland, insisting that wars of aggression were by no means universally condemned at the outbreak of World War II. Schmitt's attempt to place sole responsibility for Nazi crimes in the hands of a tiny group of the Nazi elite was typical among Germans after the war: a very small group of criminals (Hitler, Josef Goebbels) was made responsible for the evils of Nazism, whereas the vast majority of Germans were depicted as innocents who had been mesmerized by a band of devils. Of course, this interpretation was opportune, especially in light of the fact that most members of the tiny band of evildoers held responsible for the war were dead by war's end anyhow (Hitler, Rudolf Hess, Roland Freisler, and others). Given that this text was published only after Schmitt's death and that Schmitt's *published* writings from this period are unrepentant, I am not sure how much one is to make of his admission that some crimes were committed by the Nazis.

18. Schmitt, "Nationalsozialismus und Rechtsstaat," 714.

19. Schmitt, "Dreihundert Jahre Leviathan," *Universitas: Zeitschrift für Wissenschaft, Kunst und Literatur* 7 (1950): 180.

20. Schmitt, *Glossarium: Aufzeichnungen der Jahre 1947–51*, 146, 278; Schmitt, *Die Lage der europäischen Rechtswissenschaft*, 30.

21. Schmitt recalls the etymological origins of the concept of amnesty: "Amnesty means forgetting," and only by means of forgetting the purported crimes of Nazism can Germany allegedly put an end to the "civil war" of which denazification constitutes the latest stage of "continued injustice" ("Amnestie—Urform des Rechts," *Christ und Welt* 2, no. 45 [1949]: 1–2).

22. Schmitt, "Der Führer schützt das Recht," *Positionen und Begriffe im Kampf mit Weimar-Genf-Versailles.*

23. van Laak, *Gespräche in der Sicherheit des Schweigens. Carl Schmitt in der politischen Geistesgeschichte der frühen Bundesrepublik*; William E. Scheuerman, "Unsolved Paradoxes: Conservative Political Thought in Adenauer's Germany," in *Against Mass Technology and Mass Democracy: Essays in Twentieth Century German Political Thought*, ed. John P. McCormick (Durham, N.C.: Duke University Press, 1999). Schmitt's direct influence on the authors of the Basic Law was limited. See Ulrich K. Preuß, "Vater der Verfassungsväter?: Carl Schmitts Verfassungslehre und die verfassungspolitische Diskussion der Gegenwart," in *Politischen Denken Jahrbuch 1993*, ed. V. Gerhardt, H. Ottmann, M. Thompson (Stuttgart: J.B. Metzler, 1993), 117–34. Also: Bernhard Schlink, "Why Carl Schmitt?" *Constellations* 2, no. 3 (1996): 429–41. Yet his subsequent influence on jurisprudence in the Federal Republic has been significant (Maus, *Bürgerliche Rechtstheorie und Faschismus: Zur sozialen Funktion und aktuellen Wirkung der Theorie Carl Schmitts*).

24. John Ely, "The *Frankfurter Allgemeine Zeitung* and Contemporary National

Conservatism," *German Politics and Society* 13, no. 2 (1995): 81–121, for a discussion of Schmittian discourse in Germany's premier conservative newspaper.

7. CARL SCHMITT AND THE ORIGINS OF JOSEPH SCHUMPETER'S THEORY OF DEMOCRATIC ELITISM

1. There is a vast literature on Schumpeter's influence on postwar political analysis and, in particular, neoconservative social and political thought in the United States. See Peter Bachrach, *The Theory of Democratic Elitism: A Critique* (Boston: Little, Brown, 1967); David M. Ricci, "Democracy Attenuated: Schumpeter, the Process Theory, and American Democratic Thought," *Journal of Politics* 32, no. 2 (May 1970): 239–67; Nicholas Xenos, "Democracy as Method: Joseph A. Schumpeter," *Democracy* 9, no. 4 (October 1981): 110–23. Schumpeter has also played an important role in rational choice theory; I address this aspect of his work later.

2. Weber, *Economy and Society*, 657.

3. Weber, *Economy and Society*, 979. I should add that Weber himself ultimately accepted a modified version of this view, in accordance with what I have described earlier in this study as the *limited indeterminacy thesis*. Although skeptical of the extreme legal formalism endorsed by some modern legal thinkers, Weber sought to defend its underlying spirit.

4. I have also discussed this topic in my *Between the Norm and the Exception: The Frankfurt School and the Rule of Law*, 13–38, 67–96. For an approach less critical of Schmitt, see G.L. Ulmen, "The Sociology of the State: Carl Schmitt and Max Weber."

5. Schmitt, *Legalität und Legitimität*, 94.

6. This is a heated issue in the Weber literature. For a start, see Wolfgang Mommsen, *Max Weber and German Politics, 1890–1920*, trans. Michael S. Sternberg (Chicago: University of Chicago Press, 1984), esp. 381–89, where Mommsen discusses Weber's influence on Schmitt.

7. In this view, the true entrepreneur represents a "leading personality" [*Führerpersönlichkeit*]. Joseph Schumpeter, "Sozialistische Möglichkeiten von heute" ["Socialist Possibilities for Today"], *Archiv für Sozialwissenschaft und Sozialpolitik* 48 (1920–21): 318.

8. Max Weber, *The Protestant Ethic and the Spirit of Capitalism*, trans. Talcott Parsons (New York: Routledge, 1992), 18–19.

9. Weber, *The Protestant Ethic and the Spirit of Capitalism*, 181.

10. Weber, *The Protestant Ethic and the Spirit of Capitalism*, 181.

11. Weber, *The Protestant Ethic and the Spirit of Capitalism*, 20–21.

12. Weber, "Socialism," in *Max Weber: Selections in Translation*, ed. W. G. Runciman, trans. E. Matthews (Cambridge: Cambridge University Press, 1992), 252. For a helpful discussion of Weber's views of socialism, see Wolfgang Mommsen, *The Political and Social Theory of Max Weber: Collected Essays* (Chicago: University of Chicago Press, 1989), 53–73.

13. Joseph Schumpeter, *The Theory of Economic Development* (Cambridge,

Mass.: Harvard University Press, 1934), 57 n. 1. More generally, on the intellectual relationship between Weber and Schumpeter, see Jürgen Osterhammel, "Varieties of Social Economics: Joseph A. Schumpeter and Max Weber," in *Max Weber and His Contemporaries*, ed. Wolfgang Mommsen and Jürgen Osterhammel (London: Allen and Unwin, 1987), 106–26; Richard Swedberg, "Introduction," in Joseph A. Schumpeter, *The Economics and Sociology of Capitalism*, ed. R. Swedberg (Princeton, N.J.: Princeton University Press, 1991), 45–46; the Weber-Schumpeter nexus is thematized in many passages of Richard Swedberg, *Schumpeter: A Biography* (Princeton: Princeton University Press, 1991). Schumpeter himself wrote an interesting eulogy for Weber, "Max Weber's Work," in 1920. It has been reprinted in Schumpeter, *The Economics and Sociology of Capitalism*, 220–29.

14. Schumpeter, *Capitalism, Socialism and Democracy*, 3rd ed. (New York: Harper and Brothers, 1950), 125. Rationalization does, however, come up against anthropological impediments; the vast majority of humanity in this view is incapable of fully embracing rational habits (Schumpeter, *Capitalism, Socialism, and Democracy*, 129, 144–45). As will become evident, this point is crucial for Schumpeter's critical view of modern political and social democratization.

15. The basically pacific nature of capitalism is a main theme of Schumpeter's "The Sociology of Imperialism," also reprinted in Schumpeter, *Economics and Sociology of Capitalism*, 141–219.

16. Schumpeter, *Capitalism, Socialism, and Democracy*, 127.

17. This is one of Schumpeter's favorite themes; it is repeated in many of his writings. See *Capitalism, Socialism, and Democracy*, 131–64; also "Can Capitalism Survive?," "An Economic Interpretation of Our Times: The Lowell Lectures," and "The Future of Private Enterprise in the Face of Modern Socialistic Tendencies," reprinted in Schumpeter, *Economics and Sociology of Capitalism*, 339–405.

18. This element of Schumpeter's work was one of the reasons why it gained so much attention during the 1940s, when socialism—in one form or another—indeed seemed to constitute for many the likely outcome of developmental trends within Western civilization. Not surprisingly, Schumpeter's belief in the inevitability of socialism has been extensively criticized in recent years. See Arnold Heertje, ed., *Schumpeter's Vision: Capitalism, Socialism and Democracy After Forty Years* (New York: Praeger, 1981); and *Capitalism and Democracy: Schumpeter Revisited*, eds. Richard D. Coe and Charles K. Wilbur (Notre Dame: University of Notre Dame Press, 1985).

19. Schumpeter, *Capitalism, Socialism, and Democracy*, 172–73.

20. Schumpeter, *Capitalism, Socialism, and Democracy*, 219.

21. For Weber, charisma refers "to a certain quality of an individual personality by virtue of which he is considered extraordinary and treated as endowed with supernatural, superhuman, or at least specifically exceptional powers or qualities . . . [O]n the basis of them the individual concerned is treated as a 'leader' " (Weber, *Economy and Society*, 241). This description could easily fit Schumpeter's entrepreneur. See Edward A. Carlin, "Schumpeter's Constructed Type—The Entrepreneur," *Kyklos* 9 (1956): 27–43. Swedberg similarly notes, "that there exist some

similarities between Schumpeter's heroic entrepreneur and Weber's charismatic leader is obvious" (*Schumpeter: A Biography*, 35). It is revealing that Schumpeter is dismissive of Weber's "protestant ethic thesis," and by implication Weber's emphasis on the religiously inspired "ascetic" rationalism of the early modern capitalist entrepreneur (Schumpeter, *Business Cycles: A Theoretical, Historical, and Statistical Analysis of the Capitalist Process* [New York: McGraw-Hill, 1939], 228).

22. Schumpeter, *Theory of Economic Development*, 93. Also see *Capitalism, Socialism, and Democracy*, especially 132–33, where Schumpeter's description of the entrepreneur emphasizes his "individual decision and driving power." Schumpeter is *not* arguing that capitalist ownership necessitates the exhibition of entrepreneurial skills. Entrepreneurship refers to a series of special traits, which some property owners obviously do not possess. Of course, "everybody knows the type of old respectable firm, growing obsolete . . . and slowly and inevitably sinking into limbo" despite its entrepreneurial roots ("Social Classes in an Ethnically Homogeneous Environment," in Schumpeter, *Economics and Sociology of Capitalism*, 243). Nonetheless, there is a special relationship in this account between capitalism and entrepreneurship: a capitalist economy allows those with entrepreneurial skills to become proprietors.

23. In his final years, Schumpeter hoped that economics would correct this failing by focusing proper attention on the entrepreneur ("Comments on a Plan for the Study of Entrepreneurship," in Schumpeter, *Economics and Sociology of Capitalism*, 406–28). It is hard to avoid the conclusion that Schumpeter's argument here rests on a truncated conception of rationality. His main point is that the entrepreneur cannot be conceived as engaging in predictable forms of technical rationality; for this reason, the entrepreneur is "irrational." Clearly, a richer conceptualization of the nature of rationality might have allowed Schumpeter to avoid this conclusion. Of course, creativity and unpredictability hardly entail a *lack of* rationality, as Schumpeter might be interpreted as arguing.

24. Nathan Rosenberg, "Joseph Schumpeter: Radical Economist," in *Schumpeter in the History of Ideas*, ed. Yuichi Shionoyo and Mark Perlman (Ann Arbor, Mich.: University of Michigan Press, 1994), 48. For textual support for this interpretation, see Schumpeter, *Theory of Economic Development*, 79–83. This element of Schumpeter's thought is ignored by those, like Anthony Downs and Gary Becker, who have enlisted Schumpeter into the ranks of "rational choice" political analysis. In some ways, Schumpeter *does* argue for an economic analysis of politics in which political action is explained by means of formal models of rationality borrowed from economic theory. But those who focus on this facet of Schumpeter's work conveniently ignore the fact, first, that he repeatedly emphasized the significant *failings* of approaches that *universalize* the experience of the "rational economic man," and second, that he was doubtful of the scope of rational action *especially* in the political realm. Formal modeling has obvious appeals for those of us engaged in political science. The problem, however, is first, whether formal models are capable of grappling with novel and innovative forms of action, and second, whether formal models based on the "rational economic man" are appropriate for spheres of activ-

ity fundamentally dissimilar from the market. See the acknowledgments of Schumpeter's influence in Gary Becker, "Competition and Democracy," *Journal of Law and Economics* 1 (1958): 106; and Anthony Downs, *An Economic Theory of Democracy* (New York: Harper Brothers, 1957), 29. More generally on Schumpeter's relationship to rational choice, see William C. Mitchell, "Schumpeter and Public Choice, Part I: Precursor to Public Choice?" *Public Choice* 42, no. 1 (1984): 73–88; Mitchell, "Schumpeter and Public Choice, Part II: Democracy and the Demise of Capitalism: The Missing Chapter in Schumpeter," *Public Choice* 42, no. 2 (1984): 161–84; Manfred Prisching, "Schumpeter's Irrational Choice Theory," *Critical Review* 9, no. 3 (Summer 1995): 301–24. Emily Hauptmann has argued in support of the proposition that modern rational choice analysis reproduces the profound hostility to democratic politics found in Schumpeter's political theory (*Putting Choice Before Democracy: A Critique of Rational Choice Theory* [Albany: SUNY Press, 1996], especially 9–13).

25. Schumpeter's reworking of Weber's theory does generate one problem missing from Weber's original account: why is capitalist civilization so "rationalistic" if its most important figure, the creative entrepreneur, is anything but the embodiment of ascetic rationalism described by Weber? In my reading of Schumpeter, he provides no adequate answer to this question. At times, a eulogy for the charismatic entrepreneur exists uneasily along with an equally respectful eulogy for the rationalism of classical capitalist civilization.

26. Schumpeter, "Social Classes in an Ethnically Homogenous Environment," *Economics and Sociology of Capitalism*, 246.

27. Schumpeter, "Sozialistische Möglichkeiten von heute," 318.

28. Schumpeter typically argues for the inevitability of socialism, before proclaiming that entrepreneurship has yet to be fully obliterated and that socialism may still take a substantial period of time before emerging. Thus, many of his specific comments on the details of economic policy lead him to embrace views that we would describe today as "free market." See, for example, "An Economic Interpretation of Our Times: The Lowell Lectures," reprinted in Schumpeter, *Economics and Sociology of Capitalism*, 363–72, where he rails against the anticapitalist implications of progressive taxation. His sympathetic review of Hayek's *The Road to Serfdom* is also telling in this respect: see Schumpeter, "Review of Hayek, *The Road to Serfdom*," *Journal of Political Economy* 54 (1946): 269–70.

29. As will become clear in the discussion of his democratic theory, this aspiration is hardly altogether alien to Schumpeter, either.

30. Schumpeter, *Theory of Economic Development*, 82.

31. Schumpeter, *Theory of Economic Development*, 93.

32. Schumpeter, *Theory of Economic Development*, 89.

33. Schumpeter, *Capitalism, Socialism, and Democracy*, 168, 300–1.

34. Cited in Swedberg, "Introduction" to Schumpeter, *Economics and Sociology of Capitalism*, 16.

35. Swedberg, "Introduction," 14.

36. Schumpeter, "Sozialistische Möglichkeiten von heute," 318. The implica-

320   *Notes: Chapter 7*

tions of this argument for the details of socialization proposals under discussion in postwar Germany and Austria are then outlined on 351–60.

37. For example, in Schumpeter's contributions to the Socialization Commission, "his criterion for the public enterprise, in the manner of private enterprise, was efficiency, with provisions for incentives for management and workers" (Robert Loring Allen, *Opening Doors: The Life and Work of Joseph Schumpeter*, vol. I [New Brunswick, N.J.: Transaction Books, 1991], 163–64.

38. Schumpeter, "Sozialistische Möglichkeiten von heute," 328.

39. Schumpeter, "Sozialistische Möglichkeiten von heute," 327–30.

40. Schumpeter, "Sozialistische Möglichkeiten von heute," 330.

41. Schumpeter, "Sozialistische Möglichkeiten von heute," 328.

42. Schumpeter, "Sozialistische Möglichkeiten von heute," 327.

43. Schumpeter, "Sozialistische Möglichkeiten von heute," 325.

44. Schumpeter, "Sozialistische Möglichkeiten von heute," 327.

45. Schumpeter, "Sozialistische Möglichkeiten von heute," 331.

46. Schumpeter, "Sozialistische Möglichkeiten von heute," 308.

47. Schumpeter, "Sozialistische Möglichkeiten von heute," 326–28.

48. Carl Landauer, "Sozialismus und parlamentarisches System: Betrachtungen zu Schumpeters Aufsatz 'Sozialistische Möglichkeiten von heute,' " *Archiv für Sozialwissenschaft und Sozialpolitik* 48 (1922): 748–60. Landauer offers a detailed summary of Schumpeter's main theses, as well as a critical response to Schumpeter's claim that political and social democratization inevitably must cripple parliamentarism.

49. This is one reason why interpretations of Schumpeter's democratic theory as essentially Weberian, in my view, are too simple. For one example of this genre, see David Held, *Models of Democracy* (Stanford, Calif.: Stanford University Press, 1987), 143–85. Schumpeter is indebted to Weber in many ways, but Schumpeter's hostility to classical liberal parliamentarism is far more profound than Weber's. Weber was anxious about the future of liberal parliamentarism and sought, as mentioned earlier, to supplement it with plebiscitary leadership; nonetheless, he fought to preserve core elements of liberal parliamentarism, and in many ways he clearly saw English parliamentary life as a model for political reconstruction in Germany after World War I. Weber was famously disgusted by the political involvement of the irresponsible "literati." In light of this fact, I find it difficult to fathom Weber endorsing Sorel's attack on popular rule with the same enthusiasm as Schumpeter.

50. M. J. Bonn, *Die Auflösung des modernen Staates* (Berlin: Verlag für Politik und Wirtschaft, 1921); and M.J. Bonn, *Die Krise der europäischen Demokratie* (Tübingen: Mohr, 1925), translated as *The Crisis of European Democracy* (New Haven, Conn.: Yale University Press, 1925).

51. See Herbert von Beckerath, "Joseph Schumpeter as a Sociologist" (1950), in *J.A. Schumpeter: Critical Assessments*, ed. John Cunningham Wood (New York: Routledge, 1991).

52. Allen, *Opening Doors: The Life and Work of Joseph Schumpeter*, vol. 1, 203; Erwin von Beckerath, *Wesen und Werden des faschistischen Staates* (Berlin: Springer, 1927).

53. Schmitt makes reference to Bonn in many of his works, and Bonn corresponded with Schmitt on the issue of parliamentary decay. Bonn was also one of Schmitt's promoters in the German university system, helping him gain positions at Munich, Bonn, and then at the University of Berlin in 1928. Some of Bonn's correspondence with Schmitt is cited in Ellen Kennedy, "Introduction: Carl Schmitt's *Parlamentarismus* in Its Historical Context," xxxvi–xxxvii. I should note that I am indebted to Kennedy's introduction for bringing the importance of Schumpeter's 1920 essay to my attention. Unfortunately, her discussion of it there is problematic, particularly in light of her utterly misconceived reading of Schumpeter as a left-wing thinker who embraced Marxism (xxvi–xxvii and xlvi n. 50). Indeed, Schumpeter integrated Marxist ideas, *but only in order to criticize them* from the right.

M. J. Bonn was Jewish and was forced to leave Germany when the Nazis took power. His postwar reminiscences about Schmitt, whom he described as his "most brilliant colleague," at Bonn, make fascinating reading for those interested in Schmitt's biography (M. J. Bonn, *The Wandering Scholar* [New York: John Day, 1948], 330–31).

54. Carl Schmitt, "Wesen und Werden des faschistischen Staates" (1929), reprinted in Schmitt, *Positionen und Begriffe im Kampf mit Weimar-Genf-Versailles*, 109–15.

55. In a letter from Schumpeter to Schmitt dated March 16, 1926, Schumpeter extends his best wishes to Schmitt and his new bride (against the wishes of the Catholic Church, Schmitt married his second wife on February 28, 1926). In a postcard of September 8, 1927, Schumpeter apologizes to Schmitt and his wife for not having been able to attend a social event to which Schumpeter had been invited. Both pieces of correspondence are on file at the Carl Schmitt Archives, Nordrhein-Westfälisches Hauptstaatarchiv, Düsseldorf. I am grateful to Professor Joseph Kaiser for providing access to this correspondence.

56. The letter, from February 19, 1948, appears in Carl Schmitt, *Glossarium: Aufzeichnungen der Jahre 1947–1951*, 101.

57. Carl Schmitt, "Der Begriff der modernen Demokratie in seinem Verhältnis zum Staatsbegriff" (1924); and "Zu Friedrich Meineckes 'Idee der Staatsräson,' " (1926), both reprinted in Schmitt, *Positionen und Begriffe im Kampf mit Weimar-Genf-Versailles*, 45–66. See also Schmitt, "Der Begriff des Politischen," *Archiv für Sozialwissenschaft und Sozialpolitik* 58 (1927): 1–33.

58. Based on the dates of the correspondence, Schumpeter must be referring to "The Concept of the Political," though the essay is never directly mentioned by name. Both letters are on file at the Carl Schmitt Archives, Düsseldorf.

59. Richard Thoma, "Zur Ideologie des Parlamentarismus und der Diktatur," *Archiv für Sozialwissenschaft und Sozialpolitik*, 53 (1925): 212–17.

60. Schmitt, "Der Begriff des Politischen," 32; Schmitt, "Völkerrechtliche Formen des modernen Imperialismus" (1932), 162; Schmitt, *Die Kernfrage des Völkerbundes*, 36.

61. Ernst Fraenkel, *The Dual State*, 201–2.

62. Schumpeter, "The Sociology of Imperialism," 143.

63. Schmitt's 1948 letter to Helmut Schelsky potentially provides some support for this interpretation: Schmitt notes that at the close of the 1927 version of "The Concept of the Political" the reader will find evidence of the influence [*Wirkung*] of Schumpeter's "last conversation" with Schmitt in "1926/27" (?) (Schmitt, *Glossarium: Aufzeichnungen der Jahre 1947–1951*, 101). Schmitt left Bonn for Berlin in 1928; Schumpeter went to Harvard in 1932.

64. In the introduction to the original 1923 edition of *The Crisis of Parliamentary Democracy*, Schmitt cites those who have influenced his account, including the works of his friend M. J. Bonn (92 n. 4). Among the first references is one to Carl Landauer's article on Schumpeter, in which the author both summarizes Schumpeter's diagnosis of the "crisis of parliamentarism" and offers a critical response to it. Most striking about the literature cited by Schmitt here is that it tends to emphasize the problems posed for parliamentary democracy by social and economic developments.

65. Schmitt, *The Crisis of Parliamentary Democracy*, 66.

66. Schmitt, *Positionen und Begriffe im Kampf mit Weimar-Genf-Versailles*, 313.

67. Indeed, the scholarly paraphernalia of this section of Schumpeter's study is extremely scarce; Schumpeter seems most indebted to Gustav Le Bon, Graham Wallas, and, most importantly, Vilfredo Pareto. Part of this stems from the author's attempt to offer an accessible, "popular" work. Part of it, however, also derives from the fact that some of the inspirations for his ideas would have shocked an American audience.

68. Schumpeter, *Capitalism, Socialism, and Democracy*, 241–45. Schumpeter adds that "the United States excludes Orientals and Germany excludes Jews from citizenship; in the southern part of the United States Negroes are also often deprived of the vote" (244). In the context of his argument here, this *might* be taken as suggesting that Nazi Germany rests on some "democratic" elements. Like Schmitt, Schumpeter robs the concept of democratic equality of any commitment to universal civil and political rights.

69. For Schumpeter, "a large element of democracy" entered into "autocracies, both *dei gratia* and dictatorial, of the various monarchies of a non-autocratic type." Schumpeter, *Capitalism, Socialism, and Democracy*, 246.

70. Schumpeter, *Capitalism, Socialism, and Democracy*, 256–64.

71. Schumpeter, *Capitalism, Socialism, and Democracy*, 247–49, 264–68. See also: Joseph A, Schumpeter, "Vilfredo Pareto," in his *Ten Great Economists: From Marx to Keynes* (New York: Oxford University Press, 1951), 139.

72. Schumpeter, *Capitalism, Socialism, and Democracy*, 263. Schmitt, of course, was also fascinated by the possibilities for modern mass propaganda that modern technology provided.

73. Schumpeter, *Capitalism, Socialism, and Democracy*, 251.

74. Weber famously sought to moderate his own decisionism by means of the "ethic of responsibility."

75. Schumpeter, *Capitalism, Socialism, and Democracy*, 282. Schumpeter's 1942

study also represents an attempt to resolve some of the problems raised by his 1920 essay. One of the main theses of *Capitalism, Socialism, and Democracy* is that democracy—either in capitalism or socialism—is still possible, *if* we abandon the ambitious legacy of rationalistic liberalism and embrace his "democratic method" as an alternative. in *Capitalism, Socialism, and Democracy*, Schumpeter is struggling with the question of what form of popular rule is still possible *given* the basic irrationality of most people and the inevitability of the "match towards socialism." His "theory of democratic elitism" represents his answer to this question: "socialism and democracy may be compatible *provided the latter be defined as it has been*" in the chapter on democratic elitism [Schumpeter's own emphasis] (*Capitalism, Socialism, and Democracy*, 411).

    76. Schumpeter, *Capitalism, Socialism, and Democracy*, 269.

    77. Schumpeter, *Capitalism, Socialism, and Democracy*, 270.

    78. Schmitt, *Legalität und Legitimität*, 93.

    79. Schumpeter, *Capitalism, Socialism, and Democracy*, 284–85 [emphasis added].

    80. What Schmitt says about this topic, even during the 1920s, is not particularly encouraging. See, for example, his attack on the (purportedly) privatistic and antipolitical liberal institution of secret, individual voting (*Die Verfassungslehre*, 243–46).

    81. Kirchheimer, "Constitutional Reaction in 1932," 78.

    82. Schumpeter, *Capitalism, Socialism, and Democracy*, 285.

    83. Schumpeter explicitly excludes only military coups, as well as "the acquisition of political leadership by the people's tacit acceptance of it or by the election *quasi per inspirationem*." He quickly expresses reservations about the latter two exclusions, however, concluding that the first is still common in mass political parties dominated by the boss, whereas the second concerns a mere electoral "technicality" (!). Such qualifications potentially bring him closer to Schmitt's rather vague model of a plebiscitary election than might at first appear to be the case (*Capitalism, Socialism, and Democracy*, 271).

    84. Schumpeter, *Capitalism, Socialism, and Democracy*, 271–2. Unfortunately, Schumpeter is vague here on the issue of *how much* individual freedom is implied by his "democratic method."

    85. Schumpeter, *Capitalism, Socialism, and Democracy*, 296.

    86. Swedberg, *Schumpeter: A Biography*, 15, 192–93. This admiration is expressed loud and clear in Schumpeter's essay, "Vilfredo Pareto," in *Ten Great Economists: From Marx to Keynes*, 110–42.

    87. Allen, *The Life and Work of Joseph Schumpeter*, vol. 1, 208. Tom Bottomore has convincingly shown that Pareto influenced Schumpeter's analysis of social classes and many other elements of his thinking (*Between Marginalism and Marxism: The Economic Sociology of J.A. Schumpeter* [New York: St. Martin's Press, 1992], 53, 76, 107, 111).

    88. Schumpeter, "Vilfredo Pareto," in *Ten Great Economists: From Marx to Keynes*, 137–38.

89. Vilfredo Pareto, *Sociological Writings*, ed. S. E. Finer, trans. Derick Mirfin (New York: Praeger, 1966), 274. Significantly, Schmitt was probably familiar with some of Pareto's writings, though his writings provide no evidence that he systematically engaged with Pareto's ideas until *after* World War II. (See the bitter entries from his diary from July 22–23, 1948: Schmitt, *Glossarium: Aufzeichnungen der Jahre 1947–1951*, 180–82.)

Pareto's gloss on elite circulation often takes on unambiguously ethnicist and even protoracist connotations (*Sociological Writings*, 133, 159). Although these themes play a relatively secondary role in Schumpeter's work, they are not altogether absent. In a 1927 essay, Schumpeter concedes that he was once influenced by "the racial theory of classes," and still believes that "racial differences" are significant for the analysis of class formation. Still, racial differences are "not the heart of the matter," and thus their analysis can be bracketed in any discussion of the class structure ("Social Classes in an Ethnically Homogeneous Environment," in *Economics and Sociology of Capitalism*, 230).

90. Schumpeter, *Capitalism, Socialism, and Democracy*, 289.

91. Substantial biographical evidence from the 1930s and 1940s suggests that Schumpeter was an iconoclastic political reactionary with a soft spot for elements of the authoritarian right. After Hitler's takeover, Schumpeter criticized the American press for its purportedly indiscriminate attacks on the new regime in Germany (Schumpeter was no refugee; he came to Harvard in 1932 primarily for career reasons); for Schumpeter, Franco's movement was "really the most national and democratic imaginable and means nothing else but the revolt of the very soul of Spain against barbarism and crime" (cited on 223), and he seems to have toyed with conservative Catholic models of corporatist planning. Not surprisingly, he despised Franklin Delano Roosevelt and the New Deal, speaking at one point of Roosevelt's ten-year "dictatorship" (cited on 148) (Swedberg, *Schumpeter: A Biography*, 147–51, 169–71, 222–23).

92. For a classic statement of these criticisms, see Carole Pateman, *Participation and Democratic Theory* (Cambridge: Cambridge University Press, 1970).

93. Schmitt surely would have dismissed Schumpeter's emphasis on elite *competition* as reliance on an economic category unsuitable to the core of authentic political experience. For Schmitt, such recourse to concepts of competition in politics represents a characteristically liberal quest to subordinate political experience to fundamentally economic modes of analysis. For Schmitt, Schumpeter's model surely does injustice to the political (Schmitt, *The Concept of the Political*, trans. George Schwab, 28).

94. Pareto, *Sociological Writings*, 320. Interestingly, Schumpeter downplays Pareto's fascist preferences (Schumpeter, "Vilfredo Pareto," 118).

95. On Pareto's relationship to fascism, see *Pareto and Mosca*, ed. James Meisel (Englewood Cliffs, N.J.: Prentice Hall, 1965).

96. Soviet-style state socialist regimes are probably the most obvious example of this.

97. Heller, "Bemerkungen zur Staats- und rechtstheoretischen Problematik der Gegenwart," *Archiv des öffentlichen Rechts* 55 (1929): 337–38.

98. Schumpeter, *Capitalism, Socialism, and Democracy,* 251.

99. Interestingly, "Schumpeter repeated over and over in his diary, 'Democracy is government by lying' " (Swedberg, *Schumpeter: A Biography,* 193).

8. THE UNHOLY ALLIANCE OF CARL SCHMITT AND FRIEDRICH A. HAYEK

1. For one noteworthy exception: Renato Cristi, "Hayek and Schmitt on the Rule of Law," *Canadian Journal of Political Science* 17, no. 3 (1984): 521–36. Cristi rightly argues that "[s]ome of Schmitt's basic assumptions have penetrated his [Hayek's] philosophy of liberty, effectively determining the content of his argumentation" (523).

2. See Heinrich Potthof, "Das Weimarer Verfassungswerk und die deutsche Linke," *Archiv für Sozialgeschichte* 12 (1972): 433–86.

3. Schmitt, *Unabhängigkeit der Richter, Gleichheit vor dem Gesetz und Gewährleistung des Privateigentums nach der Weimarer Verfassung,* 23.

4. Schmitt, *Unabhängigkeit der Richter,* 23. In the immediate aftermath of World War II, when the specter of socialization again momentarily loomed large in Germany, Schmitt again rolled out these criticisms of individual legal acts ("Rechtstaatlichen Verfassungsvollzug" [1952]), in Schmitt, *Verfassungsrechtliche Aufsätze,* 452–86.

5. Schmitt, *Unabhängigkeit der Richter,* 4, where Schmitt notes that the thesis of his study is that the proposed legal acts by the left "violate numerous positive determinations of the Weimar Constitution." Schmitt in this book is speaking as a jurist interpreting the Weimar Constitution, which he believes to contain a substantial liberal [*bürgerlich*] element.

6. It is important to recall that many classical defenders of the generality of the legal norm clearly suggested that it was compatible with substantial forms of legal *specialization* and *intervention* in socioeconomic affairs. Jean-Jacques Rousseau writes that "when I say that the object of law is always general, I mean that the law always considers subjects as a body and actions in the abstract, never a man as an individual or a particular action. Thus the law can very well enact that there will be privileges, but it cannot confer them on anyone by name. The law can create several classes of citizens, and even designate the qualities determining a right to these classes, but it cannot name the specific people to be admitted to them" (Rousseau, *On the Social Contract,* ed. Roger Masters [New York: St. Martin's Press, 1978], 66). Similarly, Hegel defended the idea of the generality of the legal norm, but he saw it as being consistent with extensive state intervention in the economy (Hegel, *Philosophy of Right,* para. 211). Even Locke, who is particularly influential for Schmitt's discussion of this theme in *The Crisis of Parliamentary Democracy,* is more ambiguous than Schmitt lets on. True, Locke warns his reader repeatedly of the dangers of "indeterminate resolutions" and "extempory, arbitrary decrees," but simply to *assume*—as Schmitt seems to—that Locke must have been thinking of forms of state action like those common in the modern welfare state suggests a

rather anachronistic reading of seventeenth-century English liberal thought. John Locke, *Two Treatises on Government*, ed. Peter Laslett (Cambridge: Cambridge University Press, 1967). Although Schmitt's delineation of general law from individual measures does reproduce some elements of classical modern jurisprudence, his formulation obscures why writers like Rousseau were concerned about legal generality in the first place: they wanted *like rules for like cases.* This is important: when stated in this manner, it *might* suggest the legitimacy of some *individual* legal acts when a democratic government is confronted with a genuinely peculiar or "individual" situation—when a large corporation or bank is on the verge of bankruptcy, for example. Of course, such acts have become relatively widespread in the era of the contemporary interventionist state. To conflate them with acts of "revolutionary violence" seems, at the very least, to trivialize the perils of revolutionary dictatorship. For a somewhat more satisfying account of the problems posed by traditional views of liberal general law, see Kent Greenawalt, *Law and Objectivity* (New York: Oxford University Press, 1992).

7. Schmitt, *Unabhängigkeit der Richter*, 22.

8. Schmitt, *Die Verfassungslehre*, 154. He then makes the rather obscure comment that "equality [before the law] is only possible where minimally a majority of cases can be affected" (155).

9. Ludwig Preller, *Sozialpolitik in der Weimarer Republik.*

10. Schmitt, *The Concept of the Political* (1932), 39–45, where Schmitt links his "concept of the political" to his critique of "pluralist" tendencies in the modern interventionist state.

11. This argument was intimated as early as 1930 in Schmitt, "Staatsethik und pluralistischer Staat" (1930).

12. Schmitt, *Der Hüter der Verfassung*, especially 63, where Schmitt refers to the view of democracy developed by Kelsen in *Vom Wesen und Wert der Demokratie.*

13. Schmitt, *Die Verfassungslehre*, 143–57. This criticism is especially disingenuous in light of Schmitt's own radical deconstruction of the idea of norm-based judicial and administrative action.

14. Schmitt, *Unabhängigkeit der Richter*, 23.

15. For a fine historical survey of this period, see Gotthard Jasper, *Die gescheiterte Zähmung: Wege zur Machtergreifung Hitlers 1930–1934.*

16. Gowan, "The Return of Carl Schmitt," *Debate: Review of Contemporary German Affairs* 2, no. 1 (1994): 120.

17. Schmitt, "Starker Staat und gesunde Wirtschaft: Ein Vortrag vor Wirtschaftsführen." In this crucial essay, Schmitt argues that much of the capitalist economy should be "self-administered," but he contrasts his use of this term with social democratic conceptions of worker self-management. For Schmitt, "economic leaders" [*Wirtschaftsführer*]—in other words, owners and managers—need to be given substantial autonomy in their industries and factories, and they need to be freed from *social-democratic* forms of regulation. The essay is a revealing one: first, it represents an early attempt to extend the infamous *Führerprinzip* into the economy; and second, it reproduces the view, widespread among propertied groups in Germany

in 1933, that the Nazis might succeed in guaranteeing German business far more autonomy than it had succeeded in maintaining in the Weimar period. For a helpful introduction to Schmitt's (often ignored) economic views, see Volker Neumann, *Der Staat im Bürgerkrieg: Kontinuität und Wandel des Staatsbegriffs in der politischen Theorie Carl Schmitts* (Frankfurt a.M.: Campus, 1980).

18. Schmitt is hardly the only author to claim that growing state intervention in the twentieth century has engendered increasingly discretionary forms of decision making. But even if it is true that there is at least *some* empirical support for Schmitt's claim, there is certainly no reason why it is an inevitable and irreversible facet of contemporary politics.

19. Schmitt, *Hüter der Verfassung*, 81.

20. Hayek was born in 1899 in Vienna. He completed degrees at the University of Vienna in law and political science, before becoming an intellectual accomplice of Ludwig Mises in the late 1920s. Hayek left the University of Vienna for a position at the London School of Economics in 1931, though he clearly stayed in close contact with intellectual and political developments on the continent well after leaving Vienna (Kurt R. Leube, "Friedrich August von Hayek: A Biographical Introduction," in *The Essence of Hayek*, ed. Chiaki Nishiyama and Kurt R. Leube (Stanford: Hoover Institution Press, Stanford University, 1984), xvii–xxxvi.

Schmitt was probably unfamiliar with much of Hayek's work, though a copy of his "Confusion of Language in Contemporary Political Thought" (1968) was found in Schmitt's library at his death. This essay has been reprinted in Hayek, *Economic Freedom* (Oxford: Basil Blackwell, 1991), 357–82. I have been unable to find evidence either of correspondence or of a personal meeting between Schmitt and Hayek.

21. Friedrich A. Hayek, *The Road to Serfdom* [1944] (Chicago: University of Chicago Press, 1976).

22. Hayek obviously knew of Schmitt's National Socialist proclivities in the 1930s. But he failed to grasp fully that even in the Weimar period, Schmitt's model of the rule of law was fundamentally oriented toward discrediting formalistic legal liberalism. Hayek seems to have been unfamiliar with many of those texts in which Schmitt explicitly deconstructs liberal jurisprudence (most importantly, Schmitt's early writings on legal indeterminacy). Because of this, he tends to take Schmitt's occasional dependence on an overstylized interpretation of the classical liberal rule of law at face value.

23. Hayek, *The Road to Serfdom*, 73.

24. Moreover, Hayek's implicit claim that the liberal legal order once primarily rested on such norms constitutes, at best, a sloppy contribution to legal history. Where did Hayek's pristine liberal legal universe exist? When did law ever chiefly consist of norms having the general form described by him here? Hayek is remarkably vague in answering these questions. The issue is further complicated by Hayek's nostalgia in his late writings for customary and traditional common law. Contrary to what Hayek occasionally seems to believe, it is rather dubious to claim that traditional law looked at all like the legal model—based on clear general

norms—otherwise endorsed in his theory. See Hayek, *Law, Legislation, and Liberty*, vol. 1 (Chicago: University of Chicago, 1973), especially 72–94. Hayek would do well to recall the criticisms made by many classical writers, most prominently by Bentham, of the "monstrous confusion" (Hegel) of traditional customary law. See H. L. Hart, *Essays on Bentham: Studies in Jurisprudence and Political Theory* (Oxford: Oxford University Press, 1982), especially pp. 21–39; and Gerald J. Postema, *Bentham and the Common Law Tradition* (Oxford: Oxford University Press, 1986).

25. Cited in Hayek, *Road to Serfdom*, 178.

26. Hayek, *Road to Serfdom*, 69. He also introduces (67) the peculiar concept of an "economic dictatorship," which may hearken back to Schmitt's account of an "economic-financial state of emergency" that, according to Schmitt's argument in *The Guardian of the Constitution*, justifies the extensive use of emergency powers by the Weimar Federal President in the realm of economic and social affairs.

27. Hayek, *Road to Serfdom*, 2.

28. Notwithstanding the undeniable importance of the concept of the rule of law to modern liberalism, it is surely peculiar to claim that the essence of liberalism "is a doctrine about what the law ought to be" (Hayek, *The Constitution of Liberty* [Chicago: University of Chicago Press, 1960], 103). Schmitt's view of liberalism is similarly idiosyncratic: liberalism is a "normativistic" ideology whose centerpiece is the rule of law—and the "normativism" of general law.

29. Hayek, *Constitution of Liberty*, 485 n. 1. The works cited here include *Die Verfassungslehre* and *Der Hüter der Verfassung*, and later *Die Unabhängigkeit der Richter* (487 n. 9). In a subsequent work, Hayek appreciatively cites Schmitt's statement that "there can be no 'equality before a measure' as there is equality before the law" (*Law, Legislation, and Liberty*, vol. 1, 139).

30. See also the definition provided in *Law, Legislation, and Liberty*, vol. 3 (Chicago: University of Chicago Press, 1979): "The basic conception of classical liberalism, which alone can make decent and impartial government possible, is that government must *regard* all people as equal, however unequal they may in fact be, and that in whatever manner the government restrains (or assists) the action of one, so it must, under the same abstract rules, restrain (or assist) the actions of all others. Nobody has special claims on government because he is rich or poor" (142–43).

31. As far as the latter qualification is concerned, Hayek writes that legal distinctions "will not be arbitrary, will not subject one group to the will of the others, if they are equally recognized as justified by those inside and outside the group [affected by them]" (*Constitution of Liberty*, 155). The first precondition is clearly rather minimal since legal action can still take an "individual" form even if no specific person or object is expressly named (e.g., "all citizens living in cities with a population over seven million will pay an extra tax that the federal government henceforth will describe as an NYC tax"). In order to criticize the second precondition, R. Hamowy has commented that "laws granting privileged status to select groups are commonly acquiesced in by larger majorities even when such laws run counter to their own ends" ("Law and Liberal Society: F. A. Hayek's *Constitution of Liberty*," *Journal of Libertarian Studies* 2 [Fall 1978]). In other words, the fact that a

particular legal category may be acceptable both to a substantial number of people who fall within and outside of it may not be able to provide the check on governmental arbitrariness which Hayek thinks that it can.

32. Hayek, *Constitution of Liberty*, 209.

33. Chandran Kukathas, *Hayek and Modern Liberalism* (Oxford: Oxford University Press, 1989), 148–64; R. Hamowy, "Law and Liberal Society: F. A. Hayek's *Constitution of Liberty*"; and W. P. Baumgarth, "Hayek and the Political Order: The Rule of Law," *Journal of Libertarian Studies* 2 (Winter 1978). For an (unconvincing) attempt to defend Hayek's view of general law, see John Gray, *Hayek on Liberty* (Oxford: Basil Blackwell, 1984), 64. The literature on Hayek is voluminous, but for two helpful general accounts of his analysis of the rule of law, see Gottfried Dietze, "Hayek on the Rule of Law," *Essays on Hayek*, ed. Fritz Machlup (London: Routledge and Kegan Paul, 1977); and Joseph Raz, *The Authority of Law*, 210–29. For a thoughtful critical overview of Hayek's intellectual legacy, see David Miller, "F. A. Hayek: Dogmatic Skeptic," *Dissent* (Summer 1994): 346–53.

34. Hayek, *Road to Serfdom*, xxi.

35. According to Hayek, "the reliance on abstract rules is a device we have learned to use because our reason is insufficient to master the full details of complex reality." The rule of law thus has its basis in the very core of human nature (*The Constitution of Liberty*, 66). For a critique of this portion of Hayek's argument, see Judith N. Shklar, "Political Theory and the Rule of Law," 9–16.

36. Hayek, *Studies in Philosophy, Politics, and Economics* (London: Routledge and Kegan Paul, 1967), 169.

37. Hayek, *Law, Legislation, and Liberty*, vol. 3, 194–95. The passage includes an extended quote from Schmitt's *Legality and Legitimacy* in which he argues that the pluralist party-state is "total" but "weak" because it is forced to intervene in all areas of social and economic existence in order "to satisfy the demands of all interested parties."

38. Not surprisingly, Hayek cites Schmitt's *Crisis of Parliamentary Government* at various junctures, and his argument seems to parallel Schmitt's on this issue as well (*Constitution of Liberty*, 443 n. 2).

39. Hayek, *Law, Legislation, and Liberty*, vol. 3, 13.

40. Hayek, *Law, Legislation, and Liberty*, vol. 3, 99.

41. Hayek, *Law, Legislation, and Liberty*, vol. 3, 23.

42. Hayek, *Law, Legislation, and Liberty*, vol. 3, 113.

43. Hayek, *Law, Legislation, and Liberty*, vol. 3, 113.

44. Hayek writes that "the employment of the resources at its [the state's] command will require constant choosing of the particular ends to be served, and such decisions must be largely a matter of expediency. Whether to build a road along one route or another one, whether to give a building one design or a different one, how to organize the police or the removal of rubbish, and so on, are all not questions of justice which can be decided by the application of a general rule." (*Law, Legislation, and Liberty*, vol. 3, 23–24). The passage is extremely revealing: it suggests that *even* some of the most basic tasks of government, for Hayek, may necessitate decisionistic legal forms.

45. This is another reason why the option for the minimal state makes so much sense given the broader contours of Hayek's argument. For him, "the difference between a society of free men and a totalitarian one lies in the fact that in the former" state activity is reduced as substantially as possible. Only the minimal state hides from view the underlying tensions within Hayek's account here: only in a situation in which state intervention is virtually nonexistent could a would-be Hayekian legislature not have to worry too much about this rather obvious contradiction in his theory (*Law, Legislation, and Liberty*, vol. 3, 24).

46. Most importantly, Schmitt thinks that extensive state intervention is consistent with substantial decision-making authority for private capital, whereas Hayek believes that all but the most minimal forms of state activity (and, as has been shown, perhaps even these as well) constitute a threat to private capital.

47. One might prhaps describe it as "rule by a narrow group of citizens with a substantial amount of gray hair but a rather insubstantial democratic base."

48. Both Schmitt and Hayek, not surprisingly, tend to downplay *this* facet of contemporary politics.

9. ANOTHER HIDDEN DIALOGUE—CARL SCHMITT AND HANS MORGENTHAU

1. Hans J. Morgenthau, "An Intellectual Autobiography," *Society* 15, no. 2 (1978): 67.

2. Morgenthau, "An Intellectual Autobiography," 68.

3. Morgenthau, "An Intellectual Autobiography," 67.

4. Morgenthau, "An Intellectual Autobiography," 68.

5. Morgenthau, "An Intellectual Autobiography," 68.

6. The literature on Morgenthau is extensive. For helpful discussions of his Weimar roots, see Christoph Frei, *Hans J. Morgenthau: Eine Intellektuelle Biographie* (Bern: Verlag Paul Haupt, 1993); and Jan Willem Honig, "Totalitarianism and Realism: Hans Morgenthau's German Years," in *Roots of Realism*, ed. Benjamin Frankel (London: Frank Cass, 1996), 283–313. The former study provides excellent biographical material; the latter focuses on the origins of Morgenthau's theory in the tradition of German "geopolitics." Some references to the Schmitt/Morgenthau nexus are also found in Gary L. Ulmen, "Toward a New 'Leviathan': Power in the Postwar World," in *Power and Policy in Transition: Essays Presented on the Tenth Anniversary of the National Committee on American Foreign Policy in Honor of Its Founder, Hans J. Morgenthau*, ed. Vojtech Mastny (Westport, Conn.: Greenwood Press, 1984), 17–36. Morgenthau's European roots are alluded to in Greg Russell, *Hans J. Morgenthau and the Ethics of American Statecraft* (Baton Rouge, La.: Louisiana State University Press, 1990), 9–102. Essential to the young Morgenthau's biography is also the "Postscript to the Transaction Edition: Bernard Johnson's Interview with Hans Morgenthau," in *Truth and Tragedy: A Tribute to Hans J. Morgenthau*, ed. Kenneth Thompson and Robert J. Myers (New Brunswick, N.J.: Transaction Books, 1984), especially 339–54.

7. For one study that sees the "concept of the political" as the centerpiece of Schmitt's intellectual agenda, see Matthias Schmitz, *Die Freund-Feind Theorie Carl Schmitts* (Cologne: Westdeutscher Verlag, 1965).

8. Strauss's "Comments on Schmitt's *Concept of the Political*" was originally published in German in 1932 in the renowned *Archiv für Sozialwissenschaft und Sozialpolitik*. Reliable English translations appear both in Schmitt, *The Concept of the Political*, trans. George Schwab (New Brunswick, N.J.: Rutgers University Press, 1976), 81–105; and in Heinrich Meier, *Carl Schmitt and Leo Strauss: The Hidden Dialogue*, trans. J. Harvey Lomax (Chicago: University of Chicago Press, 1995), 91–120. Meier expands on his reading of Schmitt in his *Die Lehre Carl Schmitts: Vier Kapitel zur Unterscheidung Politischer Theologie und Politischer Philosophie* (Stuttgart: J.B. Metzler, 1994).

9. Strauss, *Natural Right and History* (Chicago: University of Chicago Press, 1953).

10. Meier, *Carl Schmitt and Leo Strauss*, where Meier dismissively refers to Karl Löwith's "imaginary picture of Schmitt's political decisionism" (61). But Meier himself provides documentation suggesting that Strauss considered Schmitt a decisionist at least at some points in his career: Strauss told a friend in Berlin that Schmitt "is now [in 1934] against the decisionism of Hobbes" (cited in Meier, *Carl Schmitt and Leo Strauss*, 130).

11. Changes were also made to guarantee that the 1933 text was filled with anti-Semitic and openly National Socialist rhetoric (Herbert Marcuse, "Review of Schmitt," *Zeitschrift für Sozialforschung* 3, no. 1 [1934]: 102–3).

12. The 1932 version was also definitive in the sense that Schmitt selected it after the war (in 1963) for republication.

13. Although explicit socialist themes are virtually nonexistent in his early writings, Morgenthau later conceded his youthful left-wing sympathies ("An Intellectual Autobiography," 65–67).

14. Meier, *Carl Schmitt and Leo Strauss*, 19.

15. "Das politische steht nämlich selbständig als eigenes Gebiet neben anderen" (Schmitt, "Der Begriff des Politischen" [1927], 3).

16. Schmitt also attended a *Dozentenseminar* conducted by Weber, and parts of *Political Theology* appeared in a Festschrift for Weber (G. L. Ulmen, "The Sociology of the State: Carl Schmitt and Max Weber," *State, Culture, and Society* 1, no. 2 [1985]: 3–6).

17. Of course, fundamental differences ultimately separate Weber and Schmitt. See Scheuerman, *Between the Norm and the Exception*, 15–24.

18. Ilse Staff, "Zum Begriff der Politischen Theologie bei Carl Schmitt," 200–1, 204–5.

19. Meier, *Carl Schmitt and Leo Strauss*, 22.

20. "Der Begriff des Politischen" [1927], 9–10, where Schmitt concedes that nonpolitical motives and conflicts can constitute the starting point for political conflicts.

21. Schmitt, *Der Begriff des Politischen* [1932], 24, 62.

22. Schmitt, *Der Begriff des Politischen* [1932], 26. Compare the original formulations on pp. 3–5 of the 1927 "Begriff des Politischen," cited in 15.

23. Schmitt, *Der Begriff des Politischen* [1932], 22.

24. Hans J. Morgenthau, *Die internationale Rechtspflege, ihre Wesen und ihre Grenzen* [*The International Judicial System: Its Essence and Its Limits*] (Leipzig: Universitätsverlag von Robert Noske, 1929).

25. The Neumann-Schmitt nexus is a central theme of my *Between the Norm and the Exception*. On Fraenkel and Schmitt, see Scheuerman, "Social Democracy and the Rule of Law: The Legacy of Ernst Fraenkel," *From Liberal Democracy to Fascism: Political and Legal Thought in the Weimar Republic*, ed. Peter Caldwell and William E. Scheuerman (Atlantic Highlands, N.J.: Humanities Press, 1999).

26. Oddly, Morgenthau never explicitly refers to Schmitt's 1927 essay, though his terminology (he also talks of a *Begriff des Politischen*) echoes Schmitt's own. But Morgenthau does cite Schmitt's 1926 *Die Kernfrage des Völkerbundes* extensively.

27. *Nachlass Carl Schmitt: Verzeichnis des Bestandes im Nordrhein-Westfälischen Hauptstaatsarchiv*, ed. Dirk van Laak and Ingeborg Villinger (Siegburg: Republicas-Verlag, 1993). 465. It is also revealing that the crucial changes to the 1932 *Concept of the Political* were anticipated by scattered comments in Schmitt's writings in 1930 and 1931, that is, immediately subsequent to the appearance of Morgenthau's 1929 book (Schmitt, *Hugo Preuss: Sein Staatsbegriff und seine Stellung in der deutschen Staatslehre* [1930], 26 n. 1; Schmitt, *Der Hüter der Verfassung* [1931], 111). One of the crucial passages here is translated in Meier, *Carl Schmitt and Leo Strauss*, 22.

28. Morgenthau, *Die internationale Rechtspflege, ihr Wesen und ihre Grenzen*, 65.

29. Morgenthau, *Die internationale Rechtspflege*, 65–66. Schmitt himself later makes the same point in his critique of American imperialism, which claims a nonpolitical, "economic" stature. See Schmitt's 1932 "Völkerrechtliche Formen des modernen Imperialismus," 162–63.

30. Morgenthau, *Die internationale Rechtspflege*, 67.

31. Morgenthau, *Die internationale Rechtspflege*, 70.

32. Morgenthau, *Die internationale Rechtspflege*, 59–60.

33. Morgenthau, *Die internationale Rechtspflege*, 69.

34. Leo Gross, "On the Justiciability of Judicial Conflicts," in *A Tribute to Hans Morgenthau*, ed. Kenneth Thompson and Robert Myers (Washington, D.C.: New Republic Books, 1980), 204.

35. This is the international lawyer Charles De Visscher's accurate paraphrase of Morgenthau's position (Charles De Visscher, *Theory and Reality in International Law* [Princeton, N.J.: Princeton University Press, 1957], 7).

36. Morgenthau, *Die internationale Rechtspflege*, 70–71. This is the original theoretical source for Morgenthau's postwar hostility to an exaggerated faith in the virtues of quantitative social science. From this perspective, the quest for nomological generalizations, grounded in quantitative data, is often inappropriate if one hopes to capture the "intensity" of political experience.

37. Schmitt, *Der Begriff des Politischen* [1932], 59–68.

38. Meier, *Carl Schmitt and Leo Strauss*, 57.

39. Morgenthau, *Die internationale Rechtspflege*, 74. His formulations here probably represent a popular rendition of Freud's view of human nature. In "An Intellectual Autobiography," Morgenthau alludes to his enthusiasm for psychoanalysis during this period (67).

40. Meier, *Carl Schmitt and Leo Strauss*, 21.

41. Meier, *Carl Schmitt and Leo Strauss*, 21.

42. Schmitt, "Der Begriff des Politischen" [1927], 4.

43. Meier, *Carl Schmitt and Leo Strauss*, 24–26.

44. Morgenthau, *Die internationale Rechtspflege*, 60.

45. Morgenthau, *Die internationale Rechtspflege*, 74.

46. Morgenthau, *Die internationale Rechtspflege*, 75.

47. Morgenthau, *Die internationale Rechtspflege*, 77. The international lawyer Antonio Cassese makes a similar point when he notes that "international rules do not define in detail the processes by which treaty and customary rules come into being" (*International Law in a Divided World*, 179).

48. In this vein, Morgenthau in 1938 comments that "[i]ngeniously contrived legal clauses, as far as they do not reflect real political decisions, can at best create the illusion of solving a political problem. They can for a time disguise the political reality behind the veil of legalistic constructions, but they cannot spirit it away. And as soon as the political problem emerges from academic debates as an urgent actuality which requires to be solved, the legal formula reveals its practical futility" ("Switzerland's Differential Neutrality," *American Journal of International Law* 32 [1938]: 560).

49. This argument is also found in Morgenthau, *Politics Among Nations*, 410. Morgenthau's classic postwar study also offers an accessible summary of the immediate "results" of his 1929 inquiry for international law. Those conflicts containing an intense "political" character are described by Morgenthau as "disputes." They are nonjusticiable; that is, they cannot be effectively resolved by international courts. For Morgenthau, however, matters are complicated further by the fact that many issues that hypothetically should be justiciable are *not* because they mask underlying disputes between nation-states. Because warfare is rightly condemned in our century as a means of settling political differences, nation-states are often forced to resolve their disagreements by judicial means *when judicial devices are likely to fail*. Explosive political disputes, unlikely to gain a successful judicial resolution, often find themselves "transplanted" into the realm of justiciable conflicts; potentially violent conflicts are "repressed" and forced into the international judicial system. For Morgenthau, this explains why international courts may find it extremely difficult to resolve even those conflicts—for example, concerning international postal regulations or intellectual property rights—that at first glance seem primarily technical. Such technical disagreements may become a vehicle by which nation-states give expression to a fundamental, politically explosive dispute between them (*Politics Among Nations*, 401–10).

50. Morgenthau, *Die internationale Rechtspflege*, 107–10.

51. Hans Morgenthau, "Stresemann als Schöpfer der deutschen Völkerrechts-

politik," *Die Justiz* 5, no. 3 (1929): 169–76. This essay is an excellent summary of Morgenthau's Weimar agenda. On the one hand, he is skeptical of those who, in his view, naively exaggerate the potentialities of the existing "static" system of international law. On the other hand, Morgenthau himself demands an alternative, "dynamic" system of international law. The reference to Schmitt (176) *might* be taken as evidence that Morgenthau intends this agenda as a critical answer to Schmitt's radical hostility to international law. Within Morgenthau's theory, the half-truths of Schmitt's criticism of existing liberal international law are taken seriously, but Schmitt's dogmatic hostility to *any* ambitious system of international law is dismissed.

52. In light of Morgenthau's subsequent skepticism about ambitious forms of international organization, this section of the book is especially fascinating (*Die internationale Rechtspflege*, 148–52).

53. Schmitt, *The Concept of the Political* [1932], trans. George Schwab, 35.

54. Meier, *Carl Schmitt and Leo Strauss*, 41.

55. Morgenthau, *Die internationale Rechtspflege*, 74.

56. Morgenthau's "retirement" without financial compensation from the Frankfurt labor courts followed as a result of the 1933 "Law for the Reestablishment of the State Bureaucracy," which systematically eliminated Jews, Social Democrats, Communists, and antifascists from the civil service.

57. I rely here for biographical details on "Postscript to the Transaction Edition: Bernard Johnson's Interview with Hans J. Morgenthau" and on Christoph Frei, *Hans J. Morgenthau: Eine intellektuelle Biographie*, 51–70.

58. Hans Morgenthau, *La Notion du "Politique" et la théorie des différends internationaux* (Paris: Librairie du Recueil Sirey, 1933), 35 n. 2. Morgenthau's 1933 critique seems to have been ignored in the massive debate on Schmitt's political theory. The only reference to it that I have found is Ernst Vollrath, *Grundlegung einer philosophischen Theorie des Politischen* (Würzburg: Königshausen and Neumann, 1987), 34. Morgenthau appreciatively cites Strauss's 1932 "excellent comments" on Schmitt (46).

59. Morgenthau, *La Notion du "Politique" et la théorie des différends internationaux*, 47–48. This is an impressive reconstruction of Schmitt's discussion; Schmitt himself is much cruder on this point (*The Concept of the Political* [1932], 25–26).

60. Morgenthau, *La Notion du "Politique,"* 42, 56, 61–64. "On the family level, the typical conflict between the mother-in-law and her child's spouse is in its essence a struggle for power, the defense of an established power position against the attempt to establish a new one. As such, it foreshadows the conflict on the international scene between the policies of the status quo and the policies of imperialism" (Morgenthau, *Politics Among Nations*, 31).

61. Morgenthau, *La Notion du "Politique,"* 42–46.

62. Morgenthau, *La Notion du "Politique,"* 48–50.

63. *Wert* can be translated as "value," "meaning," or "significance"; the German word seems to possess many of the same ambiguities as its English counterpart. Morgenthau makes much of the conceptual ambiguities of the idea of politics as a distinct *Wertsphäre*.

64. Morgenthau, *La Notion du "Politique,"* 50.
65. Morgenthau, *La Notion du "Politique,"* 50–51.
66. Morgenthau, *La Notion du "Politique,"* 51–52.
67. Morgenthau, *La Notion du "Politique,"* 51.
68. Morgenthau, *La Notion du "Politique,"* 53–55, 60–61.
69. One implication of this view seems to be that one's "amicable" or "friendly" view of China might or might not be authentically political in Morgenthau's view. If this friendliness took on an "intense" significance, then it might deserve to be described as political in character. But this friendliness might also lack intensity and thus political significance in Morgenthau's sense of the term.
70. Morgenthau, *La Notion du "Politique,"* 55–56.
71. Morgenthau, "An Intellectual Autobiography," 67.
72. Compare Schmitt, *Concept of the Political* [1932], 60–61; Morgenthau, *Scientific Man Vs. Power Politics* (Chicago: University of Chicago, 1946), 9, 168–69; Morgenthau, *Politics Among Nations*, 3–4. Similar formulations can be found throughout Morgenthau's massive postwar oeuvre.
73. Morgenthau, "Positivism, Functionalism, and International Law," *American Journal of International Law* 34 (1940), 275–76. Morgenthau never, in fact, fully gave up his early belief in the merits of a strengthened international political and legal system. But he became increasingly critical of writers, especially legal positivists, who allegedly were blind to its complexities and dangers, and in addition considered such a system a real possibility for the long term but an irresponsible utopia for the short term. His postwar writings thus tend to emphasize the profound flaws of contemporary demands for a strengthened system of international governance.
74. Morgenthau, *Politics Among Nations*, 257.
75. Morgenthau, *Politics Among Nations*, 155–248, 322–64, 505–38. A similar nostalgia can be detected in Schmitt, *Der Nomos der Erde*, 111–86.
76. Compare Morgenthau, *Scientific Man Vs. Power Politics*, 169; Morgenthau, *In Defense of the National Interest* (New York: Alfred Knopf, 1951), 34, where he refers to the "profound and neglected truth hidden in Hobbes's extreme dictum that the state creates morality as well as law and that there is neither morality nor law outside the state" (Morgenthau, *Dilemmas of Politics* [Chicago: University of Chicgo Press, 1958], 80–81). See also Schmitt, *Der Leviathan in der Staatslehre des Thomas Hobbes*, 72–78.
77. Schmitt, *Der Nomos der Erde*, 62–65, 101; Morgenthau, *Politics Among Nations*, 331–34. Compare as well Schmitt's and Morgenthau's reflections on the changing relation between the European and non-European worlds: Morgenthau, *In Defense of the National Interest*, 40–68; Schmitt, *Der Nomos der Erde*, 187–212.
78. Morgenthau, *Politics Among Nations*, 134–37. Morgenthau's picture of the modern demos is hardly more flattering than Schmitt's.
79. Morgenthau, *Scientific Man Vs. Power Politics*, 67.
80. Morgenthau, *Scientific Man Vs. Power Politics*, 51. See also *Politics Among Nations*, 230–33; and *In Defense of the National Interest*, 37.
81. Morgenthau, *In Defense of the National Interest*, 53–57, where like Schmitt

he emphasizes the manner in which modern air warfare "compresses" space and time. On modern "mechanization" and "technization," see Morgenthau, *Politics Among Nations*, 352, and Schmitt, "The Age of Neutralizations and Depoliticization." Also interesting from this perspective is Morgenthau's late *Science: Servant or Master?* (New York: New American Library, 1972), the first part of which reproduces Schmitt's critical views on the modern quest for neutrality via technology, 2–3, 23, 28. Interestingly, Morgenthau notes that this section of the study grew out of "an unpublished manuscript on the philosophy of scholarship which was written in the mid-thirties" (xxi), that is, precisely when Schmitt's thinking clearly was present in Morgenthau's reflections.

82. This point is also made by Frei, *Hans J. Morgenthau: Eine Intellektuelle Biographie*, 210.

83. The Germanic term "concept of the political" is retranslated into a host of terms more acceptable to the American ear. The most important one is probably "power politics."

84. For Morgenthau, the key text here is probably *In Defense of the National Interest*, 91–158. But the Monroe Doctrine is discussed in many other contexts as well, for example: Morgenthau, *Truth and Power: Essays of a Decade, 1960–1970* (New York: Praeger, 1970), 79–80. For Schmitt's account of the explosive dialectic of American interventionism and isolationism, see *Der Nomos der Erde*, 270–85.

85. The best overview of this tradition remains Kenneth N. Waltz, *Man, the State, and War: A Theoretical Analysis* (New York: Columbia University Press, 1954).

86. Hedley Bull, "Hobbes and the International Anarchy," *Social Research* 48, no. 4 (1981): 737–38.

87. Meier mentions Strauss's observation that Schmitt's "affirmation of the political" represents an affirmation of the "seriousness" of human life (*Carl Schmitt and Leo Strauss*, 46).

88. Morgenthau's sober reflections on these and many other topical issues are found in Morgenthau, *The Decline of Democratic Politics* (Chicago: University of Chicago Press, 1962); Morgenthau, *The Restoration of American Politics* (Chicago: University of Chicago Press, 1962); and Morgenthau, *Truth and Power: Essays of a Decade, 1960–1970*.

89. On the virtues of this element of Realist thought, see Zolo, *Cosmopolis: Prospects for World Government*, 53–93. I am grateful to Aaron Hoffman for helping me sort out my thoughts on this matter.

90. For some thoughtful criticisms, see Stanley Hoffmann, "Notes on the Limits of 'Realism,'" *Social Research* 48, no. 2 (Winter 1981): 653–59.

91. Morgenthau, "National Socialist Doctrines of World Organization" [1941], in his *The Decline of Democratic Politics*, 243.

92. Strauss, "Comments on Carl Schmitt's *Begriff des Politischen*," 88.

93. Morgenthau, *Politics Among Nations*, 206.

94. Morgenthau, *Scientic Man Vs. Power Politics*, 8–9, also 175–78.

95. Morgenthau, *Politics Among Nations*, 12.

96. Schmitt, *The Concept of the Political* [1932], 48–49, 52, 70–71.

97. Meier, *Carl Schmitt and Leo Strauss*, 46, 49.

98. Schmitt, *Political Theology*, 66.

99. Meier, *Carl Schmitt and Leo Strauss*, 46–47.

100. In 1938, Schmitt is reported to have said that "[i]f the pope excommunicates a nation so therefore does he excommunicate himself" (cited in McCormick, *Carl Schmitt's Critique of Liberalism: Against Politics as Technology*, 35–36). As discussed in chapter 5, Schmitt during the 1930s distanced himself from Catholic theories that might at first glance seem similar to his concrete-order thinking. Theological themes *do* appear in Schmitt's writings from the mid-1920s; they play at best a minor role after 1926, when Schmitt was excommunicated because of marital problems. It is important to note that Schmitt's excommunication was self-willed in the sense that he seems to have been warned that a second marriage would result in his excommunication; Schmitt chose to remarry despite this warning. Meier's "theologian" left the Catholic Church well before the rise of National Socialism. For an incisive critique of the literature interpreting Schmitt as an undercover Catholic theologian during the Nazi period, see Bernd Rüthers, "Altes und Neues über Carl Schmitt," *Neue Juristischen Wochenschrift*, no. 14 (1996): 896–904.

101. See the explicit reference to an "ethic of responsibility" in *Scientific Man Vs. Power Politics*, 186.

102. Morgenthau, *Politics Among Nations*, 12.

103. In *Politics Among Nations*, Morgenthau suggests that we should interpret the idea of distinct value spheres as referring to counterfactual theoretical abstractions. In concrete empirical reality, every individual stands under a competing set of obligations. But if "I want to understand 'religious man' I must for the time being abstract from the other aspects of human nature and deal with its religious aspect as if it were the only one." The field of economics, similarly, considers humanity from an economic perspective; by no means need it deny that human beings are subjected to the imperatives of distinct value spheres (Morgenthau, *Politics Among Nations*, 12). On politics and morality, see Morgenthau, *Scientific Man Vs. Power Politics*, 168–203.

104. Morgenthau, *Politics Among Nations*, 12.

105. Morgenthau, *Scientific Man Vs. Power Politics*, 201.

106. Morgenthau, *Scientific Man Vs. Power Politics*, 202.

107. Morgenthau, *Scientific Man Vs. Power Politics*, 203.

108. Morgenthau responds to criticisms of this sort in *Dilemmas of Politics*, 80–87. In the final analysis, both Schmitt and Morgenthau begin with a Weberian model of modern society as resting on distinct value spheres; Schmitt offers a fascist reworking of this model, whereas Morgenthau, like Weber himself, seeks to make it consistent with liberalism. But both Schmitt and Morgenthau arguably accept too many of Weber's initial assumptions about politics. Many of Arendt's famous criticisms of the conceptual paraphernalia of Weber's political theory (in particular, his concept of power) could easily be applied to Morgenthau as well (Arendt, *On Violence* [London: Penguin, 1970]).

CONCLUSION: AFTER CARL SCHMITT?

1. For an incisive critique of the left's appropriation of Schmitt, see Mark Neocleous, "Friend or enemy? Reading Schmitt politically," *Radical Philosophy* 79 (1996): 13–23.

2. Paul Gottfried, "Legality, Legitimacy, and Carl Schmitt," *National Review* (August 28, 1987): 52–53.

3. Chantal Mouffe, *The Return of the Political* (London: Verso, 1993).

4. Mark Lilla, "The Enemy of Liberalism," *New York Review of Books* 44, no. 8 (May 15, 1997): 38–44.

5. One of the worst examples is surely Paul E. Gottfried, *Carl Schmitt: Politics and Theory* (Westport, Conn.: Greenwood Press, 1990).

6. As I have tried to suggest in this study, it is likewise unwarranted to exaggerate these merits. Schmitt's diagnoses of the problems of contemporary liberal democracy are often overstated and misleading. At the same time, they occasionally point to problematic empirical trends within capitalist liberal democracy.

7. For the (now classic) critique of the idea of a German "special path" [*Sonderweg*], see David Blackborn and Geoff Eley, *The Peculiarities of German History: Bourgeois Society and Politics in Nineteenth-Cetury Germany* (Oxford: Oxford University Press, 1984).

INDEX

ABOUT THE AUTHOR

William E. Scheuerman is associate professor of political science at the University of Pittsburgh. He is author of *Between the Norm and the Exception: The Frankfort School and the Rule of Law*, which won prizes from the Conference for the Study of Political Thought and Foundations of Political Theory section of the American Political Science Association. His writings have also appeared in journals such as *Constellations, Political Theory, History of Political Thought, Politics & Society, Review of Politics*, as well as in many edited volumes in both English and German.